EXPLAINING LANGUAGE UNIVERSALS

Explaining Language Universals

Edited by
John A. Hawkins

Basil Blackwell

First published 1988

Basil Blackwell Ltd
108 Cowley Road, Oxford, OX4 1JF, UK

Basil Blackwell Inc.
432 Park Avenue South, Suite 1503
New York, NY 10016, USA

British Library Cataloguing in Publication Data
Hawkins, John A.
    Explaining language universals.
    1. Universals (Linguistics)
    I. Title
    410   P204
    ISBN 0-631-15534-1

Library of Congress Cataloging in Publication Data
Explaining language universals edited by John A. Hawkins.
    1. Universals (Linguistics)   2. Cartesian linguistics.
    3. Language acquisition.   4. Semantics. 5. Pragmatics.
    6. Psycholinguistics.   7. Linguistic change.   I. Hawkins, John A.
    P204.E96 1988
    410—8819   87-36796 CIP
    p.   cm.
    Includes indexes.
    ISBN 0-631-15534-1

Typeset in 10 on 11pt Times by Joshua Associates Ltd, Oxford
Printed in Great Britain by T. J. Press Ltd, Padstow, Cornwall

Contents

Preface

Why do languages share the universal properties that they do? Why do they exhibit the parameters of variation that they do? The purpose of this volume is to address such questions and to provide new insights, clarifications, critical discussion and new data. The contributors have been asked to illustrate the reality of some major type of explanation for language universals. And the result is a state of the art volume on this centrally important topic compiled by some of the most familiar names in the field.

Discussions of these questions in the linguistic literature are currently rather fragmented. Linguists appear to be grouped into different camps, reflecting the type(s) of explanation to which they are sympathetic. Some argue for the innateness of general linguistic principles housed within a language acquisition device which enables the new-born child to acquire the particular language of his/her community with remarkable speed and despite impoverished input. Others argue for a more social, rather than a biological, foundation to language: the communicative (discourse-pragmatic) functions that language users perform are reflected in linguistic structure. Yet others appeal to the psychological demands placed upon language users in the production and comprehension of language in real time. These so-called 'processing' demands are also argued to be reflected in its structure, as are certain intrinsic properties of our human perceptual and cognitive apparatus. Finally, there are more grammar-internal explanations, whereby one part of the grammar is claimed to be explained by another. For example, properties of linguistic form may be explained in terms of their associated meanings.

And yet we have no reason to expect that all language universals should be uniformly explainable in just one of these ways. Rather, it seems more reasonable to assume that natural languages are constrained by *all* of these fundamental considerations simultaneously, simply because success-ful systems of human communication and of cognitive representation must regularly satisfy demands of *all* these types. The challenge before us is to make each of them more precise, thereby clarifying their domain of applicability, and to understand how they work together to constrain the variation space within which the set of possible human languages can occur.

It therefore seemed to me that progress would be accelerated by the publication of a volume that brought together the different types of causal factors that have been proposed in this context. The contributors have accordingly been asked to motivate some general type of explanation for which they see evidence, and to provide illustrative universal data supporting its reality, with discussion of this explanation type in relation to others.

It is fitting that several disciplines should be represented in a project such as this, given the fundamental nature of the central problem. The contributors are specialists in linguistics (generative theory, typology, syntax, semantics, morphology, the lexicon, discourse-pragmatics and historical change), psycholinguistics (language acquisition and language processing) and computer science (neural computing and artificial intelligence).

The book is divided into five sections: an introductory section on explaining language universals containing a chapter by the editor; a section on innateness and learnability with three chapters from three different disciplines; a section on semantic and pragmatic explanations, with four chapters; a section on cognitive, perceptual and processing explanations containing three chapters, again of an interdisciplinary nature; and finally a section on the diachronic dimension in explanation, with two chapters.

It is the editor's hope that these papers will stimulate even further research and progress towards our goal of understanding why languages are the way they are.

John A. Hawkins
Santa Monica, California

Acknowledgements

Most of the contributors to the present volume were participants in a research project entitled 'Explanation in Universal Grammar' that was held in the Netherlands between the summer of 1983 and the summer of 1985. The project was supported and funded by the West German Max-Planck-Institut (MPI) für Psycholinguistik, located in Nijmegen, and by the Netherlands Institute for Advanced Study (NIAS) in Wassenaar. The project was initially conceived by the editor of the present volume, John Hawkins, together with Anne Dunlea, as an interdisciplinary approach to the study of language universals, and was coordinated for its duration by John Hawkins with the assistance of Heather Holmback. There were thirty project participants (listed below), drawn both from the permanent MPI scientific staff and from many different institutions and countries. Numerous meetings, invited lectures, conferences and workshops were held both at Nijmegen and at Wassenaar, during which the participants presented their ongoing research to one another for critical feedback. There was active participation between the MPI/NIAS project and both Hansjakob Seiler's Universals group at Köln and Simon Dik's Functional Grammar group at Amsterdam University. Members of these groups presented papers at our meetings and conferences and assisted us in numerous ways with ongoing research. There was also a week-long workshop on universals and language acquisition funded by the MPI and held in August 1985, which involved numerous additional invited participants over and above those listed below. The MPI/NIAS project resulted in the publication of many papers and books by the participants, of which the present volume is just one. Papers were prepared for this volume during 1986 and were then sent around for reviewing. Revisions were received during the first half of 1987.

I would like to acknowledge the very generous financial and institutional support made available to this project both by the Max-Planck-Institut für Psycholinguistik and by the Netherlands Institute for Advanced Study. In particular, I would like to thank the (then) executive director of the MPI, Professor Dr Pim Levelt, who saw the potential significance of this venture for both psycholinguistics and linguistics and who gave us his strong support from the outset. I am also indebted to the other MPI directors, Professor Dr Wolfgang Klein and Dr William Marslen-Wilson, for their assistance. The project would not have been possible without the co-operation of NIAS, and I am therefore most grateful to the (then) director, Professor Henk Misset.

Of the sixteen contributors to the present volume, seven were supported either by salaries or by guest stipends from the MPI: Melissa Bowerman (MPI); Bernard Comrie (USC); Anne Cutler (MRC, Applied Psychology Unit, Cambridge); Lyn Frazier (University of Massachusetts, Amherst); Chris Hall (USC); John Hawkins (MPI and USC); and Edward Keenan (UCLA). Five were supported by fellowships at NIAS: Joan Bybee (SUNY, Buffalo); Teun Hoekstra (Leiden); Ekkehard König (Hannover); Jan Kooij (Leiden); and Sandra Thompson (UCLA, now UCSB). Four additional contributors have been invited to participate in the current volume, on account of their relevant expertise: Michael Arbib (USC); Jane Hill (Smith College); Michael Lee (USC); and Keith Rayner (University of Massachusetts, Amherst).

I would like to express my personal appreciation to all the contributors for cooperating so conscientiously in the preparation of this volume. In addition, special thanks must go to: Heather Holmback, who did much of the day-to-day running of the project; Anne Dunlea, who contributed equally to the project's conception; Elaine Andersen, who organized the universals and acquisition workshop together with Heather Holmback and myself; to the MPI staff who were always so helpful and friendly, especially Sylvia Aal, Marlene Arns, Ushi de Pagter, Inge Tarim, Edith Sjoerdsma and 'Mr König'; and to Ellie Cassee at NIAS, who made life so agreeable for the NIAS participants.

Since all the project participants were at least indirectly involved in preparing the current volume, through their many discussions and interactions, I would like to acknowledge them all.

The following were supported by salaries or guest stipends for varying periods from the MPI: Elaine Andersen (USC); Ruth Berman (Tel Aviv); Melissa Bowerman (MPI); Sandra Chung (UCSD, now UCSC); Eve Clark (Stanford); Bernard Comrie (USC); Anne Cutler (MRC, Applied Psychology Unit, Cambridge); Matthew Dryer (Alberta); Anne Dunlea (MPI, now USC); Ulli Frauenfelder (MPI); Lyn Frazier (University of Massachusetts, Amherst); Gary Gilligan (USC); Alex Grosu (Tel Aviv); Chris Hall (USC); John Hawkins (MPI and USC); Heather Holmback (MPI); Edward Keenan (UCLA); Pim Levelt (MPI); William Marslen-Wilson (MPI); Larry Moss (UCLA, now University of Michigan, Ann Arbor); Dan Slobin (UC Berkeley); and Alan Timberlake (UCLA, now UC at Berkeley). In addition, Johan Van der Auwera (Leuven) joined the project on a Humboldt fellowship and was given institutional support at the MPI.

The following were supported by fellowships from NIAS: Joan Bybee (SUNY, Buffalo); Teun Hoekstra (Leiden); Ekkehard König (Hannover);

Jan Kooij (Leiden); Lachlan McKenzie (FU Amsterdam); Leon Stassen (Nijmegen); and Sandra Thompson (UCLA, now UCSB).

Finally, I am grateful to Philip Carpenter and Basil Blackwell Ltd for their assistance, enthusiasm and professionalism in making this volume available to the linguistic community.

PART I

Introduction

CHAPTER 1

Explaining Language Universals

John A. Hawkins

1 Introduction

The study of language universals has been a major focus of modern linguistics for at least the past three decades. This volume addresses questions of explanation. Why do languages exhibit the commonalities and the range of variants that they do? Why are the variants of some not shared by all? Why are certain logically possible properties not found in any known language? Each of the contributors has been asked to address general questions of this sort, and to provide data supporting the reality of a major explanation type. The result is a state of the art volume on explaining language universals compiled by some of the most familiar names in the field.

Any attempt to go beyond description towards explanation for something as fundamental as language universals immediately raises philosophical and methodological issues on which there is much current debate. Linguists appear to be grouped into different camps, reflecting the type(s) of explanation to which they are sympathetic. Some argue for the innateness of general linguistic principles housed within a language acquisition device (LAD) which enables the new-born child to acquire the particular language of his/her community with remarkable speed and despite impoverished input. Others argue for a more social, rather than a biological, foundation to language: the communicative (discourse-pragmatic) functions that language users perform are reflected in linguistic structure. Yet others appeal to the psychological demands placed upon language users in the production and comprehension of language in real time. These so-called 'processing' demands are also argued to be reflected in its structure, as are certain intrinsic properties of our human perceptual and cognitive apparatus. Finally, there are more grammar-internal explanations, whereby one part of the grammar is claimed to be explained by another, for reasons essentially of internal consistency. Some of the most convincing arguments of this type explain properties of linguistic form in terms of their associated meanings, that is, they provide semantic explanations for language universals.

And yet we have no reason to expect that all language universals should be uniformly explainable in just one of these ways. Rather, it seems more reasonable to assume that natural languages are constrained by all of these fundamental considerations simultaneously, simply because successful systems of human communication and of cognitive representation must regularly satisfy demands of *all* of these types. The challenge before us is to make each of these explanation types more precise, thereby clarifying their domain of applicability, and to understand how they work together to constrain the variation space within which the set of possible human languages can occur. There is presumably *some* innate predisposition to language in humans, else why do we invariably learn it whereas other primates do not? There is also ample evidence that *some* universals are motivated by discourse-pragmatic functions, and that linguistic expressions of the relevant type have evolved in response to these functions. Languages must also be readily usable in real time, and so on. And I regard the current explanatory literature as providing a set of thoroughly good preliminary insights, whose full coverage and generality is not yet known, but which will undoubtedly have some place in a more comprehensive and integrated theory of universal grammar than we now have.

The purpose of this volume is to contribute to current issues in the explanation of language universals by providing new insights, clarifications, critical discussion and new data. In section 2 I outline what I think some of the major issues are, and in section 3 I summarize the relevance of each of the papers to these issues.

It is useful as a starting-point to consider some important differences between types of universal statements currently found in the literature, because different types of descriptive statements will require different types of explanations.

1.1 *Types of universals*

In the present context I shall distinguish three major logical types.

First, *absolute* universals, of the form 'for all languages, L, property P holds of L', that is, ∀L (P)L. Such universals define properties found (or not found) in every single language. Examples are: all languages have vowels; or all languages have pronoun systems distinguishing at least three persons and two numbers (cf. Greenberg 1966a). At a more abstract level, we can subsume the formal and substantive universals of Chomskyan generative grammar under this category (cf. section 2.1). The explanations for absolute universals must motivate the existence of the relevant properties as indispensable and necessary features of every single language (or alternatively as impossible features of every single language).

Second, *implicational* (or *parameter*) universals, of the form 'if a language has some property (or property complex) P, then it also has some property (or property complex) Q', that is, ∀L (P(L) ⊃ Q(L)). These universals set limits on langue variation, by defining permitted versus non-permitted combinations of properties. Specifically, the combination of P&Q is permitted, while *P & −Q is not. −P & Q and −P & −Q are also permitted by this statement, making three permitted co-occurrences in all. If the implication is reversible, only two co-occurrences will be permitted (P & Q and −P & −Q, but not *P & −Q or *−P & Q, cf. Hawkins 1983). Examples are: if a language has basic VSO word order, then it will have prepositions before NP within the prepositional phrase (cf. Greenberg 1966a); or (more abstractly) the Pro-drop and configurationality parameters of more recent generative theory (cf. Chomsky 1981, 1982). The explanations for such universals must account for why languages permit all and only the variants that they do within a given domain.

Third, *distributional* (or *frequency*) universals, of the form 'languages of type T are more frequent than languages of type T' (for theoretically predictable and interesting reasons)'. These univerals define frequency scales or hierarchies. Examples are: the more similar the position of syntactic heads across phrasal categories, the more languages there are (cf. Hawkins' 1983 descriptive principle of Cross-Category Harmony); the more to the left the subject stands in a VO language, the more languages there are (cf. Hawkins 1983: 157; Keenan 1979), that is, SVOX > VSOX > VOSX > VOXS; or languages without self-embedded relative clauses are more frequent than those with. Explanations for such universals necessarily involve intrinsically gradient and quantifiable causes, such as different degrees of processing difficulty or preference, degrees of structural complexity of various kinds, markedness, or cases of one linguistic principle being stronger than an opposing one to a certain extent. And relative language frequencies are then seen as consequences of the relevant causal factor (for example, processing difficulty) asserting itself to a greater or lesser extent within and across languages.

For many further examples of these universals, the reader should consult Greenberg's (1966b) *Universals of Language*, Greenberg, Ferguson and Moravcsik's (1978) *Universals of Human Language* (4 volumes), Comrie's (1981) *Language Universals and Linguistic Typology*, Shopen's (1985) *Language Typology and Syntactic Description* (3 volumes), Keenan's (1987) *Universal Grammar: 15 Essays*, Chomsky's (1981) *Lectures on Government and Binding* and Chomsky's (1982) *Some Concepts and Consequences of the Theory of Government and Binding*, to name just a few sources, together with the references cited therein.

2 Issues in the Explanation of Language Universals

Let us consider the major types of explanatory causes that are currently being proposed for these universals.

2.1   *Innateness and learnability*

Within Chomskyan generative grammar, the ultimate principles and atoms of the theory in terms of which the grammatical rules of all languages are to be written are the so-called formal and substantive universals (cf. Chomsky 1965), together with a set of parameters circumscribing permitted variation (cf. Chomsky 1981, 1982). Formal universals are those that determine the form and shape of the grammar, for example the components, rule types, principles of rule interaction or (in more recent versions) the various modules of the theory. Substantive universals refer to the contents of these rules or modules, for example, the categories and bar levels of X-bar theory (cf. Jackendoff 1977), the various distinctive features of phonology, etc. An example of parameter setting is the configurationality parameter of Hale (1983). These principles of Universal Grammar are explained, in turn, by the innateness hypothesis. That is, they are claimed to be innately represented in the human species and to be a part of our genetic endowment (cf. Chomsky 1968, 1975). Chomsky argues that the innateness hypothesis also explains the fact of language acquisition, specifically the remarkable rapidity with which children of all cultures learn language, despite (it is argued) insufficient data as input on the basis of which to learn the highly complex adult grammar. To quote one recent formulation:

> [Explanatory principles of UG] should be linked to the problem of how the child attains a rich and structured system of rules – a grammar – on the basis of degenerate and deficient data. [The] concern is to look for and specify that a-priori knowledge, available to the language-learning child, which permits language acquisition to circumvent the impoverished stimulus.
>
> (Coopmans 1984: 55)

One major respect in which the child's input is impoverished involves so-called 'negative data', that is, the child generally hears only grammatical sentences of the adult language (the positive data), and normally receives no information about what is ungrammatical (the negative data). How then does he/she succeed in inferring the boundaries of grammaticality for the sentences of his/her language, when confronted with positive data only, and when the data that he/she does not hear includes both grammatical (that is, potentially usable) and ungrammatical (unusable) sentences? In Chomsky's view, the richly specified innate knowledge of grammatical universals permits the child to infer the form and content of the rules of his/her particular language, together with the appropriate parameter settings, even with quite limited data as input. These latter act as a 'trigger experience' for the construction of a particular grammar and obviate the need for negative evidence.

The innateness hypothesis depends for its precise content, of course, on the absolute universals and parameter settings that are derived from grammatical analysis and cross-language comparison. As the theory evolves, so do assumptions about what is innate (compare Chomsky 1981/1982 with Chomsky 1965, or Saito's 1985 discussion of the configurationality parameter with Hale 1983). This is inevitable, and underscores the fact that the innateness hypothesis is supported in the first instance by the very existence of universal generalizations. But since there may be other proposed explanations for these generalizations, and since there is no possibility at this time of obtaining any direct evidence about the LAD from genetics or neurology, the major thrust of support for the hypothesis has been of this indirect kind, involving learnability. In a nutshell, language acquisition cannot be explained without appeal to an innately represented Universal Grammar, and any general learning strategies that the child might apply to the input data will be insufficient without it (cf., for example, Wexler and Culicover 1980, Baker and McCarthy 1981 for further details).

How good is this argument? On the one hand, it seems to me highly plausible that there are *some* innately represented features of language in the human species, and that these do facilitate language acquisition. On the other hand, there is a major issue that has not received the attention and critical scrutiny it deserves within the Chomskyan literature, namely: what exactly *can* the child infer from positive evidence? what kinds of learning strategies *do* children actually adopt, both in language and in other cognitive domains? and *are* these strategies systematically incapable of explaining language acquisition without the innateness hypothesis? The argument for innate grammar is based on crucial assumptions about what can and cannot be learned from positive evidence. If these assumptions need to be qualified (as Arbib and Hill this volume and Bowerman this volume argue they do), this will have far-reaching consequences for the very relevance of learnability to the innateness hypothesis.

Consider some simple examples. If the child hears only subject–verb–object (SVO) word order in a particular language in every relevant sentence uttered, it does not require much intelligence to infer the impossibility of subject–object–verb (SOV) in that language. The positive data suffice here to provide evidence about ungrammaticality. If the child hears both *he washed himself* (anaphoric reference) and *he washed him* (disjoint reference) and understands the meaning difference, he/she will be able to infer the grammaticality of *I washed myself* and the ungrammaticality of *I washed me*, given knowledge of the uniqueness of the first person singular reference. More generally, there are lots of correct hypotheses of these kinds that an intelligent organism can infer from positive evidence, and we need to know just how far such inferencing could go in the area of language acquisition.

In addition, arguments about the insufficiency of positive data can be made just as readily for sentence types in which grammaticality differences do *not* reduce to universal (and hence innate) principles as they can for those that do. The ungrammaticality of the English raising structure *Harry is possible to come* versus the grammaticality of *Harry is likely to come* reflects a highly idiosyncratic property of English (*likely* is in the class of raising triggers, *possible* is not). Yet it poses an identical learning problem to the data sets involving grammaticality distinctions that reflect universal principles. Ungrammatical sentences are not heard, so how can the child infer that such sentences are any more impossible than all the other sentences he/she doesn't hear, some of which are quite grammatical? And won't whatever mechanisms the child applies to figuring out the raising distinction (where no innateness can be invoked) simply extend to the (much smaller number of) distinctions that are purportedly guided by innate knowledge?

In short, generativists need to address the fundamental point: what can the child infer from positive evidence and what can he/she not?

There is also a somewhat premature leap from Universal Grammar to innateness in many generative discussions. There are other types of causal factors that can be invoked to explain why languages are the way they are, and the reasoning from grammar to innateness typically ignores these. We can accept, therefore, that there are some innately given linguistic principles. The issue is: what are they precisely? and what is the relation between these biologically given principles and other types of causal factors?

2.2 *Semantics*

The idea that there could be semantic explanations for grammatical universals has been vigorously pursued by Ed Keenan in many papers since the early 1970s, many of which are reprinted in Keenan (1987). The logic of his argument is as follows: certain universal facts of grammatical form (morphology and syntax) are the way they are, because of their corresponding semantic interpretations. The semantics renders the grammar predictable. The precise causal link between semantics and grammar takes slightly different forms in Keenan's different principles. A paradigm example is the Meaning–Form Dependency Principle (MFDP) (or Functional Dependency Principle) of Keenan (1979).

Keenan observes that morphological agreement across languages obeys an interesting restriction. Consider adjectives and nouns. If one of these categories agrees with the other, it is always the adjective that agrees with the noun (for example, in number or gender), and never the other way round. In addition, adjectives exhibit a form of semantic agreement with their nouns. The precise interpretation of an adjective typically varies with the choice of head noun, whereas the precise interpretation of a head noun does not usually depend on that of an accompanying adjective. Compare (1) and (2):

(1) flat tyre
    flat beer
    flat road

(2) flat road
    dusty road
    windy road

The interpretation assigned to *flat* in (1) differs radically in conjunction with *tyre* versus *beer* versus *road*. But the interpretation of road in (2) remains constant through the three examples.

More generally, Keenan argues that all function categories (which include adjectives) vary their precise interpretation with the choice of argument (the noun in (1) and (2)), but not vice versa. And if there is morphological agreement between categories, it is always the function category that agrees with the argument, rather than vice versa. The result is a strong form of internal consistency within the grammar: a dependency in form (with the adjective looking to the noun for its agreement features) mirrors a dependency in meaning. That is, a universal morphological dependency follows from a semantic dependency. This same explanation also accounts for verb agreement across languages: verbs (as function categories) often receive quite divergent interpretations, depending on the choice of accompanying subject NP or object NP (as argument), as illustrated in the different senses of *run* in (3) and (4).

(3) John ran.
    The water ran.
    The stocking ran.

(4) Harry ran the water.
    Harry ran the race.
    Harry ran an ad.

Correspondingly, it is verbs that agree with subjects and (less frequently) objects across languages, rather than vice versa.

I consider Keenan's semantic explanation for this universal of morphological agreement to be highly plausible and intuitive. And yet surface form (syntax and morphology) does not always mirror meaning in this way. For example, there is a mismatch between semantic and syntactic categories in Keenan's (1979) other major example involving cross-categorial word order correlations. There is no uniform semantic basis underlying these statistical word order universals, and Keenan is forced to propose a Dissimilation Principle whereby the top two pairs of function–argument categories in Table 1.1 are typically placed in the opposite order from the bottom two in one and the same language type. By contrast, a syntactic generalization in terms of head versus modifier status does accord well with the statistical correlations and permits a single unifying

Table 1.1 Head-modifier and function-argument predictions for statistical word
order correlations

		head–modifier (syntactic)	function–argument (semantic)
(NP)	Adj + N	modifier + head	function + argument
(AdjP)	Adv + Adj	modifier + head	function + argument
(VP/S)	Obj + V	modifier + head	argument + function
(AdpP)	NP + Po	modifier + head	argument + function

generalization: a head of phrase either consistently precedes or follows its modifiers, with more than chance frequency (cf. Hawkins 1983, 1984 and also Zwicky 1985).

Moreover, numerous rules of syntax are not in any straightforward correspondence with semantic rules and representations, for example syntactic rules that rearrange arguments from their predicates, such as raisings, rules creating ambiguities, rules of deletion. And such rules have provided the motivation all along for considering syntax at least partially autonomous of semantics.

In short, grammatical form *sometimes* conserves and reflects properties of its associated semantics, but *sometimes* does not. The challenge before us is to better understand when we can invoke Keenan's principle and intuition, and when we cannot.

Another of Keenan's principles, the principle of Conservation of Logical Structure (CLS) (cf. e.g. Keenan 1972), raises a related issue. Keenan argues that the more that syntactic structures preserve features of their corresponding logical structures, the more accessible these structures are to operations such as Relative Clause Formation. In languages like Hebrew, Persian and Welsh which preserve pronouns in the positions relativized on (giving, for example, *the student that I passed him* rather than *the student that I passed*) relativization is possible in a much larger set of environments, particularly in the intuitively more difficult structures involving coordinate and subordinate NPs, or positions low on the Keenan–Comrie (1977) Accessibility Hierarchy, etc.

Keenan's hypothesis is that pronoun retention extends the set of relativization evironments because relative clauses with pronouns correspond more closely to their logical-semantic structures than do relative clauses without such pronouns. The pronoun identifies the semantically appropriate position of the NP within the relative clause that is co-referential to the head, and so make the relationship between relative clause and head more semantically transparent. This in turn makes it easier to understand what the relative clause and head are being used to refer to.

But this means that the wider applicability of rules such as Relative Clause Formation in pronoun-retaining languages is not just a function of a more transparent relationship between surface structure and logical structure; it is the result of semantic transparency *and* processing ease (cf. section 2.4). The comprehension and production of relative clauses is facilitated by pronoun retention, and hence certain independent considerations involving real-time language processing reinforce a semantic principle (CLS) in explaining cross-linguistic differences in syntactic rule behavior.

But does semantic transparency always contribute to processing ease? The answer is surely 'no'. Imagine the case of a language whose syntax assigned distinct grammatical structures, such as different morphological affixes or word order differences, etc., to each distinct type of predicate (distinct in terms of the number and type of accompanying arguments, their obligatory versus optional status, distinct selectional restrictions à la Chomsky 1965 and semantic or case roles à la Fillmore 1968). The task of assigning meanings to surface forms in this language would be completely transparent and simple, but the number of separate grammatical forms required, and the necessary limitations on rule productivity would be quite enormous, and this language would be quite unusable. For this reason languages typically collapse semantically distinct predicates into large syntactic classes of, for example, verbs, and these classes are treated in a relatively uniform way by the syntax (cf. further Hawkins 1986: 125–7).

In this example, processing ease would appear to correlate with a lack of semantic transparency, and an argument could be made for processing as a motive for the (partial) autonomy of syntax. Thus, semantic transparency and processing ease do not always reinforce one another when explaining language universals.

2.3 Discourse-pragmatics

Some explanations for universals appeal to pragmatic aspects of meaning, that is, to those which make reference to the discourse context of an utterance (the speaker, the hearer, their shared knowledge and beliefs, previous utterances, etc.), to the speech act functions that languages perform and to those additional aspects of meaning (the implicatures of Grice 1975 and the relevance-based inferences of Sperber and Wilson 1986) that are derived from the invariant semantics of sentences when used in real discourse. For example, if every grammar contains pronouns distinguishing at least three persons and two numbers (cf. Greenberg 1966a: 96), then an explanation involving the referential distinctions that speakers of all languages must regularly make for efficient communication is, a priori, highly plausible (cf. Ingram 1978 for a more detailed formulation of this universal).

Another paradigm example has also recently been pointed out to me by Bernard Comrie (personal communication). Comrie observes that if a language has a reflexive/non-reflexive distinction on its first person pronouns (*me*/*myself*), then it also has this distinction on second person pronouns (*you*/*yourself*); if it has it on second person pronouns, it also has it on third person pronouns (*him*/*himself*, etc.). That is, some languages have a reflexive/non-reflexive distinction on all three persons (English), or on the second and third only (Huichol), or just on the third (German, cf. *ihn*/*sich*). (Cf. Faltz 1985: 120 for confirmation of this universal.)

Comrie proposes the following explanation for this distribution. The third person distinction is, he argues, the most useful in discourse. The number of potential third person referents is very large, and so the distinction between same and non-same referents (*he washes himself*/*him*) is one that it is useful to be able to capture clearly and quickly. The second person distinction is slightly more useful than the first (*you washed yourself*/*you*), given the possibility of addressing more than one addressee. But the first person distinction is almost totally useless, on account of the uniqueness of the speaker (*I washed myself*/?*me*).

This explanation appeals, ultimately, to the number of occasions on which a formal distinction is useful in actual communication. I find it highly plausible. And yet it raises a fundamental question. When can we appeal to such discourse considerations in general, and when not? After all, there are lots of useful real-world distinctions that could potentially be grammaticalized in languages which either never receive their own separate morphemes or structures, or which do so only rarely. Speakers regularly have occasion to refer deictically to objects on their left as opposed to their right side, and vice versa. Yet deictic systems across languages are not organized on this basis. The height of an object in relation to the speaker is another potentially useful distinguishing criterion, and here there are some languages that incorporate a height dimension into systems of spatial deixis (e.g. Daga and Dyirbal, cf. Anderson and Keenan 1985), but the majority operate only with a system of relative distance from the speaker (and in some cases from the hearer as well, cf. Anderson and Keenan 1985). Hence, although Comrie's explanation for his reflexive universal is very convincing, it is somewhat after the fact. If other similar motivations for the grammaticalization of real-world distinctions do not result in distinctive grammatical morphemes or structures in this way, when can we appeal to a discourse-pragmatic explanation, and when not? And can we assume that there will be a simple correlation between the degree of usefulness of some real-world distinction, and the frequency of its grammaticalization across languages?

The same issue arises when considering the expression of speech act distinctions across languages. Sadock and Zwicky (1985) show that declaratives, interrogatives and imperatives are universal sentence types, although languages differ in the degree of specificity or vagueness of these constructions, and in the extent of their distinctiveness. These speech act functions thereby contrast with many others that do not receive regular and distinctive encoding, even though they are communicatively important, and even though there are many readily imaginable ways in which they could be grammaticalized. A nice example discussed by Sadock and Zwicky (1985: 164) involves 'optatives', that is, expressions of the speaker's wishes. They write:

> There are several natural sources for a true optative sentence type: future tenses, conditional or subjunctive moods, and imperative moods. Any one of these might become specialized as an optative during the history of a language. Yet in few of the languages known to us has this specialization occurred. For the most part, the optative use of the relevant construction remains as one of a number of related uses, without any special mark. This is so in Latin . . . and in Turkish.

There are a number of pragmatic principles of word order that have been proposed, and they raise a related issue in this context. Linear ordering in so-called 'free word order' languages has been argued to be pragmatically determined. According to one standard formulation, old and given information precedes new (cf. Thompson 1978 for a summary). Givón (1983) provides a slightly different principle: old or topical information precedes new, but new may also precede old just in case the old information has been recently mentioned (within the last twenty sentences of the discourse) and is therefore accessible to memory. Givón reasons that linear ordering is determined by a pragmatic principle which he paraphrases as 'attend first to the most urgent task'. If the subject or object NP has not been previously mentioned, or has been mentioned too far back in the discourse to be readily accessible to memory, then establishing the reference is the most urgent task, prior to predicating something of this referent, and hence subject before verb and object before verb orders are preferred in Givón's text counts from diverse languages. But if subject or object have been recently mentioned, then the predicate becomes the most urgent information and is ordered first.

Now, I actually believe that there is a more general explanatory principle that motivates these data, involving language processing (cf. the principle of Order of Computation in Cutler and Hawkins 1987). But leaving this aside, notice that the word order freedom for which Thompson and Givón propose pragmatic principles typically arises at the sentence level only. The relative ordering of immediate constituents of the noun phrase, the adjective phrase and the adposition phrase is normally highly constrained and syntactically determined: the cross-categorial rules responsible for head placement (cf. table 1.1) have nothing to do with pragmatics. Nor does a language-particular rule such as the one that orders Tense + (Modal) + (*have* + *en*) + (*be* + *ing*) + (*be* + *en*) + Verb in English. So when can we invoke a pragmatic motivation for linear order, and when can we not?

Moreover, even when pragmatic considerations do motivate syntactic rearrangements, they typically interact with non-pragmatic (syntactic and semantic) principles in subtle ways, and this interaction will often obscure the pragmatic ordering principle. German provides a relevant example. In a very elegant study, Lenerz (1977) argues that the unmarked and basic syntactically determined order of indirect object (IO) and direct object (DO) in German is IO + DO. With this ordering, either NP can be pragmatically old or new information, as shown in (5):

(5)   IO + DO
      old + new
      new + old

This ordering provides, of course, no evidence of any pragmatic generalization. However, Lenerz shows that the marked order DO + IO is only possible if pragmatically new information occurs to the right and old information to the left, as shown in (6):

(6)   DO + IO
      old + new
      ?new + old

That is, a general pragmatic principle that has been derived from languages with even freer word order than German involving the placement of old before new information asserts itself in the syntactically marked construction, and only this construction provides any evidence for the pragmatic principle at all.

Lenerz uses question–answer pairs to provide evidence for this interaction of syntax and pragmatics. New information is that which is explicitly sought via a WH-question; old information is explicitly mentioned in both the question and the answer. An IO as new information can both precede and follow an old information DO, in the unmarked and marked structures respectively:

(7)   Wem   hast du   das Geld   gegeben?   (German)
        'whom-Dat have you the money given'

(8) a. Ich habe *dem   Kassierer das   Geld* gegeben.   IO + DO
        'I   have the-Dat cashier   the-Acc money given'   new + old
    b. Ich habe *das Geld dem Kassierer* gegeben.   DO + IO
                                                              old + new

But a DO as new information must follow and cannot precede an IO which provides old information, that is, both DO and IO occur in the unmarked syntactic order only:

(9)   Was hast du   dem   Kassierer gegeben?   (German)
        'what have you the-Dat cashier   given'

(10) a. Ich habe *dem   Kassierer das   Geld* gegeben.   IO + DO
     'I   have the-Dat cashier   the-Acc money given'   old + new
   b. ?Ich habe *das Geld dem Kassierer* gegeben.   DO + IO
                                             ?new + old

Corresponding to the inappropriateness in context of (10b), German also
has some ungrammatical sentences in which indefinite (and hence
typically new information) direct objects precede definite indirect objects:

(11) *Geben Sie *Milch den   Kindern*. (German)   DO + IO
     'give   milk   the-Dat children'   indef + def

We can conclude that many rules of syntax have no pragmatic motivation (for example, the rules of basic order assignment in German); and
even when pragmatic principles *are* relevant in syntax, their effects can be
constrained by independent principles, and will assert themselves only
within a subset of the options provided by these latter. What we need to
better understand is: when will pragmatic principles be reflected in the
syntax, and when not?

2.4 *Processing*

Processing explanations for language universals invoke principles of
comprehension and production that have been derived from controlled
experiments on real-time language use. These explanations appeal ultimately to two major considerations: human beings are limited capacity
machines – there are, for example, real limitations on short-term memory;
and different linguistic structures may be associated with different degrees
of processing ease or difficulty.

One structural type that has been argued to involve considerable
processing difficulty is center embedding (cf. Kuno 1973, 1974; Bever
1970; Slobin 1973). Compare the ungrammatical center-embedded
clause in English with its grammatical equivalents (involving clause-initial
and clause-final embeddings):

(12) a. *Who did *that Mary hit Bill* surprise?
    b. *That Mary hit Bill* surprised who?
    c. Who did it surprise *that Mary hit Bill*?

Dryer (1980) has found cross-linguistic support for the regular avoidance
of such center embeddings. Many SOV languages must or may employ
SVO order when the direct object is a finite sentential complement. Postposing of the complement is obligatory in German, Persian, Yaqui and
Turkish, as illustrated in the following data from Persian:

(13) a. *An zan   ₛ(ke an mard sangi partab kard) mi   danat (Persian)
         'the woman   that that man rock threw   Cont knows', i.e.
         That woman knows that the man threw a rock.

   b. An zan mi danat ₛ(ke an mard sangi partab kard).

and it is optional in Mojave, Lakhota, Latin and Wappo. All of these languages have basic SOV order. Postposing of a center-embedded sentential object is also obligatory in all VOS languages, such as Malagasay:

(14) a. *Mihevitra ₛ(fa   mitady   ny zaza Rasoa) Rabe. (Malagasy)
         'thinks   that looks-for the child Rasoa Rabe', i.e.
         Rabe thinks that Rasoa is looking for the child.

   b. Mihevitra Rabe ₛ(fa mitady ny zaza Rasoa).

On the other hand, center-embedded clauses *are* tolerated in those languages in which postposing is optional, and they are also tolerated in languages like Japanese which have optional preposing rules for heavy constituents (cf. Dryer 1980).

Another set of structures which have been argued by psycholinguists to be difficult to process are temporary ambiguities (cf. Frazier and Rayner 1982). Temporary ambiguities arise when the processor's initial decision about the structure of a string turns out to be incorrect, as in (15):

(15) *The guest expected to be late* arrived.

This sentence will be temporarily ambiguous in its left-to-right presentation: up until *arrived*, *expected to be late* can be parsed as a main clause VP or as a reduced relative clause (cf. *who was expected to be late*). The former interpretation will initially be preferred on account of general parsing principles (cf. Frazier 1978), but this preference will necessarily be revised as soon as *arrived* is encountered, resulting in a 'garden path' effect. And yet temporary ambiguities of this sort do obviously occur in languages.

These considerations pose a challenge similar to the one we encountered for semantic and pragmatic explanations: when will processing difficulty be reflected cross-linguistically in the avoidance of certain structures, and when will it not? In section 2.7 below I will suggest a way of approaching this problem. Processing difficulty is an intrinsically gradient notion, and when other causal factors are held constant we can expect to see different degrees of difficulty reflected in language frequencies and in implicational dependencies between the properties involved. Thus, Hawkins (1988) argues that the degree of processing difficulty associated with different types of center embeddings and temporary ambiguities can be quantified (cf. the principles of Early Immediate Constituents and Immediate Boundary Recognition respectively), with many correct predictions being made for implicational and distributional universals of linear order.

2.5 *Perception and cognition*

To what extent are language universals explainable as a result of human perceptual systems and of human cognition? The perception of sounds has been claimed to have a profound impact on phonological universals, cf. Lindblom et al. (1984) (and Lee this volume). It has also been claimed that the following implicational universal for color terms has a ready perceptual explanation (cf. Berlin and Kay 1969; Kay and McDaniel 1978):

(16) white   green
            > red >   > blue > brown
       black   yellow

That is, if a language has just three color terms, they will be white, black and red. If there is a fourth, it will be green or yellow, etc. Kay and McDaniel (1978) demonstrate that the focal points for basic color terms across lanaguages are determined by the neural anatomy of our color vision system. Focal colors are those that produce the most distinctive neural response, and the ranking of (16) reflects the fact that languages encode the most contrastive stimuli first (cf. Lee this volume for further details).

For many other universals, the sensory data of the world around us are cognitively analyzed and classified in similar ways across cultures, resulting in cross-linguistic patterns that reflect fundamental properties of our human cognitive apparatus. Noun classifier systems are a case in point (cf. Lee this volume).

It is important to know just how many universals of language are directly explainable by our perceptual apparatus, or by properties of the world mediated through fundamental processes of human cognition. We need to know also just how far such explanations can be taken. Most of the examples of these types involve lexical universals, such as color terms, or universals of body part terminology (cf. Andersen 1978). Do perceptual and cognitive principles extend into the grammar, and if so how and where?

Some very suggestive work in this regard has been done by Haiman (1983, 1985) on iconicity in syntax. One principle that he proposes is the Distance Principle: the linguistic distance between expressions corresponds to the conceptual distance between them. Linguistic distance refers to the physical distance between linguistic units (these units may be non-adjacent words, adjacent words, stem and affix combinations, or just a single lexical item). And conceptual distance refers to the perceived separability or inseparability of concepts and the reality they describe. So, in the area of causation, the conceptual distance between cause and result is greater in multi-word English expressions such as *cause to die* than it is in the single lexeme *kill* (cf. Bybee this volume for further details).

2.6 The diachronic dimension

Languages are not static. They change, often in quite fundamental ways even in the limited recorded time depth available to us. Linguistic science throughout the nineteenth century was preoccupied with change and evolution, being heavily influenced by paradigms of explanation that were current in the other social and natural sciences of the period. The most recent states of the Indo-European languages were explained by (i) observing earlier states of these languages, and (ii) applying reconstructed or observed laws of change to earlier states to derive more recent states, thereby explaining why these latter are the way they are. With the development of research on language universals and cross-linguistic variation has come a renewed interest in diachrony. Implicational universals have been used as an aid in historical reconstruction both in Indo-European and in other language families (cf. Givón 1971, Lehmann 1974, Friedrich 1975, Hawkins 1982), and as a predictor of possible and impossible changes (Hawkins 1979, 1983). And conversely, a number of researchers stress the diachronic dimension in the synchronic universals themselves.

This diachronic dimension consists in answering the question: how do languages evolve into the variation states to which implicational and distributional universals refer? (Absolute universals are not relevant in this context, since these properties are necessarily present in (or absent from) every single language, and so are not subject to change.) The claim is made that at least part of the explanation for universal parameters of variation is to be found in diachrony, specifically by (i) examining earlier states of languages, and (ii) by applying general laws of change to these earlier states to derive more recent states. But in contrast to the language-particular laws of change in individual Indo-European languages and families, the laws within the present context must be of greater generality if they are to subsume all language families. And indeed there have been a number of interesting attempts to define possible versus impossible pathways of change, or diachronic universals, in various areas of language, that is, to define which properties X can change into properties Y, together with the directionality of the change. Within phonology, only certain sounds can merge into others: a voiceless consonant may become voiced between vowels, but not vice-versa (cf. Foley 1977 for many examples of phonological drifts). In morphology, a bound morpheme derives historically from a free lexical or grammatical morpheme and generally inherits the same order relative to its stem that was assigned to the earlier free morphemes by the syntax – the converse shift (bound to free morpheme) does not occur (cf. Hall this volume). And for semantics it has been proposed that root modals may acquire epistemic senses later in time, but not vice versa (cf. Sweetser 1984, 1986), and that speech act verbs will emerge diachronically from descriptive verbs that do not perform speech acts, whereas speech act meanings do not develop into descriptive ones (cf. Traugott 1982, 1986).

Such universals of change make predictions for synchronic variation patterns in these various phonological, morphological and syntactic environments, and in co-occurring word meanings, as the type X properties merge into type Y: co-occurrences of X and Y are predicted (and in part explained through the diachronic principles involved), co-occurrences of, for example, type Z and Y are not. It is therefore important to know how extensive such universals of change are throughout the language system as a whole. Note that it is not the undirectionality of such changes per se that is explanatory, since at any one historical stage X may occur unshifted, or in combination with Y, or else Y may occur alone upon completion of the shift. All logical possibilities can occur. What *is* constraining for synchrony, however, is the identity of X and Y. The frequent co-occurrence of these properties is predicted, as is some possible vestige of features of X in Y even when X is no longer present synchronically, as in the morphology example.

At the same time, the diachronic dimension in explanation raises some profound methodological and theoretical issues. Consider an instructive example taken from Mallinson and Blake (1981: ch. 6). These authors summarize a number of attempts that have been made to set up diachronic links between the word order properties that were first correlated in the implicational universals of Greenberg (1966a). For example, N + Gen and Pr + NP are highly correlated, as are Gen + N and NP + Po. Mallinson and Blake observe that a head noun before genitive construction (*the back of the hut*) may shift diachronically into a prepositional phrase (*back of the hut*) in a number of languages, whereas a genitive before head would shift into a postpositional phrase (cf. further Bybee this volume). Such considerations are then invoked to explain the implicational universals themselves.

But there are problems with this line of reasoning. Synchronic word order universals provide strong support for a rather abstract notion of head of phrase (cf. table 1.1), with language frequencies reflecting consistency in the ordering of heads in relation to their respective non-heads across phrasal categories (cf. Hawkins 1983). Now, while diachronic links can reasonably be established between N + Gen and Pr + NP, etc., the number of word orders for which such diachronic links can be explanatory is far less than the total number of head ordering correlations that exist synchronically. Diachronic links of this type are only plausible for pairs of word orders that are sufficiently closely related semantically so that the one structure can merge gradually into the other, which is not many. The diachronic link theory, therefore, lacks generality.

Nor is it terribly convincing even with prepositions and genitives. The simple prepositions in English are not derived from genitives, and for most languages of the world we either have no record of earlier syntactic states or no compelling arguments for reconstructing a genitive source for adpositions in many cases at least.

In short, the diachronic link proposed here is not a diachronic universal and does not have sufficient generality to provide an explanation for a synchronic universal. (For a synchronic explanation of a processing nature for these cross-categorial head ordering facts, cf. Hawkins 1988.) This is not to deny that diachronic drifts of these types occurred: they did, and they account for some adposition facts in some languages. But this is no explanation for a universal.

The how of change will only contribute to constraining the nature and extent of cross-language variation in areas of data for which there are universal diachronic drifts. If there are no such universals of change, then successive language states will be constrained only by the wellformedness requirements of synchronic universals, and by accidents of history that are of no consequence for language universals. Nor will there be a diachronic dimension to explanation if there are certain diachronic tendencies (such as the adposition-genitive shift) which cover only a (small) proper subset of the range of synchronic data to be explained. Such diachronic tendencies will operate upon structures whose linearization is fixed by other (synchronic) principles, and will effect minor category shifts that are mere artifacts of a synchronic syntactic scheme of much greater generality. (For a drift that has been argued to oppose the predominant universal word order pattern in a language, thereby further undermining the explanatory potential of such drifts for synchronic universals, cf. Li and Thompson 1974.)

2.7 *Two general issues*

I have made a number of critical comments about the current state of the art in explaining language universals. But these criticisms do *not* cast doubt on the reality of causal factors of each of these types. Quite the reverse. Each of them *is* plausibly responsible (in part at least) for some area of linguistic data. But they are insufficient as currently proposed. Innateness is a reasonable hypothesis for some aspects of human linguistic ability, but we need greater clarity on what precisely is innate, and the argument from learnability will remain weak until more systematic attention is paid to what *can* be learned from positive evidence. Semantic transparency is plausibly responsible for Keenan's MFDP data, yet there is also considerable non-transparency or autonomy of linguistic form. Communicatively useful distinctions are grammaticalized in some cases, but not others. And so on.

There is a twofold moral to all this. First, we need to clarify and sharpen the various causal factors for universals that have been outlined in this section. What are the precise causes that researchers appeal to when explaining some set of universal data in one of these ways? How far can they be taken? How convincing are they?

Second, we need to be aware of the totality of causal factors that could be relevant in any one case, and we must consider the mutual interaction between them. In some cases the domain of explanation for one principle may be quite neutral to that of another. The purported innateness of subjacency constraints in syntax can stand or fall regardless of whether the perceptual explanation for color term universals is correct. But in other cases there may be an alternative explanation of greater generality for some common set of data. For example, a principle that is merely stipulated by the syntax may actually follow from considerations of a semantic nature. Or two arguably separate and independently motivated causal factors may reinforce one another. An example involving semantic transparency and processing ease was mentioned above (section 2.2) in connection with Keenan's Conservation of Logical Structure principle. Alternatively, two principles may be in conflict, and the resolution of the conflict may result in variation as languages opt for different solutions. In languages such as English with grammatically fixed word order, the re-arrangements motivated by pragmatic principles are severely reduced compared with 'free word order' languages, in which these pragmatic principles take priority over syntactically determined orders (at the sentence level at least). German is an intermediate case (section 2.3) with pragmatic principles asserting themselves in grammatically marked orders only (within the VP).

Most importantly, many causal principles are gradient rather than absolute. Communicative usefulness (section 2.3) is a matter of degree. There are also different degrees of processing ease or difficulty (section 2.4), of perceptual salience (section 2.5) and different extents to which semantic transparency is necessary or desirable (section 2.2). All languages share a common core of grammaticalized categories and structures, for example, the noun/verb distinction, the transitive/intransitive distinction, etc. And they all respond to each of these causal pressures to at least a minimal degree. But beyond this core, the various pressures may be realized to different extents.

Consider processing. I suggested in section 2.4 that processing difficulty is a gradient notion, with empirical consequences for language frequencies and implicationally defined co-occurrences of properties. At the extreme end of some gradient the processing difficulty may be so great that the relevant structures will be non-occurring across all languages. An example might be the absence of mirror-image structures across languages, as discussed in Chomsky (1968), or of unbounded rightward movement rules, as discussed in Fodor (1979). But otherwise the degree of processing difficulty will be reflected in the *relative* numbers of languages exemplifying the structures in question.

Why should this be? Let us assume that processing preferences join with other explanatory principles in shaping the structural options that grammars can choose from when putting together a set of wellformedness rules. A given processing principle will then define a set of preferences (cf. Hawkins 1988 and Hawkins and Cutler this volume): some structures are more highly valued than others. An overall grammar will select some (arguably roughly comparable) mix of more and less highly valued structures from the set of options potentially available to it, but I would argue that within any single set, grammars will select the unmarked and more highly valued options before they resort to the more marked and less highly valued ones. These latter will be selected only when there is some compelling reason for doing so, and only when the more highly valued options in that set have already been chosen. As a result, these more highly valued options will be grammaticalized more frequently. We can also make a prediction of an implicational nature: if some relatively easy structure is not selected for grammaticalization from a given set of options, then a more difficult one will not be either; conversely, if a more difficult structure is grammaticalized, an easier one will be as well.

Compare center embeddings with self-embeddings. The latter have been argued to be even more difficult for processing than the former: they involve a higher local ratio of non-terminal to terminal nodes (cf. Frazier 1984); and they also involve center embedding. If there is some independent motivation (of a syntactic or semantic nature) for grammaticalizing these structures, we would therefore expect grammars to exhibit a greater tolerance for center embeddings over self-embeddings: the former should be more frequent. And if some center embedding is ungrammatical, the corresponding self-embedding should be ungrammatical as well; conversely, if the self-embedding is grammatical, the center embedding will be as well.

The following data from German, in which both self-embedded (17) and center-embedded (18) relative clauses are grammatical, bear out this latter prediction:

(17)   Der Bauer $_S$(der die Kuh $_S$(die   schlechte Milch gab)
       'the farmer   who the cow   which bad   milk gave
       The farmer who killed the cow which gave bad milk

       schlachtete) ist grausam.
       killed   is cruel'
       is cruel.

(18)   Der Bauer hat die Kuh $_S$(die   schlechte Milch gab) geschlachtet.
       'the farmer has the cow   which bad   milk gave killed'
       The farmer has killed the cow which gave bad milk.

English, like many other languages, permits relative clauses to be center embedded within a higher VP or S, but it does not permit self-embeddings. As a result, center embedding is more frequent across languages. In a similar manner, quantifiable degrees of processing difficulty are argued to predict language frequencies and implicational universals of linear order in Hawkins (1988). Within each set of linear order options defined by processing preferences, languages select the more highly valued ones before they resort to those that are less highly valued.

These examples should suffice to show that talk of different degrees of processing ease and difficulty does not diminish the causality of the relevant principles. Quite the contrary. In the most extreme cases of processing difficulty, absolute predictions of non-occurrence can be made (recall the mirror-image example). But we now have a means of explaining many implicational and distributional universals as well in a principled way (cf. further Hawkins and Cutler this volume).

This gradient aspect of many causal factors also has a profound effect on the interaction between principles. Some principles are stronger than opposing ones and will assert themselves in more languages. Recall the frequency gradient $\underline{SVOX} > \underline{VSOX} > \underline{VOSX} > \underline{VOXS}$ of section 1.1. The principle that motivates Subjects Front (Keenan 1979) asserts itself with increasing effect in VO languages; in opposition to a weaker principle positioning subjects to the right of other constituents, reflected in the minority subject-final languages (Keenan 1979; Pullum 1981). And once this kind of interaction between principles is taken into account, the reality of each can be factored out from the variation data, and it may well be that the strength of *all* gradient principles is directly correlated with language frequencies, unless some opposing principle confounds the predictions in particular instances. By making the interaction between principles (and their partial conflicts) explicit, it could be that different degrees of communicative usefulness and perceptual salience, etc., are also reflected in corresponding language frequencies for the properties in question (despite the caveats above).

3 Contributions of the Present Volume

How can we contribute to these rather general issues of explanation for language universals? Obviously a lot of the questions I have raised cannot be answered at this time, in the current state of our knowledge. But it seemed to me that progress would be accelerated by the publication of a volume that brought together the different types of causal factors that have been proposed in this context. The contributors have accordingly been asked to motivate some general type of explanation for which they see evidence, and to provide illustrative universal data supporting its reality, with discussion of this explanation type in relation to others. The result is a state of the art volume that addresses the general issues outlined in section 2.7: what are the causal factors that explain language universals? how far can they be taken? and how do they interact?

The papers are provocative and authoritative. There are, as one would expect, some lively disagreements. The contributors have heard each other's views and (where relevant) read each other's papers. It is also fitting that several disciplines should be represented in a project such as this, given the fundamental nature of the central problem. The contributors are specialists in linguistics (generative theory, typology, syntax, semantics, morphology, the lexicon, discourse-pragmatics and historical linguistics), psycholinguistics (language acquisition and language processing) and computer science (neural computing and artificial intelligence). In this section I outline the themes that are addressed in the papers, in relation to the discussion of section 2.

3.1 *Themes*

What aspects of grammatical knowledge are claimed to be innate, and what is the logic of the innateness hypothesis? Hoekstra and Kooij outline the Chomskyan theory of Universal Grammar and innateness, stressing the centrality of the learnability problem.

Arbib and Hill, and Bowerman ask, on the other hand: what is learnable from positive evidence? Arbib and Hill develop a computational model of learning that operates without a built-in Universal Grammar, and test the predictions of their model on language acquisition in a two-year-old child. And Bowerman examines empirically how somewhat older children acquire subtle grammatical rules without negative data. She argues that assumptions of innate knowledge do not actually solve the negative evidence problem, that children regularly make learning errors of the type that at least some proposed innatist theories preclude and that positive evidence can be exploited in richer ways than is currently assumed. She points out (as do Arbib and Hill) that the absence of negative data poses a parallel problem for the learning of rules that differ idiosyncratically between languages as it does for universally determined properties of rules, and concludes that we need to sever the proposed theoretical link between the search for innate linguistic knowledge and the no negative evidence problem.

Keenan proposes a new semantic theory (Semantic Case Theory) capable of explaining a variety of universal generalizations, including subject–object asymmetries in quantifier scope assignments, and the distribution and interpretation of anaphors. He also contributes to the learnability problem, by showing how the semantic interpretations of complex sentences can readily be learned on the basis of the semantic interpretations of simplex sentences. König examines cross-linguistic similarities and variation patterns in concessive sentences. He argues that the universal generalizations are motivated by the meanings of concessive sentences together with the functions they fulfill in discourse. Contributing to the explanation are certain common historical drifts in the development of these complex constructions. Thompson looks at the category of adjectives across languages: some languages treat the property concepts of

English adjectives more like verbs, and others treat them more like nouns. The variation is explained as a consequence of the major discourse functions that these property concepts are used to perform: predicating a property of an established discourse referent (like verbs); and introducing a new discourse referent (like nouns). Comrie examines variation in co-reference options within conjoined clauses across languages, and accounts for it in terms of an interaction between grammar and discourse.

Lee summarizes some of the major perceptual and cognitive explanations for universals that have been proposed in the literature (in phonology and the lexicon), and presents his own cognitively based account of classifier systems across languages.

Frazier and Rayner examine the hypothesis of Yngve (1960) that left-branching structures are more difficult to parse than their right-branching counterparts (thereby explaining the existence of rightward-moving extraposition rules in a variety of languages, cf. section 2.4 above). They provide experimental results that refute the hypothesis, and propose instead that left- and right-branching structures are processed in terms of a single (though paramaterized) principle of Maximal Chunking. Hawkins and Cutler offer a processing explanation for the suffixing preference: across languages suffixal morphology is more frequent than prefixing and infixing. It is argued that lexical stems are processed before affixes, and that this motivates the preferred ordering stem + affix, even in languages in which alternative principles (specifically the Head Ordering Principle) would predict the reverse.

Hall integrates the processing considerations of Hawkins and Cutler's paper with diachronic processes of change. Affixes derive historically from separate words, and morpheme order typically reflects the earlier syntactic order of the pre-fused elements. He rejects an alternative hypothesis that the suffixing preference is the result of all language families being originally SOV in basic word order, and instead combines the processing arguments of Hawkins and Cutler with diachronic universals of morphologization, thereby providing a more complete theory that explains both why suffixes are more frequent across languages, and how they arise historically. Bybee gives a general discussion of the diachronic dimension in explaining language universals. She cites a number of areas in which diachronic processes explaining how a change occurs need to supplement synchronic principles. She then provides a detailed discussion of a universal semantic drift involving future meanings and related notions, which accounts for cross-linguistic variation in the semantics of the relevant verbs synchronically.

These papers therefore illustrate and discuss a number of types of explanations for universals. They also provide several examples of co-operation or partial conflict between principles. To cite just a few: König's paper appeals to an interaction between semantics, pragmatics and diachrony in explaining universals of concessive sentences; Comrie examines the interplay between syntax and discourse; Hall looks at the interaction of processing and historical principles; and Hawkins and Cutler examine frequency differences between languages and implicational universals that result from a partial conflict between principles (head ordering and stem-initial processing).

It is the editor's hope that these papers will stimulate even further research and progress towards our goal of understanding why language universals are the way they are.

References

Andersen, E. (1978) 'Lexical universals of body-part terminology'. In Greenberg et al. (1978), vol. 3, *Word Structure*.

Anderson, S. R. and E. L. Keenan (1985) 'Deixis'. In Shopen (1985), vol. 3, *Grammatical Categories and the Lexicon*.

Baker, C. L. and J. J. McCarthy (eds) (1981) *The Logical Problem of Language Acquisition*. Cambridge, Mass.: MIT Press.

Berlin B. and P. Kay (1969) *Basic Color Terms: Their Universality and Evolution*. Berkeley, Calif. and Los Angeles: University of California Press.

Bever, T. G. (1970) 'The cognitive basis for linguistic structures'. In J. R. Hayes (ed.), *Cognition and the Development of Language*. New York: John Wiley.

Chomsky, N. (1965) *Aspects of the Theory of Syntax*. Cambridge, Mass.: MIT Press.

(1968) *Language and Mind*. New York: Harcourt, Brace & World.

(1975) *Reflections on Language*. New York: Pantheon.

(1981) *Lectures on Government and Binding*. Dordrecht: Foris Publications.

(1982) *Some Concepts and Consequences of the Theory of Government and Binding*. Cambridge, Mass.: MIT Press.

Comrie, B. (1981) *Language Universals and Linguistic Typology: Syntax and Morphology*. Oxford: Basil Blackwell.

Coopmans, P. (1984) 'Surface word order typology and universal grammar'. *Language*, 60, 55–69.

Cutler A. and J. A. Hawkins (1987) 'Computational order as a motivation for word order'. Paper presented at the XIVth International Congress of Linguists, East Berlin.

Dryer M. S. (1980) 'The positional tendencies of sentential noun phrases in universal grammar'. *Canadian Journal of Linguistics*, 25.2, 123–95.

Faltz, L. M. (1985) *Reflexivization: A Study in Universal Syntax*. New York: Garland.

Fillmore, C. J. (1968) 'The case for case'. In E. Bach and R. T. Harms (eds), *Universals of Linguistic Theory*. New York: Holt, Rinehart & Winston.

Fodor, J. D. (1979) 'Superstrategy'. In W. E. Cooper and E. C. T. Walker (eds), *Sentence Processing*. Hillsdale, NJ: Erlbaum.

Foley, J. (1977) *Foundations of Theoretical Phonology*. Cambridge: Cambridge University Press.

Frazier, L. (1978) 'On comprehending sentences: syntactic parsing strategies'. Ph.D. diss., University of Connecticut.

(1984) 'Syntactic complexity'. In D. Dowty, L. Karttunen and A. Zwicky (eds), *Syntactic Theory and How People Parse Sentences*. Cambridge: Cambridge University Press.

and K. Rayner (1982) 'Making and correcting errors during sentence comprehension: eye movements in the analysis of structurally ambiguous sentences'. *Cognitive Psychology*, 14, 178–210.

Friedrich, P. (1975) *Proto-Indo-European Syntax*. Journal of Indo-European Studies, Monograph 1. Butte: Montana College of Mineral Science and Technology.

Givón, T. (1971) 'Historical syntax and synchronic morphology: an archaeologist's field trip'. *Papers from the Seventh Regional Meeting of the Chicago Linguistic Society*. Chicago: Chicago Linguistic Society.

(ed.) (1983) *Topic Continuity in Discourse: A Quantitative Cross-Language Study*. Amsterdam: John Benjamins.

Greenberg, J. H. (1966a) 'Some universals of grammar with particular reference to the order of meaningful elements'. In Greenberg (1966b).

(ed.) (1966b) *Universals of Language*, 2nd edn. Cambridge, Mass.: MIT Press.

C. A. Ferguson and E. A. Moravcsik (eds) (1978) *Universals of Human Language*, 4 vols. Stanford, Calif.: Stanford University Press.

Grice, H. P. (1975) 'Logic and conversation'. In P. Cole and J. Morgan (eds), *Syntax and Semantics 3: Speech Acts*. New York: Academic Press.

Haiman, J. (1983) 'Iconic and economic motivation'. *Language*, 59, 781–819.

(ed.) (1985) *Iconicity in Syntax*. Typological Studies in Language, vol. 6. Amsterdam: John Benjamins.

Hale, K. (1983) 'Warlpiri and the grammar of non-configurational languages'. *Natural Language and Linguistic Theory*, 1.1, 5–47.

Hawkins, J. A. (1979) 'Implicational universals as predictors of word order change'. *Language*, 55, 618–48.

(1982) 'Language universals and the logic of historical reconstruction'. *Linguistics*, 20, 367–90.

(1983) *Word Order Universals*. New York: Academic Press.

(1984) 'Modifier-head or function-argument relations in phrase structure? The evidence of some word order universals'. *Lingua*, 63, 107–38.

(1986) *A Comparative Typology of English and German: Unifying the Contrasts*. Austin, Tex.: University of Texas Press, and London: Croom Helm.

(1988) 'Some processing motivations for linear order universals'. MS, USC Dept of Linguistics.

Ingram, D. (1978). 'Typology and universals of personal pronouns'. In Greenberg et al. (1978), vol. 3, *Word Structure*.

Jackendoff, R. (1977) *X̄ Syntax: A Study of Phrase Structure*. Linguistic Inquiry Monograph 2.

Kay, P. and C. McDaniel (1978) 'The linguistic significance of the meanings of basic color terms'. *Language*, 54, 610–46.

Keenan, E. L. (1972) 'The logical status of deep structures'. In L. Heilmann (ed.), *Proceedings of the Eleventh International Congress of Linguists*, Bologna; reprinted in Keenan (1987).

(1979) 'On surface form and logical form'. In *Studies in the Linguistic Sciences*, vol. 8, no. 2, Dept of Linguistics, University of Illinois; reprinted in Keenan (1987).

(1987) *Universal Grammar: 15 Essays*. London: Croom Helm.

and B. Comrie (1977) 'Noun phrase accessibility and universal grammar'. *Linguistic Inquiry*, 8, 63–99; reprinted in Keenan (1987).

Kuno, S. (1973) 'Constraints on internal clauses and sentential subjects'. *Linguistic Inquiry*, 4, 363–85.

28   JOHN A. HAWKINS

(1974) 'The position of relative clauses and conjunctions'. *Linguistic Inquiry*, 5, 117–36.

Lehmann, W. P. (1974) *Proto-Indo-European Syntax*. Austin, Tex.: University of Texas Press.

Lenerz, J. (1977) *Zur Abfolge Nominaler Satzglieder im Deutschen*. Studien zur Deutschen Grammatik. Tübingen: Gunter Narr.

Li, C. N. and S. A. Thompson (1974) 'Historical change of word order: a case study of Chinese and its implications', In J. M. Anderson and C. Jones (eds), *Historical Linguistics 1*. Amsterdam: North Holland.

Lindblom, B., P. MacNeilage and M. Studdert-Kennedy (1984) 'Self-organizing processes and the explanation of phonological universals'. In B. Butterworth, B. Comrie and Ö. Dahl (eds), *Explanations for Language Universals*. New York: Mouton.

Mallinson, G. and B. J. Blake (1981) *Language Typology: Cross-Linguistic Studies in Syntax*. Amsterdam: North Holland.

Pullum, G. K. (1981) 'Languages with object before subject: a comment and a catalogue'. *Linguistics*, 19, 147–55.

Sadock, J. M. and A. M. Zwicky (1985) 'Speech act distinctions in syntax'. In Shopen (1985), vol. 1, *Clause Structure*.

Saito, M. (1985) 'Some asymmetries in Japanese and their theoretical implications'. Ph.D diss., MIT.

Shopen, T. (ed.) (1985) *Language Typology and Syntactic Description*, 3 vols. Cambridge: Cambridge University Press.

Slobin, D. I. (1973) 'Cognitive prerequisites for the development of language'. In C. A. Ferguson and D. I. Slobin (eds), *Studies in Child Language Development*. New York: Holt, Rinehart & Winston.

Sperber, D. and D. Wilson (1986) *Relevance: Communication and Cognition*. Cambridge, Mass.: Harvard University Press, and Oxford: Basil Blackwell.

Sweetser, E. E. (1984) 'Semantic structure and semantic change: a cognitive linguistic study of modality, perception, speech acts, and logical relations'. Ph.D. diss., University of California at Berkeley.

(1986) 'Polysemy vs. abstraction: mutually exclusive or complementary?'. *Proceedings of the Twelfth Annual Meeting of the Berkeley Linguistics Society; Papers from the Parasession on Semantic Typology*, 528–38.

Thompson, S. A. (1978) 'Modern English from a typological point of view: some implications of the function of word order'. *Linguistische Berichte*, 54, 19–35.

Traugott, E. C. (1982) 'From propositional to textual and expressive meanings; some semantic-pragmatic aspects of grammaticalization'. In W. P. Lehmann and Y. Malkiel (eds), *Perspectives on Historical Linguistics*. Amsterdam: John Benjamins.

(1986) 'From polysemy to internal semantic reconstruction'. *Proceedings of the Twelfth Annual Meeting of the Berkeley Linguistics Society; Papers from the Parasession on Semantic Typology*, 539–50.

Wexler, K. and P. W. Culicover (1980) *Formal Principles of Language Acquisition*. Cambridge, Mass.: MIT Press.

Yngve, V. H. A. (1960) 'A model and an hypothesis for language structure'. *Proceedings of the American Philosophical Society*, 104, 444–66.

Zwicky, A. M. (1985) 'Heads'. *Journal of Linguistics*, 21, 1–29.

PART II

Innateness and Learnability

CHAPTER 2

The Innateness Hypothesis

Teun Hoekstra and Jan G. Kooij

1 The Logic of the Innateness Hypothesis

Although a great number of different communication systems can be found among an extensive range of different species, none of these systems can be shown to have the properties that are characteristic of the speech of human beings. By contrast, all members of the human species have ready access to at least one human language. These two facts would appear to be sufficient for anyone to conclude that the language faculty is a biological endowment of the species. Yet, despite its obvious nature, the innateness hypothesis has met with considerable resistance ever since its inception.

The fact that members of other species also possess the capacity for communicating with other members of their species can hardly be adduced as an argument to deny the biological determination of the language faculty in the human species. And whereas we may certainly be convinced of an evolutionary development in the various animal species along the lines of classical evolution theory, it does not follow that their various communication systems have developed from each other in the same evolutionary sense. What we know is that the language of each species is determined by the innate structure of that species. What would have to be established to prove otherwise is that these systems have evolved from each other to an extent that is still compatible with similarities in their innate structures. Thus, along these lines one might argue that the capacity of the human species to acquire language results from its cognitive potential and that humans differ from chimpanzees and other primates in a quantitative rather than in a qualitative way: the greater complexity of human language being not a function of a specific linguistic endowment, but deriving both from an increase in cognitive potential and from a stronger environmental impetus as compared to the much simpler demands placed on apes by their environment.

It would seem that this environmental argument can easily be dismissed. True, human society requires the versatility and universal applicability of our communication system, but it seems unlikely that the complexity of human language would have arisen as a result of this communicative system, and that environmental demands would have caused the communicative system to have these properties. There is no linguistic basis for assuming a differentiation in structural complexity across languages as a function of the differentiation in complexity of human societies. It is also entirely inconceivable that, on the assumption that apes would have a larger linguistic and cognitive potential than can be met within their own communicative system, this potential would have gone unexploited up to now, given the evolutionary advantages it offers and the environmental pressures that the species has been under.

The idea that the difference between humans and apes is a matter of quantity rather than quality is in conformity with a steady, gradual interpretation of evolution. This picture, however, is an oversimplification in general, and it is certainly deceptive in this specific case. There has been a rapid expansion of the brain in humans and humanoids, which is already dramatic from the gradualist point of view, and yet it is questionable whether this increase in brain size can be held responsible for the human language faculty without further qualification. It is more likely that a function-specific organization of the brain resulted in an evolutionary gap between humans and other primates. This then would constitute a qualitative rather than a quantitative basis for the difference between the species. Leaving this matter to evolutionary biologists and neurologists, we now turn to the question of whether the linguistic activities of humans and other primates can be differentiated on a qualitative rather than a quantitative basis.

The communicative system of apes in natural circumstances does not seem to differ significantly from systems found in other animals, either in function or in complexity. In order to rule out the possibility of explaining this in terms of environmental demands and similar factors, it is important to expose apes to human language in the setting of human society and to see how they cope with the system exploited there. Research of this type has been carried out on a sufficiently large scale for at least some conclusions to be drawn. It would appear that apes do master human language to a certain extent, and this indeed suggests a quantitative difference. However, we have to be careful not to jump to conclusions. We have to examine what apes can do, and also what they cannot do.

The accomplishments of the trained apes reported in the literature are impressive. They are capable of learning a vocabulary of about 500 to 600 items. They have the capacity for self-reference. They can appreciate the symbolic value of the signs they use and exploit these to construct new messages. To give an example, if the subject has learned the signs 'door' and 'open' in the combination of 'open door', used to convey the request to open the door, he is also capable of constructing the combination 'open window', provided that the sign for 'window' has been learned as well. What these examples show is that the ape certainly has an impressive cognitive capacity and in this respect he might differ in a quantitative sense only from our species.

The process of learning a human language in apes also shows interesting resemblances to the acquisition of language by children. The first stage is characterized by one-word sentences, and gradually develops into a two-word sentence stage. Still later, subjects are reported to be able to construct three-word sentences. There, however, the resemblance stops. In the speech development of humans, no four-word stage is discernible, nor is there a five-word stage, etc. After a certain period of simple sentences of two and three words, the child's performance exhibits an explosion into the use of sentences with no fixed limit. It is precisely this that is seen as a reflex of a unique feature of human language: it is an infinite system. This systematic infiniteness is often regarded as a consequence of the infinite number of messages that the system allows us to convey. Let us call this concept 'communicative infiniteness'. Whereas human languages certainly have such communicative infiniteness, from a strictly linguistic point of view it is not a particularly interesting property. The communicative versatility of human language is a matter of performance, that is, of exploiting certain resources in order to respond to the environment in an adequate way. One of the resources that is put to use is the knowledge of the language system, but other resources contribute to it as well. The interesting property of human language that becomes evident from the example we just gave is that the system does not impose any limit on the length of sentences constructed according to the rules of the system. In this respect, the human language system is like the number system. Just as a child does not need to learn how to count from 21 to 29 once he has learned the rules of the number system, he can construct sentences of infinite length once he has mastered the system of language. Both systems are recursive and neither is accessible to apes. Natural languages do not differ in this regard, whereas they may vary with respect to communicative infiniteness, although only temporarily so.

This difference in the capacity for handling recursive systems is not a quantitative matter: one either has it or one doesn't. The fact that all languages are characterized by this recursive property reflects a predetermined faculty of the species and cannot be argued to derive from any other factor, for example, from the infinity of messages that the species is required to convey. There are several other ways in which this communicative infiniteness might be served. The uniformity of natural languages in this regard would be explained, however, if it is assumed that the property derives from our biological determination. The relevance of this particular property is not universally appreciated by all linguists. There seems to be a rather widespread tendency to take such properties for granted, but clearly such an attitude is not well-founded.

Related to this is the problematical status of the notion of learning. Surprising as it may seem, there are those who believe that innate faculties are those that manifest themselves directly at birth, whereas all other faculties that a full-grown system possesses are learned. The concept of learning is much too unspecific to disconfirm this, but the acquisition of language is undoubtedly an entirely different activity from, for example, learning topography. Birds are said to learn to fly, but it would be more accurate to say that they have the innate capacity to fly which develops on the way to maturity. Similarly, it would make more sense to speak of language growth instead of language learning. Also in this respect, the acquisition of human language by apes differs significantly from the acquisition process in children. Whereas there is teaching in the former case, no special attention is paid to the development of linguistic knowledge in human offspring. Humans master the complex system of rules without any instruction and do this in a surprisingly uniform fashion. Barring abnormalities, no variation has been reported that reflects any difference in the actual language that the child is exposed to, nor any variation in learning capacity exhibited in other domains. This uniformity, then, suggests maturation rather than a process of learning. At the same time, it suggests a fundamental similarity between the systems being acquired, a similarity that can hardly be motivated in terms of environmental demands to which the different linguistic communities have to respond, because these show considerable diversity.

The conclusion to be drawn from these considerations should be obvious. The human species is endowed with a specific language faculty that is qualitatively different from anything found in other species, but uniformly present among the members of the human species. The uniformity of acquisition and the fact that all systems underlying human languages are characteristically recursive cannot be accounted for by assuming that each of these systems is one of the possible answers to environmental demands that the species as a whole has come up with in response to general cognitive growth. The argument in this case is not different from the classical argument for genetic determination of any feature of a particular organism: the feature is too specific to be determined by external factors.

Up to now, we have only pointed to the recursiveness of the system underlying human languages. No matter how important this feature may be, one might question whether this single property suffices to counterbalance the enormous variation exhibited by the languages of the world. It is certainly true that the hypothesis of an innate linguistic program is not easily reconciled with this attested variation. In fact, this reconciliation is the very program of general linguistics to which we have turned only recently. Our knowledge is therefore still very limited. Under these circumstances it is to be expected that one is easily overwhelmed by the extent of diversity that one encounters. Impressive as it may be, the diversity should not distract our attention from the fundamental similarity that we should be able to find given the reasoning above.

Before turning to a discussion of various aspects of language that may be accounted for in terms of a fixed bioprogram, we shall first indicate the relations between such things as grammars, competence and innate endowment as they are commonly conceived within generative grammar.

In large measure these interrelations are familiar, but it may be useful to summarize them briefly.

A language L can be characterized by a set of rules. Such a characterization is traditionally called a grammar G of L. Each user of L has mastered the rules of L, that is, he is a competent speaker of L by virtue of knowledge of G. Therefore, a grammar can be interpreted as a description of the tacit knowledge of the speaker, that is, as a description of his competence. Admittedly there may be disagreement concerning the boundaries of the grammar, concerning the precise formulation of specific rules, etc., but these are issues of an empirical nature. It would seem unreasonable, however, either to deny the existence of tacit knowledge in the individual or to question the validity of interpreting a grammar as a description of this knowledge.

To say that a grammar is a description of the tacit knowledge of the individual speaker is not at variance with the idea that a language belongs to a community rather than an individual. Language itself is a derivative concept, an entity of a much larger degree of abstractness than grammar. Individuals use their language to communicate with other individuals of the same linguistic community. In this process, each speaker puts his competence to use, among other modules such as his knowledge of the world, etc. In a sense, the language of a community is made up of the languages of the individual members of the community, each of which will differ to some extent. Hence, the language of a community is even more abstract than the language of an individual. For practical purposes, linguistic research abstracts away from these variations among individuals. Accordingly, Chomsky (1965: 3) states that 'Linguistic theory is concerned primarily with an ideal speaker-listener, in a completely homogeneous speech-community, who knows his language perfectly.' Despite the obvious need for making a number of abstractions, a prerequisite for any normal scientific research, this position has given rise to unfortunate disputes, more often than not based on a lack of understanding.

A fundamental assumption of general linguistics has always been that grammars of languages show certain similarities. Indeed, this assumption constitutes the very basis for the field of general linguistics. Thus, all grammars of natural languages share a common core. Again, it is an empirical matter to establish the content of this common core, and disagreements about the validity of proposals in this domain are likely to continue, as our efforts to arrive at relevant generalizations are fairly recent and only relatively little is known. Let us refer to this common core shared by individual grammars as UG (Universal Grammar). Just as G has a realistic interpretation as a description of the competence of an individual speaker, UG is given a realistic interpretation as a description of the initial state of the knowledge of grammar (this is what used to be called the language acquisition device, LAD). The task of UG is to narrow down the notion of a possible grammar of a human language, and hence, derivatively, to describe the notion of possible human language. The ultimate explanatory power of UG is located in the account it provides for the speed of language acquisition, that is, in explaining how a child can acquire a grammar consistent with the language spoken by the community in a relatively short space of time and on the basis of rather degenerate evidence.

Opponents of this research program tend to question the latter point, that is, the claim about speed of acquisition and the poor quality of evidence available to the child. In large measure such disagreement is determined by the extent to which one is impressed by the complexity of what has to be acquired. There is a tendency to take for granted that language is the way it is and hence to disregard other conceivable options. Chomsky has frequently noted that grammatical rules are structure-dependent (cf. Chomsky 1975). This being a matter of fact, there is a tendency simply to accept it as such, that is, not to consider it as something that needs explanation, or, put differently, as something that needs to be learned. However, a child will ultimately have to master a rule such as subject–verb agreement. If his acquisition system is not endowed with the structure-dependent hypothesis, the number of logical possibilities for formulating this rule is much wider and hence the acquisition task is considerably more complicated. Just to assume that children mimic the operation performed by their caretakers without considering the basis for the child's conclusion that the operation is structure-dependent is to seriously disregard the complicated task that the child performs. Referring to the discussion above, we note that no explanation is given either for the fact that rules of subject–verb agreement are structure dependent in every language.

It is sometimes claimed that the acquisition problem is not as severely hampered by the poor quality of the data as we claim it is, as the input is initially restricted by the simple register called 'motherese' (cf. Snow and Ferguson 1977). Motherese is then assumed to provide a more adequate basis for acquisition to proceed on an inductive basis, that is, without the need for a structured set of hypotheses. However obvious this may sound, the idea is quite naive in two ways. First, the factual claim is incorrect, that is, children are exposed to a much broader data base than only motherese. Second and more importantly, however, even if such a restriction of the input were possible, it would be of little help to the child. Chomsky (1975) and Wexler (1982) have pointed out that narrowing the learner's data base cannot facilitate the construction of a grammar covering the full language. The narrower the range of data, the more hypotheses can describe them. Hence, the learning task would be compounded if such a restriction were to hold. The input would not only be random, but would also fail to be representative.

The most impressive evidence in favor of biased acquisition of grammar derives from the fact that speakers appear to possess knowledge that is underdetermined by the available evidence. The following example illustrates this. Speakers of English are capable of giving the judgments in (1). Whereas one might argue that they are capable of giving these judgments with respect to (1a)–(1c) on the basis of being exposed to such constructions, no such argument can be given with respect to (1d).

(1) a. He proved the theorem
    b. His proof of the theorem
    c. He proved the theorem wrong
    d. *His proof of the theorem wrong

The judgments in (1) would require negative evidence which is unavailable to the language user. It is also very hard to argue that there is no communicative need for a construction such as (1d). In any event, it is up to proponents of the hypothesis of unbiased learning to provide an explanation as to why the patterns in (1b) and (1c) do not generalize to (1d). Such an explanation should also explain why constructions of type (1d) are impossible in all other languages as well, assuming that they are. One might object to this argument by pointing out that in English a construction of the form in (1d) is never attested, hence that the pattern *N of NP AP* is never induced as a possible pattern of English. Notice that this objection implies the assumption that language users keep track of the patterns that they have encountered, which is a very strong assumption. Nevertheless, it is conceivable that the actual process of learning the grammar of a language does involve keeping certain patterns in memory. But in itself, this would make little sense unless patterns were not only stored but also used when one works out relevant generalizations. In this case, the generalization would be that 'gerundive' nominalizations allow predicative adjuncts whereas 'derived nominals' do not:

(1) d. *His proof of the theorem wrong
    e. His proving the theorem wrong
    f. *His destruction of the city single-handed
    g. His destroying the city single-handed

In view of the obvious parallelism in other respects between the two types of nominalization, one expects the child to arrive at a conclusion about both types, and not just about one. Drawing this conclusion presupposes awareness of differences between nominalizations that are full NPs and nominalizations that are not, in particular, for the examples under consideration, awareness of rules for predication. But these rules are quite abstract. Therefore, it is plausible that the judgment that (1d) is ungrammatical and, indeed, impossible is ultimately based on knowledge of principles of UG and not just on the non-occurrence of the pattern itself.

Notice, furthermore, that there are cases where non-occurrence of a pattern can hardly be the explanation for consistency of judgments to begin with. Consider (2a) versus (2b).

(2) a. Where did John say that we had to get off the bus?
    b. Where did John ask whether we had to get off the bus?

Both sentences are grammatical. However, while (2a) is ambiguous between a reading in which *where* has matrix scope and a reading in which it has embedded scope, (2b) can only be interpreted as a question concerning the place where John uttered a particular question (that is, with matrix scope). This piece of knowledge is shared by all native speakers, but it can hardly have been established on the basis of induction, simply because there are no data from which induction could conceivably proceed. Again, one might object that there are positive data to proceed from, for instance the fact that questions like (2b) are never answered in a way that indicates that *where* in (2b) could have embedded scope. But it would be surprising if the child were to stop there. There are many and sometimes quite complex differences in extraction possibilities between structures that are highly similar on the surface. In a fair number of these cases grammaticality judgments do not vary, and they certainly do not vary at random. The reasonable assumption seems to be that the child, on the basis of whatever relevant data he or she encounters, must try to find an answer to the question *why* there is no embedded scope for *where* in (2b), and, more generally, must try to find out which structures under which conditions are 'barriers' for the extraction of question words. Data like (2a) and (2b), no matter how carefully 'stored', are in themselves largely insufficient to provide an answer to these questions unless the child also has access to complex principles of UG that determine the (im)possibility of extraction in otherwise similar configurations.

What we are confronting then is a system which is constant through the species and which has properties that are underdetermined by the environment. These are precisely the characteristics that lead to the postulation of a property of the genotype. Obviously, as in every case of genotypical determination, environmental differences will lead to phenotypical variation. In the case of language, a distinction is made between a core grammar of each individual language which is determined by the genotype, and a language specific periphery which accounts for the variation across languages.

The logic of the situation is clear. It is the task of general linguistics to determine which properties belong to UG. Whether or not a particular property of a particular language can be assumed to derive from UG is an empirical matter, that is, claims made in this respect are falsifiable in principle. A sufficient criterion to establish any such claim would be that the property in question is underdetermined in the sense outlined above. A necessary condition, on the other hand, would be that the property is found in every language.

Although this latter condition is straightforward, it would seem to place an unnecessarily heavy demand on linguistic theory. On the one hand, it is conceivable that a property that we expect to turn up in every language fails to be present in a particular language because it is overruled by a language-particular mechanism. Obviously, claims to this effect require careful consideration, as the idea in itself endangers the testability of any claim of universal scope. On the other hand, languages may vary in certain ways on a theme that is nevertheless universal. A case in point is the subjacency condition proposed in Chomsky (1973). In its original form, the condition was formulated as in (3).

(3) no transformational rule may involve X and Y in the structure
$...X...[_A...[_B...Y...]...]...X...$ if A, B are either NP or S

Interestingly, this condition is not an empirical generalization, as it is in conflict with the very data of English that motivate it; there are numerous constructions in which landing site and extraction site for a movement operation are more than two S boundaries apart. Thus, whereas the condition is obeyed in (2b), the embedded scope interpretation of (2a), taken at face value, constitutes a violation. We will assume here that the violation is indeed apparent only, because successive cyclic movement of a WH-element is possible if the dependent clause contains the complementizer *that* but not if it contains the WH-operator *whether* (with the further assumption that the complementizer *that* in English does not block extraction of an adjunct phrase like *where*).

There are more apparent violations of subjacency, and to the extent that the condition does make the correct predictions, then, it is hard to see how it could be learned as such. It is reasonable, therefore, to assume that subjacency is part of UG. However, as Rizzi (1978) has argued, the condition in the formulation in (3) does not make the correct predictions for Italian. Rather than taking this evidence as falsifying the subjacency condition, Rizzi argues that the condition should be maintained with a slight modification concerning the set of categories that function as bounding nodes: NP and S in English, NP and S′ in Italian. Such an option, called a parameter, allows for variation across languages that is still determined by UG. UG can thus be thought of as specifying a number of parameters, the values of which can be set differently by different languages. What must be learned in these cases are the different values, whereas the type of bounding condition that subjacency represents belongs to the innate structural constraints on the syntax of human languages. Awareness of such fundamental principles, of course, will be triggered by sets of data, but that by no means implies that the principles can be deduced from the data.

This perspective on UG is of relatively recent date, so that no well-established set of parameters is available as yet, although many interesting proposals can be found in the recent literature, including Chomsky (1986) where another modification of subjacency is proposed in the light of recent developments in GB theory. It is possible, in principle, that subjacency will be replaced in the course of time by some other condition, call it C, that more satisfactorily accounts for the fact that within a given structure S no two elements E1 and E2 may be 'related' in some structurally defined sense of the term because they are 'too far apart', where 'too far' again has to be made precise in terms of what is known and what can be made explicit about the syntax of human languages. But for the time being we can regard subjacency as one attempt among others to define a characteristic of UG in the sense described above.

One may object, at this point, that the ultimate goal of general linguistics as we see it is overly ambitious, and is, moreover, often kept out of sight in the practice of syntactic or phonological analysis, in comparing languages and in the presentation of results. While this latter may be true, it does not constitute a principled objection. As for the former point, it would seem to us that the goal is set by the nature of human language – or, more precisely, by the proper definition of the difference between 'language' and 'grammar' – by the facts of language acquisition and by the exigencies of scientific theory commonly accepted elsewhere. There seems to be no a priori reason to assume that the construction of a theory of UG in our sense is more ambitious than the construction of such a theory on the basis of syntactic or phonological evidence from a large number of languages. On the contrary, it is a natural assumption that what does and what does not count as evidence for a theory of UG amongst all these data can be determined only on the basis of a far more abstract theory of UG as outlined above.

2 On What Counts as an Explanation

The innateness theory is a hypothesis, to be sure, and not a belief, and, as we stated before, it seems to be the most reasonable hypothesis in view of the phenomena defining the empirical domain of linguistics as a science. We may well ask, therefore, why the hypothesis has met with considerable disbelief and scepticism.

An initial asnwer to this question is that there seems to be a strong bias in the study of the design features of human beings to the effect that those aspects of human design which have to do with the development and nature of man's cognitive capacities are preferably viewed as 'acquired' in the course of a more general intellectual or cognitive development, whereas the more obviously biological endowments, such as, for example, the capacity to walk, are preferably viewed as 'innate'. For some reason, which may go far back into the history of western philosophy, this position is felt to be a comfortable one, in spite of the fact that there is enough evidence to the contrary. To some extent, and in a more sophisticated form, the position still influences research into language acquisition and into man's linguistic capacity in general. As Marshall states (1980: 134): 'All available computational models of any interest presuppose a strongly constrained hypothesis space and a well-defined input "language". But when we turn to the learning theories currently available in a (quasi-)

physiological format, we find associative theories of the most classical kind.' Lieberman's book on language and evolution (1984) provides a good example of precisely that. While he does not deny that some capacities that are involved in the acquisition of language may be innate, he tries, on the one hand, to define the capacity to acquire syntax as derivative of sensori-motor capacities developed in the course of evolution, and, on the other hand, to ascribe those linguistic capacities that he does recognize as species-specific to the workings of a 'general purpose' computer in the human brain. The following passage, in an approving comment on computer simulation of language acquisition, is quite typical (pp. 50–1): 'The computer programs used in these experiments . . . use the general associative ability of the distributed neural model to deduce the rules of grammar that underlie the input sentences.'

Lieberman's reasoning illustrates an a-priori that is not uncommon. Inasmuch as man's capacity for language is biologically determined, it is supposed to be 'biological' in the traditional sense of physical growth and sensori-motor development (for example, in the case of Lieberman, the capacity for production and perception of speech sounds). Inasmuch as the capacity for language cannot reasonably be claimed to be biological in this restricted sense only, it is assumed, and often without much argumentation, that it is an instantiation of a more encompassing cognitive capacity (say, the capacity for logical thought), which enables us to 'learn' things and 'handle' problems. The idea that there might be such a thing as an innate universal grammar which determines the nature and manifestations of this cognitive capacity and which, furthermore, is quite distinct from other cognitive abilities still seems to be almost offensive. Nevertheless, this idea receives support both from research into the communicative capacities of apes and from language acquisition as well as from the partial, tentative, but undeniable successes to date in constructing fragments of what we have called UG.

The major mistrust of explanations in terms of innate principles of UG seems to be that such explanations are not 'external' in some sense, in particular, that they do not relate in any obvious way to the variety of principles that constitute human symbolic behavior as we experience it and that they have no immediate link with other cognitive capacities of the species. The observation is correct, but the criticism is not. On several occasions (e.g. Chomsky 1980) Chomsky has warned against the belief that a statement about universal grammar (the formulation of a structural possibility or a structural constraint supposedly valid for all languages) gains in validity if it can be formulated in terms of a generalization outside of language, for instance if it can be directly tested for 'psychological reality'.

First of all, if we take linguistics seriously we can ill afford to leave the permanent impression that we view the categories of our theory of grammar as convenient abbreviations for something more interesting that has yet to be discovered, though this is the distinct impression one sometimes gets. Secondly, in order to establish connections with other cognitive capacities – which is desirable if we take the biological point of view seriously also – we have to know a lot more than we do about both human language and other cognitive capacities of humans. And finally, in view of the specificity of the knowledge of language attained by adult humans and in view of the imperfect evidence available to the child, we expect that a subset of the principles of UG will never be reduced to some more encompassing principle in any interesting and explanatory way, because they are 'linguistic' *tout court*. This is the thrust of the argument for 'modular' approaches towards the study of cognitive processes and capacities: we have a specialized brain, whether we like it or not.

Nevertheless, precisely because our knowledge on this point is wanting, it is perfectly reasonable to ask the question in what direction we should look for the possible connection between principles of UG and cognitive capacities in general or the constitutive principles of linguistic behavior in particular. To our mind, the choice that apparently is the obvious choice to some people is the least promising: an explanation for structures and constraints that determine UG in terms of communicative purposes or principles of human interaction. While such principles certainly invite investigation because they belong to language in the broad sense of 'one's communicative resources as a human', and while the investigation may throw light on particular aspects of the form and meaning of linguistic elements, the principles that actually determine the interactive use of language seem to be quite remote from the principles of grammar. As we shall argue below in some detail, sentence types – in the structural sense of 'type' – are multifunctional in the communicative sense. There can hardly be a more glaring contrast than that between what we have labeled 'systematic infiniteness' and 'communicative infiniteness'. Or, from another point of view, the chances that the latter aspects of human symbolic behavior converge with communicative behavior in other animals seem to be much larger than the chances of convergence for the linguistic systems underlying this behavior.

A more promising line of research appears to be the investigation of the correlations between the linguistic representation of syntactic and morphological structures and models for the processing of organized sequences of elements; for example, the experimental study of the inter-relations between models for on-line processing and abstract models of grammar as pursued in recent psycholinguistic approaches to parsing (e.g. Frazier 1978). From the biological point of view, a further link would still have to be established between the workings of performance models and the actual neurological 'hardware', which at present seems to be a too formidable task. In evaluating the results of the study of actual parsing it should be kept in mind that parsing models and models of grammatical structure are not interchangeable objects. Thus, it is somewhat strange to see Lieberman (1984) claim that a transformational model of *grammar* can be dispensed with because the ATN *parsing model* can do without transformations; apart from the fact that the claim is factually incorrect, as his own illustration of the workings of the ATN parser shows, it is based on a serious confusion of the distinct modules that are – possibly – involved in the actual understanding of sentences in a natural language. Nevertheless, if one wants to know whether some principle of UG like 'subjacency' has any external explanation, or whether some linguistic phenomenon does have an entirely non-linguistic explanation, the answer will emerge from a confrontation of models of grammar and models of processing rather than from research into 'communicative strategies'.

Consider a fairly trivial example first. Many languages exhibit structures of the type that are commonly referred to as 'Topicalization' where some element is moved towards the left-peripheral position of the sentence and where the remaining part of the sentence can be construed as some form of 'predication' on the topicalized element. Many problems about this type of structure are unsolved: for instance, what has been called 'Topicalization' sometimes clearly involves a 'gap' in a structurally definable sense, left by the topicalized element (for example, if it is an argument), whereas in other instances of 'Topicalization' the left-peripheral element which restricts the domain of interpretation of the rest of the sentence may well be generated in situ (for instance, if it is a sentential adverb), which, of course, would mean that under some definitions this type of structure would not be an instance of Topicalization proper, though the logical form of the sentence would be similar. Also, it is not clear in the case of at least some languages whether 'Topics' in the more restricted sense coincide with what are 'subjects'. Nevertheless, for a number of languages it is fairly well established that there is a left-peripheral non-argument position in the sentence that serves as a landing site for different types of constituents.

This being so, a question that one could ask is why languages tend to organize sentences in such a way that the element 'about which' the rest of the sentence is a predication precedes and the predication follows. Disregarding VSO languages for the moment, this is also true of subject and predicate in the more formal syntactic sense; in the majority of natural languages predicates follow their subjects, and within the sentence, again, it appears that predicative constructions of the small clause type are equally linearized along the subject first, predicate after principle. A good example of the latter is provided by Dutch. Compare

(4) a.   Jan vond zijn broer dronken op   straat
         John found his brother drunk   on the street

     b. *Jan vond dronken zijn broer op   straat
         John found drunk   his brother on the street

where (4b) is ungrammatical under the intended interpretation that John's brother is the one who is drunk. The question now is whether the principle 'subject, or topic first, predicate after' is in any way natural in the sense that it can be explained on independent grounds. In terms of information processing, one is inclined to answer in the affirmative: it is natural that, given the linear organization of elements of speech into sentences, the information which is the pivot is presented first and the information which says something about the pivot comes after. While probably correct, the answer is not helpful as an explanation before we have established that there are principles of information processing independent of natural language which point towards the same conclusion; as long as we do not have such principles, the answer is vacuous. This, probably, is what Marshall (1980: 113) is referring to when he says that explanations of universal principles of language in terms of more general principles of cognition tend to be expressed 'in a formalism that is a vague variant of those found in linguistics (or worse, in predicate calculus)'.

More interestingly, it can often be shown quite easily that one general cognitive principle cannot be the explanation even for such a relatively testable phenomenon as the presentation of information. Suppose, for the sake of argument, that a general principle such as 'pivot first' has been established. We might then conclude, first of all, that the order of the elements *zijn broer* and *dronken* in (4a) is predicted and hence does not have to be entered as a separate statement in the grammar. Second, we might conclude that this aspect of linear order is not part of universal grammar but is imposed on universal grammar by a more general principle, say P. Now, consider Topicalization. We have seen that predicative elements in Dutch like *dronken* in (4a) have to follow their subject; hence, (4b) is ungrammatical, but in (4c), in which *op straat* is an adjunct, the phrase *zijn broer* can follow the adjunct grammatically:

(4) c. Jan vond op   straat zijn broer
    John found on the street his brother

But under Topicalization, the order 'predicate first, subject after' becomes fully acceptable; (4d) has one interpretation where, as intended, John's brother is the one who is drunk.

(4) d. Dronken vond Jan zijn broer op   straat
    drunk   found John his brother on the street

This sentence, apparently, disregards the principle 'subject first, predicate after' but is in conformity with the principle 'topic first, comment after'. A modest conclusion from these examples is that languages have at least two ways of organizing the information: a syntactic principle and a semantic/pragmatic principle, and that the more general principle that we have been assuming, 'pivot first', cannot or does not have to be satisfied in both dimensions of sentence structure. Thus, some useful connection between a principle of UG and another, cognitive principle which is independent still has to be established, let alone any explanatory link between the two. Actually, of course, the situation in examples (4a)–(4d) is much more complex; in particular, the structure of (4d) and the formulation of

Topicalization in general cannot be adequately described in terms of linear order and 'first position in the sentence' at all, since we have to assume hierarchical structure in addition to linear order, just as for the explanation of antecedent–anaphor relations we must assume notions like 'command' rather than 'precede'. And this is exactly what we expect. Given that, on the surface, sentences are linear sequences of elements of speech and that, on the other hand, UG has a number of ordering principles such as head first/last, subject first, topic first, adjuncts and modifiers left/right, to mention only a few, one cannot very well expect that the actual ordering of elements in a particular type of sentence will necessarily reflect any one independent principle of 'presentation of information' to any interesting degree, since too many different principles of organization at the level of UG have to be satisfied, ultimately, within one and the same linear dimension. Our conclusion is not, we should add, that one should not try to find a more general principle of perception or processing that might be connected to ordering principles in UG for, for example, certain left–right asymmetries in sentences. But if such a principle could be found, and the connection could be established, one would still need to see what it explains.

3 On What Constitutes an Explanandum

From what has been said so far, it will be clear that the explanation of so-called language universals constitutes only a derivative goal of generative theory. The primary explanandum is the uniformity of acquisition of a rich and structured grammar on the basis of varied, degenerate, random and non-structured experience. The starting assumption for constructing an explanatory theory is that the acquisition is determined by genetically encoded principles that vigorously restrict the hypothesis space available to the child. These principles need to be sufficiently abstract, however, to allow for the fact that a child can learn any language it is exposed to. The existence of language universals is thus predicted by the theory. We can even go one step further. We noted above that the strongest evidence in favor of the innateness hypothesis derives from those aspects of a grammar that are underdetermined by the available evidence, that is, the primary linguistic data. These aspects, then, must logically be determined by some property of UG. The properties ascribed to UG accordingly not only predict the existence of language universals, but constitute necessary conditions for the occurrence of quite specific linguistic phenomena.

This situation contrasts sharply with the one found in the context of what is referred to by such labels as typology, universal grammar, etc. – work that has evolved within the tradition of Greenberg. The explananda for these theories are the language universals themselves. What constitutes a language universal in this framework is not determined by some theory but on an inductive basis. If some phenomenon is found time and time again in the languages of the world, it is perforce a language universal and therefore requires explanation. There are no external criteria that decide whether the particular property found in a particular sample holds as a matter of accident, or reflects a deep grammatical regularity, or is a universal for reasons outside of grammar or of our linguistic capacity. There are no necessary or sufficient conditions to determine whether the attested property is part of the explanandum. By the same token, there is no a priori idea about the kind of explanation that is to be given for the observed regularity. Thus, various kinds of explanations are entertained in the context of typological research, including functional, cognitive and pragmatic explanations.

This liberal stance regarding possible explanations is an immediate consequence of the absence of a theoretical foundation for the explananda. This is not to say that functional or other types of explanation should be rejected out of hand. On the contrary, it may very well be the case that quite a few phenomena that are recurrent in the languages of the world are not determined by linguistic principles at all. From the point of view of generative grammar, however, a theoretically determined selection can be made among the total set of such phenomena, whereas there is no such external criterion within the typological approach. By the same logic, generative grammar does not aim at providing an explanation for every universal phenomenon.

Consider the following simple example from the domain of phonology. A good candidate for a substantive universal seems to be that every language has an [a]. This could not, if true, ever be established on the basis of examination of a single language, no matter how deep the examination. At the same time, the fact that the language the child is exposed to has an [a] is not something that could only be established on the basis of negative evidence, since positive evidence will be abundantly available. Hence, there would be no explanatory benefit in claiming that the occurrence of [a] is determined by some innate principle.

This yields quite a different perspective on the possible contribution of innateness from the one given in Hawkins (1985: 583). The following passage is worth quoting in full:

> many factors presumably interact to explain their shared properties [that is, those of linguistic systems], and to constrain the range of variation. But of all these factors, the one that is hardest to argue for is innateness. We can observe the functions that languages perform; we can argue for or against particular explanations of form in terms of meaning; we can undertake psychological performance experiments; and we can observe historical changes. But we cannot look into the head of the newborn child and find the innate principles of grammar. Hence innateness should not be the principle to which we appeal first, but rather LAST, after other possibilities have been

seriously explored. If these are lacking, innateness becomes a more plausible explanation.

Although we appreciate this open-mindedness regarding allowable explanations, as well as Hawkins' attempt to conceive of the typological and generative approaches as complementary, we strongly object to the role Hawkins has reserved for innateness. Conceived of in this way, essentially as an explanation in the last resort, innateness is reduced to a principle that is actually beyond investigation. This is in fact the appreciation of many linguists in the typological school (e.g. Comrie 1981a: ch. 1). In their view, innateness can be called on to explain each regularity for which the researcher is unable to come up with an alternative explanation and indeed, this would be the single permissible criterion for an explanation in terms of innateness. But as we argued above, there is a theoretical basis for deciding whether or not a particular aspect of grammar can be assumed to be determined by UG.

The difference between the two approaches in their primary explanatory goals entails a difference in methodology: whereas hypotheses about UG within generative grammar can be based on detailed investigation of a single language in principle, the consideration of a fair range of languages is a *conditio sine qua non* in typological approaches, for the simple reason that the explananda for the latter approach can only be detected on the basis of a survey of a fair number of languages. Claims made within generative grammar can and have to be tested against other languages of course, although such testing must be carried out in a careful fashion. The typological approach also requires consideration of a broader corpus of languages, but given the inductive nature of the generalizations, the testing of hypotheses is in fact much more difficult. Given an inductive generalization derived from the study of a particular sample, any explanation is relatively certain to cover a significant proportion of all other languages as well, merely because the hypothesized explanation has to take into consideration the number of languages already studied. This should be a truism: the larger the data base that led to the postulation of a certain hypothesis, the smaller the predictive power becomes. Seen in this way, then, one cannot maintain that explanations of linguistic phenomena in the typological approach have by definition more validity.

It should be noted that the restriction to one or few languages in the generative approach is not a matter of principle. The relevant point is that it is possible to arrive at deep principles on the basis of careful consideration of a single language. Comrie (1984: 156) is in error when he concludes that the fact that a much larger range of languages has recently been considered in generative grammar is to be construed as an indication that generative theory has changed in any relevant sense, let alone that he could rightfully claim that this 'shift to a broader data base therefore calls into question the consistency of the programme'.

It is instructive, in this context, to examine the comparison between the generative approach and the typological approach made by Comrie (1981a). In this discussion he rejects the possible explanatory contribution of the innateness hypothesis. In our view, he misrepresents the motivation for the hypothesis. He states that generative grammar 'maintains that, in addition to relatively concrete levels of syntactic representation, there are also levels of representation that are considerably more abstract, considerably removed from the surface-structure analysis. . . . When the existence of such abstract representations is taken into account in discussing the way in which children acquire their first grammar, a potential problem arises' (p. 2). The problem would be that the child cannot induce these abstract structures and hence, some set of innate ideas is postulated as an explanation for the fact that children nevertheless learn to speak.

The essential point of misrepresentation is situated in the statement that generative grammar *maintains* that there are abstract levels of representation: the existence of these levels results from linguistic argumentation and not from a priori assumptions about the nature of language or about innateness. If adoption of the innateness hypothesis itself *followed* from the postulation of abstract levels of representation (which seems to be Comrie's reasoning), then Comrie would have to argue against abstract representations, not on a priori grounds, but on the basis of linguistic argumentation. To the extent that he has done that, we feel that, again, a serious misunderstanding is involved. Consider his criticism (Comrie, 1981a: section 1.1.3) that levels of representation in UG in the generative sense are (sometimes) abstract or remote to the extent that they have no directly testable reflex in the actual surface structures of a sample of languages, or of any language for that matter. Comrie, apparently, feels that such a move takes grammar beyond the level of testability, but wrongly so.

Topicalization, again, is a case in point here. It has been argued that, for some given SVO language, the landing site for topics at the left periphery of the sentence is different from the position taken by the subject. On the surface, however, the 'first position in the sentence' in a structurally defined sense of 'first' is either occupied by the topic or by the subject if, for instance, the language has a verb second requirement. In each actual surface structure, then, the difference between these two left-peripheral positions does not 'show'. The difference can be motivated using linguistic argumentation, for instance, because there are different constraints on preposing as investigated in Reinhart (1983). The difference between these two 'initial positions' is, in some sense, abstract but whether the move is satisfactory or not depends, we would say, on its success in explaining structures and their acquisition, not on the degree of immediate concreteness of the structures posited.

Let us summarize the main points. Before we can begin to evaluate explanations we have to know what it is that has to be explained. The position of generative grammar is, in this respect, clear and consistent:

what we have to explain are the principles underlying the child's ability to learn any language at all. A subset of these principles belongs to UG and is innate. Which principles of grammatical or phonological structure are innate is an empirical question, and so is the question of the level of abstraction that is involved. It follows from this position that explaining a property P by assuming that it is innate is no more or less interesting and no more or less highly valued than assuming that it follows from, say, the way in which language functions as an instrument of communication or thought. Whether, in fact, the latter kind of explanation is appropriate depends entirely on the data to be explained and cannot be established on a priori grounds.

Let us consider the communicative category of questions. From a functional point of view it is no accident that all languages have the means to ask questions: question words, particles, movement rules, intonation patterns or any combination of these. In that sense, then, we are dealing with a universal category. More likely than not we will find that both in their syntactic form and in their logical form question sentences will show profound similarities with other non-question sentences that involve the use of operators but otherwise serve altogether different communicative purposes. Thus, for a number of languages, we will find that sentences in which question words are moved towards a left-peripheral position show properties that are similar to the rules and constraints involved in Topicalization and in the formation of WH-relative clauses. Functionally, however, these are quite different structures.

What this means is that the formal properties of constructions used for a particular functional category X generalize in a particular language to constructions that are functionally of a different type. And in addition there is no particular formal category that generalizes across languages to serve the particular functional category X. Why that should be disappointing is unclear; rather the correct conclusion appears to be that we are moving one step further towards an understanding of the design of natural language.

This implies that the typology of question sentences in a large sample of languages is up in the air, notwithstanding its own merits, until the typological generalizations are confronted with an in-depth syntactic analysis which, predictably, will lead to a profound alteration of the first round of generalizations. In the light of the syntactic analysis applied, these tentative generalizations will turn out to be not a homogeneous set of properties of question sentences but a heterogeneous set: some will dissolve into separate generalizations corresponding to distinct modules of the grammar – some will remain mysterious for the simple reason that we have not yet moved far enough towards understanding the properties of syntax or of logical form, for that matter, and some may turn out to be pragmatic. Typologically, for example, it is interesting that some languages do not move their question words towards a left-peripheral position in the sentence, but it requires a fair amount of syntactic analysis before we can establish whether a putative division into two types of question formation has any significance for Universal Grammar.

This brings us to a further difference between the two approaches which is quite fundamental and which may be helpful in clarifying the reasons behind other differences. The question is: what constitutes a significant linguistic unit of analysis? The answer given in the tradition of generative grammar is relatively clear, or, more precisely, has become increasingly clearer in recent years: there is no reason to assume that particular types of constructions will show similarities across languages.

A good example is provided by the case of passive. In early transformational approaches, the traditional category of passive was accepted as a relevant unit of analysis, without much other motivation than the plain fact that traditional grammar recognized it as such. Hence, a passive transformation was postulated to describe the properties of this construction. During the early seventies, Relational Grammar rejected the transformational treatment of the passive construction because the formulation of the rule for English failed to generalize to other languages. But RG held on to the assumption that passive constitutes a relevant unit of analysis and developed a set of primitives that would allow for the formulation of cross-linguistically relevant generalizations concerning this unit. Within generative grammar itself, the basic assumption of passive as a linguistically relevant category was given up in favor of a conspiracy analysis of the passive construction in English. 'Passive' thus reduced to a descriptive category with no corresponding category in the theory of grammar. The make-up of this descriptive category in English results from the interplay of several components and wellformedness conditions (Case theory, theta theory, ECP, binding theory). Consequently, these componential factors constitute the linguistically relevant units entering into predictions pertaining to other languages. Commonalities between 'passive' in English and in other languages are only expected to the extent that each of the relevant components contributes to the make-up of a certain sentence type in the same way. It should be noted that this particular approach to 'passive' (or rather non-approach) was motivated on the basis of detailed linguistic argumentation concerning only few languages. Some of the conclusions concerning passive can even be established simply on the basis of a single language. We give two well-known examples.

A traditional description of 'passive' states that 'the object of the active construction is made the subject of the corresponding passive construction, while the former subject becomes an optional adjunct'. The examples in (5) and the Dutch examples in (6) show that rendering the former subject as an adjunct phrase is not necessarily connected with 'promotion' of the object to subject.

(5) a. the enemy's destruction of the city
    b. the destruction of the city by the enemy

(6) a. dat de hond blaft
         that the dog barks
     b. dat er door de hond wordt geblaft
         that there by the dog is barked

Similarly, the example in (7) shows that it is not only objects in passives that are 'promoted' to subjects.

(7) a. X believes the theorem to be wrong
     b. the theorem is believed to be wrong
     c. *X seems the theorem to be wrong
     d. the theorem seems to be wrong

That this particular analytical conclusion is arrived at in generative grammar is not related to the 'single or few languages' approach, at least not in principle. Nor is there a principled reason why the many languages approach should not embrace this conclusion, but in actual practice, this type of result of grammatical analysis is not often used by those working in the typological approach. Typically, cross-linguistic generalizations made within this framework are based on traditional linguistic categories, for example, passivization, relative clause formation, causative constructions, etc. Therefore, two things may be expected.

First, explanations of a functional nature will suggest themselves for generalizations found in the domains considered. This is expected since the domains considered are more or less defined in terms of functional categories. A domain such as 'passive' is first and foremost a category in which one argument (the subject of the active clause) is either left implicit or expressed in an adjunct phrase, and a concomitant phenomenon is that the object is often realized as a subject. Hence, functional characterizations of passive will be offered along either of the following lines: (i) the passive is used when reference to the agent is not appropriate for some reason or other; (ii) whereas the active voice focuses on the action, the passive voice focuses on the resultant state (cf. Comrie 1981b). To take another example, consider the following quotation: 'The claim found in some discussions of Turkish that Turkish does not have relative clauses is thus in one sense correct, but from a wider perspective, it is clear that the Turkish construction [. . .] *fulfils precisely the same function* as the English relative clause' (Comrie 1981b: 136, emphasis added).

Second, it is to be expected that no formal generalizations will be found which hold consistently for the domain of investigation. Indeed, the variation in the formation of relative clauses between languages is considerable. Hence, generalizations found in this domain are likely to be determined by their common function and therefore be open to functional explanations. From a formal point of view, the variation may be taken to indicate that 'relative clause' is not a relevant category cross-linguistically, if only for the reason that some of the structures under consideration do not conform to the definition of clause. In languages that prepose all modifiers of N, including the 'relative clause', this more often than not is the case. What we can establish, rather, is that there are constructions which involve WH-movement. Relative clauses in English constitute one such construction and we expect to find similarities with other constructions which also involve WH-movement, both within English and in other languages. We expect that relativization is possible in the same contexts where WH-interrogatives are possible in English, because WH-interrogatives also involve WH-movement. However, if relative clauses in some other languages are formed without the operation of WH-movement, there is no reason to expect to find formal similarities between relative clauses in that language and relative clauses in English.

These remarks should not be construed as claiming that no relevant generalizations will be encountered under the many languages approach. We merely wanted to stress that entirely different points of view are involved here, and that this has strong implications, on the one hand, for the types of explanations which are relevant within these frameworks, and on the other hand, for the way in which relevant categories for cross-linguistic investigation are determined. We thus disagree with Comrie's view that differences between the two approaches primarily involve (i) the data base, (ii) the abstractness of the categories and (iii) the types of explanations advanced. This blurs the more fundamental difference. The fundamental difference lies in the explanandum, and it is this fundamental difference which implies other differences, such as those discussed by Comrie and other proponents of the typological approach.

4 Conclusions and Outlook

In the above, we have tried to remove some misunderstandings about the innateness hypothesis as we see them because we feel that a discussion about the goals of Universal Grammar cannot very well proceed as long as some basic points have not been clarified. In our view, the enterprise called Universal Grammar follows logically from the fundamental goal of linguistics: the construction of a theory which explains the acquisition of knowledge of a linguistic system that differs qualitatively from other known forms of 'symbolic behavior' among animals. On the basis of the evidence available, a subset of the principles that constitute this knowledge of a language and that allow for its acquisition must be innate. Examples of the nature of linguistic knowledge among humans such as (1) and (2), above, can easily be multiplied and all point in the same direction: adult humans know things about their language which they cannot possibly have learned in the relevant sense of the term, and which pertain to the structure of the linguistic system itself and not to the way it is put to use. The principles under consideration here are not principles of 'appropriateness', 'relevance' or 'communicative strategy' though these also undoubtedly belong to the communicative capacity that humans acquire.

What is innate about the human linguistic capacity first and foremost relates to aspects of the linguistic system that are too often taken for granted. There is no obvious logic to the ungrammaticality of (1d) or to the fact that (2b) is ungrammatical under one of the two interpretations that (2a) allows, or to the fact that the latter ungrammaticality may be felt to be less 'serious' than the former. Such phenomena, then, require an explanation within the theory, and since humans have access to any natural language, it follows that the theory must be universal. This is the first point to underscore: the theory is not universal because we feel an obligation to answer the question why such and such phenomena are the way they are in English, Japanese or Tamil; if we want an answer to questions of this kind, the only thing we can do is proceed with the construction of a theory of Universal Grammar as defined above, with the expectation that some questions about the variety of languages around the world can be made more precise.

Constructing the theory of UG will involve a fair amount of abstraction, not willfully, but inevitably. The explanation for the difference between sentences (2a) and (2b), above, already requires representations of syntactic form that are abstract, compared to the actual sequence of spoken elements (say, a 'trace' of *where*), and takes account of the fact that some human languages *do* allow for the formation of questions that are utterly impossible in English, but do so in a non-random fashion. This, we feel, should be uncontroversial. What can be discussed is the degree of abstractness of representations, as the history of generative grammar shows – and, in all fairness, it should be added that what this history shows so far is that the degree of abstraction allowed for in the prevailing version is quite moderate, certainly when compared with the options available. What we should underline, rather, in this context is that notions that are more familiar than 'trace' or 'COMP' and which therefore, possibly, sound less abstract, are actually more abstract in the sense of 'remote from the phenomena' in that they use a functional label for grammatically quite diverse structural properties. We have given several examples of this; another example would be the way the term 'Topic' is applied and exploited in a serious and informative article by Davison (1984).

Third, we have argued that what is and what is not universal can be established only on the basis of a theory of UG in the above sense, and that, consequently, what is and what is not relevant within the many phenomena that appear to be universal in an absolute or statistically significant sense cannot be decided on the basis of these data themselves. In practice, this may be the greatest source of divergence between the generative and the typological approach.

Generally, the problem with the search for explanations of linguistic universals is not only that we know so little, but also that we are too impatient, and inclined to look for immediate and somehow independently 'plausible' justifications for linguistic generalizations. This is misguided. The substantive, statistical or implicational universals that have been found are data: challenging, fascinating, but still – to a large measure – awaiting interpretation in the context of a theory. The logic of the innateness hypothesis entails that in trying to find an explanation for these as well as other data we begin by looking at the hardest linguistic evidence available: the bits and pieces of what has so far been achieved in constructing a theory of Universal Grammar.

Note

We would like to thank Frits Beukema, Berend Hoff and Harry van der Hulst for their helpful comments on an earlier version, and John Hawkins for his comments on the pre-final draft. The paper was prepared during our stay at NIAS in Wassenaar, which we hereby gratefully acknowledge.

References

Chomsky, N. A. (1965) *Aspects of the Theory of Syntax*. Cambridge, Mass.: MIT Press.
  (1973) Conditions on transformations. In S. Anderson and P. Kiparsky (eds), *A Festschrift for Morris Halle*. New York: Holt, Rinehart & Winston.
  (1975) *Reflections on Language*, New York: Pantheon.
  (1980) *Rules and Representations*. New York: Columbia University Press.
  (1986) *Barriers*. Cambridge, Mass.: MIT Press.
Comrie, B. (1981a) *Language Universals and Linguistic Typology. Syntax and Morphology*. Oxford: Basil Blackwell.
  (1981b) 'Aspect and voice: some reflections on perfect and passive'. In P. J. Tedeschi and A. Zaenen (eds), *Tense and Aspect. Syntax and Semantics*, vol. 14. New York: Academic Press.
  (1984) 'Language universals and linguistic argumentation: a reply to Coopmans'. *Journal of Linguistics*, 20.1, 155–64.
Davison, A. (1984) 'Syntactic markedness and the definition of sentence topic'. *Language*, 60.4, 797–846.
Frazier, L. (1978) 'On comprehending sentences: syntactic parsing strategies'. Unpub. diss., University of Connecticut.
Hawkins, J. A. (1985) 'Complementary methods in Universal Grammar: a reply to Coopmans'. *Language*, 61.3, 569–87.
Lieberman, P. (1984) *The Biology and Evolution of Language*. Cambridge, Mass.: Harvard University Press.
Marshall, J. C. (1980) 'On the biology of language acquisition'. In D. Caplan (ed.), *Biological Studies of Mental Processes*. Cambridge, Mass.: MIT Press.
Reinhart, T. (1983) *Anaphora and Semantic Interpretation*. London: Croom Helm.
Rizzi, L. (1978) 'Violations of the WH island constraint and the subjacency condition'. In L. Rizzi, *Issues in Italian Syntax*. Dordrecht: Foris Publications, 1982.

Snow, C. and C. Ferguson (1977) *Talking to Children; Language Input and Acquisition*. Cambridge: Cambridge University Press.

Wexler, K. (1982) 'A principle theory of language acquisition'. In E. Wanner and L. R. Gleitman (eds), *Language Acquisition: the State of the Art*. Cambridge: Cambridge University Press.

CHAPTER 3

Language Acquisition:
Schemas Replace Universal Grammar

Michael A. Arbib and Jane C. Hill

1 Introduction

Chomskians hold that what makes it possible for the child to acquire its language in a few years on the basis of degenerate and inadequate data is the existence of an innate universal grammar. By contrast, we model language acquisition in terms of a dynamic process involving multitudinous changes in the child's stock of schemas with continuing experience. Our model demystifies the unimportance of negative data by providing a theory of the way in which positive evidence is exploited which is richer than that offered by generative theories. We suggest that universals are to be seen not as guiding the process of language acquisition, but rather as being descriptive of regularities that arise from the intricate interactions of a multitude of schemas acting and changing as the child comes to better and better exploit language for communication with and about its world.

2 Performance vs. Description: from the Beginning or from the End?

Just as there is initial structure in the visual system that helps determine the kinds of things we see and the way we see them – recent data on the 'many visual systems' are especially compelling in that respect (Cowey 1981; Zeki 1984) – so there can be no argument that, as evidenced by data on lesions in Broca's and Wernicke's areas inter alia, the human brain is genetically specified with a network of mechanisms that makes language possible. But to say that the human capacity for language is embodied in such structures does not imply that language acquisition is based on universal grammar rather than, say, the possession of innate mechanisms to relate word perception to visual perception, or to produce sentences using mechanisms evolved from those producing other types of co-ordinated, skillful movements. It is in the light of such considerations that we have suggested elsewhere (Arbib and Caplan 1979; Arbib 1982) that language principles are not to be understood in isolation from sensori-motor processes. In this connection, it is instructive to quote the remarks of Arbib, Caplan and Marshall (Arbib et al. 1982: 430–1) on the paper by Galaburda (1982) in their volume:

Galaburda's evolutionary perspective on comparative anatomy emphasizes the division of cortical areas into discrete patches with distinct input and output pathways and attendant, distinctive, staining properties. In applying neuroanatomical techniques to human autopsy material, Galaburda finds an unusually high accumulation when staining with lipofucsin granules in a number of areas that are linked (through lesion analysis and neurophysiological testing) to language function. The staining selects Area 44 from the classical Broca's area, and Tpt from the Wernicke region. We thus have what appears to be the first *cellular* marker for the language areas. Moreover, in the opercular region, Area 44 alone receives direct projections from posterior auditory fields, and Area 44 and Tpt are neatly connected by fibers coursing the arcuate fasciculus. We are reminded of Geschwind's hypothesis that such a connection is an important part of the substrate for language organization in the brain. But there is one catch: The projections shown in the last sentence but one were shown in anatomical studies of the rhesus monkey. We are forced once again to place neurolinguistics in a broader neurophsychological perspective in which we can come to understand the role of these not-quite-language areas in rhesus, and thus better understand the evolutionary pedigree of our own language abilities.

Chomsky argues (Beckwith and Rispoli 1986) that we do not learn to grow arms and that we also do not learn to have language in any very interesting sense and then asserts that there are not going to be principles of learning any more than there will be principles of growth – the organs become what they do become because of genetic instructions that give them particular directions and because of the way in which the intrinsic structure relates to the environmental context which is all pre-programmed. We leave it to the embryologists to defend themselves against the slur that there are no principles of growth. Here, we want to look briefly at recent results which show that the genetic program for brain growth is open to experience in a way that reverses the thrust of Chomsky's argument – it is not that the growth of language is as fixed and preprogrammed as the growth of a hand; rather it is that the theory of growth is itself beginning to develop so that it can address the subtleties of neural development in a way which may begin to make contact with our understanding of *real* learning. Hubel and Wiesel (1965) showed that cats raised with an artificial squint would 'lose' stereopsis, while Hirsch and Spinelli (1970) and Blakemore and Cooper (1970) showed that cats raised in an impoverished environment would 'lose' part of their normal complement of 'edge detectors'. However, Hirsch and Spinelli went further, showing that cats could be so trained that visual cortex neurons would be specified for 'new' features not present in the normal animal. Moreover, Spinelli and Jensen (1979) have shown that the allocation of cells to different subsets of the sensory world can be modified on the basis of early experience. Fregnac and Imbert (1978) have shown that cells of visual cortex came in three varieties – totally pre-wired, biased and totally uncommitted. The theoretical models of these phenomena by such authors as von der Malsburg (1973), Amari (1980) and Bienenstock et al. (1982) make it clear that we have a situation in which innate structure provides the basis for, rather than precluding the operation of, powerful learning mechanisms.

Universal grammar is exciting as a *description* of general properties of adult syntax but we reject the claim that the setting of parameters can quickly outline the grammatical structure of all human languages, even from 'unrelated families'. Certainly, there is no reference work which marshalls the evidence in a single place where experts could evaluate it. Our concern is that *even if the* **description** *were true*, this would provide no argument for Chomsky's use of 'parameter setting' as a theory of language acquisition – any more than Kepler's description of planetary orbits justifies a theory of dynamics that holds that planets determine their trajectories by setting the major and minor axes of an ellipse. Each language has idiosyncracies of syntax that fill far more pages of the grammar books than do those general principles subsumed by 'parameter settings', and learning grammar is a very small part of learning a language. The child must learn to segment the sound stream and master the idiosyncracies of the morpho-phonology of his language; to this must be added the learning of a huge vocabulary as well as a large stock of idioms, phrases and metaphors. By the time we have found explanations for the ability to learn all these, the mechanisms thus uncovered may have obviated the need for a set of parameterized universal principles. We do not wish to dismiss the existence of grammaticality judgments but we do claim that by examining computational models of language acquisition we may discover routes to language competence, including grammaticality judgments, that do not require a universal grammar, and such routes may in fact be discovered by focusing on language performance.

Another way of characterizing Chomsky's approach is that it proceeds *backwards* from a characterization of adult grammar to see how the child might arrive at this characterization. Our approach, by contrast, is to work *forward* from the evidence that the child provides toward some characterization of the adult language. We have already stressed that the richness of the world's languages exhibits far greater variation than is captured by the addition of parameter setting to a fixed stock of universals. We view the acquisition of language in a larger cognitive sense than does Chomsky. Our neo-Piagetian approach is to view the child, motivated by an innate desire to communicate, as actively constructing language, aided by innate cognitive schemas and mediated by the perceptive apparatus through which all humans perceive the world. To motivate our use of the term neo-Piegetian, consider that, in *Language and Learning: The Debate between Jean Piaget and Noam Chomsky* (Piattelli-Palmarini 1980), Chomsky's rejection of Piaget is based more on disdain for Piaget's lack of formal precision than on any reasoned critique of the body of data the Piagetians have accumulated or the way in which Piaget's informal concepts address them. Certainly, we find Piaget at his weakest when he tries to force his rich observations into the Procrustean bed of his *groupements*; while his description of mental development, though stimulating, lacks specific mechanisms and is overly complacent in its trust in the unfolding of stages of ever-greater sophistication (see Arbib 1987 for a critique based on the roles of instruction and historical contingency in the acquisition of concepts of logic and mathematics). However, we shall suggest below that one may provide models of language acquisition that are informed by a 'computational neo-Piegetian' view of construction rather than by an appeal to innate principles of universal grammar, in that they combine a Piagetian attention to the child's 'unfolding' of cognitive structure with the rigor of a computational model.

Chomsky's position is based on the view that language is too complex to be learned in the sense that one learns mathematics, or learns to play chess. Yet all normal children acquire a native language by the time that they are around five years old. Moreover, every child produces myriad original sentences. By what processes can these facts be explained? In 1965 Chomsky posited a need for a set of evaluation criteria for choosing between the presumably infinitely many hypotheses about language structure that might be compatible with the linguistic input data. The need for these evaluation criteria has since been obviated by his assumption of a set of language universals and a set of parameters that narrow the hypothesis space. Chomsky defined a universal grammar to be a system of principles which characterize the class of biologically possible grammars. Emphasizing the biological foundations of language, Chomsky likens the 'growing' of language to the growing of any other organ of the body (Beckwith and Rispoli 1986). The child will hear the language of his or her environment and the discovery, for example, that this language uses subject–object–verb word order might act as a trigger for a set of related assumptions such as that the language uses a case system. Universal grammar then has highly restricted options and a few parametric variations.[1] Chomsky sets the debate in terms of the 'setting up' of adult language rather than in terms of the dynamic changes that the child's language undergoes during the process of acquisition.

Our book *From Schema Theory to Language* (Arbib et al 1987) looks at language from a perspective in which performance, rather than competence or syntax, takes center stage, and builds on insights from brain theory and artificial intelligence (AI) to sketch the evolution of schema theory as it models three phenomena of language performance: language understanding by aphasics; language learning by a two-year-old (to be discussed in some detail below); and scene description. It is the second of these that will focus our discussion here. Hill (1983; see also Arbib et al. 1987, Part III) found that the language of a two-year-old changes week by week, and offered a computational model of the learning mechanism which could underlie such changes. The model is a repetition-and-response model which explains both how the two-year-old child that she studied responds to adult utterances, usually with a truncated form of that utterance, and how the child's linguistic and conceptual structures may change with each such 'repetition'. It is important to note that the repetitions differ markedly from adult syntax, but do have a coherent structure whose unfolding the model addresses. *Every* adult utterance can serve to modify the child's evolving representation, and thus the model is not vitiated by Chomsky's observation that children receive little in the way of *explicit* syntactic error feedback and seem resistant to what they do receive. As we shall see below, the model requires no negative evidence, and yet successfully hypothesizes a process of dynamic change of an evolving set of word classes and grammatical templates, rather than the all-or-none acquisition of adult grammaticality. The learning process is highly dynamic, and what is learned depends upon what has been learned before, so that the same adult input data presented at different times to the model result in different patterns of learning. Thus, for the learning processes posited here, it is far from true that there is a poverty of data or that the child had no relevant experience. Hearing hundreds of sentences a day and using billions of neurons to do so, surely the wonder is that the child takes so long! However, our real claim is that the child is not so much trying to model adult criteria for syntactic wellformedness as coming to interact with, perceive, represent and communicate about its world in ever more complex ways. Chomsky does not help us unravel these intertwined processes of construction.

We agree with Chomsky that some machinery has to be innate in the brain – but the question is whether it involves learning-principles governing a rich set of interacting subsystems, or whether it involves setting a few parameters. As support for basing language acquisition on mechanisms incorporating universal grammar, Chomsky argues (Beckwith and Rispoli 1986) that to learn whether your language is 'head first' or 'head last', English or Japanese, it is enough to hear three-word sentences like 'John saw Bill' or 'John Bill saw.' If you hear one, 'John saw Bill', you have a 'head first' language – so it is just a matter of setting parameters in a very highly constrained situation. However, from our cognitive viewpoint, this begs a multitude of questions. We must first ask 'How does the child learn to recognize John and "John", Bill and "Bill", and recognize what action "saw" denotes, and who saw whom?' 'How does a complex perceptual structure get mapped into a simpler structure of words?' 'How can the child recognize the order of the words in an utterance that it hears?' All this reinforces our point that a psychology of language must explain so much of language learning that is not explained by universal grammar that it is moot whether an adequate theory of such learning would have any lacunae that Universal Grammar must necessarily fill. Once one has the mechanisms for all these processes, one can then address the question whether the discoveries attendant upon the 'head last' vs. 'head first' distinction must be learned by parameter setting or are 'automatically' given by the very processes necessary to observe it.

3 Computational Models and the Importance of Errors

The approach to language acquisition embodied in both models to be described here is to work forward from the evidence that the child provides toward some characterization of the adult language. We ask not only under what conditions a language can be learned by a computational model, but also does the model learn the language in the same way that the child does? To define 'in the same way', particular attention must be paid to the 'errors' that children make since child speech that differs from adult speech yields clues concerning the processes that the child uses to understand and produce speech. An equally important clue to the child's processes are those errors which the child typically does not make. One frequently noted phenomenon is the over-generalization of the plural of nouns and of the past tense of verbs in English. Such phenomena need explanation. Rumelhart and McClelland's model (see section 6) deals specifically with the learning of past-tense forms in English. Hill's model (to which we now turn) learns these forms within the context of learning word classes and syntactic constructs. The model learns to understand and generate sentences of ever greater complexity as does the child. Moreover, to provide a satisfying explanation of the course of language acquisition the model must make the same kinds of errors that the child makes, and must eventually correct the errors after further learning has occurred. As we shall see, both models proceed without the need for negative evidence. It is gratifying to see that the basic paradigm which was initially used in Hill's model to learn word classes and a simple template grammar could be quite naturally extended to the learning of past-tense forms of verbs in English. We offer these two models as examples of the different sorts of answers which computational models may suggest to traditional questions, thanks to an approach to language acquisition based on a set of dynamic processes rather than a set of static rules.

4 The Hill Model

Figure 3.1 shows the components of Hill's model. The model takes as its input adult sentences together with indications (provided by the modeler,

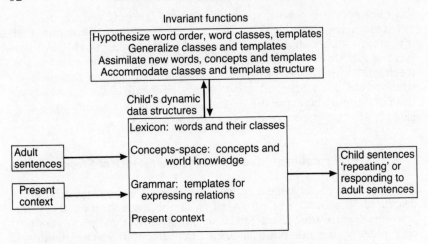

FIGURE 3.1 Basic components of the Hill model of language acquisition

where relevant) of the physical context in which the sentences are uttered. Output from the model is a representation of child-like sentences repeating or responding to the adult input in accordance with the current state of the model's linguistic capacity. The child's knowledge is represented by dynamic data structures encoding the child's lexicon, the child's grammar, the conceptual knowledge of the child and the physical context of the dialogue. The model is given a basic lexicon and a set of concepts with a mapping between the two. No assumptions have been made about the ultimate form of the adult grammar nor about what must be built into the model, but a precise account is kept of the knowledge and processes found necessary even for this elementary level of language understanding and production. Processes attend to the adult input and use rules of salience to focus on examples within the adult data which are used as the basis for language growth. The input data is in no way especially coded for the model, but is generally taken from language acquisition corpora of adult–child dialogue. The world knowlege is encoded in a semantic net as are the grammar templates and the lexicon. The model uses its language experience (that is, the processing of the input sentences) to build a grammar which is at first a flat template grammar but which eventually evolves into a procedural grammar which may be described, if one chooses, by a set of recursive context-free phrase structure rules. The model embodies five assumptions:

1 The child has schemas for and talks about relations.
2 The child has schemas for and employs word order in his utterances.
3 The child employs processes of concatenation and deletion.
4 The child forms classes of concepts and words.

5 The classifying process causes successive reorganizations of the information stored.

Thus we do *not* assume that the lexical classes of adult grammar are innate. Rather, we posit a process of *classification through word use* whereby words that are used in similar ways come to be assigned to the same class, thus extending from members of the class to further members of the class certain patterns (templates) of word use. The initial grammar is given by a set of templates, consisting of a 'relation' and a 'slot', which is free of any characterization of the adult grammar which will emerge but is not yet present. Hill observed a brief stage in which the child concatenated two-word templates with a common word, as in

little bear baby bear

but these soon give way to such three-word templates as

little baby bear.

The four-word utterances with repeated lexical items occurred in such a brief interval that Hill hypothesized that the three-word utterances were arrived at by (1) concatenating the two templates 'little bear' and 'baby bear', and (2) collapsing the concatenated relations into a single three-word utterance by deleting the first occurrence of the repeated word. Some evidence that the concatenation best captures the semantics of such three-word utterances in the young child is given by the finding of Matthei (1979) that the child interprets 'the second green ball' as 'the ball which is second and green' – in fact, several children, when presented with an array in which the second ball was not green, actually rearranged the balls in order to make the situation conform to their interpretation of the words.

From an adult sentence such as 'daddy gave the toy to the boy' the model might initially respond with a single word such as *toy*. A subsequent presentation of the same sentence might cause the model to acquire a template for *gave toy* where *gave* would be classified as a relation-word and *toy* as a slot-filler. Yet another presentation of the sentence might cause the model to learn the template *Daddy gave* where *Daddy* was a slot-filler, and eventually the template (*slot 1 gave slot 2*) might be learned for *Daddy gave toy*. What is learned in each presentation of the input depends upon the language experience of the model and what has been learned so far. Thus learning is highly dynamic in that each time the same input sentence is presented to the model a different set of grammar rules and additional lexical class information may be learned.

No information is given the model about word classes, but hearing sentences such as 'mommy gave the toy', 'John gave the book', 'Sue gave the puzzle', would eventually cause the model to put *toy*, *book* and *puzzle* all together in a word class of words which stand for possible objects of the relation-word *gave*. Note that it would not matter if the input sentences were far more complex than those used here for illustration. If the model is focusing on the word *gave* then a sentence such as 'Mommy gave the toy to Sue while she went into the store to buy groceries' would have just the same effect as the short sentences used above. By this process word classes are derived from the model's ability to produce language. The process results in a multiplicity of overlapping and intersecting word classes. The model requires schemas for word classification and template classification in order to grow, but the actual classes remain flexible. Processes of generalization eventually also permit the classifying of relation-words which might permit, for example, *giving* and *bringing* to be relation-words that could be classed together as words which have similar syntactic properties.

Successive reorganizations of the grammar and the lexicon occur as learning takes place. This process of gradual broadening of word classes and grammatical rules from applying to specific examplars to applying to sets of specific examplars and thence to more general categories has been defended by Kuczaj (1982) and Maratsos and Chalkley (1980). In this fashion the model suggests one way in which language based initially on cognitive knowledge can grow into a syntactic system which will be increasingly independent of its semantic and cognitive foundations. It is important to note that the although the rules embedded in processes within the model are simple, their interaction is complex enough to necessitate the use of a computer model.

5 Dynamic Rule Schemas and the Use of Weighted Hypotheses

Why does the child not end up with an overly generalized grammar or lexicon? There is much discussion in the literature concerning the kinds of generalizations and overgeneralizations that children make (e.g. Brown 1973; deVilliers and deVilliers 1979). We believe that it is important to focus on the errors that children make because of the insights which they yield concerning the processes that the child employs in language acquisition. Bowerman (1974) states this position very clearly. A study by Bybee and Slobin (1982) presents a careful examination of the acquisition of irregular past-tense forms of verbs in English. If, however, we permit no overt and specific correction of the child's errors, then how shall we explain why errors of overgeneralization do not persist into adult speech?

It is especially interesting to explore the use of verbs in English in the developing language of the child since learning English is intimately tied to the learning of verbs. DeVilliers (1985) has found evidence that input language has a significant impact on the child's developing language with respect to verbs. The mother's use of verbs is a high predictor of the child's use – it is not the frequency of the mother's use, but rather the variety of verb forms in the mother's use which is significant. This is interpreted to mean that the child is monitoring the input for clues about the proto-typicality of forms of individual verbs. Wide differences in the use of verbs between subjects were found in the samples considered in her study. Verbs with a variety of heard uses were used with greater confidence by the child even in unheard contexts. Hill's model simulates this monitoring process. De Villier's analysis did not address the issue of overgeneraliza-tion but it does lend credence to our processes which rely on the informa-tion gleaned from the input by focusing on different constructs at different times for the learning of forms. Thus whether one concludes that the input has an impact on the language learning of the child depends on whether one monitors the course of development over fine time slices, or whether one simply looks at the end product (adult language).

Consider the verb *break*. It is an empirical fact that children at the earliest stage of language acquisition typically learn the word *broke* and seem to use it correctly. One may assume that such forms have been learned by rote. Then at a subsequent stage of development the child will start to use the word *breaked*. Is this because the child has formed a general schema for forming the past tense of verbs? Eventually of course children learn that *break* is an irregular verb and does not obey the general rule in the forming of its past tense. But the puzzle is that for a period of time, sometimes for years, both forms exist in the child's vocabulary. How can this period of imbalance between the erroneous and the correct forms be explained? It cannot be explained if the language mechanisms are expressed in terms of explicit rules which the child either does or does not know.

One answer to this question is proffered by our computational model which attaches a weight representing the degree of confidence that is associated with each hypothesis about word forms or grammar rules. (The use of weights to direct learning in computational models is by no means new; see, e.g., Kelley 1967.) Each time an adult sentence is presented to the model, it is searched for possible instantiations of the available set of hypotheses; and the child's output also represents an instantiation of a particular hypothesis. The crucial point is that this process of instantiation involves a competition which depends on the current weights associated with the various hypotheses, and that these weights are themselves changed in the process. The weight associated with a hypothesis is increased each time that hypothesis is instantiated in the adult speech input. The weight is similarly increased, but to a lesser degree, each time a hypothesis is employed in the child-like output. In this way more frequently matched constructs are preferred over (given more weight than) less frequently matched contructs. Hypotheses must be reinforced to survive. If new hypotheses, however, are to start with very low weights they will have trouble 'catching up' with earlier hypotheses. For this reason, separate recency values are employed whose function it is to cause more recent hypotheses to be favored for testing.

We illustrate the use of weights in the learning of past-tense forms. In order to observe the correlation between past-tense and -*ed* endings, the model must be given a representation of time-past in its cognitive knowledge, and the ability to identify action verbs in its lexicon. The model forms past-tense entries in its lexicon for all action verbs simply by adding -*ed* endings. Each of these forms is initially given a modest confidence factor. The model then proceeds to modify the confidence factors of the past-tense forms depending on its language experience. The confidence factor of a form is incremented each time that the model recognizes a past-tense form in the adult input; a smaller increment is added each time that the model produces a past-tense form. This general scheme has the advantage that for a period of time when confidence factors are approximately in balance, two or more constructs can co-exist, as for example in the case of the past-tense overgeneralization *breaked* and the correct form *broke*. Since the choice of past-tense form depends upon the history of the model, no a priori conclusions can be drawn about the specific past-tense forms which are learned, but depending upon the input data, the model (1) may keep an erroneous -*ed* ending, (2) may proceed through a period of instability in which the output vacillates between an erroneous -*ed* ending and the correct irregular form, or (3) may discard the erroneous form and replace it by the irregular form (see Hill 1986 for further description of the model with regards to past-tense forms).

A paradigm such as ours may thus be sensitive to the input data and may exhibit varied behavior without the need for negative evidence. Dynamic rule schemas and confidence factors have been used to model the phenomena of generalization, overgeneralization and subsequent correction of overgeneralized forms. Thus we need not talk of rules or individual cases which have been learned or have not yet been learned but rather of a continuum in which rule procedures are either strong or weak.

Other issues which the same model explores are what variation occurs in the model as specific constraints are built in or omitted, how input filters can focus on different aspects of the input data over time and how variation in meaning representation and sets of semantic features can affect the learning process. Recently, Hill has begun to explore the effects of encoding phonological data in the input to the model. A pilot study conducted with Ann Peters (building on the studies by Peters 1985a, 1985b and Wilson and Peters 1984) has shown that in order to model her corpus of data collected from a blind child, the inclusion of primary and secondary stress and of intonational boundaries is of great importance.

6 The Rumelhart and McClelland Model

To further advance our argument, we now discuss Rumelhart and McClelland's (1986) model of how children may learn the past-tense forms of verbs in English. Since these past-tense endings exhibit a highly idio-syncratic structure peculiar to English, a model of their acquisition can make no appeal to Universal Grammar. The point again is that, once we have modeled the 'non-Chomskian' processes involved in this phase of language acquisition, we have increased the inductive evidence for our schema-based approach to language acquisition in general. The present model is at a finer grain than Hill's model, approaching the learning of past-tense verb forms from the phonological level. It is an example of a 'connectionist' model, in that knowledge is not encoded in a small set of explicit rules, but is embedded in the connections between a large number of simple processing units (neuron-like, but not to be confused with actual neurons in the child's brain). The model interactively activates subsections of the network of these simple units. As in a neural network, each unit sums its inputs, excitatory and inhibitory, from other processing units to determine its output which can then affect other processing units. The continued interaction of these excitatory and inhibitory effects causes the network to converge on a decision about a hypothesis – through distributed interactions, not through the sovereignty of any single rule.

The Rumelhart and McClelland model learned the past tense of some 420 verbs in English, some regular and some irregular. The model explains the period of instability between correct and incorrect forms, and moreover the model output evidences a rough correlation between the difficulty of learning particular forms and the observations of Bybee and Slobin (1982) concerning the course of learning in the child. How difficult a word form is to learn in the model depends upon the corpus as a whole. What is crucial here, and in agreement with the Hill model, is that (i) cognitive science must address the time course of mental development, not just adult competence; and (ii) the model makes no appeal to explicit representation of a general rule. Rather, the decentralized interaction of many components, representing different verbs, yields a coordination of their behavior which is *describable* by a rule, but which in no way is the *expression* of any such rule, innate or otherwise. We believe that the development of models such as these will have a large impact on future work in language acquisition.

The occurrence of errors of overgeneralization and their subsequent correction is totally unexplained by any of Chomsky's theories. Such phenomena are not deemed important by Chomsky and if noticed at all are dismissed as belonging to 'pre-language' (cf. Wanner and Gleitman 1982 on the 'tadpole/frog' hypothesis). Chomsky speaks of the child making mistakes because he 'simply doesn't yet know how a parameter is set' (Beckwith and Rispoli 1986). But, in fact, few of us who have not read the Chomskian canon even know that the parameters exist (if indeed they do). If we use the more careful phrasing 'the child's behavior does not yet exhibit the regularities describable by the setting of the parameter', we leave open the hypothesis that such regularities are, as suggested above, descriptive rather than causal.

7 And Yet, There Are Rules

Since the Hill model deals only with very early stages of language acquisition it is open to the criticism that the subtleties of language which are yet to be learned by the model are precisely the areas of language acquisition addressed by Universal Grammar. We do not believe this to be the case, but we cannot yet offer a full-fledged computational model of language acquisition. We offer this model as an illustration of the kinds of processes which may enable language acquisition to be bootstrapped by gleaning example templates from adult input, given innate schemas of the kind we have posited thus far. Our weighting schemes provide an answer to the problem of the lack of negative evidence, and our focusing mechanisms suggest how the input data may be used. Our use of the distributional data encoded in the child's own production data, based initially on cognitive knowledge, suggests a way in which word classes may come to be formed. At the very least the model illustrates a manner in which all the input data may be processed, yet with only selected portions of that data focused upon at different times. By contrast, the theory of Universal Grammar is based on no attempt to constructively assess the data on, or models of, language acquisition developed to date, and fails to address those issues of language as a medium of communication that are of concern to many cognitive scientists.

To highlight what we have shown, we close by discussing two passages from Hoekstra and Kooij's contribution to this volume, for they are, alas, typical of the 'method' of those who advance Universal Grammar as a 'model' of language acquisition. In the first passage, they downplay the argument that a string of words might be judged ungrammatical in English because the pattern to which it conforms is never induced as a possible pattern in English, noting that 'this objection implies the assumption that users keep track of the patterns that they have encountered, which is a very strong assumption.' Since this appears to be the basic assumption in our model, we must both defend it and undermine Hoekstra and Kooij's argument. First, note that current versions of Universal Grammar require that each word have a complex entry in the lexicon, and no claim is made that these entries are innate. Thus the proponent of Universal Grammar is committed to having the child learn a great number of patterns, for surely it is not too strong an assumption that language users keep track of the words that they have encountered. Second, just as we might not expect the user to remember every occasion on which he had heard a word and yet still to have encoded in memory a 'spanning set' sufficient to establish the lexical entry and a set of usages for each word, so is our argument unweakened if we allow the Hill model to have a 'spanning set' of patterns rather than a complete set of patterns ever encountered. Third, we stress that the Hill model presents the first stages in the acquisition of patterns of ever greater abstraction and generality, so that the adult's grammaticality judgment is not based on an exhaustive search of every string of words ever encountered, but rather involves rapid access to patterns at the appropriate level of generality through word classes at that level – but word classes built up through experience (our notion of 'classification through word use'), rather than given as a priori universals.

Later on in the same section from which we have just quoted, Hoekstra and Kooij ask us to consider (2a) versus (2b):

(2) a. Where did John say that we had to get off the bus?
    b. Where did John ask whether we had to get off the bus?

Both sentences are grammatical. However, while (2a) is ambiguous between a reading in which *where* has matrix scope and a reading in which it has embedded scope, (2b) can only be interpreted as a question concering the place where John uttered a particular question (that is, with matrix scope). This piece of knowledge is shared by all native speakers, but it can hardly have been established on the basis of induction, simply because there are no data from which induction could conceivably proceed.

But where is the evidence that 'this piece of knowledge is shared by all native speakers'? It certainly is not shared by all two-year-old native speakers. Perhaps Hoekstra and Kooij mean 'all *adult* native speakers'. But if so, and even if they are correct, where is the explanation for the transition that occurs in the individual child from ignorance to knowledge? By parameter setting? But where is the explicit description of what the child's language would look like before and after the parameter is set? And where is the corpus collected from a large number of children showing the magical moment at which the crucial datum sets the parameter? We would assert that there is no one crucial datum. Rather, the child is exposed to a vast array of data which include qustions whose patterns are reflected by (2a) and (2b). The very patterns that enable the child to master the words 'ask' and 'say', 'that' and 'whether' are the same patterns which give the child 'the data from which induction could ... proceed' whose existence Hoekstra and Kooij deny. But they deny it without *any* empirical analysis of how the language of the child changes with experience.

We have *shown* that simple patterns can evolve into complex patterns in a way which matches patterns of language acquisition in a two-year-old child. We *claim*, as a target for future research, that our model, can be extended (not by the formation of word patterns alone, but [cf. figure 3.1] through the continuing interaction of the lexical space, grammar space and cognitive space of the child) to cover such phenomena as the distinction between (2a) and (2b). Yes, an adult (and one trained in linguistic terminology at that) can learnedly discern patterns in (2a) that can be distinguished as matrix scope vs. embedded scope, but this adds no weight at all to the claim that such knowledge is embedded in an innate Universal Grammar, and that without 'knowing' matrix scope vs. embedded scope innately, the child could not acquire the ability to distinguish (2a) from (2b). In our society, children initially learn language through using it without any necessary reflection upon its patterns. Eventually, the child does come to reflect with pleasure on these patterns, as well as to experience, with less pleasure, the explicit presentation of grammatical rules in the classroom. But this does not concede an explanatory role for Universal Grammar in language acquisition. We argue that the rules are structures whose acquisition is made possible by the prior acquisition of language, not innate structures that make the acquisition of language possible.

Note

A number of the arguments presented here are based on those in Arbib (1986) and Hill and Arbib (1984).

1 But are the options highly restricted, and are the variations indeed few? The problems with this approach are well illustrated in the companion article by Hoekstra and Kooij (this volume). They give '(1d) *His proof of the theorem wrong' as an example of a construction of a type impossible in all languages – yet it is in fact correct in Chinese (on omitting 'the'). Again, they note that the use of a parameter is required to 'save' the subjacency principle for Italian, but then note that even this is not enough to make the principle of universal application. One may thus be excused for favoring a mechanism which can generate schemas to embody experienced regularities over a theory of language acquisition which is little specified beyond positing the necessity for a baroquely epicyclic data base parametrized to express variations in the thousands of human languages that the child will never learn.

References

Amari, S. (1980) 'Topographical organization of nerve fields'. *Bull. Math. Biol.*, 42, 339–64.
Arbib, M. A. (1982) 'Perceptual-motor processes and the neural basis of language. In Arbib et al (1982).
    (1986) 'Minds, modules and schemas: a response to Chomsky'. *New Ideas in Psychology*, 4, 203–10.
    (1987) 'A Piagetian perspective on the construction of logic'. *Synthese* (in press).
    and D. Caplan (1979) 'Neurolinguistics must be computational. *Behav. Brain Scis.*, 2, 449–83.
    D. Caplan and J. C. Marshall (eds) (1982) *Neural Models of Language Processes*. New York: Academic Press.
    E. J. Conklin and J. C. Hill (1987) *From Schema Theory to Language*. Oxford: Oxford University Press.
Beckwith, R. and M. Rispoli (1986) 'Aspects of a theory of mind: an interview with Noam Chomsky'. *New Ideas in Psychology*, 4, 187–202.

Bienenstock, E. L., L. N. Cooper and P. W. Munro (1982) 'Theory for the development of neuron selectivity; orientation specificity and binocular interaction in visual cortex'. *J. Neuroscience*, 2, 32–48.

Blakemore, C. and G. Cooper (1970) 'Development of the brain depends on the visual environment'. *Nature*, 228, 477–8.

Bowerman, M. (1974) 'Learning the structure of causative verbs: a study in the relationship of cognitive, semantic, and syntactic development'. In *Papers and Reports on Child Language Development*, no. 8 (ed. E. Clark). Stanford University Committee on Linguistic.

Brown, R. (1973) *A First Language: the Early Stages*. Cambridge, Mass.: Harvard University Press.

Bybee, J. and D. Slobin (1982) 'Rules and schemas in the development and use of the English past tense'. *Language*, 58, 265–89.

Chomsky, N. (1965) *Aspects of the Theory of Syntax*. Cambridge, Mass.: MIT Press.

Cowey, A. (1981) 'Why are there so many visual areas?' In F. O. Schmitt, F. G. Worden and F. Dennis (eds), *The Organization of the Cerebral Cortex*. Cambridge Mass.: MIT Press.

deVilliers, J. (1985) 'Learning how to use verbs: lexical coding and the influence of the input'. *Journal of Child Language*, 12, 587–95.

— and P. deVilliers (1979) *Early language*. Cambridge, Mass.: Harvard University Press.

Fregnac, Y. and M. Imbert (1978) 'Early development of visual cortical cells in normal and dark-reared kittens: relationship between orientation selectivity and ocular dominance'. *J. Physiol.*, 278, 27–44.

Galaburda, A. M. (1982) 'Histology, architectonics, and asymmetry of language areas'. In Arbib et al. (1982).

Hill, J. C. (1983) 'A computational model of language acquisition in the two-year-old'. *Cognition and Brain Theory*, 6, 287–317.

— (1986) 'A computational model which addresses errors of overgeneralization and their subsequent disappearance'. *Proceedings of the Eight Annual Conference of the Cognitive Science Society*, University of Massachusetts at Amherst, August.

— and M. A. Arbib (1984) 'Schemas, computation and language acquisition'. *Human Development*, 27, 282–96.

Hirsch, H. and D. N. Spinelli (1970) 'Visual experience modifies distribution of horizontally and vertically oriented receptive fields in cats'. *Science*, 168, 869–71.

Hoekstra, T. and J. G. Kooij (this volume) 'The innateness hypothesis'.

Hubel, D. H. and T. N. Wiesel (1965) 'Binocular interaction in striate cortex of kittens reared with artificial squint'. *J. Neurophysiol.*, 28, 1041–59.

Kelley, K. (1967) 'Early syntactic acquisition'. Ph.D. diss., University of California at Los Angeles, 1967; also published as Report no. P-3719, The Rand Corporation, Santa Monica, Calif., November 1967.

Kuczaj, S. A., II (1982) 'On the nature of syntactic development'. In S. Kuczaj (ed.), *Language Development*, vol. 1, *Syntax and Semantics*. Hillsdale, NJ: Erlbaum.

Maratsos, M. and M. Chalkley (1980) 'The internal language of children's syntax: the ontogenesis and representation of syntactic categories'. In K. Nelson (ed.), *Children's Language*, vol. 2. New York: Gardner Press.

Matthei, E. (1979) 'The acquisition of prenominal modifier sequences: stalking the second green ball'. Ph.D. diss., Dept of Linguistics, University of Massachusetts at Amherst.

Peters, A. (1985a) 'The role of imitation in the syntactic development of a blind child'. Paper presented at the Society for Research in Child Development Tornoto, April.

(1985b) 'Routines as loci for language development'. Paper presented at the Boston University Conference on Child Language, October.

Piatelli-Palmarini, M. (ed.) (1980) *Language and Learning: The Debate between Jean Piaget and Noam Chomsky.* Cambridge, Mass.: Harvard University Press.

Rumelhart, D. E. and J. L. McClelland (1986) 'On learning the past tense of English verbs'. In Rumelhart and McClelland (eds). *Parallel Distributed Processing: Explorations in the Microstructure of Cognition,* vol. 2. A Bradford Book and Cambridge Mass.: MIT Press.

Spinelli, D. N. and F. E. Jensen (1979) 'The mirror of experience'. *Science*, 203, 75–8.

von der Malsburg, C. (1973) 'Self-organizing of orientation sensitive cells in the striate cortex'. *Kybernetik*, 14, 85–100.

Wanner, E. and L. Gleitman (1982) *Language Acquisition: The State of the Art.* Cambridge: Cambridge University Press.

Wilson, B. and A. Peters (1984) 'What are you cooking on a hot?': A blind child's "violation" of "universal" constraints'. Paper presented at the Boston University Conference on Child Language, October.

Zeki, S. (1984) 'The specialization of function and the function of specialization in the visual cortex'. In P. F. Baker (ed.), *Recent Advances in Physiology.* Churchill Livingstone.

CHAPTER 4

The 'No Negative Evidence' Problem: How Do Children Avoid Constructing an Overly General Grammar?

Melissa Bowerman

The story of language acquisition is, to a large extent, the story of how children make linguistic generalizations. Traditionally, the emphasis in describing this process has been on how learners go beyond the specific utterances they hear to draw out regularities that will enable them to produce and understand an infinite number of novel sentences. However, in the last few years the converse question has also come under intense scrutiny: how do children avoid generalizing too broadly, ending up with grammars that not only generate all the well-formed constructions of their language but a number of ungrammatical ones as well?

The problem of how children avoid constructing an overly general grammar was first posed in 1971 by Martin Braine. Braine used the problem to argue against the nativist position set forth by Chomsky (1965) and in favor of the idea that language is learned largely from scratch. It was later revived by Baker (1979), who, in an interesting turn-around, made it the cornerstone of the argument that children must be guided by innate constraints in their acquisition of language. That both nativist and empiricist theorists have been able to adapt the puzzle to their own use indicates that the problem transcends party lines. Indeed, I believe it constitutes one of the most intriguing and difficult challenges for all students of language acquisition.

By now, a range of solutions has been proposed for the problem. My goal in this chapter is not to advance still another hypothesis but rather to take stock of where we now stand in our efforts to crack the puzzle. My focus is on how children learn rules that have lexical exceptions, since these constitute a core learnability problem to which different theoretical approaches have offered very different solutions.

1 Statement of the Problem

According to Chomsky's (1965) account of language acquisition, the child's task is to construct an internal grammar. The learner does this by using incoming language data, together with innate linguistic knowledge, to formulate hypotheses about possible grammatical rules. He then tests these hypotheses against further data, discards or revises them as necessary, and eventually applies an evaluation metric to surviving candidate grammars in order to select the best one.

Braine (1971b) observed that there is a critical discrepancy between the kind of data needed for a hypothesis testing procedure to work and the kind of data children actually receive. Hypothesis testing requires feedback about the correctness of predictions, pointed out Braine. In particular, it requires evidence not only about what *is* an instance of what is to be learned (an acceptable sentence of the language, in this case), but also about what is *not* an instance. Negative evidence is essential for the learner to revise hypothesized rules that are overly general, since these rules will generate all acceptable instances (sentences) and err only in that they generate unacceptable instances as well (sentences that fluent speakers find ill-formed).

Language is full of partial regularities that might suggest attractive but ultimately overinclusive hypotheses to children. Consider, for example, the following sentences (adapted from Baker 1979):

(1) a. Dad told a story to Sue.
    b. Dad told Sue a story.
(2) a. I gave a book to John.
    b. I gave John a book.
(3) a. Jim showed the model to Bob.
    b. Jim showed Bob the model.
(4) a. Mom baked a cake for Jack.
    b. Mom baked Jack a cake.

A child exposed to sentences like these might come to see a relationship between the (a) and (b) versions. He might conclude that, given a sentence of the (a) form, he can convert it into the (b) form (corresponding to various linguists' proposed rule(s) for an optional Dative Movement transformation). The child would accordingly produce many well-formed novel (b) sentences such as *I sent my cousin a birthday present* and *Linda knitted me a sweater*. But he would also produce sentences that fluent speakers find unacceptable, for example the (b) forms below:

(5) a. Dad said something nice to Sue.
    b. *Dad said Sue something nice.
(6) a. I reported the death to the police.
    b. *I reported the police the death.
(7) a. Mary donated a book to the library.
    b. *Mary donated the library a book.

(8) a.   Jim demonstrated the model to Bob.
    b. *Jim demonstrated Bob the model.
(9) a.   Mom buttoned the coat for Jack.
    b. *Mom buttoned Jack the coat.

If the child is testing a hypothesized rule of Dative Movement, how does he learn that *say*, *demonstrate*, etc., are exceptions to the rule? This would seem to require someone telling him that sentences like those above are not acceptable; otherwise he would have no reason to alter his hypothesis. But do children in fact get information of this type? After reviewing the available data (e.g. Brown and Hanlon 1970), Braine concluded that negative evidence is rare in the input to children; moreover, children appear to be relatively impervious to what little correction they do receive. In consequence, argued Braine, the hypothesis testing approach cannot be correct. The child must acquire language with procedures for which positive evidence alone – that is, exposure to sentences of the language – is sufficient. The procedures proposed by Braine will be considered in a later section of this chapter.

2 A Nativist Response

Although nativists did not respond immediately to Braine's challenge, the problem was eventually taken up and refocused in an important article by Baker (1979). Baker agreed that children get no reliable and systematic evidence about what is not a sentence and that they must be prepared to learn from positive evidence only. He argued, however, that this situation is not damning to the innatist program in general, but only to grammatical frameworks that allow types of rules that children could not acquire from positive evidence alone. He also observed that the 'no negative evidence' problem – as the puzzle has gradually come to be called – is a challenge not only to nativist theorizing, as argued by Braine, but also to empiricist approaches to language acquisition that invoke learning by generalization. Sentences (5a)–(9a) are 'similar' in many important respects to sentences (1a)–(4a). Why then do fluent speakers balk at (5b)–(9b), given that (1b)–(4b) are acceptable? What blocks this generalization?

2.1 *Benign versus embarrassing exceptions*

Baker pointed out that not all overgeneralizations a child might make are troublesome for a theory of language acquisition. He distinguished between rule exceptions that are 'benign', in that errors involving them can in principle be corrected without negative evidence, and those that are 'embarrassing', because their correction seems logically to depend on evidence of a type that children do not regularly receive.

Benign exceptions are irregular forms in an inflectional or other paradigm. If children overgeneralize a rule of (say) past tense or plural marking, producing forms like *runned* or *foots*, positive evidence alone – in this case consistent exposure to the irregular adult forms *ran*, *feet*, etc. – is in principle sufficient to show them that their form is wrong.

For an embarrassing exception, however, there is *no exact, irregular counterpart*, and therefore no positive evidence that the form is an exception to the rule. Consider dative alternation, for example. The child who on a particular occasion considers saying sentence (5b) might hear sentence (5a) instead. But this cannot be taken as evidence that (5b) is not possible, any more than hearing (1a) counts as evidence against the wellformedness of (1b). Sentences of both kinds can co-exist.

In general, observed Baker, benign exceptions involve rules proposed to be *obligatory*, whereas embarrassing exceptions involve rules characterized as *optional*. He emphasized that the 'no negative evidence' problem affects a large proportion of the rules proposed in classical transformation theory.

2.2 Baker's solution: innate constraints on the child

Baker took the 'no negative evidence' problem as strong evidence that children must be *innately constrained* in their acquisition of language, and a number of other theorists have since followed his lead (for example, see chapters in Baker and McCarthy 1981). If certain hypotheses about language structure are incorrect, but, once made, could not be corrected except by evidence of a type that is not available in the learner's input, then there must be something that keeps children from making them in the first place. Different investigators have suggested different types of constraints, depending in part on their theoretical orientation and also on the domain of grammar they are concerned with.

Baker's proposal was to limit the grammatical rules allowed by linguistic theory to those that can be learned by children on the basis of positive evidence alone. Constraints on permissible grammatical rules can also, of course, be phrased in terms of constraints on the child – that is, children are seen as so constituted that they will not entertain, as a possible grammatical rule, any rule which, if incorrect, could not subsequently be corrected on the basis of positive evidence alone.

According to Baker, the appropriate constraints on grammatical rules were offered by the *lexicalist* approach to linguistic theory, which was just beginning to attract widespread attention at the time he wrote (see also Roeper et al. 1981). Lexicalists called for reducing the power of the syntactic component of grammar in favor of a richer lexicon. For example, they argued that regularities with lexical exceptions (and certain other properties) should not be treated as syntactic transformations. Instead, the partial regularities that transformations like Dative Movement and Passive had been designed to capture should be represented within the lexicon.

A special device for doing this is the lexical redundancy rule, proposed by Jackendoff (1975). This kind of rule does not derive one construction from another, but instead simply captures a passive generalization across lexical items that are already fully specified in the lexicon. For example, a redundancy rule representing the relationship between 'shifted' and 'non-shifted' datives would state that corresponding to the subcategorization frame [_ NP$_1$ to NP$_2$] is the frame [_ NP$_2$ NP$_1$]. Items to which the rule applies are marked accordingly, and items to which it does not apply are left unmarked.

If there are no general syntactic rules relating shifted and non-shifted datives, actives and passives, etc., then children do not have to learn exceptions to the rules. Instead, they proceed conservatively. Predicate by predicate, they wait for positive evidence that the form can appear in a given syntactic context. They will notice that *give*, for example, appears in both the subcategorization frame [_ NP$_1$ to NP$_2$] and the frame [_ NP$_2$ NP$_1$]. But they will observe *say* only in the frame [_ NP$_1$ to NP$_2$]. If learners never encounter a form in certain contexts, they will not make the corresponding entry in their mental lexicons. Their grammars will therefore never contain overly general rules with embarrassing lexical exceptions.

3 A Second Nativist Proposal: the Subset Principle

Before evaluating Baker's proposal, let us take a quick look at a second, qualitatively different approach to constraining the child from the outset. Recall that Baker called for restricting the types of rules children can entertain. Other investigators have appealed instead to a built-in order for generating hypotheses: the focus is not on what rules a child can conceive of, but on which rule she considers first when more than one rule is conceivable.

This approach, proposed initially by Dell (1981) and formalized by Berwick (1985; Berwick and Weinberg 1984) under the name 'the Subset Principle', exploits the fact that the grammars generated or sanctioned by candidate grammatical rules (or constraints, or parameters) may stand in a subset–superset relation to each other; that is, the grammar generated by one rule may be a proper subset of the grammar generated by the other rule. The proposal is that since learning must proceed from positive instances only, children must first hypothesize the *narrowest possible grammar* compatible with the evidence observed so far. If the grammar is too narrow, the learner will eventually discover this through positive evidence (that is, sentences in the input that the grammar does not account for). She will then posit the next larger grammar compatible with the data as she now perceives it. The learner must never hypothesize a grammar that is too general, since without negative evidence there is no way to cut back to the correct, narrower grammar.

Berwick has applied the Subset Principle to a wide variety of problems in grammar construction, including rules with lexical exceptions like Dative and Passive. See also Wexler and Manzini (1987) and Smith (1981) for related applications to parameter-setting and word formation, respectively.

4 Overproductivity: a Problem for both 'Innate Constraints' Approaches

Several questions can be raised on purely theoretical grounds about the adequacy of both the lexical redundancy rule approach and the Subset Principle as solutions to the 'no negative evidence' problem.[1] There is, however, a compelling empirical reason for questioning them as well: children *do* overgeneralize rules with 'embarrassing' exceptions, producing errors that should not occur if these approaches were correct.

At the time Baker wrote, evidence concerning such errors was sparse, so the hypothesis that children simply do not make them was perhaps not unreasonable. However, as linguists have increasingly based their theorizing on the assumption that children do not formulate overly general grammars, and so must be innately constrained, child language scholars have begun to emphasize that the critical errors do occur. New experimental work has also confirmed that children generalize more broadly than Baker, Berwick and others have supposed.

The major systematic body of evidence about the relevant errors in children's spontaneous speech comes from my diary records of my two English-speaking daughters, which I have supplemented with comparable examples from other children. The errors include overgeneralizations of dative alternation, causative verb formation, passivization, locative alternation (*spray/load*-type verbs) and *un*-prefixation (Bowerman 1974, 1982a, 1982b, 1983). Some examples are shown in table 4.1.

Spontaneous speech data are backed up by experimental evidence that children often judge ungrammatical 'shifted' datives as acceptable (Mazurkewich and White 1984; these investigators also list a few dative errors from children's spontaneous speech). Similar results for unacceptable causatives are presented by Hochberg (1986). There is also experimental evidence that children are able to create never-heard passives, shifted datives and causative forms for novel verbs (Pinker et al. 1987; Pinker 1987; Maratsos et al. 1987), which goes counter to Baker's proposal that children are conservative, waiting for positive evidence before listing a new subcategorization frame for a verb in their mental lexicon.

How damaging is such evidence to the program of solving the 'no negative evidence' problem by innately constraining children in such a way that their grammars never become overly general? Before drawing conclusions, let us consider two possible lines of counterargument.

Table 4.1 Some overgeneralizations of rules with lexical exceptions[a]

A   Dative Alternation

1	C	3; 1	I *said her* no.
2	C	2; 6	Don't *say me* that or you'll make me cry.
3	L	7; 8	Shall I *whisper you* something?
4	C	2; 6	I want Daddy *choose me* what to have. (Re: what kind of juice to have at breakfast.)
5	M	5+	*Choose me* the ones that I can have.
6	C	3; 4	*Button me* the rest. (Request to have remaining snaps on her pyjamas fastened.)
7	—	6; 0	Mommy, *open Hadwen* the door. (Mazurkewich and White 1984)
8	—	2; 3	I'll *brush him* his hair. (Mazurkewich and White 1984)

B   Lexical Causatives (The regularity to which the verbs below are exceptions is exemplified by intransitive/transitive pairs like *The stick broke* / *I broke the stick*.)

9	J	6+	Do you want to see us *disappear* our heads? (Then, with a friend, she ducks down behind couch.)
10	—	2; 8+	I don't want any more grapes; they just *cough* me. (Braine 1981a)
11	R	5; 9	I want to *comfortable* you. (R lying on sofa with mother, cuddling her.)
12	E	3; 0	Don't *giggle* me. (As father tickles her.)
13	E	3; 2	Will you *climb* me up there and hold me? (Wants mother to help her climb a pole.)
14	E	3; 7	I'm gonna put the washrag in and *disappear* something under the washrag. (Playing in tub with small toys and a container into which she puts washrag.)
15	C	3; 6	Did she *bleed* it? (After her sister falls and hits head on edge of table.)
16	C	4; 3	It always *sweats* me. (Refusing sweater.)
17	M	5; 8	*M*: These are nice beds. *Mother*: Yes, they are. *M*: Enough to *wish* me that I had one of those beds.

C   Passive

18	E	3; 8	Both are going to be *go-ened* in! (= gone in. Watching one child sit down on potty and another on toilet.)
19	C	3; 6	Until I'm four I don't have to be *gone*. (= be taken to the dentist.)
20	C	3; 6	If you don't put them in for a very long time they won't get *staled*. (Reference to crackers in a bread box. Passive of novel causative; see B above.)
21	C	4; 3	Why is the laundry place *stayed* open all night? (= kept.)

Table 4.1 (*cont.*)

22	H	4; +	He's gonna die you, David. (Turns to mother.) The tiger will come and eat David and then he will be *died* and I won't have a brother any more.
23	E	5; 2	Mommy will get *lightninged*. (= struck by lightning)
24	C	5; 6	I don't want to be *dogeared* today. (Asking for her hair not to be arranged in 'dogears'.)
25	C	8; 9	A child wanted her doll to be *mummied*. (= made into a mummy; mummified)

D Locative Alternation (The regularity here is exemplified by sentence pairs like these:

        a   b
... spray paint on the wall / spray the wall with paint.
... load hay into the wagon / load the wagon with hay.
... spread butter on the bread / spread the bread with butter.

Hall (1965) proposed deriving the *b* forms from the *a* forms with an optional transformation for verbs of a certain semantic class. Certain verbs in this class are exceptions, however, in that they are 'fixed' in either the a-pattern (e.g. *pour*, *spill*, *steal*) or the b-pattern (e.g. *fill*, *cover*, *rob*).

b-verb in a-pattern:

26	E	4; 5	I'm gonna *cover* a screen over me.
27	E	5; 0	Can I *fill* some salt into the bear? ('the bear' = a bear-shaped salt shaker.)
28	C	4; 9	She's gonna *pinch* it on my foot. (Protesting as E approaches with a toy.)

a-verb in b-pattern:

29	E	2; 11	(Waving empty container near mother.) *E*: Pour, pour, pour. Mommy, I *poured* you. *M*: You poured me? *E*: Yeah, with water.
30	E	4; 11	(Mother asks if E is going to finish toast.) I don't want it because I *spilled* it of orange juice.
31	C	6; 5	(Telling of TV episode.) *C*: Once the Partridge Family got *stolen*. *M*: The whole family? *C*: No, all their stuff.

E Reversative *un*-prefixation.

32	E	3; 11	How do you *unsqueeze* it? (Coming to mother with clip earring dangling from ear; wants it off.)
33	E	3; 10	*Mother*: I have to capture you. (Grabbing E in a game.) *E*: *Uncapture* me!

Table 4.1 (*cont.*)

34	C	4; 7	C:	I hate you! And I'm never going to *unhate* you or nothing! (Angry after request is denied.)
			Mother:	You're never going to unhate me?
			C:	I'll never like you.
35	C	4; 5		(C has asked mother why pliers are on table.)
			Mother:	I've been using them for straightening the wire.
			C:	And *unstraighting* it?
36	C	5; 1		He tippitoed to the graveyard and *unburied* her. (Telling ghost story.)
37	C	7; 11		I'm gonna *unhang* it. (Taking stocking down from fireplace.)

ª Child's age is given in years; months. Sources as indicated, plus Bowerman 1983, for dative alternation and passives (I am grateful to Eric Kellerman for example 3); 1982a, 1982b, 1983 for lexical causatives; Bowerman 1982b for locative alternation and reversative *un*- prefixation.

4.1 *Limited productivity for lexical redundancy rules?*

Lexicalists who have not been specifically concerned with the 'no negative evidence' problem have suggested that although lexical redundancy rules are typically passive (that is, not called on in sentence production or comprehension), speakers might occasionally use them productively (e.g. Jackendoff 1975). Tolerance for productivity would appear to be necessary to accommodate the evidence that *adult* speakers sometimes produce passives, shifted datives, etc., with novel verbs. Perhaps, then, examples like those in table 4.1 should be dismissed under an escape clause that allows speakers an occasional burst of creativity with what is basically a passive generalization over existing lexical entries.

This defense is untenable. First, only a small portion of children's errors such as those shown in table 4.1 involves novel verbs whose properties are in principle open to creative negotiation. For the most part they are everyday verbs whose syntactic and morphological privileges are well known to fluent speakers. We are still left, then, with the problem of how children identify them as exceptions to a particular rule. More generally, the very existence of a 'creativity' escape clause destroys the advantage claimed in the first place for the lexicalist approach as a solution to the 'no negative evidence' problem. Once the door is opened a crack to productivity, how does the child know where to stop? (See also Wasow 1981 on this point.)

4.2 *Errors as analogies, not rule-governed productions*

A second way to deal with errors like those in table 4.1 within the innate constraints framework is to argue that they do not actually reflect rule use. Instead, they are on-the-spot analogies in which the child momentarily 'borrows' the legitimate syntactic or morphological privileges of a verb that is semantically similar to the one in question (see Maratsos 1979: 335 for suggestions along this line). If this is correct, there is no problem for either the lexicalist solution or the Subset Principle. The child really *does* know the syntactic or morphological privileges of the form in question; his grammar is not overinclusive.

It seems possible that some of children's errors are passing analogies rather than the output of established rules. But is this true in all cases of errors involving 'embarrassing' lexical exceptions? The 'analogy' interpretation for errors of a given genre seems most plausible when the errors are very rare, and there are semantically closely related forms to serve as models for the analogy. Errors of this type in my data include incorrect choices of verb complement, for example *Christy insisted me to make a house* (= insisted that I should make . . .; E age 7; 3; cf. *forced, persuaded, told*). But the 'passing analogy' interpretation seems strained for errors that occur more frequently and involve many different lexical items, many of which lack close semantic neighbors that undergo the rule. In my data these include novel causatives, locatives and passives. Errors with shifted datives are not frequent in my data, but ill-formed shifted datives were ofted judged grammatical by Mazurkewich and White's (1984) subjects, which is difficult to explain by reference to passing analogies.

If, as the data strongly indicate, at least some genres of children's overgeneralizations involving 'embarrassing' lexical exceptions are rule-governed and not mere analogies, then theoretical proposals for constraints that will prevent such overgeneralizations from ever occurring are on the wrong track. Instead, we must shift our attention to the procedures children use for cutting back on overgeneral rules.

5 The Criteria Approach: Conditions on Rules

An interesting hypothesis about these procedures has recently been proposed by Mazurkewich and White (1984) for dative alternations, and expanded by Pinker (1984: ch. 8; 1987) to cover causatives, passives, locative alternations and *un*- prefixation as well. This approach is based on the assumption that rules with lexical exceptions do not apply to an arbitrary set of verbs, but rather to verbs of a coherent class, characterized by shared semantic, morphological and/or phonological criteria (hence the label 'Criteria' approach; Pinker 1987). Children may initially overgeneralize, but they eventually identify the criteria that define the lexical class appropriate to the rule. When they do, they limit productive use of the rule to lexical items of the right class, and errors cease.

For dative alternation, for example, the child learns that 'shiftable' indirect objects must be 'prospective possessors' of the entity named by the direct object and that the verb itself must be of 'native [Germanic] stock', not Latinate (Mazurkewich and White 1984; Pinker 1984; these authors draw on Goldsmith 1980, Green 1974, Oehrle 1976, and Stowell 1981). For causativization of an intransitive verb or adjective, the causation must be direct (for example, physical), and the agent, manner and goal of causation must be stereotypic or conventional for the act in question (Pinker 1984, drawing on Shibatani 1976, Gergely and Bever 1986 and others). And for reversative *un*-prefixation, a 'covert semantic class' identified by Whorf (see Bowerman 1982b) is relevant: verbs that can be *un*-ed share 'a covering, enclosing, and surface-attaching meaning ... hence we say "uncover, uncoil, undress, unfasten, unlock, unroll, untangle, untie, unwind", but not "unbreak, undry, unhang, unheat, unlift, unmelt, unopen, unpress, unspill"' (Whorf 1956: 72).

This approach has some similarity to the Subset Principle, since both strategies appeal to subset–superset relations among possible rules of grammar. However, it differs importantly in that children are not expected to identify or automatically prefer, from the beginning, the grammatical rule that generates the smallest grammar; instead, they must work to identify the criteria that define the target subsets. Although the Criteria approach clearly invokes learning in a way that the Subset Principle does not, the approach is nevertheless compatible with – and may well require – some strong nativist corollary assumptions about how children identify the conditions on rules.[2]

The Criteria approach has the clear advantage over both the 'lexical redundancy rule' strategy and the Subset Principle that it can accommodate the overgeneralizations that children actually make. And there is evidence that children are indeed capable of restricting a rule that is initially overly general to verbs of the 'right' semantic class (see Bowerman 1982b on *un*- prefixation). Nevertheless, I am doubtful that it is the right answer to the 'no negative evidence' problem.

One difficulty is that it is hard to understand why children would go to so much work to identify conditions on their rules (Fodor and Crain 1987; Randall, 1987). Why should they bother to hypothesize possible constraints and check whether these constraints correctly predict the adult words that undergo a rule, especially given that, with their overly general rule, they can already understand all adult utterances of the relevant form? And how would they know which conditions to consider in connection with which rules?

A second difficulty, discussed immediately below, is that the subsets proposed for rules with lexical exceptions are themselves dotted with gaps: items that fully conform to the semantic/morphological conditions on the rule, but that still do not undergo the rule.

5.1 Gaps in the subsets

For dative alternation, such an item is *choose* (see examples 4–5 in table 4.1). Many speakers find something distinctively odd about 'shifted' indirect objects with *choose*, as in *I chose you a book at the library sale*.[3] Yet *choose* satisfies the putative semantic/morphological restrictions on verbs that allow dative alternation, since (i) it is of native stock and (ii) the beneficiary of an act of choosing is the 'prospective possessor' of the object named by the direct object. (Many speakers who regard 'shifted' indirect objects with *choose* as unacceptable find them perfectly normal with *pick out*, which is semantically almost identical to *choose*.)

For lexical causatives there are gaps in English like 'to *cough/*laugh/ *comfortable/*vomit someone'. There seems to be no principled reason why a too-big bite can *choke* or *gag* us but not *cough* us (see example 10 in table 4.1), why we can *cheer* someone *up* but not *laugh* or *giggle* her (for example, with tickling or a joke) (example 12) and why we can *quiet* or *burp* a baby but neither *comfortable* (or *comfy*) her when she is uncomfortable (example 11) nor *vomit* her when she is nauseated (for example, with a finger). The acts of causation specified by the latter verbs do not seem any less 'direct' or 'conventional' than those specified by the former.

For *un-* prefixation, the verb *squeeze* is an inexplicable exception (example 32). You can squeeze somebody's hand but you can't *unsqueeze it, even though *squeeze* falls into Whorf's covert class of 'centripetal' verbs. (Note, for example, that you can both *clench* and *unclench* your teeth or fists; *squeeze* is similar to *clench* in specifying a continuous pressure toward a center point.)

Gaps in a target subset – let's call them 'negative exceptions' – constitute a grave challenge to the Criteria approach. The approach can tolerate exceptions, but only if they are positive – that is, items to which a rule applies even though they do NOT belong to the target class. These latter exceptions are generally regarded as tractable because in principle they could be learned on the basis of exposure to positive evidence. For example, children could learn that *assign* allows dative alternation – even though it is Latinate – through hearing sentences like *The teacher assigned John a desk in the back row*. However, there is no comparable evidence to mark *squeeze*, *choose*, *cough*, etc., as exceptions that *cannot* undergo rules whose conditions they otherwise satisfy. They are invisible holes within their subsets. How do children identify such holes?

5.2 Partitioning subsets more finely

In very recent work, Pinker (1987) argues that where there have appeared to be negative exceptions to target subsets (as argued above and in Bowerman 1987), the semantic or other constraints on the items that can undergo a particular operation have not yet been adequately pinned down. Since it is often difficult or impossible to identify a single subclass per rule that satisfactorily includes all and only the desired lexical items, Pinker now proposes that for each rule there may be *sets* of coherent subclasses of items that do and do not undergo the specified operation. In other words, if we slice up the lexicon more finely, alleged 'negative exceptions' will disappear.

Drawing on work by Levin (1985) and Rappoport and Levin (1985), Pinker outlines a number of candidate subclasses. For example, he proposes that dative alternation applies to 'verbs of giving' (*give, pass, send* . . .), 'verbs of future having' (*offer, promise, bequeath* . . .), 'verbs of successful communication' (*tell, show* . . .) and a couple of other subclasses. However, it does *not* apply to 'verbs of choosing' (*choose, select, pick* . . .), 'verbs of manner of speaking ' (*shout, whisper* . . .) and a few other subclasses that were encompassed by the class previously specified as relevant for dative alternation in Pinker (1984).

Similarly, causativization applies only when the resulting transitive verb specifies a 'cause of a change of physical state' (*open, melt, shatter* . . .), 'cause of motion in a particular manner' (*float, roll, bounce* . . .), 'coerced or encouraged locomotion in a particular manner' (*walk, gallop, run, jump* [your horse] . . .) and 'enabling and accompanying of willful transportation in some manner' (*fly, boat, motor* [someone to New York] . . .). It does *not* apply to verbs specifying 'motion in a direction' (cf. **I went my son to school; *I rose the flag*) and verbs of 'internally caused acts' (**Bill vomited Jill, *Fred laughed the baby, *John died Harry*), although there may be suppletive forms with the same meaning (*I took my son to school, I raised the flag, John killed Harry*), and some verbs are 'positive exceptions', in that they causativize even though they belong to a class whose members in general do not (*Mom burped the baby*, 'internally caused act'; *Mary dropped the ball*, 'motion in a direction').

Do these changes strengthen the viability of the Criteria solution to the 'no negative evidence' problem for rules with lexical exceptions? Although the fit of the subclasses to the data appears at first glance to be better, I believe that this is somewhat illusory: repartitioning has simply redistributed problems to places where they seem superficially to do less damage; it has not eliminated them.

Recall that the motivation behind partitioning lexical items into smaller semantic classes was to get rid of alleged negative exceptions like (**choose* + indirect object' and causative **cough*, since the original version of the Criteria approach was not able to account for how a child could identify them. These items have now been excised from the original target subclasses in a principled way, by being declared members of semantically coherent subclasses of their own, none of whose members undergo the rule (except as positive exceptions). These 'negative' subclasses are in turn used in defining the boundaries of the new, multiple 'positive' subclasses to which the rule *does* apply.

For example, 'verbs of locomotion in a particular manner' can causativize, unless they also happen to be members of the non-causativizing class of 'verbs of motion in a direction'; this accounts for why *climb*, apparently a perfectly good verb of locomotion, does not causativize. *The riders walked/galloped/*climbed their horses up the hill* (Pinker, personal communication). Similarly, 'verbs of future having' can undergo dative alternation, but this class must be construed so as to omit 'verbs of choosing', even though the one for whom something is chosen could reasonably be viewed as a 'future haver'.

Now, the problem for a plausible theory of language acquisition is to explain how children could learn the critical negative subclasses that serve to define and delimit the positive subclasses. I will argue that the cost of eliminating negative exceptions in the way proposed is to so increase the number of new *positive exceptions*, relative to the size of the now smaller subclasses, that many of the necessary generalizations about what classes do not undergo a rule are likely to be unlearnable.

An example will illustrate the problem. As noted above, in Pinker's (1987) version of the Criteria approach the child must learn that 'verbs of motion in a direction' do not causativize. This will account for the cessation of causative errors with inherently directional verbs like *climb*, *go* and *rise*. But could a child in fact learn this? There are many positive exceptions to the generalization – that is, many 'verbs of motion in a direction' that DO causativize: for example, *drop*, *lower*, *sink*, *topple*, *recline*, *dip*, *tilt* (direction of motion 'down'); drain ('out and down'), *exude* ('out'); *lift*, *levitate* ('up'); *transfer* ('across' [Latin *trans*-]); *withdraw* ('away'); *filter*, *percolate* ('through'), *retract* ('back'). Most of the other critical negative subsets outlined by Pinker also have positive exceptions.

In principle, of course, positive exceptions to negative subsets are learnable through positive evidence. The problem, though, is that there must not be so many positive exceptions that the boundary between items that can and can't undergo the rule is hopelessly blurred. The threat posed by positive exceptions is a function of their number relative to the number of items correctly predicted by the criteria for distinguishing positive and negative classes. If they are few, and the number of correctly predicted items is large, a robust learning system can still make the generalization. But as the number of exceptions rises or the size of the classes falls, the generalization becomes steadily weaker.

In the earlier version of the Criteria model, in which there was a single critical subclass for rule application and a residual negative class of items to which the rule did not apply, the classes were large enough that some positive exceptions could be tolerated. But in the present version, the single split has been replaced by *multiple subclasses*, both positive and negative; this means that the size of the classes against which any positive exceptions must be weighed has dropped sharply. Consequently, even a few positive exceptions can so severely pollute the generalization that it is unlikely a child would ever consider it.

In sum, efforts to make the Criteria approach work as a solution to the 'no negative evidence' problem have veered from the Scylla of unlearnable negative exceptions, as argued in the last subsection, to the Charybdis of too many positive exceptions, as just discussed. Is it possible that the approach can be strengthened by still further attempts at partitioning aimed at reducing the number of positive exceptions to tolerable levels? I think this is unlikely.

I do not question the claim that the sets of words that undergo rules like dative alternation or causativization are not arbitrary; there are clearly correlations, often very strong, between certain meanings and eligibility for certain rules. But is the nature of language such that there *necessarily* are systematic principles governing which words do and do not undergo a particular rule? The Criteria approach insists that this is the case. Wasow (1977), however, presents a different view:

> I assume that if a tree satisfying the structural conditions of a transformation is prohibited from undergoing the structural change, then some explanation is called for, but *a lexical item that does not undergo a lexical rule whose conditions it satisfies is perfectly normal*. Transformations are crucial to the generation of all and only the sentences of the language (and hence have infinite domains); in contrast, lexical rules express subregularities within a finite lexicon ... Hence, I assume (following Jackendoff, 1975) that *lexical rules ... will typically have unsystematic exceptions*. (p. 331, emphasis added)

The Criteria approach to the 'no negative evidence' problem recognizes and can tolerate only *one* kind of unsystematicity in lexical rules: positive exceptions. But there seems to be no principled reason to rule out the opposite kind of unsystematicity: negative exceptions. If Wasow's view is correct, as I believe it is, then drawing and redrawing subset boundaries to get rid of negative exceptions is a futile exercise. Negative exceptions may be just as characteristic of the lexicon as positive exceptions. If so, children must have techniques for identifying them. And if they do have such techniques, they could presumably apply them directly to *all* lexical items to which a rule has been overgeneralized, rather than first eliminating some items through the discovery of appropriate subclasses before bringing in stronger methods to detect any remaining stragglers.

In summary, it is not clear that children's identification of lexical subclasses plays any necessary role in their retreat from an overly general grammar, although the process of discovering correlations between lexical rules and the meanings of the lexical items that typically undergo them is an interesting aspect of language acquisition in its own right (see Bowerman 1982b).

6 Principles of Universal Grammar

One question about the Criteria approach to the 'no negative evidence' problem, as mentioned earlier, is whether it is plausible that children would go to all the effort of identifying conditions on a rule, given that their overly general version of the rule accounts perfectly well for all the utterances they hear and allows them to create new ones. Some theorists have argued that we need stronger principles than the Criteria approach provides to explain what would cause a child to reject a successful but overly general rule – in particular, principles of Universal Grammar (Grimshaw 1987; Randall 1987).

Principles of Universal Grammar are assumed, by theorists who work within this framework, to be built into the human capacity for language. Thus, if a child's rule should be incompatible with such a principle, this would trigger automatic rejection. But, we may ask, if the child had a principle that would eventually lead to rejection of a rule, why would this principle not operate from the beginning to prevent the rule from ever being constructed? The answer is that the child may not at first 'realize' that the principle applies to the forms on which he errs. When he discovers that it does, errors will cease.

There is a danger to this logic, as noted by Matthews (1983): it can be used to reconcile the 'innate constraints' approach with any data, no matter how uncooperative. To avoid being totally *ad hoc* in appealing to a particular principle to explain the cessation of certain errors, an investigator must at least propose a plausible account of why the child does not at first realize that the principle applies, and of what triggers the realization that it does apply. An intriguing proposal that attempts to satisfy these basic requirements has been made by Randall (1985, 1987) to explain how children eventually restrict dative alternation to verbs of the right class.

The proposal comprises two key ingredients. First, Randall argues that verbs that do and do not undergo dative alternation differ in their basic argument structure: verbs that take the double-object form (the *give*-class) have three mandatory arguments, whereas those that do not take double objects have only two (*donate*-class), although they can optionally take a third, the dative object. This difference in argument structure can be seen from differences in the way verbs of the two types behave in a variety of syntactic contexts; most saliently, it is perfectly normal for *donate*-class verbs to appear without a dative argument, whereas this is more marked for *give*-class verbs, requiring special contexts where the missing dative argument can be inferred.

The second critical ingredient of Randall's proposal is the claim that children are innately equipped with a principle central to X-bar theory (Jackendoff 1977), which dictates that obligatory elements are attached inside of optional elements, relative to the phrasal head and its projections. This means that optional arguments cannot precede obligatory arguments in the predicate of an English sentence: *Pablo invited* (**to the art opening*) *Doris*; *Dylan spent* (**on drink*) *a lot of money*. Notice that this principle rules out shifted datives with *donate*-class verbs, according to Randall, since the dative argument of these verbs, unlike that of *give*-class verbs, is optional, and so must appear *after* the obligatory argument.

What children are lacking at first, argues Randall, is an understanding of the basic argument structure of *donate*-class verbs. They assume that *both* the direct object *and* the dative object arguments are obligatory; hence, the double-object construction that reverses the order of these two arguments is permissible. Once they discover that the dative object is optional for these verbs – possibly through observing that the verbs can occur without dative objects in unmarked discourse contexts – the principle that obligatory arguments attach inside optional elements serves to eliminate errors.

This principle is so strong that it will also rule out certain double-object constructions that English in fact allows, in particular those with 'beneficiary' arguments such as *Mom baked Jack a cake*. *Bake*, *knit*, etc., do not subcategorize for a beneficiary. Why then do these verbs allow the double-object construction? Randall (1987 and personal communication) proposes that there is a lexical rule of English that converts two-argument verbs like *bake* into three-argument verbs like *give*, subject to certain semantic conditions (the beneficiary must be the 'prospective possessor' of the thing baked, knitted, etc.). These new three-argument verbs are free to appear with 'shifted' datives, since all their arguments are obligatory.

Children would construct this lexical rule as follows. When they discover that the beneficiary of verbs like *bake* is optional, they at first simply rule out the double-object construction for these verbs entirely, since it would violate the universal principle of attachment. Then they would learn, one by one from positive evidence, that *bake*, *knit*, etc., in fact can take the double-object construction. After they have assembled a collection of such 'exceptions', all of which share the 'prospective possessor' property, they recognize that there is a pattern to the exceptions and formulate a lexical rule to account for it. This will allow them to create double-object constructions for novel verbs of cooking, creation, etc., as long as the semantic condition on the rule is met. Although this account makes reference to a semantic criterion, it does so in a much more restricted way than Mazurkewich and White's (1984) and Pinker's (1984, 1987) approach. Most of the work of eliminating undesired double object constructions is done by a universal constraint on the syntactic realization of verb argument structure; semantics is brought in only after the grand cutback has taken place, in order to capture what all the positive exceptions to the cutback have in common.

Randall's proposal raises a number of immediate questions. For example, why should children at first assume that *donate*-class verbs have three obligatory arguments, especially since (1) the critical evidence that they have only two arguments – sentences without a dative object like *John said something nice*; *Mary chose a dress* – is surely available in the input all along, and (2) to judge from their spontaneous speech, children seem more disposed to think that *obligatory* constituents are *optional* than that *optional* ones are *obligatory* (Brown 1973). (Notice that if children did not assume that *donate*-class verbs have three obligatory arguments, but only two, the universal principle of attachment would apply immediately and no overgeneralizations of dative alternation would occur – a wrong prediction.)

More generally, it is important to ask whether a solution of the same general type as Randall proposes for datives can be found for all rules with lexical exceptions. For example, is there a universal principle that accounts for why some verbs of English causativize and others do not? One particular difficulty may be to formulate principles that are strong enough to block undesirable generalizations in one language without at the same time ruling out, or gratuitously rendering as 'marked' or unusual, what appear to be the wholly normal constructions in other languages (Bowerman 1983).

If the proposal that the 'no negative evidence' problem for rules with lexical exceptions can be solved through appeal to principles of Universal Grammar is to be viable, it is essential that comparable explanations for other rules with lexical exceptions can be found. As long as there are rules with lexical exceptions for which such an explanation cannot be constructed, children must have some other techniques for identifying lexical exceptions. And if they have such techniques, children can presumably apply them to any rule with lexical exceptions; it thus becomes superfluous to call upon principles of Universal Grammar.

Two possible candidates for such very general techniques are 'preemption' and 'discovery procedures'. Let us consider their strengths and weaknesses.

7 'Benign Exceptions' Reconsidered: the Role of Preemption

Almost every investigator who worries about the 'no negative evidence' problem has assumed that at least part of the answer lies in preemption: when children formulate overly general rules, they eventually give up overgeneralized forms if they are consistently faced with positive evidence for other forms expressing the same meanings.[4]

A precondition for preemption is that there must be a conventional adult counterpart for a child's overgeneralized word or construction: that is, a form that means what the child's form means and that occurs consistently in the same contexts. This precondition is met most clearly in cases of inflectional overregularization (*runned/ran*; *foots/feet*, etc.). Some overgeneralized causatives also have plausible preempting counterparts (for example, causative **die/kill*; **come/bring*), as do a very few locative verbs (*rob/steal jewels from the bank; *steal/rob the bank of its jewels).

But what about causative *disappear or *climb, or *"choose + indirect object"? For these there are no obvious candidate preempting forms: they are 'embarrassing exceptions' by Baker's (1979) definition. Nevertheless, some researchers have suggested that the notion of preemption might be stretched to cover overgeneralizations of these types as well. For example, Clark (1987) proposes that children will give up their overgeneralized causatives like *"to disappear (something)' in favor of 'to make (something) disappear', since in every context where they would say the former, they hear adults say the latter.

A stretch is involved here because make disappear is not a perfect semantic match to causative disappear (as kill is, for example, to causative die). In general, lexical causatives and their periphrastic counterparts differ with respect to the directness and conventionality of the act of causation specified (compare, for example, John stood the baby up [direct physical causation] with John made the baby stand up [indirect causation, e.g. through giving an order]). The weight of this meaning distinction, pervasive throughout English, ought to work against children's willingness to let periphrastic causatives like make disappear preempt nonexistent lexical causatives like disappear. Still, we might be willing to accept this solution, if only for lack of a better idea.[5]

But, even if it is correct, this extended view of preemption buys us only a little more help with the 'no negative evidence' problem, not a cure. For the approach to work, there must at least be a consistent relationship between the child's overgeneralized form and an adult counterpart, even if that counterpart is not identical in meaning to the overgeneralization. This condition is indeed met with causative disappear and its periphrastic counterpart.

But what about errors with reversative un-, for example? Here the child meets with no consistent alternatives in the adult input. For instance, in contexts where unsqueeze would be appropriate, if it existed, adults might say loosen, ease up, release, let go, remove, and so on. None of these is in direct semantic competition with unsqueeze, since none of them specifies or requires that the event referred to is the reversal of an act of 'squeezing'. Nor should the child take the existence of such forms as having any bearing on the possibility of unsqueeze: reversative un- forms coexist harmoniously with various related constructions, for example unwrap and take the wrapper off, unzip and pull the zipper down, unload and empty.

For overgeneralizations of the type shown in table 4.2 (for example, *untie it off; see Bowerman 1982b), the problem is even more severe. These sentences are based on a highly productive construction pattern of English that specifies the combination of a causing event and a resulting change of state or location: for example shoot your enemy dead, pat the baby dry, wipe the table clean, eat oneself into a stupor, pull your socks up,

Table 4.2 Resultative overgeneralizations

1	C	3; 8	I *pulled* it *unstapled*. (After pulling stapled booklet apart.)
2	C	3; 10	*Untie* it *off*. (Wants mother to untie piece of yarn and take it off tricycle handle.)
3	C	4; 0	I'm *patting* her *wet*. (Patting sister's arm after dipping her own hand into a glass of water.)
4	C	6; 2	It's hard not to knock them down 'cause whenever I breathe I *breathe* them *down*. (Having trouble setting up a paper village; when she exhales, the houses fall down.)
5	E	3; 11	I took my bunny out . . . I *pinched* him *out* with [= by] his fur. (Telling how she reached into bedroom through door, and extracted her toy rabbit by pulling on a bit of fur.)
6	E	6; 3	His doggie *bited* him *untied*. (Telling how tied-up man in a TV show was freed.)
7	M	5; 6	Are you *washing* me *blind*? (As mother wipes corners of her eyes.)
6	M	5; 10	Feels like you're *combing* me *baldheaded*. (As mother combs her hair.)
7	A	4; 3	When you get to her, you *catch* her *off*. (A is on park merry-go-round with doll next to her. Wants a friend, standing nearby, to remove doll when it comes around to her.)
8	R	4; 9	I'll *jump* that *down*. (About to jump on bath mat M has just put on top of water in tub.)

cut your hair off, *chop a tree down*. However, the pattern is subject to constraints that are still incompletely understood (Green 1972; Mc-Cawley 1971; Randall 1983; Simpson 1983). How do children come to appreciate that there are any restrictions at all, much less what these restrictions are?

The special difficulty is that novel utterances of this type – both those that are acceptable to adult ears and those that sound odd – are usually 'one time only' constructions, designed to fit a certain passing configuration of cause and effect such as pulling on a book and the book's becoming unstapled, or combing the hair and becoming bald. This means that learners do not have repeated opportunities to observe 'the way other people express this particular meaning.' Even if a particular configuration of cause and effect should arise quite frequently (say, 'untying a rope' so that it 'comes off' of something, as in example 2), the alternatives a child might hear from an adult – such as *untie the rope and take it off*, *take the rope off by untying it*, or just plain *take the rope off* – have no bearing on the grammaticality of the child's version, just as the verb *empty* has no bearing on the well-formedness of *unload*. As Fodor and Crain (1987) point out, a learner cannot take every sentence he hears as precluding all sentences that express somewhat related messages; natural languages are too rich for this.

In summary, children make a number of overgeneralizations for which preemption, even if interpreted liberally, fails to provide a correction.

8 Braine's Discovery Procedures Proposal

Braine's original (1971b) empiricist proposal for how to solve the 'no negative evidence' problem has received relatively little attention. According to this approach, the language learner is equipped with 'discovery procedures' that register the properties of incoming sentences. As properties are repeatedly registered, they are passed along a series of intermediate memory stores until they reach permanent memory. Since general properties are characteristic of more sentences than are specific properties, they will be encountered the most often and will reach permanent memory first. Further acquisition involves registering more detailed information – for instance, about the syntactic contexts in which specific lexical items appear. Specific knowledge comes to stand before general knowledge. This means that if a general rule that has arrived in permanent memory has lexical exceptions, it will be overridden, where necessary, by information about the syntactic and morphological behavior of individual words.

This solution has certain advantages. One is that although a rule that is initially overgeneralized will eventually no longer cause problems for familiar lexical items, it is still available. It can therefore be applied to novel words whose properties have never been registered, which is necessary if we are to account for productivity with the passive, etc.

Another advantage is that the learning system has a 'sieve-like' property: only properties that are encountered repeatedly in the input get retained and passed along to permanent storage, and any pattern that is not repeatedly instantiated eventually decays and drops out of the intermediate stores, never making it into permanent memory. This means that occasional errors by the child's conversational partners do no harm. (In contrast, in Baker's (1979) lexicalist approach, a single exposure to a faulty sentence like *Don't say me that* could cause the child to add a wrong subcategorization frame that could never be expunged; see note 1.)

Finally, Braine's model provides a way to formalize native speakers' strong intuition that they do not use familiar lexical items in certain ways simply because they have never heard them used that way. Baker's 'lexical redundancy rule' account also captures this intuition, but, unlike Braine's model, it does not allow for children's overgeneralizations or for productivity with novel lexical items.

Despite these advantages, Braine's account makes the wrong prediction about the *timing* of children's overgeneralizations. If overgeneralizations of a particular pattern are made at all, they should be made early, before word-specific information has been registered. Once such information *has* been registered, the errors should drop out. In fact, however, most of children's overgeneralizations follow the opposite course (see Bowerman 1982b for discussion). The child first treats individual lexical items, whether exceptional or unexceptional with respect to some rule, with remarkable syntactic and morphological accuracy. This lexically specific stage of learning is followed by the extraction of general rules. Once a generalization is made, errors begin. The errors thus do not reflect initial ignorance of the handling of specific words, which could be corrected simply by further learning of the relevant details, but rather the *overriding* of lexically specific knowledge.

To deal with this problem, Braine (in press) has recently suggested that there may indeed be special circumstances that cause a specific pattern to be learned before a general one. Sometimes, for example, 'the categories of the general pattern may not be available to the [child] at the time the specific pattern is being learned, so that the specific pattern has a long lead through the filter system.' Whenever a specific pattern is learned first, for whatever reasons, 'it may not take precedence over a later-acquired general pattern.' This means that early specific knowledge does not block the later onset of overregularizations involving the same forms.

This modification is too sketchy at present for proper evaluation. One obvious question is how the learning system 'knows' whether information about a specific pattern has preceded or followed information about a general pattern: where and how is information about the relative progress of different patterns stored and evaluated? A second critical question is how overgeneralizations that have been preceded by lexically specific knowledge are eliminated. Must the same lexically-specific information be relearned *after* the generalization, this time coming to override it? A third question is how Braine's learning system would handle the learnability puzzles posed by rules which, if overly general, could not be corrected by learning about the contexts in which specific lexical items can occur.

For example, consider again overgeneralizations of the resultative pattern, shown in table 4.2. One of the constraints on sentences of this type, as Green (1972) has pointed out, is that the 'result' must not be expressed with a past participle (compare, for example, *She combed her hair SMOOTH/*UNTANGLED; She cooked the roast DRY/*BURNED/ *OVERDONE; he smashed the box FLAT/*BROKEN*).[6] (This accounts for the ungrammaticality of examples 1 and 6.) Children following Braine's learning strategy might conclude that *untangled*, *burned* and *broken* cannot appear as result complements, because they have never observed them in these positions. But since this information is specific to particular words, there is nothing to stop the learner from creating resultatives with the past participles of novel or newly learned verbs. How do children form a general block against ALL past participles as result complements, regardless of past opportunities to observe a particular participle's behavior? (See Bowerman 1987: 461 for discussion of the problem of identifying properties shared by items that do *not* undergo a rule.)

Conversely, why does the child who follows Braine's strategy eventually come to regard sentences like *Whenever I breathe I breathe them down* and *I pinched him out with his fur* (examples 4 and 5 in table 4.2) as peculiar? The problem here is not with the specific lexical items, but with their interaction. For example, both *down* and *out* occur frequently as result complements (for example, *blow/chop/push NP DOWN*; *pull/yank/press NP OUT*), and *breathe* and *pinch* both occur as main verbs in resultative sentences (*BREATHE NP in/out*; *PINCH NP black and blue/to death*). Why then do they resist occurring together? We cannot solve this puzzle within Braine's framework by arguing that these words have never been heard together in this construction (i.e., by appealing to information specific to the contingencies between TWO lexical items). To do so would be to lose sight of the fact that the child whose learning system we are trying to characterize must end up with a productive rule that allows him to create *novel combinations* of main verb and result complement.

It is not clear whether these problems can be solved within Braine's general framework. Clearly the model will require more work before its potential as a solution to the 'no negative evidence' problem can be properly evaluated.

9 Does the 'No Negative Evidence Problem' Really Exist?

In view of all the difficulties I have raised for various approaches to the 'no negative evidence' problem, the reader might have concluded that children must get negative feedback after all. Perhaps the 'no negative evidence' problem is just a myth.

Several investigators have argued for a resolution to the problem along these lines. They concede that children do not get many *explicit corrections* of their grammar, but they argue that learners do get negative feedback in the form of misunderstandings, requests for clarification, repetitions and recastings (e.g. Demetras et al. 1986; Hirsch-Pasek et al. 1984). I do not think the answer lies in this direction, however, for the following reasons.

First, researchers who argue that children do get negative evidence from their speaking partners have not distinguished in the necessary way among feedback to different categories of ungrammatical child utterances. Whenever negative feedback is observed for child utterances that are imperfect by adult standards, it is indiscriminately taken to count against the seriousness of the 'no negative evidence' problem. But most of this feedback is simply irrelevant. Many utterances, especially among younger children, are ungrammatical not because the speaker's rules are overly general but because the speaker hasn't yet constructed the necessary rules at all. (Omissions of grammatical morphemes are a case in point.) Adult misunderstandings, recastings and the like might or might not hasten rule construction in these cases, but they do not bear on the problem of how children cut back on overly general rules.

Even where such feedback does follow errors resulting from overly general rules, these errors often involve 'benign' rule exceptions, which in principle could be corrected by preemption and so do not require negative feedback. I suspect that the amount of negative evidence that remains after we eliminate these two types of irrelevant feedback is not very great, especially since overgeneralizations of the types discussed in this chapter are produced by relatively old children and rarely cause misunderstanding (as noted also by Mazurkewich and White 1984).

Second, listener misunderstandings, requests for clarification, repetitions and recasts are not reliably diagnostic of ungrammaticality on the speaker's part: they follow well-formed utterances as well as those that are ungrammatical (Hirsch-Pasek et al. 1984). If a child's first impulse on hearing such responses is to question the adequacy of his grammar, he would continually be trying to revise perfectly acceptable rules. It seems unlikely that children are so readily led astray. Even if a child does on occasion question his grammar, only recasts give information about where the problem lies–misunderstandings, repetitions and 'what' questions are silent about what is wrong.

In sum, the 'no negative evidence' problem is not a myth, but a very real and serious challenge for the construction of an adequate theory of language acquisition.

10 Conclusions

Many linguists have assumed that the lack of negative feedback to children creates a logical problem for language acquisition that can be solved only by reference to innate constraints that prevent children from ever formulating overly general grammars. The data discussed in this chapter show that this assumption is untenable. Children do construct overly general grammars, yet somehow they are able to recover. How this recovery is accomplished is still uncertain.

It is possible, as some proponents of Universal Grammar have argued, that recovery is effected through innate linguistic constraints that come into play *after* rather than before the critical overgeneralizations have been made. But evidence for this is as yet slight. Existing hypotheses make questionable assumptions about why the proposed innate knowledge does not block the child's overgeneralizations from the beginning. In addition, no proposals have been developed to deal with most of children's error genres, and it is not clear that this will be possible, especially in view of cross-linguistic variation, even among closely related languages, in what lexical items constitute exceptions to a particular rule.

At present, I think it is most likely that children cut back on rules that are too broad with the help of relatively general learning mechanisms that apply across a wide range of error types. However, developing a plausible account of such mechanisms has proved remarkably difficult, and I have raised a number of problems for the three approaches of this type considered in this chapter: Criteria, Preemption, and Discovery Procedures.

Despite these criticisms, and also those I have leveled at Baker's verb-frame-by-verb-frame approach, the Subset Principle, and the Universal Grammar hypothesis, I believe we have made significant progress in the last few years in understanding the 'no negative evidence' problem. I hope that this chapter may contribute to its eventual resolution by highlighting some of the subtle and complex difficulties that future research on this puzzle will have to address.

Notes

Portions of this chapter have been adapted from my discussion chapter 'Commentary: mechanisms of language acquisition', in B. MacWhinney (ed.), *Mechanisms of Language Acquisition* (Hillsdale, NJ: Erlbaum, 1987). They are used here with permission of the publisher. I am grateful to Janet Randall and Lee Ann Weeks for helpful comments on an earlier draft.

1 One problem is that these approaches do not seem sufficiently robust against misleading input (Bowerman 1983). Children are often exposed to errors in the speech they hear, especially if they have a parent who is not a native speaker of the language they are learning. For example, Dutch adults often make shifted dative errors with *say* and *suggest* when speaking English (parallel structures with the Dutch cognate verbs are grammatical). Once having registered an incorrect syntactic frame for a verb, how could a child ever get rid of it? In addition, as Fodor and Crain (1987) point out, the Subset Principle solution to the 'no negative evidence' problem has an unattractive corollary. When the output of one rule is a proper subset of the output of another rule, then the narrower rule is typically more complex than the broader one since it is annotated for one or more constraints on application that the broader rule does not respect. This means that if children always start out by hypothesizing the narrowest rule possible, their first rules are routinely more complex than their later ones. But it clashes with our intuitions to imagine that children move consistently from more complex to less complex rules – that language acquisition proceeds by the successive removal of constraints on rule application.

2 For example, to make the Criteria approach work, Pinker (1984, pp. 333–341) credits children with foreknowledge of (1) a finite, universal set of features, possibly hierarchically organized, that are potentially relevant to constraining the class of lexical items to which a given rule applies, 2) the 'Unique Entry' principle (see footnote 4), violations of which will lead children to sample from among the potential constraints mentioned in (1) if they have not already done so spontaneously, and (3) a universal set of notions like 'passive', 'causative', and 'inchoative' that define the levels of the word-formation paradigms across which the 'Unique Entry' principle operates.

3 I base this claim on an informal survey of about twenty native speakers of English, most of whom rejected examples like these. Failure to find 100 percent agreement is not surprising: for every rule with lexical exceptions there are items about which speakers disagree or are uncertain. This is not important for my argument. As long as there are mature speakers who find such examples odd, we must explain how in their grammars the lexical item involved came to be excepted from the rule under examination.

4 There are both nativist and empiricist accounts of how preemption works. Some theorists argue that there is some property 'in the child' that rejects the idea that two forms should have exactly the same meaning. For example, Pinker (1984) postulates a 'Unique Entry' principle, according to which children resist having more than one entry in an inflectional or derivational paradigm unless they are faced with strong positive evidence that both forms exist. Clark's (1987) 'Principle of Contrast' is even stronger, stating that children assume that every two forms differ in meaning, and will resist acquiring or retaining two forms that seem synonymous. A contrasting, 'empiricist' hypothesis explains preemption as the outcome of *competition* among alternative forms for expressing the same meaning (MacWhinney 1987; Rumelhart and McClelland 1987): over time, the conventional adult form gains in activation strength and the child's overregularized form weakens until it dies out entirely. Grounds for deciding between these alternative views are at present unclear (see Bowerman 1987 for discussion).

5 See also Pinker (1981), Maratsos and Chalkley (1981) and Bowerman (1983) for the related proposal that children may identify items that are exceptions to their overly general rules through continually failing to encounter those items in discourse contexts where they 'expect' them; this is sometimes called 'indirect negative evidence', following Chomsky (1981: 9).

6 *Closed* and *shut* seem to be the only exceptions to this constraint (cf. Green 1972).

References

Baker, C. L. (1979) 'Syntactic theory and the projection problem'. *Linguistic Inquiry*, 10, 533–581.
 and McCarthy, J. J. (1981) *The Logical Problem of Language Acquisition*. Cambridge, Mass.: MIT Press.
Berwick, R. (1985) *The Acquisition of Syntactic Knowledge*. Cambridge Mass.: MIT Press.
 and A. Weinberg (1984) *The Grammatical Basis of Linguistic Performance*. Cambridge, Mass.: MIT Press.
Bowerman, M. (1974) 'Learning the structure of causative verbs: a study in the relationship of cognitive, syntactic, and semantic development'. *Papers and Reports on Child Language Development* (Stanford University Department of Linguistics), 8, 142–78.
 (1982a) 'Evaluating competing linguistic models with language acquisition data: implications of developmental errors with causative verbs'. *Quaderni di Semantica*, 3, 5–66.
 (1982b) 'Reorganizational processes in lexical and syntactic development'. In E. Wanner and L. R. Gleitman (eds), *Language Acquisition: The State of the Art*. Cambridge: Cambridge University Press.

(1983) 'How do children avoid constructing an overly general grammar in the absence of feedback about what is not a sentence?' *Papers and Reports on Child Language Development* (Stanford University Department of Linguistics), 22, 23–35.

(1987) 'Commentary: mechanisms of language acquisition'. In B. MacWhinney (ed.), *Mechanisms of Language Acquisition*. Hillsdale, NJ: Erlbaum.

Braine, M. D. S. (1971a) 'The acquisition of language in infant and child'. In C. Reed (ed.), *The Learning of Language*. New York: Scribners.

(1971b) 'On two types of models of the internalization of grammars'. In D. I. Slobin (ed.), *The Ontogenesis of Grammar*. New York: Academic Press.

(in press) 'Modeling the acquisition of linguistic structure'. In Y. Levy, I. M. Schlesinger and M. D. S. Braine (eds) Categories and Processes in Language Acquisition. Hillsdale, NJ: Erlbaum.

Brown, R. (1973) *A First Language*. Cambridge, Mass.: Harvard University Press.

and C. Hanlon (1970) Derivational complexity and order of acquisition in child speech. In J. R. Hayes (ed.) *Cognition and the Development of Language*. NY: Wiley.

Chomsky, N. (1965) *Aspects of the Theory of Syntax*. Cambridge, Mass.: MIT Press.

(1981) *Lectures on Government and Binding*. Dordrecht: Foris.

Clark, E. (1987) 'The principle of contrast: a constraint on language acquisition'. In B. MacWhinney (ed.), *Mechanisms of Language Acquisition*. Hillsdale, NJ: Erlbaum.

Dell, F. (1981) 'On the learnability of optional phonological rules'. *Linguistic Inquiry*, 12, 31–7.

Demetras, M. J., K. N. Post and C. E. Snow (1986) 'Feedback to first language learners: the role of repetitions and clarification questions'. *Journal of Child Language*, 13, 275–92.

Fodor, J. D. and S. Crain (1987) 'Simplicity and generality of rules in language acquisition'. In B. MacWhinney (ed.), *Mechanisms of Language Acquisition*. Hillsdale, NJ: Erlbaum.

Gergely, G. and T. Bever (1986) 'Related intuitions and the mental representation of causative verbs in adults and children'. *Cognition*, 23, 211–77.

Goldsmith, J. (1980) 'Meaning and mechanism in language'. In S. Kuno (ed.), *Harvard Studies in Syntax and Semantics* III, Department of Linguistics, Cambridge, Mass.: Harvard University Press.

Green, G. (1972) 'Some observations on the syntax and semantics of instrumental verbs'. *Proceedings of the Chicago Linguistic Society*, 8, 83–95.

(1974) *Semantics and Syntactic Regularity*. Bloomington, Ind.: Indiana University Press.

Grimshaw, J. (1987) 'Discussion: Session on "Acquisition of verbs and argument structure"'. Boston Child Language Conference, October.

Hall, B. (1965) 'Subject and object in modern English'. Doctoral diss., MIT (Published under B. Partee, [same title], New York: Garland, 1979).

Hirsch-Pasek, K., R. Treiman and M. Schneiderman (1984) 'Brown & Hanlon revisited: mothers' sensitivity to ungrammatical forms'. *Journal of Child Language*, 11, 81–8.

Hochberg, J. G. (1986) 'Children's judgements of transitivity errors'. *Journal of Child Language*, 13, 317–34.

Jackendoff, R. (1975) 'Morphological and semantic regularities in the lexicon'. *Language*, 51, 639–71.

(1977) $\bar{X}$ *Syntax: a Study of Phrase Structure*. Cambridge, Mass.: MIT Press.

Levin, B. (1985) 'Lexical semantics in review: an introduction'. In B. Levin (ed.), *Lexical Semantics in Review*. Lexicon Project Working Papers 1. Cambridge, Mass.: MIT Center for Cognitive Science.

McCawley, J. D. (1971) 'Prelexical syntax'. In R. J. O'Brien (ed.), *Georgetown University Round Table on Language and Linguistics*. Washington, DC: Georgetown University Press.

Maratsos, M. (1979) 'How to get from words to sentences'. In D. Aaronson and R. Reiber (eds), *Perspectives in Psycholinguistics*. Hillsdale, NJ: Erlbaum.

— and M. Chalkley (1981) 'The internal language of children's syntax'. In K. E. Nelson (ed.), *Children's Language*, vol. 2. New York: Gardner Press.

— R. Gudeman, P. Gerard-Ngo and G. DeHart (1987) 'A study in novel word learning: the productivity of the causative'. In B. MacWhinney (ed.), *Mechanisms of Language Acquisition*. Hillsdale, NJ: Erlbaum.

Matthews, P. H. (1983) Review of Hornstein and Lightfoot (eds), *Explanation in Linguistics: The Logical Problem of Language Acquisition* (1981). *Journal of Child Language*, 10, 491–3.

Mazurkewich, I. and L. White (1984) 'The acquisition of the dative alternation: unlearning overgeneralizations'. *Cognition*, 16, 261–83.

Oehrle, R. T. (1976) 'The grammatical status of the English dative alternation'. Doctoral dissertation, MIT.

Pinker, S. (1981) Comments on the paper by Wexler. In C. L. Baker and J. J. McCarthy (eds), *The Logical Problem of Language Acquisition*. Cambridge, Mass.: MIT Press.

— (1984) *Language Learnability and Language Development*. Cambridge, Mass.: Harvard University Press.

— (1987) 'Resolving a learnability paradox in the acquisition of the verb lexicon'. *Lexicon Project Working Papers 17*, Center for Cognitive Science, MIT. (To appear in R. L. Schiefelbusch (ed.), *The Teachability of Language*.)

— D. S. Lebeaux and L. A. Frost (1987) 'Productivity and constraints in the acquisition of the passive'. *Cognition*, 24.

Randall, J. (1983) 'A lexical approach to causatives'. *Journal of Linguistic Research*, 2, 77–105.

— (1985) 'Negative evidence from positive'. In P. Fletcher and M. Garman (eds), *Child Language Seminar Papers* (Proceedings of the 1985 Child Language Seminar, University of Reading).

— (1987) 'Indirect positive evidence: overturning generalizations in language acquisition'. Indiana University Linguistics Club.

Rappoport, M. and B. Levin (1985) 'A case study in lexical analysis: the locative alternation'. Unpub. MS, Center for Cognitive Science, MIT.

Roeper, T., S. Lapointe, J. Bing and S. Tavakolian (1981) 'A lexical approach to language acquisition'. In S. L. Tavakolian (ed.), *Language Acquisition and Linguistic Theory*. Cambridge, Mass.: MIT Press.

Rumelhart, D. E. and J. L. McClelland (1987) 'Learning the past tenses of English verbs: implicit rules or parallel distributed processing'. In B. MacWhinney (ed.), *Mechanisms of Language Acquisition*. Hillsdale, NJ: Erlbaum.

Shibatani, M. (1976) 'The grammar of causative constructions: a conspectus'. In M. Shibatani (ed.), *The Grammar of Causative Constructions*. New York: Academic Press.

Simpson, J. (1983) 'Resultative attributes'. In A. Zaenen, M. Rappoport, and

B. Levin (eds), *Papers in Lexical-Functional Grammar*. Indiana University Linguistics Club.

Smith, C. (1981) Comments on the paper by Roeper. In C. L. Baker and J. J. McCarthy (eds), *The Logical Problem of Language Acquisition*. Cambridge, Mass.: MIT Press.

Stowell, T. (1981) 'Origins of phrase structure'. Unpub. Ph.D. diss., MIT.

Wasow, T. (1977) 'Transformations and the lexicon'. In P. W. Culicover, T. Wasow and A. Akmajian (eds), *Formal Syntax*. New York: Academic Press.

Wasow, T. (1981) 'Comments' on C. L. Baker 'Learnability and the English auxiliary system'. In C. L. Baker and J. J. McCarthy *The Logical Problem of Language Acquisition*. Cambridge, Mass.: MIT Press.

Wexler, K. and M. R. Manzini (1987) 'Parameters and learnability in binding theory'. In T. Roeper and E. Williams (eds), *Parameter Setting*. Dordrecht: Reidel.

Whorf, B. (1956) *Language, Thought and Reality* (ed. J. Carroll). Cambridge, Mass.: MIT Press.

PART III

Semantic and Pragmatic Explanations

CHAPTER 5

On Semantics and the Binding Theory

Edward L. Keenan

1 Introduction

This article concerns natural language applications of a formal semantic theory called *Semantic Case Theory* (SCT) (Keenan 1987a).

Section 2 formally defines the semantic cases (*nominative* and *accusative*) needed to interpret transitive Ss and shows how our pretheoretical notions of 'logical subject (object)' and 'quantifier scope' may be characterized in these terms.

Section 3 presents the axioms of SCT and empirically investigates ways in which languages syntactically and morphologically present their nominatively and accusatively interpreted NPs. I demonstrate here the existence of *VP-nominative* languages – ones whose transitive Ss present a hierarchical structure like English [NP[V NP]] but in which, in distinction to English, the VP internal NP is interpreted nominatively rather than accusatively.

Section 4 extends the class of NP interpretations with a language independent (semantic) definition of *anaphor* and initiates a theory of anaphora based on that definition. The definition may be taken as an explication of our pretheoretical notion of 'referentially dependent' (Chomsky 1986: 93, 144). The theory of anaphora developed here is contrasted with that of the Binding Theory as presented in Chomsky (1986).[1]

2 Semantic Case Theory

2.1 *NPs with intransitive predicates*

We shall first consider how NPs are semantically interpreted when they combine with simple intransitive predicates (P_1s) to form main clause sentences (Ss). Then I introduce *semantic cases* as ways of *extending* these NP interpretations to their occurrences in transitive contexts.

Semantically we shall think of (main clause) Ss as (interpreted as) True or False in a given situation. A situation is in part specified by giving a domain D of (possibly mental) objects which we think of ourselves as speaking about. Given a situation, a simple P_1 such as *sings* determines a subset SING of D, those objects with the property of singing (in that situation). Such subsets of D will be called *properties* and P_1s will be interpreted as (= denote) properties.

NPs which combine with simple P_1s to form Ss will be called *initial*. Consider the interpretation of the initial NPs in (1).

(1) a. Some teacher is asleep
    b. Every student laughed.

(1b) is True (in a situation) just in case each object with the STUDENT property is also one with the LAUGH property, that is, STUDENT is a subset of LAUGH. (1a) is True just in case TEACHER has a non-empty intersection with SLEEP, that is, there is at least one object which is both a teacher and is asleep.

We may then semantically represent NPs like *some teacher* as functions which associate truth values (True, False) with properties. For example, the EVERY STUDENT function associates True with a property p if and only if STUDENT is a subset of p. Such functions will be called *basic* functions. Some other initial NPs interpreted by basic functions are:

(2) Every boy but not every girl, no boy's cat, all but two boys, every boy but Tom, neither John nor any student, more male than female students, most of John's friends, fewer boys than girls, more of John's than of Mary's articles, John

For extensive empirical discussion of this way of interpreting NPs see Keenan and Stavi (1986). Let us only note further the case of proper nouns. Given a situation, we think of *John* as determining an element b of D (the 'John-object'), and an S like *John sings* is true iff b is an element of SING. Thus *John* is interpreted by that basic function[2] which sends a property p to True iff b is an element of p.

One might imagine that all initial NPs can be semantically represented by basic functions, but in fact they are just a special case of the more general class of interpretations needed for initial NPs. (3) exhibits some non-basic NPs:

(3) you, I, my cat, every friend of mind, the same student, this cat, she, most of the papers he wrote, a different cat

The interpretation of these NPs depends on information given external to the NP itself. In this sense interpretations of these NPs will be said to be *open* (in contrast to those of the NPs in (2) which are *closed*). More generally, an interpretation of a language is a function which assigns semantic objects (properties, etc.) to occurrences of expressions. An interpretation is *open* at an expression (occurrence) if the choice of semantic object it assigns to it depends on information given external to the expression itself. In intransitive contexts, the dependency is on information given in the non-linguistic context of utterance, so open NPs in such contexts will be called *deictic*.[3] But as more complex syntactic contexts are considered the information on which an open interpretation of an NP depends may be given elsewhere in the linguistic context.

Interpretations of deictic NPs are not radically different from those of basic NPs. Given context information a deictic NP like *you* will denote the same sort of basic function as denoted by *Fred*. Thus *You are quiet* has the same truth value as *Fred is quiet* when context identifies the addressee as Fred.

We may then represent open interpretations of initial NPs as functions from contexts (whatever they are) into basic functions. For example, THIS STUDENT will assign to each context c a basic function (THIS STUDENT) (c). In general the functions denotable by initial NPs will be called *initial* functions. Such functions are either open (deictic) or closed (basic).[4]

2.2 *Transitive verbs and semantic cases*

We interpret transitive verbs like *kiss* as binary relations in the domain D, that is, as sets of ordered pairs of elements of D. So to say that an object b bears the KISS relation to an object d is just to say that the pair (b, d) is an element of the KISS set.[5] Main clause Ss formed from a transitive verb and two independent (basic) NPs will be called (*basic*) *transitive S* s.[6]

Observe now a surprising complexity difference in the interpretation of basic intransitive Ss and basic transitive ones: The truth value of the former is uniquely determined by the function denoted by the NP and the property denoted by the P_1. But given denotations for a P_2 and two NPs, the interpretation of a transitive S built from them is underdetermined in two ways. First we must specify which of the NPs is 'logical subject' and which 'logical object', and then given that, we must specify which NP is semantically within the scope of the other.

For example, given the binary relation KISS and the basic functions EVERY STUDENT and SOME TEACHER, two S meanings constructable from these elements are expressed in (4b–c). In both, *every student* denotes the 'logical subject' and *some teacher* the 'logical object'. The S meanings differ in that *some teacher* has 'narrow scope' in (4b) and 'wide scope' in (4c).

(4) a. Every student kissed some teacher
b. Every student has the property that there is a teacher who he kissed
c. Some teacher has the property that every student kissed him

The two other S meanings are those obtained when *some teacher* is taken as 'logical subject' and *every student* as 'logical object'.

I shall illustrate how SCT formally represents these pretheoretical notions in terms of the two interpretations of (4a). While the formal details can be set aside in the later sections, the existence of our formal explication is important. In SCT these notions are not unexplicated primitives.

To represent the 'object narrow scope' reading in (4b) we want to say that EVERY STUDENT has (= assigns True to) the property [KISSED SOME TEACHER]. To obtain this property from the binary relation KISS and the basic function SOME TEACHER we shall extend the domain of the latter so that it also takes binary relations as arguments, mapping them to properties in the appropriate way. This way of extending basic functions is called their *accusative extension*.

Thus the accusative extension (not yet formally defined) of SOME TEACHER is a function which takes both properties and binary relations as arguments. Its value at properties has already been given. Its value at a binary relation, like KISS, will be a property, namely the set of objects in D which bear the KISS relation to some teacher (that is some object in the TEACHER set).

Similarly the accusative extension of JOHN sends KISS to the set of objects which bear the KISS relation to John (that is, the 'John object'). The accusative extension of MORE STUDENTS THAN TEACHERS sends KISS to the set of those objects b in D which meet the condition that the number of students that b bears KISS to is greater than the number of teachers that b bears KISS to. Formally:

(5) For F a basic function, F_{acc} is that extension of F which sends each binary relation R to the set of objects b which are such that F itself holds of the set of things b bears the relation R to. That is, $F_{acc}(R) = \{b: F(R_b) = True\}$

F_{acc} is called the *accusative extension* of F, and the function ACC sending each basic function F to its accusative extension is a *semantic case*. Note that for any property, p, $F_{acc}(p) = F(p)$.

The reader may compute that the 'object narrow scope' reading (4b) of (4a) is correctly given by (6) below:

(6) (EVERY STUDENT) [(SOME TEACHER)$_{acc}$(KISS)]

That is, this interpretation of (4a) is given by first applying the accusative extension of *some teacher* to the binary relation KISS, obtaining a property, and then applying the basic function denoted by *every student* to that property. This representation is equivalent to $(\forall x)$ (if x is a student then $(\exists y)$ (y is a teacher and x kissed y)).

Consider now the 'object wide scope' reading of (4a) expressed in (4c).

Here we want to say that the basic function SOME TEACHER has a certain property, the property an object has iff every teacher kissed it. To determine this property from the binary relation KISS and the basic function EVERY STUDENT we shall extend that basic function so that it takes that relation to that property. This way of extending a basic function F is called its *nominative extension* and noted F_{nom}.

Informally, the nominative extension of EVERY STUDENT sends a binary relation like KISS to the set of objects which every student kissed. The nominative extension of JOHN sends KISS to the set of objects JOHN kissed. Formally we define:

(7) For F basic, F_{nom} is that extension of F which sends a binary relation R to the set of objects b which are such that F itself holds of the set of things which bear the relation R to b. That is, $F_{nom}(R) = \{b: (F(R^b) = True\}$.

The function NOM sending each basic function to its nominative extension is our second example of a semantic case.

As with accusative extensions, nominative extensions of basic functions take the same values at properties as does the basic function itself. Thus the 'object narrow scope' reading (4b) of (4a) may be given by (8a) below, and the 'object wide scope' reading is given by (8b).

(8) a. $(\text{EVERY STUDENT})_{nom}[(\text{SOME TEACHER})_{acc}(\text{KISS})]$

 b. $(\text{SOME TEACHER})_{acc}[(\text{EVERY STUDENT})_{nom}(\text{KISS})]$

The analysis in (8b) is equivalent to $(\exists y) [(y \text{ is a teacher}) \text{ and } (\forall x) (\text{if } x \text{ is a student then } x \text{ kissed } y)]$.

Thus we see that merely given two NPs such as *every student* and *some teacher* and a P_2 such as *kiss*, there are up to four [7] ways a transitive S formed from these elements may be semantically interpreted. Two are given by (4b–c). In each of those *every student* is interpreted by its nominative extension and *some teacher* by its accusative one. The two interpretations differ with respect to which of these extended functions take KISS as argument. Equally two further interpretations are obtained when *every student* is interpreted accusatively and *some teacher* nominatively.

Observe that our formal characterization of the interpretative possibilities for (4a) does not mention notions like logical subject and narrow scope. Rather these pretheoretical notions are characterized in terms of the formal analysis. The logical subject of the transitive S is the NP interpreted by its nominative extension. The NP with narrow scope is the one whose interpretation takes the binary relation as argument.

Lastly we note that case extensions make sense in an obvious way when applied to deictic functions. The nominative extension of the deictic function THIS BOY is that deictic function sending each context c to the nominative extension of [(THIS BOY)(c)]. Semantic case extensions then are defined for all initial functions, both basic and deictic.

3 Natural Language Applications

3.1 Axioms of Semantic Case Theory

We have seen above that there may be as many as four ways of interpreting a transitive S merely given the denotations of the transitive verb and those of two NPs. But basic transitive Ss (henceforth batSs) in English are not four ways ambiguous or vague. (9a) below has only two truth conditionally distinct readings and (9b) only one.

(9)   a.   Every student kissed some teacher
     b.   John kissed David

Clearly then interpretations of English satisfy constraints over and above what is given by the initial denotations of NPs and P_ns. One way to state the constraint is:

(10)   *English Scope and Case Constraint*
     In basic transitive Ss of the form [NP[V NP]] the VP-internal NP is always interpreted by its accusative extension, the other NP by its nominative extension

Note that (10) constrains the case in which NPs may be interpreted but it does not specify which of these functions takes the binary relation as argument. Thus, in the absence of further constraints, we predict that batSs in English are *scope ambiguous* (either NP denotation may take the transitive verb denotation as argument) but not *argument ambiguous* (that is, *John* in (9b) is uniquely interpreted as nominative, so (9b) cannot have the same meaning as *David kissed John*, in which *John* must by (10) be interpreted accusatively).

Below we shall discuss comparable interpretative constraints in a variety of languages. Each of these constraints is language-specific in that it states semantic properties of expressions of *that* language. On the other hand, these constraints exhibit significant similarities. These I shall factor out and present as the axioms of Semantic Case Theory. They are semantic universals: constraints which, I claim, are satisfied by the ways speakers of all languages interpret transitive Ss. I shall present these universals in terms of the English S & C, justifying that certain properties are general while others are not.

First, not all languages permit scope ambiguities in their batSs. J. Huang (1982), T. Lee (1986) and J. Aoun and A. Li (1987) all support that Chinese batSs have only the accusative narrow scope reading (though

Aoun and Li note the existence of scope ambiguities in passives). The Chinese S & C may in fact be given as for English above with the additional stipulation that the accusative extension take the binary relation as argument.

Second, the English S & C requires that both independent NPs in a basic transitive S be interpreted by case extensions of their initial functions. This I take as axiomatic:

(11) *Case Existence* (CE)

In basic transitive Ss the independent NPs are interpreted as case extensions of the basic functions they denote

I shall take a moment to justify the axiomatic status of Case Existence as it is a very strong empirical claim (Keenan 1987a, henceforth K-87) and will play an important role in the theory of anaphora developed in section 3.

Consider a trivial case in which CE would be violated. Suppose that interpretations for English allowed that *John* be interpreted as a case extension of *Fred* when *John* occurred in transitive contexts. For example, *Mary kissed John* would mean 'Mary kissed Fred'. Then in a situation in which *John* and *Fred* denote different basic functions it is easy to show that the interpretation of *John* in a batS fails to be a case extension of its initial function, violating Case Existence.

Thus CE is a meaning stability axiom. It says that the interpretations of basic NPs in transitive contexts cannot vary wildly from their interpretations in intransitive ones. In fact (see the Argument Structure Theorem in K-87) it says that the interpretations of basic NPs in transitive contexts are essentially the same as in intransitive ones, all differences being induced by the transitive verb denotation.

Consider a less trivial way in which Case Existence may fail. Suppose that English allowed the basic NP *John* in transitive contexts to be interpreted with the meaning of the reflexive pronoun *himself*. So *Every student admires John* would be interpreted with the meaning that *Every student admires himself* actually has. This would violate CE as follows.

First, an adequate interpretation of the reflexive in transitive contexts is given by the function SELF from binary relations to properties defined in (12):

(12) $\text{SELF}(R) = \{b : (b, b) \in R\}$

An S like *Every student admires himself* will then be interpreted as $(\text{EVERY STUDENT})_{nom}(\text{SELF}(\text{ADMIRE}))$, which is True just in case for each object b with the student property, b bears the ADMIRE relation to b. Now, following K-87 we may show:

(13) *Thm* SELF is not a case extension of any basic function[8]

From the theorem then we know that *John* in transitive contexts may not be interpreted by SELF since it would fail to be a case extension of its (or any) basic function. This observation is generalized in section 3 to show that basic NPs may not be interpreted anaphorically in transitive contexts. As basic NPs are 'r-expressions' in the Binding Theory sense we see that Case Existence covers part of the effect of Principle C of the BT.

More generally, suppose that Case Existence systematically failed. Then even if we knew what objects were in the KISS relation and we could correctly interpret both *John* and *every student* in all intransitive Ss we would have no idea at all what *John kissed every student* meant. This is patently implausible.

Third, the English S & C guarantees that the two NPs in transitive Ss are interpreted in different semantic cases. This I also take as axiomatic:

(14) *Case Distinctness* (CD)[9]

Any interpretation of the independent NPs in a basic transitive S interprets them in distinct cases

There is nothing logically nonsensical about the failure of CD. If both NPs in *John kissed David* were interpreted nominatively it would just mean that the S was argument ambiguous. On the JOHN narrow scope reading it would be true iff David has the property that John kissed him, and on the JOHN wide scope reading it would be true iff John has the property that David kissed him.

But note that satisfying CD does not guarantee the absence of argument ambiguities. They may arise when a transitive S admits of two interpretations, each of which satisfies CD (and CE). Thus the possibility in (15) is not ruled out by CE and CD.

(15) a. John   kissed David
          nom   acc (interpretation 1)
          acc   nom (interpretation 2)

This possibility *is* blocked by the English S & C, but as we shall see it is allowed by the S & Cs of certain other languages. The role of CD then is to constrain the ways argument ambiguities may arise: No given interpretation permits them, but an S may be argument ambiguous in virtue of admitting distinct interpretations with different assignments of semantic case.

Fourth, the English S & C identifies the NPs it case interprets in terms of the structure of the batS in which they occur. Thus given two (unambiguous) batSs with the *same* structure (including subcategories of the NPs and verb), the corresponding NPs must be assigned the *same* semantic case. So the interpretative possibility in (16) is blocked.

(16) a. John kissed David
       nom   acc

    b. David kissed John
       acc   nom

If (possibly different) interpretations could assign case as indicated in (16) this would say that which NP was nominative ('logical subject') would be unpredictable from the structure of the S. (It would also say, K-87, that these two Ss are logically equivalent.)

To guarantee that isomorphic batSs in an arbitrary L assign case to the corresponding NPs in the same way (without committing ourselves a priori to the claim that batSs in all Ls have the same structure) we shall avail ourselves of the traditional notion of *paradigm*: a fixed structural frame in which different lexical items can be substituted preserving the form. Thus:

(17) *Case Structure* (CS)[10]

Semantic case interpretation is preserved under grammatical substitutions of the P_2 and independent NPs

CS guarantees for example that the case interpretation of the first NP in each of the Ss in (18) is the same (whatever it is).

(18) a. John kissed David
    b. Harry kissed David
    c. Harry kissed John
    d. David kissed John

Thus *John* in (16a) (=18a) and *David* in (16b) (=18d) must have the same case, whence by CE and CD so must *David* in (16a) and *John* in (16b).

Case Existence, Case Distinctness and Case Structure are the only properties of transitive S interpretations that I am prepared to take as universal at present. Before turning to the statements of S & Cs in other languages, however, a few general comments regarding the empirical nature of these axioms and the English S & C will be helpful.

(i) Given the axioms, the statement of the S & C for any given L need only mention L-specific properties. The S & C is understood to be the conjunction of the axioms with the S & C as given. Often it is sufficient to stipulate the case of just one NP, the other being thus in the other case by CE and CD.

(ii) The English S & C only covers batSs of a certain form and is thus incomplete. In giving S & Cs for other Ls I concentrate on the widely attested S types but make no attempt at completeness.

(iii) Determining the correctness of a given S & C is an empirical matter. A given statement may be falsified by showing that it fails to predict speakers' judgments of argument ambiguity or scope ambiguity.

(iv) Commonly different structural features converge on the same assignment of semantic case. For example, the English S & C could be given as: 'Interpret the immediate preverbal NP nominatively' or 'Interpret nominatively the NP with which the verb agrees.' From the point of view of language users (and learners) this redundancy is useful (and, as Chomsky 1986: 181 notes, characteristic of biological systems).

(v) Modulo redundancy the relevance of a given structural property to determining semantic case interpretation may be checked by forming a different batS with the same NPs and P_2 in which that structural property is absent (as we did in analyzing (16a–b)). If a change in the property induces a change in argument structure (for example, one S means 'John loves Mary' and the other means 'Mary loves John') then the property is relevant (though it may follow from others).

(vi) With a further condition the remarks in (v) extend to cross-language comparisons of case interpretation: For example, *given* the English S & C, suppose that the Japanese S & C determined the case interpretations in (19a) as indicated.[11]

(19) a. Hanako-ga Taroo-o nagutta
              acc   nom   hit
        b. Taroo hit Hanako

Then, if *Hanako*, *Taroo* and *nagutta* have the same denotations as their English glosses and *Hanako (Taroo)* is interpreted in the same case in (19a) as it is in (19b) then (19a) and (19b) must have the same truth value. But this is, in fact, false. Thus the Japanese S & C is wrongly stated if the assumptions about the sameness of denotations hold.

Finally let me emphasize an obvious but important point. Semantic cases and semantic scope are defined solely in terms of binary relations and functions of a certain sort. They make no reference at all to how P_2s and NPs denoting such relations and functions are presented syntactically. Logically then the syntactic structure of a transitive S and semantic case and scope interpretation are *independent*. It is an empirical matter whether there are any universal correlations between specific aspects of syntactic structure and semantic case assignment. If it turned out that in all Ls, the nominatively interpreted NP preceded the accusatively interpreted one (or vice versa) this would be empirically significant as nothing in the semantic analysis of case is relevant to that claim.

3.2 Language specific case constraints

We investigate here the Case Constraints[12] (CCs) in several languages. I argue that (i), based on judgments of argument ambiguity, there are many languages in which morphological marking on NPs and verbs is criterial in stating CCs and VP constituency is not. And (ii), VP-nominative languages exist.

I will say that a language L 'has a VP' if its batSs present one NP in constituency with the verb to the exclusion of the other. If constituency with the verb is sufficient to determine the semantic case of the NP then L's Case Constraint will be called *configurational*. There are two logical possibilities here: the VP internal NP is interpreted nominatively (and L is called *VP-nominative*), or it is interpreted accusatively (and L is called *VP-accusative*).

3.2.1 *Morphological case marking and argument ambiguities* We begin with the obvious example of Warlpiri (Hale 1983; Jelinek 1984).

(20) Warlpiri Case Constraint (WCC)

In basic transitive Ss interpret a -*ngku* (-*rlu*) suffixed NP as nominative if there is one; otherwise interpret a -Ø suffixed one as nominative.[13]

(20) tells us that in (21a) *karnta* 'woman' is unambiguously nominative (and so by CE and CD 'man' is accusative). In (21b) 'child' is nominative and 'man' accusative.

(21) a. Karnta-ngku ka -Ø -Ø ngarrka-Ø nya-nyi
        woman-erg pres-she-him man   -abs see-nonpast
        'The woman sees the man'

    b. Kudu- Ø ka- Ø- la ngarrka-ku pada-ni
        child- abs pres- he-him man   -dat wait- nonpast
        'The child is waiting for the man'

As is well known from Hale's work, all six relative orders of the two NPs and verb in (21a) are about equally acceptable preserving the translation (the position of the Aux '*ka-*' is fixed). So change in word order does not induce a change in argument structure, so word order is not criterial for determining semantic case. But interchanging the suffixes -*ngku* and -Ø (zero) in (21a) does induce a change in argument structure, the resulting S meaning 'The man sees the woman.' So morphological NP marking is criterial for semantic case interpretation.

Equally 'VP constituency' is not relevant. Even if Warlpiri had a VP (and all workers agree that it does not at observable structure) each configurational CC incorrectly predicts that interchanging the -*ngku*/-Ø suffixes in (21a) induces no change in argument structure since no change in VP constituency results.

I note, following the detailed and convincing exposition in Jelinek, that semantic case assignment in Warlpiri can also be stated in terms of the pronominal affixes on the Aux plus statements of the form '-*ngku* marked NPs if present have the same case as that assigned to the first affix.' This approach preserves the claims above concerning the relevance of morphological marking and the irrelevance of VP constituency.

The morphological case marking system in Warlpiri is quite efficacious. Despite the great word order freedom there appear to be no batSs in Warlpiri which are argument ambiguous. Observe moreover (characteristic of morphological case marking languages) that there is no one to one correspondence between semantic case and morphological case: -Ø marked NPs may be interpreted accusatively, (21a), or nominatively, (21b).

Other languages which arguably lack a VP and have their CCs given in terms of morphological markings on NPs are Latin, Korean, Hindi, Md.E. Armenian and Malayalam. In the latter case, as Mohanon (1982) shows, morphological NP marking is criterial and is not redundantly coded in terms of linear order (which is free, clause internally), or VP constituency (which he convincingly argues against).

(22) Malayalam Case Constraint (MCC)

   In batSs interpret a -e (-ye) marked NP accusatively if there is one; otherwise interpret some inanimate -Ø marked NP accusatively

The MCC correctly predicts the lack of argument ambiguity in (23) and the presence of such ambiguity in (24).

(23) Kutti- Ø annay   -ye kantu
    child-   elephant-   saw
    'The child saw the elephant' *'The elephant saw the child'

(24) Kallǝ -Ø kuppi-Ø potticcu
    stone - bottle- broke
    'The stone broke the bottle' or 'The bottle broke the stone'

Merely interchanging the NP affixes in (23), which preserves grammaticality, induces a change in argument structure, the result meaning 'The elephant saw the child.' So NP markings are criterial for semantic case assignment and word order is not. And even if Malayalam had a VP, constituency with the verb in (24) cannot determine its semantic case since both are possible.

A further example of interest here is Japanese. Chomsky (1986), Saito and Hoji (1983) and Hoji (1987) argue that Japanese has a VP, whereas Farmer (1984), Whitman (1987) and the much earlier work of Hinds (1974) argue against. But this issue turns out to be irrelevant to the statement of the Japanese Case Constraint. (I am indebted to George Bedell for most of the discussion of the Japanese data below.)

(25) Japanese Case Constraint (JCC)

   In a batS, interpret an -o marked NP accusatively if there is one; otherwise interpret a -ga marked NP nominatively.

The JCC (see note 11) uniquely determines case assignment in (26) and tells us, correctly, that (27) is argument ambiguous.

(26) Taroo-ga Hanako-o nagutta
    Taroo   Hanako hit
    'Taroo hit Hanako' *'Hanako hit Taroo'

(27) Taroo-ga Hanako-ga suki-da
    Taroo   Hanako   likes
    'Taroo like Hanako' or 'Hanako likes Taroo'

The ambiguity is preserved if either -*ga* is replaced by -*wa*. And as in (24), neither configurational CC predicts the ambiguity in (27), so VP constituency appears irrelevant to semantic case assignment.

An importantly different type of CC which cannot be given configurationally at S-structure is exemplified by Navaho (Platero 1982; Frishberg 1972; Sapir and Hoijer 1967). Here the CC is sensitive both to (non-pronominal) verbal morphology and to semantic relations between the NPs. In general batSs in Navaho have the form in (28).

(28) $[NP_1 NP_2 \text{ x-V}]$, where $x = yi$- or $x = bi$-

The choice of prefix *yi*- or *bi*- is sensitive to certain 'Chain of Being' properties of the NPs. If the prefix is *bi*- then NP_1 cannot be a bare inanimate NP, the lowest position on the Chain of Being Hierarchy given by:

(29) Chain of Being Hierarchy (CBH)
    Human > Animate > demonstrative inanimate > bare inanimate-human

Frishberg investigates twenty-two transitive sentence types which vary with regard to the position of the NPs on the CBH and the acceptable choice of verbal prefix. In our terms, her results are exactly predicted by the Nahavo Case Constraint in (30):

(30) Navaho Case Constraint
    In batSs of the form [NP NP x-V], interpret the first NP nominatively if x = *yi*- and interpret that NP accusatively if x = *bi*- *and* the position of that NP on the CBH is greater than or equal to that of the other NP

Observe that when the prefix is *bi*- and NP_1 is not greater than or equal to NP_2 on the CBH then semantic case assignment is not uniquely determined. Thus in such a case the sentence is predicted to be argument ambiguous, and this is correct as (31) from Frishberg illustrates.

(31) shilį́į́   shinaai   bi-ztał
     my horse my brother -kick
     'My horse kicked my brother' or 'My brother kicked my
     horse'

In our terms the CC given in Platero (1982: 295), adapted from the one in Hale et al. (1977), does not predict the argument ambiguities observed in Frishberg. Nor is the ambiguity predicted if Navaho is either VP-nominative or VP-accusative.

3.2.2 *VP-nominative languages*   I turn now to two Ls which arguably have a VP but in which the VP internal NP is interpreted nominatively. The first is Toba Batak (Malayo-Polynesian; Sumatra) studied extensively in Schachter (1984a, 1984b), on which the analysis below is based.

Transitive Ss in Toba are verb initial with the form in (32), illustrated in (33).

(32) [[x-V NP]NP], where x = M- or x = D-

(33) a. Mang-ida si Ria si Torus
        -see art Ria art Torus
        'Torus sees Ria' *'Ria sees Torus'
    b. Di-ida si Ria si Torus
        -see art Ria art Torus
        'Ria saw Torus' *'Torus saw Ria'

Both verb forms in (33) are transitive in requiring two NPs to form an S, but the main clause Ss are not exactly semantically equivalent, though as Schachter notes translating them merely as present (M- forms) and past (D- forms) is not quite accurate. A better though vaguer statement would be that main clause D- forms are perfective, and so often translatable as past, whereas main clause M- forms are imperfective and so often translated as simple present, generic or habitual. The distinction is a little loose and not at all preserved in subordinate clauses.

(34) Toba Batak Case Constraint (TBCC)
    In batSs interpret the immediately postverbal NP as accusative if the verb prefix is M- and nominatively if the prefix is D-

Schachter (1984b) argues extensively and convincingly that, regardless of the choice of prefix, the postverbal NP in Toba forms a syntactic constituent with the verb. Summarizing his evidence: adverbials may not intervene between the verb and its following NP. Only the second NP can be extracted (relativized, questioned by movement, etc.), the first cannot be moved away from its verb. Nor does the first NP undergo pronominalization by deletion in discourse, in distinction to the second. Further, Emmorey (1984) shows that the nuclear pitch accent always falls on the last stressed syllable of the predicate regardless of the syntactic type of predicate (AP, PP, etc.). This rule treats the postverbal NP in (32) as the final element of the predicate, again regardless of the choice of prefix. Finally, observe that expressions of the form [x-V NP] may coordinate (regardless of the choice of x!).

(35) [Di-tuhor si Ore jala di-lompa si Ruli] mangga
      buy art Ore and cook art Ruli mangos
      'Ore buys and Ruli cooks mangos'

(36) [Di-antuk si Ria jala man-ipak si Rotua] si Bissar
      hit art Ria and kick art Rotua art Bissar
      'Ria hit Bissar and Bissar kicked Rotua'

In sum, the evidence that [x-V NP] in (33a–b) forms a syntactic constituent is stronger than that a transitive verb and its postverbal NP in English form a constituent. D- sentences in Toba then are VP-nominative.

A second example of VP-nominative Ss is given by (Tamazight) Berber. Saib (1975), Penchoen (1973), Abdel-Massih (1971), Guerssel (1986), Guerssel and Hale (1987) and my own native speaker work in 1975 are drawn on freely below. I also draw on Sadiqi (1986), Ennaji and Sadiqi (1986) and Ennaji (1985), who study the closely related dialect of Ayt Hssan.

All sources treat Berber as a strict head first language with basic transitive S order V + NOM + ACC. In the discussion below I use the term 'subject' to refer to the nominative NP in a transitive S and the only independent NP in an intransitive S.

Direct evidence that the postverbal nominative NP forms a constituent with the transitive verb is given by the distribution of NPs in the 'construct state'. (See Borer 1984 for discussion of these forms in Md. Hebrew.) NPs in Berber occur in one of two morphological forms: the free (= citation) form and the construct form. Grammars (Penchoen 1973: 19–21) derive the construct form from the free from by modifying the vowel in the first syllable. (See Guerssel 1987 for an insightful non-traditional analysis.[14]) Proper nouns appear to have only one form. The following examples will be used in the discussion:

Free form: aryaz 'man' arba 'boy' tarbatt 'girl'
Construct: uryaz   urba   terbatt

A noun occurs in the construct form if it meets one of the conditions (37)–(41) below; otherwise it occurs free.

(37) *Genitive complements of noun heads*

a. axam uryaz   b. axam n terbatt
   tent man   tent of girl
   'the man's tent'   'the girl's tent'

c. illi   -s uryaz-ad
   daughter-his man -this
   'this man's daughter'

d. zəg- guguɣ (n) irumiyən zi- tmazirt
   since- leaving (of) French   from-country
   'since the French left the country'

(38) *Objects of quantity words* (numerals, 'much', 'many', etc.)

a. yun uryaz   b. ša   uryaz
   one man   some man

The preposition *n* 'of' often occurs between the quantity word and the noun. The quantity word itself may function as an NP: *ur ɣur-i ša* lit.: 'not to-me some' = 'I don't have any.' Plausibly then these structures are special cases of (37). Note that modifying adjectives, even when they occur preverbally (rare), do not govern the construct state on their heads *yararyaz* 'bad man'.

(39) *Objects of prepositions*

a. i-   terbatt   b. tama (n) uryaz
   to/for (the) girl   near (of) (the) man

Guerssel (1987) shows that most of the independent 'prepositions' like *tama* are in fact nouns, so these cases are just further examples of (37).

(40) *Postverbal NP in intransitive Ss*

a. i- zyert urba   b. lla t- alla terbatt
   he-tall boy   imp she-cry girl
   'The boy is tall'   'The girl is crying/cries'

(41) *Postverbal NP in transitive Ss*

a. i- annay urba tarbatt   b. t- annay terbatt arba
   he-saw boy girl   she-saw girl   boy
   'The boy saw the girl'   'The girl saw the boy'
   *'The girl saw the boy'   *'The boy saw the girl'

Considering only the first four cases it seems clear that an NP is in the construct state just in case it is the complement of the head of its phrase and so certainly forms a constituent with it. Moreover, we would not hesitate to make the same claim for the postverbal

NP in transitive Ss if it were interpreted accusatively. But our earlier discussion shows it is unproblematic to interpret such an NP nominatively. For example, the interpretation of (41a) may be given by $(GIRL)_{acc}[BOY_{nom}(SEE)]$.

Morphological evidence then directly supports a process of construct state assignment under conditions of lexical government by noun heads, prepositions, transitive and intransitive verbs, henceforth called C(onstruct)-*governors*.

Right adjacency is a necessary condition for construct state assignment. Topicalized NPs occur to the left of their C-governors and are not in the construct state (see Shlonsky and Sigler 1987 for insightful discussion).

(42) a. aryaz, i- annay tarbatt
man, he-saw girl
'The man saw the girl'

b. axam uryaz ad i- meeqqur
tent man this it-big
'The tent of this man, it is big'

c. aryaz ad, axam-nns, i- meeqqur
man this tent- his, it-big
'This man, his tent, it is big'

Note that in (42b) the topicalized NP 'the tent of this man' is in the free form, as reflected by the *a*- initial consonant on the head, and its complement 'this man' is as expected in the construct state. In the double topicalization in (42c) 'this man' is not right adjacent to its head and thus occurs free.

Further facts support that mere right adjacency to a C-governor is not sufficient to induce construct marking, but that the right adjacent element must form a constituent with the governor. In (42a) 'girl' is right adjacent to the verb 'saw' but remains in the free form. This follows if it does not form a (VP) constituent with the verb.

Equally when a nominative NP is extracted, as in relative clauses, Wh-questions and Clefts, the accusative NP does not assume the construct form. Plausibly again this is because it has not moved into the nominative position forming a constituent with the transitive verb.

(43) aryaz nna i- annay-n tarbatt
man dem part-saw -part girl
'the man who saw the girl'

Further, like VSO languages generally (Chung 1983), Berber is a subject pro drop language. Verbs agree with their construct NPs in person, number and gender. And we observe that in Ss like (44a–b) the accusative NP is free.

(44) a. ur ssin- əx aryaz i- taddart
       not know- 1sg man in-house
       'I don't know the man in the house'

   b. i- ssifəd amazan
      he-sent   messenger (construct state = umazan)
      'He sent a messenger'

Various analyses of such constructions treat the full NP subject position as either not present at all or else filled with a null expletive. In either case the accusative NP will not form a VP constituent with the transitive verb and thus, predictably, not be in the construct form. Equally in transitive imperatives (Ennaji 1985: 283) the subject addressee phrase is absent but the accusative NP does not go in the construct state.

By contrast, in Passive and Raising to Subject structures which (on current theories) do move an NP into the subject position we expect that that NP will be in the construct state. This expectation is borne out:

(45) a. i- ttcu uqqzin aysum
       he-ate dog   meat (−con)
       'The dog ate meat'

   b. i- ttw- attc uysam
      it-pass-eat meat (+con)
      'The meat has been eaten'

Raising to Subject, only attested for two verbs (Sadiqi 1986: 152) also supports the claim. The proper noun *Mamma* in (46b) (Wager 1976) triggers fem. sg. verb agreement, as opposed to the impersonal masc. sg. form in (46a). (46c) from Abney 1987 shows the postverbal NP in the construct state as expected.

(46) a. i- dher   is t-ssen   Mamma ad t-ez   utsu
       it-appears that she-knows Mamma fut she-makes couscous
       'It appears that Mamma knows (how) to make couscous'

   b. t- dher Mamma is   t-ssen   ad t-ez   utsu
      she-appears Mamma that she-knows fut she-makes couscous
      'Mamma appears to know (how) to make couscous'

   c. i- dher uryaz is-   t- i- zru Bassu
      he-seems man   Comp-him he-saw Bassu
      'The man seems that Bassu saw him'

As further support for the coherent pattern presented above consider first that notional indirect objects are always constructed with a preposition, as in (47).

(47) ad i- us   uryaz aɣrum i- lmsakin
     fut he-give man bread to-poor
     'The man will give bread to the poor'

Thus in nuclear Ss all NPs required by the predicate occur in the construct state except the accusative. In this respect the accusative NP resembles the nominative one in English Ss. It is the only one whose form (?case) is not determined locally – either by the verb or a preposition.

The freedom of accusatives is further reflected in the fact that they are freely extracted, whereas extraction of other arguments is subject to a licensing condition: Their governors occur in a marked form. In the case of subjects, both transitive and intransitive, the verb goes in a participial form *i-...-n* (sg.) or *-nin* (pl.) losing its gender agreement, as illustrated in (43). In the case of indirect objects the prepositional *i-* is retained in a marked form *mi-* and fronted, (48a). (And more generally when objects of type (39a) Preps are extracted the Prep is retained and fronted, following the relative or focus marker.) But when accusatives are extracted, as in (48b), no marked form of its nominative VP is present, nor is a clitic pronoun retained (in distinction to topicalization cases).

(48) a. tarbatt nna mi i- sfa   uryaz lektab
         girl   rel to he-gave man book
         'the girl to whom the man gave the
         book'
     b. tarbatt nna i- nnay uryaz
         girl   rel he-saw man
         'the girl that the man saw'

(Possessor NPs are not directly extractable but are construed as datives taking the long form *mi* of the preposition *i-* 'to'. 'The woman whose husband died' is literally 'the woman to whom the man died' (Penchoen 1973: 69; Ennaji 1985: 49).

Fourthly, an overt (untopicalized) nominative NP is rather rigidly fixed in the immediate postverbal position (Sadiqi 1986: 10) as all the examples illustrate. But the relative order of the accusative NP and indirect objects is freer. According to Johnson (1966: 49) the more highly specified of the two will occur in final position. Compare (49) with (47).

(49) ad i- us   uryaz i- lmsakin aɣrum uasnat
     fut he-give man to-poor   bread (of) yesterday
     'The man will give to the the poor the bread of
     yesterday'

The absence of word order alternation between nominatives and accusatives then supports that the nominative forms a constituent with the verb.

A fifth piece of evidence comes from existential/possessive (E/P) Ss. We observe first that pronominal accusatives and PPs behave as clitics, attracting to an element of the verbal complex (including an overt Comp). The host is often an aspect marker like *lla* or *ad*. But when such are not present the clitic goes immediately postverbally (not blocking construct state assignment to the subject). The E/P S below is illustrative:

(50) t- əlla ɣur-s tfunast
     she-exist to-him cow (fem, +construct)
     'He has a cow'

Note that 'cow' is in the construct state and triggers verb agreement. Moreover, when extracted it triggers the participial form of the verb (Penchoen 1973: 70), confirming its status as subject.

Now, in the particular case of E/P Ss the verb is optional (a 'designated element case' of recoverable deletions). In such Ss, however, the subject cannot form a constituent with the verb, so we expect it to be in the free form, which is correct:

(51) ɣur-s tafunast
     to-him cow (−construct)
     'He has a cow'

A last piece of suggestive evidence is given in Choe (1987). She observes that Berber presents many TV (transitive verb) + Subject idioms, but virtually no TV + accusative idioms. For example, from the TV 'hit', which forms ordinary transitive Ss like 'The man hit the boy' we may form 'idioms' like 'A sneeze hit' (the cat), 'Toe-stubbing hit' (the boy), in which the parenthesized items occur as accusatives.

These facts are suggestive but inconclusive. To infer from semantic facts to syntactic ones we need some empirically established principles of correlation. In the case at hand the obvious suggestion is 'Only constituents can be interpreted idiomatically.' But no sooner said than counterexemplified. The idiomatic italicized items below are not constituents.

(52) a. We *cooked* John*'s goose*
     b. We *took the wind out of* his *sails*

(53) a. We *threw* him *to the dogs*
     b. We *put* him *on the spot*

Similarly in Ss like *Weariness overtook him*, *Misfortune befell him*, *Panic seized him*, *Sleep overcame him*, *Disease cut him down in the prime of life* the abstract nature of the subject triggers a non-literal interpretation of the verb thus yielding a semantic relation between the TV and its subject not present between the TV and its object. The examples are not dissimilar to Choe's but do not justify considering the TV + Subject a syntactic unit.

More generally Keenan (1984) exhibits a battery of semantic properties which tie accusatives to their verbs in distinction to nominatives. But no conclusions regarding syntactic constituency follow. Choe's facts then remain suggestive.

In sum, Berber presents strong evidence that the nominatively interpreted NP forms a constituent with the transitive verb to the exclusion of the accusatively interpreted one. Berber then is a second example of a VP-nominative language.

3.2.3 'Explaining' VP-nominative languages[15]

As the existence of VP-nominative languages appears to violate both current and traditional grammatical practice (see Hinds 1974 for some enlightening discussion of other traditions) let me suggest a plausible mechanism whereby a language might reasonably come to be VP-nominative.

The suggestion is just the generalization of the observations concerning construct state NPs in quantity expressions and (many) PPs. Synchronically they may be analyzed as noun complements of nouns. I suggest then that historically Verb + Subject constructions in Berber also originate as nominal ones. So historically 'John hits Bill' is an equative S like 'John's hitting (one) (is) Bill' and 'John laughs' is historically a kind of existential like 'John's laughing (is).' The constituency of transitive subjects with their verbs is explained on the grounds that historically they are possessors of the verb.

This suggestion is at least not prima facie implausible. Generative grammar (e.g. Chomsky 1986: 64) has revealed strong similarities between possessors in NPs and subjects of Ss. They behave similarly with regard to control of anaphors and infinitives (*John's criticism of himself / John criticized himself; John's desire to leave / John desired to leave*). They behave similarly with regard to blocking extractions. And in many subordinate positions possessives and tensed Ss occur almost in free variation: *We worked hard before John's arrival / before John arrived; John's leaving / That John left surprised me*.

If this historical analysis is correct, it would account for the similarities between Pred + Subj structures and Possessive structures already observed in Berber. It would in addition account for the fact that predicates agree in gender with their subjects and that subject agreement clitics and possessor clitics are morphologically similar (in particular in the plural, both genders) (Penchoen 1973: 25–7).

Direct diachronic evidence is lacking for Berber, but is available for the genetically related Middle Egyptian (daughter language Coptic). Callender (1975a, 1975b) (see also Schenkel 1975) provides quite striking evidence that Verb + Subject structures in M.E. developed from nominal forms. Several of the forms are reconstructed as nominative, accusative or genitive case forms of nominals in Proto-Afroasiatic. Moreover, all of the eight verb 'bases' take their subject pronominal forms from the possessor series. Callender explicitly argues that the nominal construction was basic and the verbal one built upon it (see his Appendix 1). Equally Prep + NP constructions are formed on the Head + Possessor one. The following examples from Callender (1975a) illustrate some of these points.

(54) a. pr   -i   b. m   r?   n(y) wbnw -f
       house-my   from mouth of   wound-his

      c. m3 -n -i   sw   d. ist wn   hjmt-f
         saw-of-my it   lo exist wife -his
         'I saw it'   'Now he has a wife . . .'

This historical development of M.E. supports the plausibility of a similar development in Berber. Moreover, even superficial inspection of bound morphology shows that Berber and M.E. are reasonably closely related.[16]

In fact, given Callender's analysis we might expect it to have reflexes in other Afroasiatic languages. And this is the case in Md. Hebrew. Borer (1984) draws on the similarities between pronominal clitics on prepositions and those in construct state possessive structures. But the pronominal 'agreements' on past tense verbs show the same similarities (S. Mordechay, personal communication), and both past and present tense verbs agree with their subjects in gender. And as in Berber, numerical constructions in Hebrew exhibit construct state morphology.

Once the historical plausibility of regarding transitive subjects as possessors is accepted it becomes surprisingly easy to find further candidates for such a development. Some quickly sketched examples relevant to the concerns of this paper are:

(i) *Isthmus Zapotec* (Oto-Manguean, S. Mexico; Pickett 1960, 1975) is a strict head first [V + NOM + ACC] language which presents a complete formal identity of VERB + Subj, Head + Poss and Prep + NP constructions. Aside from some obvious Spanish borrowings, the 'prepositions' of Zapotec are synchronically body part nouns: 'to' is the word for 'face, eye'; 'on, on top of' is 'head', 'in, inside of' = 'belly', 'next to' = 'side', 'behind' = 'back'. The pronominal clitics on verbs, heads of possessives and 'prepositions' are identical and fairly rich. Two numbers and three pesons are distinguished, with inclusive/exclusive forms in 1st pl. In the third person, both sg. and pl., three 'genders' are marked: human, non-human animate and inanimate. The third person clitics occur in complementary distribution with full NP subjects, possessors, 'objects' of prepositions. Zapotec does possess independent pronouns, but they are used for apposition, topicalized structures and *accusative* NPs.

(ii) *Jacaltec* (Mayan; Craig 1977) is a strict head first [V + NOM + ACC] language, in which the TV + Subj, Head + Possessor and Prep + NP constructions occur in the order given and show the same agreement/

clitic morphology. Certain intransitive S types are constructed directly on the historical model suggested for Berber. For example, 'I have money' is literally 'Exist my money' (Craig 1977: 27). More detailed similarities with Berber are tantalizing: When objects of prepositions are extracted the preposition is retained, either pied piped (but postposed to the extracted element) or stranded; when transitive subjects are extracted the verb loses its agreement and takes a special affix -$n(i)$. Accusatives by contrast are freely extracted leaving no pronominal trace and requiring no licensing conditions.

Jacaltec also presents TV + Possessive Subject idioms in which the possessor is referential but the V + head are idiomatic:

(55) x- s- cha' ha- wi' ha- way sunil-bal tz'ayic
asp-it-suit 2sg-head 2sg-sleep all-extent day
'You would like to sleep all day'

Note that the main verb shows third person transitive subject agreement with 'your head' but that it is the second person possessor which controls the agreement on the non-finite (aspectless) lower verb 'sleep', clearly a case of possessor NPs exhibiting control properties of subjects of S.

These idioms appear structurally similar to the *cook John's goose* type in English except that the latter are V + accusative constructions whereas the former are V + nominative ones.

(iii) *Batak and W. Malayo-Polynesian* (W.MP). The VP-nominative Ss in Toba, [[di-V John]Mary] = 'John V'd Mary', show clear traces of nominal origins for the TV + Subject. If the nominative NP in such Ss is a first or second person pronoun it replaces the *di-* prefix in the same form it has when functioning as a possessor on a noun head. So 'I saw Mary' looks literally like 'My-see(ing) (is) Mary' (The copula is null).

Quite generally W.MP languages provide synchronic support for the nominal origin of many of the verb forms. In the non-actor focus forms in Tagalog (Philippines) the pronominal agents are drawn from the possessor series. In Malagasy (Madagascar) both pronominal and full NP passive agents attach to the verb with the overt morphology with which possessors attach to their heads. In Rukai (Taiwan), P. J. K. Li (1973) notes the use of both 'subject' and possessor pronominals on the verb, yielding pairs like *eat-I the fish* and *eat-my the fish* for 'I ate the fish.'

Overall then the case that Verb + Subject structures may derive historically from nominal ones in which the subject is a noun complement is plausible and receives much support. That subjects may form a constituent with transitive verbs then is much less startling than current linguistic practice suggests.

4 Semantic Case Theory and the Binding Theory

SCT is only a theory of how simple Ss are interpreted. But it is built on a fundamental semantic asymmetry, that between nominative and accusative interpretations, and it is reasonable to query whether other subject–object asymmetries can be reduced to this one or are independent. We consider here just the following asymmetry in Standard English:

(56) a. Every student criticized himself
     b. *Himself criticized every student

(56a) is a meaningful sentence and has its truth conditions given by: (EVERY STUDENT)$_{nom}$[SELF(CRITICIZE)]. By contrast (56b) does not have this meaning, having no meaning at all.

Within a BT framework these facts are characterized in terms of syntactic asymmetry between the two NPs. *Himself*, an anaphor by stipulation, must be coindexed with a C-commanding NP. (56a) provides such an NP but (56b) does not. Nor does (57) which the BT thus blocks for the same reason as (56b).

(57) *Himself is being obnoxious

How might we represent these facts in SCT terms? Observe first that given the interpretation of *himself* as SELF and the interpretative fact in (58) we can already account for (57).

(58) *Himself, herself* lack extra-linguistic deictic interpretations in Standard English

The reasoning is as follows: Suppose that the S in (57) were grammatical. Then *himself* would be initial (by definition). From (58) it must be a basic NP. By Case Existence its interpretation in (56a) must be a case extension of the basic function which it denotes. But by (13) SELF is the case extension of no basic function. Thus *himself* is not initial, that is, the S in (57) is ungrammatical.

In this reasoning our use of the fact that *himself* is interpreted as SELF corresponds to the BT assumption that *himself* is an 'anaphor'. But in distinction to the BT we need the claim that *himself* lacks a deictic interpretation. Thus the SCT allows that there could exist a language like St.Eng. except that in addition to its anaphoric interpretation as SELF *himself* could also be interpreted deictically. In such languages SCT does not predict the ungrammaticality or uninterpretability in (57). I exhibit languages of this sort below.

Our reasoning above does not, however, extend to (56b) since *himself* is not initial there. In fact, logically, it is quite possible to interpret (56b) as a paraphrase of (56a). Simply apply SELF to CRITICIZE and then apply the accusative extension of EVERY STUDENT to the resulting property. (The first step is the same as that used to get 'subject narrow scope' readings). The truth value of (EVERY STUDENT)$_{acc}$ at SELF(CRITICIZE) is the same as that of (EVERY STUDENT)$_{nom}$ at that property, so (56b) and (56a) are equivalent.

As (56b) does not allow this interpretation the interpretative constraints on St.Eng. must be extended beyond the axioms of SCT and the English Case Constraint. We shall then require that interpretations of English satisfy the *Nominative Reference Condition* below. The underlying idea of the NRC is that the referential possibilities of nominative NPs in transitive Ss are the same as those of the only independent NP in intransitive Ss.

To state this idea more rigorously let us write *basic* (T) for the result of replacing each independent NP occurrence in T by a basic NP. Then, where T is a transitive S, an independent NP occurrence in T is said to be *structurally nominative* (*accusative*) iff the basic NP which replaces it in basic(T) may be interpreted by its nominative (accusative) extension.[17]

(59) *Nominative Reference Condition* (NRC)
      In main clause transitive Ss a structurally nominative NP is interpreted by a nominative case extension of an initial function

The judgment in (56b) now follows since *himself* there is structurally nominative but its only interpretation SELF is not a case extension of an initial function.

4.1 Comparing the BT with NRC

Both the BT and SCT + NRC provide accounts for the asymmetry in (56) and the judgment in (57). Below I provide several reasons for preferring the SCT based account.

(i) The BT blocks (56b) and (57) for the same reason, whereas the SCT-based approach requires more (the NRC) to block (56b) than (57). As there is a logical possibility of a bound reading in (56b) not present in (57) more *should* be required to block it.

(ii) Considerations of descriptive adequacy favor the SCT-based approach over the BT one. They make the same predictions for English, as the structurally nominative and the C-commanding NP coincide. But they make different predictions for VP-nominative languages, and the evidence supports the SCT theory. For Toba Batak observe (Schachter 1984b):

(60) a. [Di-ida si Torus] dirina
          -see art Torus self
          'Torus saw himself'

    b. *[Di-ida dirina] si   Torus
        see self   art Torus

(60b) shows that the structurally nominative NP cannot be the reflexive despite being asymmetrically C-commanded by the accusative. Note that it is not the case in Toba that anaphor distribution is determined by some sort of left–right override to the C-command conditions in BT. In M-sentences the structural accusative precedes the nominative one and we find, as expected, that anaphors precede their antecedents in such Ss.

(61)   a.   [Mang-ida dirina] si   Torus
            -see self   art Torus
           'Torus sees himself'
       b.   *[Mang-ida si   Torus] dirina
            -see art Torus   self

Similarly reflexives in Berber support the NRC over the BT:

(62)   a.   i-   wwet urba ixf-   nns
           he-hit   boy   head-his
           'The boy hit himself'
       b.   *i-wwet ixf-   nns arba
           he-hit   head-his boy
           'Heself hit the boy'

As per the NRC the reflexive in (62b) cannot be structurally nominative, despite being asymmetrically C-commanded by 'boy'.

VP-less languages also support the SCT approach. The NRC applies, correctly, to these Ls whether there is a VP or not. But the BT requires one. Otherwise the NPs in a transitive S would C-command each other and Principle C blocks a full NP coindexed with a C-commanding anaphor. But such a prediction is clearly incorrect. Consider (63) from Warlpiri (Hale 1983).

(63)   Ngarrka-ngku ka-   Ø- nyanu nya-nyi
        man   -erg Pres-he-self   see- nonpast
        'The man sees himself'

The Warlpiri CC (20) identifies the -*ngku* marked NP as nominative, and since it is basic (63) satisfies the NRC.

More problematic for the BT are languages like Korean, Hindi, Md. Eastern Armenian and Kannada (Bhat 1978: 65). These Ls are basically verb final with fairly free NP order preverbally. Semantic case is deter-mined morphologically with Korean exhibiting topic marking as in

Japanese. The problem is that the freedom of NP order is retained by reflexives.[18] From Korean (H. S. Lee, personal communication):

(64) a. Caki-casin-eke Kim-ŭn   silmanghaŏssta
         self   -dat Kim-NOM disappointed
         'Kim was disappointed in himself'
     b. *Caki-casin-ŭn   Kim-eke silmanghaŏssta
         self   -NOM Kim-dat disappointed

Here -(n)ŭn is the topic marker replacing the morphological nominative suffix -i (-ka). The relative order of the two NPs in each case may be changed preserving the judgments. Further examples of this sort using verbs with different morphological case paradigms may be found in O'Grady (1985) and Park (1986).

Similarly in Hindi (S. Ali, personal communication) both orders are possible in (65) and in each case only the structurally accusative *Radha*- can be replaced by the reflexive *aapne*-.

(65) a. Ram-ne Radha-ko   mara
         Ram-erg Radha-dat/acc hit
         'Ram hit Radha'
     b. Radha-ko Ram-ne mara

And in Md. Eastern Armenian (G. Mardirussian, personal communication) both orders of full NPs preverbally are possible in (66) and in each case the reflexive pronoun *inkəiran* may replace the accusative.

(66) Mard-ə   erekh-i- n khangarav
     man -def child -acc-def disturbed
     'The man disturbed the child'

These examples are compatible with the NRC as the structurally nominative NP is basic. But where the reflexive precedes the nominative it cannot form a constituent with the verb. Within a GB approach various appeals could be made here to unobservable structure, but in my judgment they all weaken the explanatory appeal of the BT account. Why should conditions crucial to the interpretation of anaphors be allowed to be violated in the structures speakers observably use? The SCT + NRC approach yields the correct results without appeal to such structures.

(iii) Generalizing from the interpretation of *himself*, SCT permits a language independent definition of *anaphorically interpreted* ((76) below). This definition allows us to account for semantic generalizations in English which must be handled by independent mechanisms within the BT. It also enables us to lexically characterize certain differences in anaphora paradigms between languages and to overcome a methodological insufficiency in the BT approach. Namely, a theory of anaphora may not directly constrain the distribution of lexical items but only the availability of anaphoric interpretations of those items. For essential anaphors like St.Eng. *himself* the two coincide, but this is not the general case.

I first illustrate the problems and then give the definition of anaphor. Consider the anaphora paradigm in (67):

(67) a. Every student$_i$ loves his$_{ij}$ mother
 b. His$_{i,*j}$ mother loves everyone$_j$
 c. Himself$_{*i,*j}$ loves everyone$_j$

The NRC predicts the 'crossover' restrictions in (67b) (given the definition of anaphor). Thus the NRC blocks the anaphoric readings in (67b) and (67c) for the same reason. (The deictic reading (*i) of (67c), allowed in the languages discussed below, is independently blocked by the language particular (58)).

By contrast the BT does not predict the restriction in (67b). Independent mechanisms which tie the restriction to LF movement of *everyone* are invoked (see May 1985: 6). Thus the BT does not capture the interpretative similarity in (67b) and (67c).

Concerning lexically based anaphora paradigms and the methodological problem mentioned above, consider the following from Fijian, a [V + ACC + NOM] language.

(68) a. a   mokuti koya o ira kece
      past hit   3sg.   pl. all
      'Everyone hit himself' or
      'Everyone hit him'
 b. a   mokuti jone o koya
      past hit   John 3sg.
      'He hit John'
      *'John hit himself'

In (68a) the structurally accusative *koya* may be interpreted either anaphorically or deictically (like *his mother* in (67a)). But when structurally nominative as in (68b) it is only interpretable deictically (like *his mother* in (67b)). Fijian lacks lexical essential anaphors – items which must be interpreted anaphorically, like St.Eng. *himself*. In this respect it is like other Oceanic languages such as Tongan, Samoan, Tahitian, Iai and Chamorro as well as N. Frisian, Middle English and Gilbertese cited in Keenan 1976).

The differences between Fijian and St.Eng. here are lexical, and should follow from the lexical specifications of *koya* and *himself*. But this is not feasible within the BT as *koya* is not classifiable as an NP. It is not an anaphor since it may be free in a simple main clause; it is not a pronoun since it may be bound there, and it is not an r-expression since it may be bound.

What must be constrained in Fijian is the range of interpretations available to *koya* in transitive contexts. The word itself occurs freely there.

Comparable but more problematic anaphora paradigms are instantiated in Irish English, Japanese and Turkish below.

In Irish English (J. McCloskey, personal communication) the expressions *himself* and *herself* may be interpreted anaphorically as in St.Eng. But in addition these expressions may be interpreted deictically to mean 'the most prominent individual in context'. Thus an office worker might say to another who arrives late 'Careful. Himself is in a foul mood today' meaning 'The boss is in a foul mood today.' However, the availability of these two interpretations follows the pattern of Fijian above. In Ss like *Everyone respects himself* the structurally accusative *himself* may be interpreted either deictically or anaphorically (as SELF). But in Ss like (69) the structurally nominative occurrence of *herself* (the first one) may only be interpreted deictically.

(69) Herself is getting herself ready.

If the BT classed *herself* in Irish as an anaphor then (69) should be blocked for the same reason as (56b). If not, then the coreferential interpretation of the second occurrence of *herself* in (69) is predicted impossible. Both options are incorrect.

Note that in Irish English the deictic interpretation of (67b) is acceptable. Only the anaphoric interpretation is blocked. Comparable claims hold for Japanese and Turkish below.

In Japanese, as discussed in Sakaguchi (1985) (also in Kuroda 1965, Akatsuka 1976, Inoue 1976 and Sportiche 1986), the 'reflexive' *zibun* may be interpreted deictically as Speaker or Addressee according as the S is declarative or interrogative (imperative). (70c) is from N. Akatsuka (personal communication).

(70) a. Hanako-ga   zibun-o   utagatte-iru
       Hanako-nom   -acc doubts
       'Hanako doubts herself' or 'Hanako doubts Speaker'
    b. Zibun-ga   Hanako-o   utagatte-iru
       -nom Hanako-acc doubts
       'Speaker doubts Hanako' *'Hanako doubts herself'
    c. Zibun-wa zibun-o hazukasiku omotte orimasu
                        shamefully think   be (humble)
       'Speaker is ashamed of self'

(70a–b) exhibit the interpretative paradigm of Fijian (68) and (70c) presents the BT with the same problem as the Irish (69).

In Turkish (M. Enç 1983, 1987 and personal communication) the lexical item *kendisi* behaves like Fijian *koya* but in addition Turkish presents an essential anaphor *kendi*.

(71) a. Herkes-Ø   (ayna- da) kendisi-(n)i gördu
    everyone-nom mirror-loc   -acc saw
    'Everyone saw himself (in the mirror)' or
    'Everyone saw him/her (in the mirror)'
  b. Kendisi-Ø   (ayna- da) kendisi-(n)i gördu
      -nom mirror-loc   -acc saw
    'He/she saw self (in the mirror)'

Replacing *kendisi* with *kendi* in (71b) we obtain only an anaphoric reading. (Note the absence of Principle B effects in (71b).)

As with Fijian, the Irish, Japanese and Turkish examples show that a theory of anaphora may not in general constrain the distribution of lexical items but only the range of interpretations available to these items.

4.2 *Defining 'anaphor'*

The definition I provide in (76) below is compatible with the intuition of 'referentially dependent' used in Chomsky 1986 and determines easily applicable tests of anaphoricity. To build the intuition behind the definition consider the interpretative differences between (72a–b):

(72) a. John kissed himself
  b. John kissed every student

We should like to find a test which shows that the interpretation of *himself* in (72a) is dependent on that of *John* in a way in which that of *every student* in (72b) is not.

To get at this difference observe first that if *John* is replaced by *Bill* in either S the resulting one may have a different truth value than the original. But suppose we know that Bill kissed exactly the same objects that John kissed. In that case the truth value of (72b) and of *Bill kissed every student* must be the same. But that is not sufficient to guarantee that *John kissed himself* and *Bill kissed himself* have the same truth value. If Bill kissed just Peter, John and Frank, and those are just the objects John kissed then *Bill kissed himself* is false and *John kissed himself* is true.

In other words, EVERY STUDENT cannot distinguish among individuals who kissed the same things. But SELF can. Thus whether EVERY STUDENT puts an object b in the set it associates with KISS does not depend on what object b is, it only depends on what objects b bears the KISS relation to. By contrast, whether SELF puts b in the set it associates with KISS does depend on what object b is. In deciding whether to put b in the set, SELF must know both what objects b bears KISS to *and* that it is b that bears KISS to those objects.

These observations yield the following anaphoricity tests.

(73) *Accusative Extensions Condition* (AEC)

To decide whether an NP X of arbitrary complexity is interpretable as an accusative extension of a basic function, verify that whenever John kissed exactly the same objects Bill hugged then *John kissed X* and *Bill hugged X* have the same truth value

(74) *Accusative Anaphor Condition* (AAC)

To decide whether X as above is an accusative anaphor verify that it fails the AEC above but satisfies the following weaker condition: If John kissed exactly the same objects he (John) hugged then *John kissed X* and *John hugged X* have the same truth value

These tests are formally justified by theorem (75) and the definition in (76).

(75) *Thm* A function F from binary relations to properties is the accusative extension of a basic function iff for all binary relations R, S and all objects a, b

if $R_a = S_b$ then a $\in$ F(R) iff b $\in$ F(S) [$R_a =_{df}$ {x: aRx}]

(76) a. A function F from binary relations to properties is an *accusative anaphor* iff for all binary relations R, S and all objects b

if $R_b = S_b$ then b $\in$ F(R) iff b $\in$ F(S)

b. F is a *proper accusative anaphor* iff it is an accusative anaphor and is not an accusative extension of a basic function

Corresponding to theorem (75) we have the nominative version obtained by replacing R_a with R^a and S_b by S^b (where R^a is by definition {x: xRa}). The same replacement in (76) yields the definition of *nominative anaphor*.

These definitions define properties of NP *interpretations*. They extend to NPs themselves as follows: An NP is said to be +*anaphor* iff it has occurences interpreted as proper (nominative or accusative) anaphors. An NP is called an *essential anaphor* if all occurrences are interpreted as proper anaphors. For example, Turkish *kendi*, St.Eng. *himself* and Korean *caki-casin* are essential anaphors. Fijian *koya*, Irish *himself* and Japanese *zibun* are not, but they are +*anaphor*.

4.3 Consequences of the definition

(i) We may now characterize the anaphora paradigms in the languages discussed in (68)–(71) by stipulating the interpretations of the relevant lexical items: Fijian *koya* is marked [+3(+deictic, +anaphor)] meaning it may be interpreted either deictically or anaphorically, third person in all cases. St.Eng. *himself*, Turkish *kendi* and Korean *caki-casin* are simply [+3 anaphor], whence all occurrences are interpreted anaphorically. Irish *himself* is [+3 anaphor, +male deictic: 'ranking individual in context']. And Japanese *zibun* is [+anaphor, +deictic: 'source of point of view of the utterance']. (For further features needed see Enç (1987).)

Any of the indicated interpretations of these items is available unless blocked by general constraints such as the NRC. The judgments in (68)–(71) follow.

(ii) The definition expands our concept of anaphor in English. For example, the structurally accusative NPs in (77) and (78) pass the test in (74).

(77) John criticized both himself and Paul / himself and no one else / everyone but himself / no one but himself / neither himself nor the other students who came late

(78) a. Each student tackled [a problem that
      i. no one but himself could solve]
      ii. only himself and the teacher could solve]
      iii. was chosen by a student other than himself]

Thus St.Eng. has denumerably many syntactically complex anaphors. In (78a.i) *a problem that no one but himself could solve* is + anaphor, indeed an essential anaphor. It properly contains another complex anaphor, *no one but himself*, which in turn properly contains a lexical essential anaphor. A detailed investigation of these anaphors remains to be done. They have some properties in common with the 'pictures of each other' cases discussed in Chomsky 1986: 174ff in that they are long distance, and replacing the lexical anaphor *himself* by *he/him* does not force judgments of disjoint reference. But they also differ:

(79) a. *John thought that Mary criticized himself
    b. John thought that Mary criticized everyone but himself
    c. Each student thought that Mary would ask a question that
      i. no one but himself could answer
      ii. only himself and Paul could answer
      iii. *himself could answer

Thus only the lexical anaphor *himself* must be bound to the closest available subject. The complex anaphors then are similar to the lexical long distance ones in Japanese (Akatsuka 1976: 53) and Kannada (Bhat 1978: 56).

These data suggest a reevaluation of long distance anaphora in English. Namely, in general it is possible, but subject to a lexical exhaustion constraint, perhaps one similar to that on across the board Pied Piping shown in (80).

(80) a. every man whose mother and whose father John knows
     b. *every man who and whose father John knows

(iii) An important feature of our definition is that + anaphor NPs are, like basic NPs, directly interpreted. For example, EVERYONE BUT HIMSELF is that function sending each binary relation R to $\{b: R_b = D - \{b\}\}$. Thus our approach enables us to exhibit properties that anaphors and basic NPs have in common – they may both take binary relations as arguments satisfying the accusative anaphor condition in (76). It is thus unsurprising on this view that NP anaphors *are* NPs and may coordinate with them, as in *John criticized himself and everyone else*.

By contrast BT approaches give little or no account of what NP anaphors have in common with basic NPs. On views which, in effect, translate them as bound variables they appear completely different from quantified NPs which are variable binding operators. Even on the revisions of BT suggested in Chomsky (1986: 175) it is unnatural to expect that reflexives and quantified NPs may form complex NPs like *everyone but himself* or *himself and everyone else*.

5 Conclusions, Extensions and Speculations

Very many difficult issues concerning both scope assignment and anaphora possibilities have been simply excluded from consideration here in virtue of limiting ourselves to transitive contexts. The adequacy of an SCT-based approach to these questions then will depend on how successfully the NRC and the definitions of semantic case and +anaphor can be extended to more complex contexts. Preliminary work here is encouraging:

Wh-questions and crossover

In intransitive contexts we may think of interrogative NPs such as *who*, *which student*, *whose cat and whose dog* as functions from properties to question denotations. Their interpretations in transitive contexts are just the isomorphic images of the case extensions of non-interrogative NPs. In Ls such as Chinese (Huang 1982) in which transitive declaratives and interrogatives are syntactically isomorphic then the crossover judgments in Qs like *His doctor examined who*? follow in the same way they do for quantified NP accusatives in English, as in (67b).

Reciprocals

We have limited our considerations here to 'first order' predicates, ones expressing properties of or relations between individuals (rather than sets of individuals). Reciprocals form higher order predicates. For example, *love each other* expresses a property that a group of individuals might have, but doesn't make sense when predicated of a single individual. Modulo this difference in logical order, our anaphora tests apply in a natural way to reciprocals. To check that *each other* is a higher order anaphor verify that (81a) and (81b) have the same truth value whenever each element of the subject set {John, Bill} kissed exactly the same objects he hugged.

(81) a. John and Bill kissed each other
      b. John and Bill hugged each other

Acquisition of anaphors

The axioms of SCT are clearly deficient in one respect: Case Existence only applies to closed (= basic) NPs. Nothing explicit is said about the interpretation of initially open (= deictic) NPs in transitive contexts, though one limiting result does follow: If an initial NP is interpreted anaphorically in a transitive context then it is interpreted deictically in the intransitive context.

Conceptually this link between anaphoric and deictic interpretations is principled. What we have been calling initial deictics are just initial NPs whose interpretations depend on information not given by the NP itself. By the assumptions on the linguistic context the dependency must be extralinguistic. But in transitive contexts this need not be the case. Expressions external to the NP in question may provide the information on which the open interpretation depends.

Thus the distinction between anaphoric and extralinguistic deictic is created by the context the transitive verb determines and we are justified in considering anaphoric interpretations of initially open NPs as special cases of open interpretations.

Thus the Fijian child who interprets *koya* 'he, him' anaphorically in transitive contexts is just applying the knowledge already obtained in learning that *koya* in intransitive contexts is open.

What requires special learning on this view are the essential anaphors (St.Eng. *himself*). Their interpretations cannot be projected from initial contexts as they do not occur there and cannot be interpreted anaphorically there. Thus the St.Eng.-speaking child is faced with a learning task not faced by Fijian (M. English, N. Frisian, . . .) speakers.

Interestingly this view of anaphora receives experimental support by Wexler and Chien (1985). They tested St.Eng.-speaking children from ages 2.6 to 6.6 on their ability to correctly identify possible antecedents of essential anaphors and pronouns (*him*, *her*). They found that throughout this period, with little improvement, the children often interpreted the pronouns with local subjects as antecedents, in violation of Principle B. That is, they were behaving like little Fijian speakers. By contrast, performance on reflexives started off poorly and consistently improved achieving about 90 percent correct responses at age 6.6.

Both these results confirm the view presented here. Initial deictics were interpreted anaphorically, and the learning of essential anaphors was a significant learning task.

Consequences for UG

If the approach taken here can be refined and extended to something like the range of data considered within the Binding Theory (a forbidding task!) this will have some challenging implications for our conception of UG (= our innate, linguistic endowment).

For example, we have shown, for the limited class of structure types considered, that the interpretation of quantified NPs and the representation of quantifier scope ambiguities does not *require* a level of LF.

More seriously the work here calls into question the UG status of that part of the BT covered by SCT + NRC. The anaphora facts we accounted for relied on the NRC and the axioms of SCT, mainly Case Existence. But these are naturally understood as special cases of a very general ability to generalize. Case Existence says we generalize the interpretation of basic NPs from initial contexts to more complex ones, and the NRC says we generalize the interpretative possibilities of initial NPs to structurally nominative ones. The ability to generalize from simple cases to more complex ones does not seem to be specifically linguistic.

But we should note in this regard that the status of the NRC is far from established. Generalizing it to more complex contexts will require revisions. And it lacks the intuitive appeal of the axioms of SCT. To be sure it guarantees an 'anchor' for anaphors but so would generalizing the referential possibilities of initial NPs to structural accusatives. I have as yet seen no clear examples of such anaphorically ergative languages. If there are none, or only few, what would explain that? Why generalize here at all? If either NP in a transitive S could be an anaphor its antecedent would have to be the other. Indeed if the analysis of Samoan given by Chapin (1970: 369) extends to anaphorically interpreted items with quantified NP antecedents we will have a counterexample to the NRC. So the NRC may be just one among many options which languages may choose to restrict the interpretations of NPs in complex contexts.

Notes

1 I take Binding Theory in the following weak form (where *bound* means coindexed with a C-commanding NP and *free* = not bound):

Principle A: Anaphors are bound in some domain   D-ana
Principle B: Pronouns are free in some domain   D-pron
Principle C: r-expressions are free

Following Chomsky (1986: 171) D-ana may be different from D-pron. I assume they both include main clause transitive Ss.

2 Formally, for each b in D define the basic function I_b, called the *individual generated by* b, as that function which sends a property p to True iff b is in p. A basic function F is an individual iff $F = I_b$ for some object b. Proper nouns are constrained to denote individuals. It is easily seen that given an individual there is exactly one object b which generates it. These are the 'John objects' referred to later.

3 I ignore here for simplicity the possibility that the initial NPs may referentially depend on the P_1. It is hard to find such cases with simple P_1s. Possibly the *it* in *It is raining*. More interesting cases arise as the predicate becomes more complex: In (i) the reference of *they* seems to be something like 'whoever is in charge of raising taxes'. In (ii) it seems to be 'the Chinese'.

(i)   They're raising taxes again
(ii) They eat a lot of rice in China

Cases of 'arbitrary reference' can probably be subsumed under the class of closed interpretations but have a clear interest in the present context: namely, they constitute another possible interpretation for 'reflexives' in particular in environments where they are not bound. See Rappoport (1986) for such uses in Russian.

4 Observe that closed interpretations may be represented as the special case of open ones which are constant. Further work will possibly yield multiple 'indices' on which interpretations may depend, in which case openness will be a gradable property.

5 Often written (b KISS d). The notation is misleading as it suggests, irrelevantly, that the first member of the pair (b, d) is somehow attached to the first NP in a transitive S.

6 An NP occurrence is *independent* in E iff it is not a proper constituent of any other NP occurrence in E. The independent NP occurrences in (in)transitive Ss correspond to 'arguments' in GB approaches, but here no primitive notion of argument is assumed.

7 I ignore here the binary quantifiers explored in Keenan 1987b. It is shown there that, limiting ourselves to first order properties, in Ss like *Every student answered a different question* the NP *a different question* cannot be interpreted as a function from binary relations to properties at all. Rather, the pair (*every student*, *a different question*) directly determines a function from binary relations to properties.

8 More precisely: There is no basic function F such that for all binary relations R, $F_{acc}(R) = SELF(R)$. Ditto for F_{nom}.

9 Thanks to Fritz Hamm for discussion of this axiom.

10 Thanks to Leonard Faltz for discussion of this axiom.

11 Following current practice I ignore the fact that in main clause Ss one of the NPs would have its postposition replaced with the topic marker -*wa*. Since -*wa*, -*ga* and -*o* are distinct it is clear that the JCC in (25) could be stated directly on forms using -*wa*. However, the statement is more complex and the one given does not make it clear that the correct statement will have to mention the identity of the transitive verb. Comparable remarks obtain for Korean with its topic marker -(*n*)*ŭn*.

12 In what follows I largely ignore questions of scope interpretation, mainly because the facts of interest relate to argument ambiguities but also in part for lack of data. Noteworthy though is that of the several languages where I have data only Chinese appears to block scope ambiguities in basic transitive Ss. Moreover, the detailed experimental work of T. Lee (1986) shows that even by the age of eight Chinese-speaking children still exhibit a very significant tendency to get two scope readings, having only about 60 percent adult competence in this respect.

13 Statements of CCs will of course be more complex when three-place predicates are considered. In addition the CCs I give are often only partial in the sense of not covering all syntactic types of BatSs. Still the class I do cover is large and includes the common S types adduced for the languages in the literature.

14 Guerssel's analysis raises several interesting issues, but it still preserves the distinction between +/− construct state, though in a different form.

15 Note the ethnocentric bias in the question. Had we begun our linguistic analyses on the basis of Berber and Middle Egyptian we might well now be explaining why the nominative NP in English wasn't bound to the verb.

16 For example: the feminine ending on nouns in M.E. is -*t*, in B. it is *t*- . . . -*t*; the passive affix on verbs in M.E. is -*tw*, in B. it is *ttw* (tensed *t*); the causative prefix on verbs in M.E. is *s*-, in B. it is *ss*-. Even the preposition *n* 'of' is the same in the two Ls, but it has a more widespread use in M.E. where it attaches verb bases to the 'subject' agreements. It also occurs as an independent preposition outside of genitive constructions.

17 This is a well definition by the Case Structure axiom. Note that no notion of a 'position' which exists independently of an NP that fills it is invoked. Such a notion is moot in free word order languages.

18 Hale (1983) citing unpublished work of Whitman claims that Japanese does not follow the Korean (Hindi, Armenian, Kannada) paradigm.

References

Abdel-Massih, E. T. (1971) *A Reference Grammar of Tamazight*. Center for N. Eastern and N. African Studies, University of Michigan, Ann Arbor.

Abney, S. (1987) 'Extraction and pseudo-objects in Berber'. In Guerssel and Hale (1987).

Akatsuka (McCawley), N. (1976) 'Reflexivization: a transformational approach'. In Shibatani (1976).

Aoun, J. and A. Li (1987) 'Syntax of scope'. MS, Dept of Linguistics, USC Los Angeles.

Bhat, D. N. S. (1978) *Pronominalization*. Deccan College, Pune, India.

Borer, H. (1984) *Parametric Syntax*. Foris: Dordrecht.

Bresnan, J. (ed.) (1982) *The Mental Representation of Grammatical Relations*. Cambridge, Mass.: MIT Press.

Callender, J. (1975a) *Middle Egyptian*. Malibu, Calif.: Undena Publications.

(1975b) 'Afroasiatic cases and the formation of Ancient Egyptian constructions with possessive suffixes'. *Afroasiatic Linguistics*, 2.6, 1–18.

Chapin, P. (1970) 'Samoan pronominalization'. *Language*, 46.2, 366–78.

Choe, H. S. (1987) 'An SVO analysis of VSO languages and parametrization: a study of Berber'. In Guerssel and Hale (1987).

Chomsky, N. (1986) *Knowledge of Language*. New York: Praeger.

Chung, S. (1983) 'The ECP and government in Chamorro'. *Natural Language and Linguistic Theory*, 1.2, 207–45.

Craig, C. (1977) *The Structure of Jacaltec*. Austin, Tex.: University of Texas Press.

Enç, M. (1983) 'Anchored expressions'. In *WCCFL* 2, ed. Barlow et al. Stanford Linguistics Association, Stanford University.

(1987) 'Pronouns, licensing and binding' MS, Dept. of Linguistics, USC Los Angeles.

Emmorey, K. (1984) 'The intonation system in Toba Batak'. In Schachter (1984a).

Ennaji, M. (1985) *Contrastive Syntax: English, Moroccan Arabic and Berber Complex Sentences*. Königshausen Neumann.

and F. Sadiqi (1986) 'The syntax of cleft sentences in Berber'. *Studies in Language*, 10.1, 53–77.

Farmer, A. (1984) *Modularity in Syntax*. Cambridge, Mass.: MIT Press.

Frishberg, N. (1972) 'Navaho object markers and the great chain of being'. In J. Kimball (ed.), *Syntax and Semantics*, vol. 1. New York: Seminar Press.

Guerssel, M. (1986) 'On Berber verbs of change: a study of transitivity alternations'. Lexicon Project Working Papers # 9, Center for Cognitive Science, MIT.

(1987) 'The status of the lexical category "Preposition" in Berber'. In Guerssel and Hale (1987).

and K. Hale (eds) (1987) *Studies in Berber Syntax*. Lexicon Project Working Papers # 14. Center for Cognitive Science, MIT.

Hale, K. (1983) 'Warlpiri and the grammar of non-configurational languages'. *Natural Language and Linguistic Theory*, 1.1, 5–49.

L. Jeanne and P. Platero (1977) 'Three cases of overgeneration'. In P. Culicover, T. Wasow and A. Akamajian (eds), *Formal Syntax*. New York: Academic Press.

Hinds, J. (1974) 'On the status of the VP node in Japanese'. *Language Research*, 9.2, 44–57.

Hoji, H. (1987) 'Weak crossover and Japanese phrase structure'. In Imai and Saito (1987).

Huang, J. (1982) 'Logical relations in Chinese and the theory of grammar'. Ph.D. diss., MIT.

Imai, T. and M. Saito (eds) (1987) *Issues in Japanese Syntax*. Dordrecht: Foris.

Inoue, K. (1976) 'Reflexivization: an interpretative approach'. In Shibatani (1976).

Jelinek, E. (1984) 'Empty categories, case, and configurationality'. *Natural Language and Linguistic Theory*, 2.1, 39–77.

Johnson, M. J. (1966) 'Syntactic structures of Tamazight'. Ph.D. diss., Dept of Linguistics, UCLA.

Keenan, E. L. (1976) 'The logical diversity of natural languages'. In *Origins and Evolution of Language and Speech*. New York: Academy of Sciences. Reprinted in Keenan (1987c).

(1984) 'Semantic correlates of the ergative/absolutive distinction'. *Linguistics*, 22, 197–223. Reprinted in Keenan (1987c).

(1987a) 'Semantic case theory'. To appear in the Proceedings of the Sixth Amsterdam Colloquium, ed. J. Groenendijk and M. Stokhof.

(1987b) 'Unreducible n-ary quantification in natural language'. In P. Gardenfors (ed.), *Generalized Quantifiers: Linguistic and Logical Approaches*. Dordrecht: Reidel.

(1987c) *Universal Grammar: 15 Essays*. London: Croom Helm.

and J. Stavi (1986) 'A semantic characterization of natural language determiners'. *Linguistics and Philosophy*, 9, 253–326.

Kuroda, S. Y. (1965) 'Causative forms in Japanese'. *Foundations of Language*, 1, 30–50.

Lee, T. (1986) 'Acquisition of quantificational scope in Mandarin Chinese'. *Papers and Reports on Child Language Development*, no. 25, Leland Stanford Junior University.

Li, P. J. K. (1973) *Rukai Structure*. Institute of History and Philology, Academia Sinica Special Publication 64 Taipei.

May, R. (1985) *Logical Form: Its Structure and Derivation*. Cambridge, Mass.: MIT Press.

Mohanon, K. P. (1982) 'Grammatical relations and clause structure in Malayalam'. In Bresnan (1982).

O'Grady, W. (1985) 'An argument for discontinuous VPs in Korean'. *Language Research*, 21.4, 451–61.

Park S. H. (1986) 'Parametrizing the theory of binding: the implications of *caki* in Korean'. *Language Research*, 22.2, 229–53.

Penchoen, T. (1973) *Tamazight of the Ayt Ndhir*. Los Angeles: Undena Publications.

Pickett, V. (1960) *The Grammatical Hierarchy of Isthmus Zapotec. Language Supplement*. Language Diss. no. 56, vol. 36, no. 1, pt 2.

(1975) 'Isthmus Zapotec: a typological sketch'. MS, Dept of Linguistics, UCLA.

Platero, P. (1982) 'Missing noun phrases and grammatical relations in Navaho'. *IJAL*, 48.3, 286–306.

Rappoport, G. (1986) 'On anaphor binding in Russian'. *NLLT*, 4.1, 97–121.

Sadiqi, F. (1986) *Studies in Berber Syntax*. Königshausen: Neumann.

Saib, J. (1975) 'Berber as a VSO language' MS, Dept of Linguistics, UCLA.

Saito, M. and H. Hoji (1983) 'Weak crossover and move α in Japanese'. *Natural Language and Linguistic Theory*, 1.2, 245–61.

Sakaguchi, M. (1985) 'Coreference relations in Japanese'. MA diss., UCLA.

Sapir, E. and H. Hoijer (1967) *The Phonology and Morphology of the Navaho Language*. Berkeley and Los Angeles: University of California Press.

Schachter, P. (ed.) (1984a) *Studies in the Structure of Toba Batak*. UCLA Occasional Papers in Linguistics, no. 5, Dept of Linguistics, UCLA.

(1984b) 'Semantic role based syntax in Toba Batak'. In Schachter (1984a).

Schenkel, W. (1975) *Die Alte Egyptische Suffix-Konjugation*. Wiesbaden: Harrossowitz.

Shibatani, M. (1976) *Japanese Generative Grammar*. Syntax and Semantics, vol. 5. New York: Academic Press.

Shlonsky, U. and M. Sigler (1987) 'Unexceptional and exceptional case marking'. In Guerssel and Hale (1987).

Sportiche, D. (1986) 'Zibun'. *Linguistic Inquiry*, 17.2, 369–74.

144   EDWARD L. KEENAN

Wager, J. (1976) 'Complementation in Berber, Swahili and French'. MS, Dept of Linguistics, UCLA.
Wexler, K. and Y. C. Chien (1985) 'The development of lexical anaphors and pronouns'. *Papers and Reports on Child Language Development* no. 24, Leland Stanford Jr University.
Whitman, J. (1987) 'Configurationality parameters'. In Imai and Saito (1987).

CHAPTER 6

Concessive Connectives and Concessive Sentences: Cross-Linguistic Regularities and Pragmatic Principles

Ekkehard König

1 Introduction

Together with terms like 'conditional', 'temporal', 'causal', etc., the term 'concessive' belongs to the terminological inventory that traditional grammar makes available for the characterization and classification of adverbials and adverbial clauses. Any attempt to give a cross-linguistic characterization of concessive relations and the way they are expressed in the world's languages is constrained by the fact that we do not have enough relevant information from a representative sample of languages. This situation could be due to several factors: First, there may simply not be any concessive markers in a language other than the adversative conjunction corresponding to English *but*. An elaborate inventory of concessive expressions, as found in European languages, presupposes, it seems, a certain tradition of argumentative writing. Second, available reference grammars may simply fail to provide the relevant information. Concessive relations have always aroused less interest than conditional or causal ones in both theoretical and descriptive studies, since the latter play a much more important role in scientific argument. And third, the formal means available in a language for expressing concessive relations may be more or less identical to those used for other functions without explicit mention being made of this fact in the relevant grammar.

The subsequent discussion, though based on a sample of seventy languages,[1] will therefore exhibit a certain bias towards European languages as well as those languages on which detailed information in the relevant area happens to be available. The cross-linguistic generalizations that will be made below relate primarily to the formal make-up of concessive connectives, the affinity to other notional domains that this make-up suggests and the historical origins of these connectives. The 'explanations' that will be offered are basically pragmatic ones.

2 Basic Distinctions

There is good evidence for the assumption that 'concessive' or 'adversative' relations can be expressed in all languages. The formal means that are typically employed to signal these relations include the following: prepositions (e.g. Engl. *in spite of*), conjunctions (e.g. Engl. *although*), conjunctional adverbs (e.g. Engl. *nevertheless*), affixes added to the verb (e.g. Malayalam -*enkil* -*um*) and asyndetic linking of two clauses, frequently reinforced by one of the other markers (e.g. Tibet. gerund + *na-yan*). Since there is no generally accepted formal, or informal, analysis of concessive relations available, it seems best to base such an analysis on a comparison with two related notions, viz. 'causality' and 'conditionality'.

Like the two clauses of a causal construction, the two clauses that enter into a concessive relation have a factual character. In other words, sentences of the general form (1a–b) entail both of their component clauses:

(1) a. q because p
     b. although p, q

Anybody asserting sentences of this general form is committed to the truth of poth p and q (cf. Reichenbach 1947: 329). In addition to the requirement that the two clauses be true, the truth conditions of causal constructions also include the condition that there be some general correlation, connection or link between the propositions expressed by these clauses. This connection is frequently analyzed in terms of a counterfactual conditional (cf. Sæbø 1986):

(2) $\sim p > \sim q$

(3) a. I did not go out because it was raining.
     b. If it had not been raining, I would have gone out.

Concessive sentences also imply a connection between the two propositions linked in such sentences. In this case, however, this implication has the status of a presupposition (or conventional implicature) rather than an entailment (cf. König 1986) with roughly the content that there is a general incompatibility between the two propositions in question. For a concrete example like (4a) this concessive presupposition can roughly be spelled out as (4b), or perhaps as (4c):

(4) a. Although John had no money, he went into this expensive restaurant.
     b. If one has no money, one normally does not go into an expensive restaurant.

   c. If John has no money, he normally does not go into an expensive restaurant.

If we abstract from the content of the two clauses, that is, if we consider concessive sentences of the form (1b), the relevant presupposition can therefore be formulated as follows, where p′ and q′ denote types of eventualities,[2] instances of which are described by p and q:

(5) If p′, then normally ~q′

In other words, asserting a concessive sentence of the form (1b) amounts to asserting two propositions p and q against the background assumption that the eventualities p′ and q′, which p and q describe an instance of, do not normally go together.[3] Additional properties of concessive relations are revealed by a comparison with those expressed by conditional connectives. Such a comparison shows that in addition to conditional and concessive sentences most languages have developed a sentence type (viz. 'concessive conditionals') that shares properties with both of the two former categories:

(6) a. Whether or not he finds a job, he is getting married.
    b. Whatever I say, he doesn't listen to me.
    c. Even if I try very hard, I won't manage.

Both formal and semantic properties identify concessive conditionals, whose general form in English is given in (6), as being basically conditionals. In contrast to simple conditionals, however, they relate a series of protases (or antecedents) to an apodosis (consequent). This series can be specified by a disjunction as in (6a), by a free-choice quantifier as in (6b),[4] or by a scalar expression as in (6c). European languages typically have a wide variety of 'free-choice' expressions, whose common property is that they signal a free choice in the substitution of values for a variable in the antecedent, thus specifying a series of protases. In sentences of type (6c) such a series is specified by asserting a conditional relationship for an extreme, unlikely value on a scale. By implication this relationship can also be assumed to hold for other, less extreme values on the same scale. Given that concessive conditionals relate a whole series of protases to an apodosis, a series which may comprise the whole spectrum of possibilities within a parameter (that is, p and ~p; (∀x) (I say x)), all of them are sufficient ones. As a consequence, concessive conditionals typically entail their apodosis.[5] Another property that they share with concessive sentences of type (1b) is that they, too, may carry an implication of incompatibility between two situations. Among the protases related by such conditionals to an apodosis, there is at least one case (either p or ~p in (6a), or one substitution instance for 'I say x' in (6b)) that is in conflict with the apodosis. Concessive conditionals can thus be shown to share semantic properties with both conditionals and concessives and it is therefore not surprising that some grammars group them together with the former and some with the latter construction. In most European and indeed in many other languages, however, a distinction between these three sentence types can clearly be drawn and many grammars do in fact make these distinctions along the lines proposed in this paper.

The concessive presupposition described in (5) provides the basis for various uses that can be made of concessive sentences. Such uses can be distinguished depending on the role the 'minor assertion' p plays in the context, depending on whether the concessivity relates to causal or epistemic notions and depending on the order of minor (p) and major assertion (q). A distinction that is frequently drawn is the one between 'external' and 'internal' concessive (or 'adversative') relations (cf. Halliday and Hasan 1976: 250ff). Borkin (1980: 50ff) draws a parallel distinction between 'dissonance of an empirical nature', as in (7a), and 'dissonance of a rhetorical nature', as in (7b):

(7) a. Even though he had not eaten for days, he looked strong and healthy.
    b. Even though this solution would be harmful to our enemies, the damage done to us would be even greater.

The second example does not express any factual conflict, but a conflict between the conclusions supported by two arguments.

Other uses that could be distinguished are illustrated by the following examples: Concessive sentences can be used to anticipate a potential counterargument, to warn somebody against drawing the wrong conclusions[6] and to restrict the validity of a previous statement:

(8) a. Even though this decision won't solve all our problems, it will certainly improve our situation.
    b. On the ride home he stayed away from Agravain. He could not avoid him, though, once they were back in Camelot. (M. Stewart, *The Wicked Day*, p. 234)
    c. He is very intelligent, although some of the things that he says are a bit silly.

These distinctions partly cut across and partly complement the one between 'external' and 'internal' concessive relations. How many different kinds of concessive relations should be distinguished and whether they are formally differentiated in a consistent way has never been answered satisfactorily even for a single language, let alone within a comparative context. This issue will not be pursued in this context. Rather, the fundamental concessive relation described in (5) is meant to capture the flexibility that seems to exist in all natural languages with respect to the terms that can enter into this relation.

Another simplifying assumption that will be made in this paper concerns the question of delimiting concessive relations, that is, the meaning of E. *although*, *even though*, *nevertheless*, etc., from 'adversative relations', that is, the meaning of E. *but*. Many investigators have struggled with this problem and have come to the conclusion that a clear distinction between these two types of relations or types of connectives does not exist and I will therefore speak indiscriminately of 'concessive' or 'adversative' relations.

3 Properties of Concessive Clauses

Concessive sentences are remarkably different from other sentences with adverbial clauses in a number of ways. The differences begin with the very term that is traditionally employed. In contrast to terms like 'causal', 'instrumental', 'conditional' or 'temporal', the term 'concessive' does not denote a two-term relation, but a possible use of a sentence or clause. The following description of marked differences between concessive sentences and other complex sentences with adverbial clauses is based on an in-depth study of some European languages rather than a cross-linguistic comparison (cf. König 1985a, 1985b, 1986).

(i) In contrast to other adverbial clause types, concessive clauses cannot be in the scope of an operator such as *only*, *also*, *too*, or *even*:

(9) a.   q, only because p
    b.   q, only if p
    c.   q, only in order that p
    d.   *q, only although p

Concessive connectives tend to take maximal scope and are therefore not easily accepted within the scope of another operator. This can be clearly observed in the following two sentences, whose near-equivalence is the result of different composition, 'not (q because p)' vs. 'not-q, although p':

(10) a.   This house is no less comfortable because it dispenses with air-conditioning.
     b.   This house is no less comfortable, although it dispenses with air-conditioning.

Concessive relations can only be affected by a focusing, metalinguistic negation operator 'not a, but b' (cf. Horn 1985b) which not only identifies an expression as being the wrong choice of words, but also offers a correction:

(11) It is not in spite of but because of the renunciation of worldly pleasures that the Amish are happier than other people.

The resistance of concessive connectives to being within the scope of another scope-bearing element can also be correlated with the fact that concessive sentences exhibit some properties of coordinate structures and may express a separate speech act perspective different from that of the main clause (cf. König and Van der Auwera, forthcoming). Notice, finally, that in those cases where focusing operators like *even* seem to combine with concessive clauses (for example, *even though* p, q), they are actually part of the concessive connective.

(ii) Asyndetic types of clause linking, absolute constructions, as well as nearly all adverbial clauses may be interpretatively enriched and receive a concessive interpretation (cf. König 1986):

(12) a. Fred was already drunk, early as it was in the night.
    b. This is an interesting, if complicated, solution.
    c. There was a funny smile on Dickie's face, as if Dickie were pulling his leg by pretending to fall in with his plan, when he hadn't the least intention to fall in with it. (P. Highsmith, *Ripley*, p. 75)
    d. Il était d'accord, tout en gardant ses objections fondamentales.

In the preceding examples, an unspecific adjectival construction, a conditional clause, a temporal clause and a 'gerund' are all interpreted concessively. Sentences, on the other hand, that are explicitly marked as concessives can never be reinterpreted in the sense of any other adverbial relation, however suitable the context might be. In other words, concessive relations are a dead-end street for interpretative augmentation.

(iii) Combinations of non-finite and finite clauses like the so-called absolute constructions in English (cf. Stump 1985), the adverbial participles in Russian or the Italian gerundio may all receive a concessive interpretation in addition to being interpretable in the sense of any other adverbial relation, given the right context. Of these interpretative options, the concessive one typically requires more supportive marking than the others. Compare the following English examples:

(13) a. ?Not having any money, he went into this expensive restaurant.
    b. Not having any money, he nevertheless went into this expensive restaurant.

The first sentence hardly makes any sense, since it tends to receive a causal interpretation that is not compatible with general background knowledge. The additional supportive marker *nevertheless* clearly leads to a concessive interpretation in the second case.

(iv) Among the interesting properties of concessive sentences that investigations of these structures in individual languages have revealed one might also want to mention a pragmatic aspect, that is, a typical use of such sentences, characterized by the traditional term 'concessive'. Concessive sentences are typically used if someone agrees with the premise of an argument, but rejects the conclusion. By using concessive sentences in this way, one accepts not only the premise, but also what Toulmin (1958) calls the 'warrant' of an argument, that is, the connection between the eventualities mentioned which justifies using the premise for the conclusion. This can be illustrated with Toulmin's famous example (cf. Klein 1980):

(14) a. Harry was born on the Bermudas. Therefore, he is a British citizen.
     b. Although Harry was born on the Bermudas, he is not a British citizen.

In using (14b) to reject the conclusion of (14a), a speaker accepts and thereby 'concedes' the premise of this argument in addition to accepting the first speaker's assumption about the connection between being born on the Bermudas and being a British citizen. It will be shown below that such typical uses of concessive sentences have left their mark on the forms that such constructions may take in various languages.

4 Some Cross-Linguistic Generalizations

Against the background of these properties revealed by in-depth studies of individual languages, the following cross-linguistic statements can be made, which are supported by all of the languages of the present study or are at least compatible with what we know about them.

(a) Not all languages seem to have specific concessive connectives like E. *despite*, *although*, *nevertheless*, though they all seem to have a counterpart for the adversative conjunction *but*. This 'distribution' accords with the fact that the conjunction *but* is less specific in its interpretation than the other connectives and may always be used to paraphrase them.

(b) In contrast to the markers of other adverbial relations (for example, conditional, causal, temporal, manner), concessive connectives have a fairly transparent formal make-up and etymology (cf. *if*, *when*, *as* vs. *although*, *even though*). Concessive connectives are complex in nature, their components are easy to identify and can easily be related to another, original – or at least earlier – meaning (cf. König 1985c; Harris, forthcoming).

(c) Concessive connectives seem to have developed fairly late in the history of the languages for which we have evidence. There were few, if any, clearly concessive markers in Old English (cf. Burnham 1911; Quirk 1954: 14), Old High German (cf. Mensing 1981) or Old French (cf. Lerch 1929; Herman 1963). In older stages of the Romance languages a limited number of subordinators carried a wide range of meanings. Among these, *makarie* (cf. Gk. *makarie* 'blessed') came closest to being analyzable as a concessive marker. But even this connective is basically a free-choice expression and was used in the sense of both 'would that' and 'although'. And although we do find connectives with a clear concessive meaning in classical languages like Latin (e.g. *quamquam, tamen, tametsi, ut, cum*), they all had another more basic use (time: *cum*, manner: *ut, quam, tam*) or they were at least based on such a more basic meaning (*quamquam* 'however') (cf. Harris, forthcoming). Similar observations can be made with respect to Greek and Sanskrit.

(d) All languages seem to have a construction, or at least had at some stage in their historical development, that can be used both as a marker of concessive conditionals and of concessive sentences proper. Free-choice expressions, in particular, are used as concessive connectives in a wide variety of languages and the differentiation between concessive conditional and concessive interpretation is often left to the context, the mood (subjunctive vs. indicative) or some other marking of the verb. In Norwegian, for instance, *selv om* is by far the most frequent concessive connective, but this expression is also used in the sense of 'even if' in counterfactual concessive conditionals like the following:

(15) Selv om de hadde blitt regn, ville vi ha dratt på fisketur.
'Even if it had been raining, we could have gone fishing.'

In those languages where a clear distinction can be made between concessive conditionals and concessives (e.g. *even if* vs. *even though*), this distinction was established fairly late.

(e) The late development of concessive connectives and late differentiation between concessive conditionals and concessives has an ontogenetic parallel. Investigations into the acquisition of English and a few other languages have shown that concessive connectives (including the adversative conjunction *but*) are acquired late, certainly much later than conditional connectives, which are acquired fairly late themselves (Braunwald 1985; Bowerman 1986).

(f) As already mentioned, concessive connectives are often composite in nature and have a very transparent etymology. In most cases, other, more basic meanings and uses of the components can easily be identified and concessivity can thus be related to other semantic domains. By investigating the affinity between concessivity and other domains, we can identify various historical sources and historical developments for these connectives. Furthermore, a typology of concessive connectives and concessive constructions can be set up: On the basis of their etymology, their historical development and the other more basic uses that their components have, five types of concessive connectives can be distinguished (cf. König and Eisenberg 1984; König 1985c).

(i) Members of the first group derive from such notions as 'obstinacy, spite, contempt', etc., that is, from notions originally only applicable to human agents or experiencers:[7]

(16) E. *in spite of*, *despite*, *regardless*; Fr. *en dépit de*, *au mépris de*, *malgré* (cf. *bon gré mal gré*; 'willy nilly'); G. *trotz*, *trotzdem*, *wider* 'against'; Sp. *a pesar de* (cf. *pesar* 'sorrow, regret'); D. *ondanks* (cf. *ondank* 'ingratitude', originally 'thoughtlessness'), *in weerwil van* ('against someone's will'); Dan. *trods*, *til trods for*; Fin. *huolimatta* (*huolimaton* 'careless, heedless, negligent', *huoli* 'care') Serb. Croat. *uprkos* (*prkos* 'spite'); Arab. *ragman* (*ragama* 'compel'); Turk. *raǧmen*; etc.

(17) a. He went out in spite of the bad weather.
   b. Er ging trotz des schlechten Wetters aus.
   c. Il est sorti malgré le mauvais temps.

(ii) Secondly, there is a close relationship beween concessivity and free-choice quantification. Concessive connectives in many languages contain a component that is also used as a free-choice quantifier (like E. *-ever*, *any*) or as a universal quantifier (like E. *all*). In addition, all connectives are assigned to this type which directly express the notion of volition and/ or 'free choice' like Russ. *chot'a* (*chot'et'* 'wish, want') or Lat. *licet* 'it is permitted, although'.[8]

(18) E. *although*, *albeit*, *for all*, *all the same*, *however*, *anyway*; G. *bei all*, *allerdings*, *wiewohl* 'how-well'; Lat. *quamquam* ('however, cf. *quisquis* 'whoever'); Fr. *toutefois*, *tout ... que*, *(com)bienque*; Rom. *măcar că* ('be it'); South Am. Sp. *ojalá* (Arab. 'and may God will it'); Port. *conquanto* ('with how(ever) much'); Finn. *vaikka* (cf. *vaikka kuka* 'whoever', *kuka* 'who'); Hung. *habár* (cf. *ha* 'if', *ki* 'who', *bárki* 'whoever'); Russ. *vsë-taki* ('all-thus'), *chot'a* 'although' (cf. *chot'a bi* 'even if, take for example, say') Aceh. *bôh* 'even though, it does not matter if' (cf. *bôh ... bôh* 'no matter whether ... or whether'); Maasai *hoo* 'any, much as, although'; Vietn. *dû* 'whatever, however, whether, although'; Mokilese *mihnda ma* 'never mind, although, in any case'; Margi *kwá*, *kó* 'wh-ever, either ... or, although'.

(19) a. (Finn.) Tulen, vaikka olen sairas.
      'I'll come, although I am ill.'
   b. (Finn.) (A) Koska kirjoitat minulle kirjeen?
      'When will you write me?'
      (B) Vaikka heti.
      'If you like now.'

(iii) In many languages, concessive connectives are composed of a conditional (e.g. G. *wenn*), originally conditional (e.g. E. *though*, G. *ob*) or temporal connective (e.g. Fr. *quand*; Finn. *kun*) and/or an additive or emphatic focus particle like E. *also*, *even*, *too*.[9] The focus particle is typically affixed either to the verb (e.g. Dravidian, Tibetan, Korean) or to the conjunction (e.g. Finnish, Bengali, Indonesian). This type of connective, probably the most frequent in the world's languages, provides further evidence for the assumption that (concessive) conditionals are an important source for the development of concessive constructions. This assumption is also supported by the fact that concessive connectives co-occur with the subjunctive mood in many languages (e.g. French), although this co-occurrence is totally unmotivated for this 'factual' construction.

(20) E. *even though*, *even so*; G. *wenn-gleich*, *ob-schon*, *ob-wohl*, *ob-gleich*, *wenn* ... *auch* ('if – also/even/well'); Lat. *et-si* 'and/also if'; Gk. *ei-kai* 'and-if'; Fr. *quand même* ('when even'); Finn. *jos-kin* ('if-also'), *sitten-kin* ('then-also'); Serbo Croat. *i-ako* ('also-if'); Turk. *cond.* + *de* 'also'; Farsi *agarče* ('if-?'); Bengali *jodi-o* ('if-even'); Sanskrit *yadiapi* ('if-even/also'); Malayal. *-enkil-um* ('if-also'); Turk. conditional + *de* 'also'; Abkhaz conditional + *gʼə* 'even'; Zulu *noma* (*na 'even'* + *uma* 'if'); Ewe *né hã* ('and if'); Sotho *le ha* ('and/even if'); Turkana *tà* + conditional; Amharic *bɨ* ... *V* ... *m* ('if ... V ... also'); Jap. *keredomo* (*mo* 'also'); Korean V + (*i*)*ru* + *do* 'although' (*do/to* 'also'); Tibet. V + *yan* ('even, *both* ... *and*'); Lahu *thô* 'even if/though'; Tagal. *man* 'even, even though'; Indonesian *we* + *lau* + *pun* ('and if even'); etc.

(21) (Malayalam) maṛa peyyuka-āṇe-enkil-um, J. purattu pokunnu.
       rain fall+Inf -aux-if-even, out go
       'Even though it is raining, John is going out.'

   (iv) Concessive relations can be expressed in many languages by emphatically asserting the truth of one of a pair of clauses linked in some fashion. Expressions with the meaning 'true, fact, well, indeed' are frequently grammaticalized as concessive connectives. As a result of such processes of grammaticalization, former truth predicates and similarly emphatic predicates may become positionally restricted. (cf. E. *true* vs. the parenthetical expression *it is true*) and combinations of such connectives with a single clause typically no longer function as complete sentences, but require a continuation with *but q* (cf. E. *true p but* ...; G. *zwar p aber* ...). Furthermore, truncation, clipping or phonological attrition are frequently concomitant features of such grammaticalization (cf. G. *zwar* < *es ist wahr* 'it is true'). If connectives of this origin are affixed to conditional markers (e.g. G. *obzwar*, It. *sebbene*, Nahuatl *immanel*) members of our fourth type of connective are difficult to distinguish from the ones listed in (iii). Further evidence for a clear affinity between concessivity and an emphatic assertion of truth[10] is provided by the fact that emphatic adverbs and particles like *wohl*, *schon*, *ja* in German frequently occur in adversative or concessive contexts and typically acquire such a meaning:

(22) G. Zeit hat/hätte er wohl/schon/ja/durchaus, aber er will uns nicht helfen.
'He has got the time all right, but he doesn't want to help us.'

The following examples illustrate this affinity:[11]

(23) E. *true*; G. *zwar*, *gleichwohl*, *wiewohl* ('how + well'); D. *wel*, *evenwel*; Fr. *certes*, *avoir beau*; It. *sebbene*; Hung. *ugyan* 'true, well'; Finn. *kylläkai*; Swed. *visserligen*; Lat. *quidem* 'certainly, true, indeed, however'; Skt. *satyám* 'truely, indeed, true . . . but'; Nahuatl *in-tlá-nel*, *im-ma-nel* ('adjunctor + if + in fact/really'); Aceh. *bit* 'true, even so'; Korean *či* 'thing, fact, although'; Jap. *no ni* ('fact + essive'); Mandarin Adj/V *shi*. Adj/V 'it is Adj/V to be sure but . . .'; *gùrán* 'of course, to be sure, true . . . but'; Bah. Indonesian *sungguh-pun* 'true-even'.

(24) a. (It is) true he is old, but not helpless
   b. Sungguhpun badannja ketjil, tetapi amat kuat. (Kähler 1965: 181)
   true-even this body small   but   very strong
   'True his body is small,   but it   is very strong.'

(v) Members of the fifth type of concessive connective all imply remarkable co-occurrence or co-existence of two facts as part of their literal meaning. The implication may be expressed in different ways:

- by asserting that one eventuality *p* does not prevent, stand in the way of or affect another eventuality *q*. All connectives of this subgroup contain a negative affix as part of their formal make-up (e.g. Fr. *p n'empêche que* q)
- by asserting simultaneity of two eventualities or unhindered continuation of one eventuality (*q*) given another (*p*) (e.g. Sp. *aunque*)
- by asserting concomitance of two facts. Members of this subgroup contain the relevant counterpart of E. *with* (e.g. Turk. *bununla beraber*)

(25) E. *nevertheless*, *notwithstanding*, *just the same*, *even now*, *still*, *yet*, *while*, *regardless*; G. *dennoch*, *indessen* ('meanwhile'), *zugleich* 'at the same time, nevertheless', *unbeschadet* 'unharmed'; Norw. *enda* 'still, although'; Lat. *nihilominus*, *cum* 'when, although'; Fr. *cependant* ('meanwhile'), *encore que*, *toujours est-il que*, *n'empêche que* ('doesn't prevent'), *n'en V. moins pas* ('V not less for that'); Sp. *aunque* (*aun* 'still'), *con todo* ('with all'); Hung. *mégis* ('still-too'); Turk. *iken* 'while', 'though', *bununla beraber* ('together with this'); Jap. *nagara* 'while, although'; Vietn. *cɐ* 'continuing without interruption, definitely, in spite of'; Quileute *-t'e* 'with, although'; Mandarin *hài* 'still, nevertheless'; Tagalog *pa . . . na* ('already . . . still');

Indonesian *sekali* 'at the same time, once'; *sekali-pun* ('even')
'although'; Norw. *imidlertid* 'however'; Swed. *ändå* 'still (temp.),
nevertheless'.

These affinities between concessivity and other notional domains
manifested in the synchrony of a wide variety of languages provide
important information on the historical development of concessive
connectives in all languages, which is corroborated by historical evidence
available for Indo-European languages (cf. Klare 1958; König 1985a;
Harris forthcoming). Concessive connectives and constructions seem
to be quite generally based on expressions or constructions having
another, more basic meaning and use. Furthermore, they may naturally
derive from several sources. As a consequence, a wide variety of
concessive connectives may be available in a language.

Given that concessivity derives from other, more basic notions, at least
one of the following semantic changes may be assumed to have occurred
in all languages:

(i) a process of bleaching through which concrete notions like 'spite',
'contempt', 'ingratitude', originally only applicable to arguments
denoting human beings lost their concrete meaning and were
predicated of propositions thus developing the more abstract,
concessive meaning.

(26) a. He went out in spite of the rain.
b. In spite of the bad weather the harvest was quite good.

(ii) a process of strengthening through which an 'open' concessive
conditional assumed a factual character. This could be the result of
the antecedent being given in the preceding context (that is, p; even if
p, q) or of an emphatic factual particle (like E. *all*, G. *gleich*, *zwar*,
etc.) being added to the conditional marker (cf. König 1985a for a
more detailed discussion).

(27) a. (German) Ob p (oder nicht -p), q
'Even if (whether) p (or not -p), q'
b. Ob-gleich/schon/zwar p, q
'Even though p, q'

(iii) a process of conventionalization through which the conversational
implicatures carried by the assertion of simultaneity or unhindered
continuation came to be part of the conventional meaning of an
expression.

(28) It is midnight and he is still working. (temporal > concessive)

5 Explanation

The cross-linguistic generalizations made in the preceding section about concessive sentences are primarily concerned with connectives, their formal make-up, their historical development and the affinities to other semantic/pragmatic domains. In trying to account for these cross-linguistic facts, it seems advisable to stress the correlations between the various facts considered, and to use the term 'explanation' cautiously. The proposals to be made here are very tentative.

Correlations can certainly be established between the composite nature of concessive connectives, their relatively transparent etymology, their late development in the history of a language and their late acquisition. The latter two facts are yet another manifestation of the close parallels in phylogenetic and ontogenetic aspects of human development. And given these two facts it is not surprising that concessive connectives should have a more transparent formal make-up than markers of any other adverbial relation. Ultimately, however, there seems to be a more basic fact which has led to these properties: concessive relations are based on a prior experience of compatibility, correlation, connection or causality between two eventualities as expressed by other, conditional or causal, connectives. The assertion of two facts against the background assumption of their general incompatibility must be based on prior knowledge of compatibilities and connections. And it is this derived character of concessive meaning that is reflected in the form of the connectives, and in their development and acquisition. This derived character is further reflected in the fact that concessive relations are a dead-end street for any kind of interpretative enrichment.

The most important cross-linguistic generalization to be explained in this section concerns the affinities between concessivity and other notional domains that manifest themselves in the form of the relevant connectives. The cross-linguistic evidence presented in this paper suggests that concessive relations are based on such concepts as 'free-choice quantification', 'conditionality', emphatic assertion of 'co-occurrence' or such relational concepts like 'spite' or 'contempt' in the same way that the concept of existence is closely tied to that of location (cf. Lyons 1967). The 'explanation' that is offered here for these affinities takes the form of general principles of semantic change. These postulated principles of semantic change, on the other hand, are seen as the result of general, pragmatic principles of language use and interpretative enrichment.

Very little needs to be said about the first group of connectives, listed in (16) E. *in spite of*, etc. which directly express the notions of dissonance and conflict and derive from predicates originally only attributable to arguments denoting human agents or experiencers. As a result of a general process of 'bleaching' leading from concrete to more abstract meanings (cf. Kronasser's Law; Kronasser 1952) these relational concepts were also applied to propositions thus giving rise to concessive connectives.

The second and third group of connectives, listed in (18) E. *although* . . . and (20) E. *even though* . . . can be assumed to be the result of essentially the same semantic changes. Both types of connectives show that concessive sentences may derive from concessive conditionals. The properties shared by these two types of sentences that make this change plausible, as well as the differences between them have already been briefly described: Concessive conditionals relate a series of protases, specified either by a disjunction, by a universal or free-choice quantifier or by a scalar expression (for example, by a scalar particle like *even*) to an apodosis. Just like genuine concessive sentences, they typically entail their apodosis, though not their protasis or 'antecedent'.[12] Another property that concessive conditionals share with concessive sentences is that they, too, imply a general dissonance or incompatibility between one of the conditions specified in the antecedent (that is, the extreme case) and the consequent. Thus the only change that has to take place in order to derive concessive sentences from concessive conditionals concerns the status of the protasis: one of the set of conditions specified in the protasis of a concessive conditional has to be selected and it has to assume a factual character.

Now it is a well-known fact that concessive conditionals and indeed conditionals in general may assume such a factual character if the antecedent is explicitly given in the preceding context or is assumed to be given due to general background knowledge. The following examples of 'resumptive' and 'thematic' conditionals illustrate this point (cf. Haiman 1978: 29; Akatsuka 1986; Funk 1985: 366ff):

(29) a. (A) I was in France for a year.
         (B) If you were in France for a year, your French must be excellent
     b. If I seemed unkind, it was because I was distracted.
     c. If this is in your idea of solving the problem, I might as well go.

(30) It was the loneliness of the neighbourhood . . . that kept the house next to theirs empty (p) . . . The house stood two hundred yards from the Bartleby's and Alicia liked looking out of the window now and then even if it was empty.[13] (q, even if p)

In cases like (29a) and (30) the protasis is given in the preceding context and is thus entailed by the dialogue as a whole. As a result, the concessive conditional in (30) becomes indistinguishable from a concessive sentence.

The connectives listed in (18) and (20) can thus be assumed to be the result of the following process: originally markers of a construction that could be used to express either a concessive conditional relationship or under specific conditions also concessive relations were frequently used in factual contexts like (29) or (30). This factuality gradually came to be associated with the connectives themselves, which developed into genuine concessive connectives. In addition to being the result of such a re-interpretation in certain contexts, concessive sentences may also have developed by a process called 'strengthening' in the relevant literature (cf. König 1985a, c for a more detailed discussion). This term refers to the introduction of emphatic particles like E. *all* (*be it* + *all*> *albeit*; *all* + *though*> *although*), G. *wohl, zwar, gleich, schon* or Fr. *tout* into a (concessive) conditional protasis, which also results in a factual interpretation for the clause. As a consequence of the development of a formally marked concessive construction, the originally versatile concessive conditionals were restricted to non-factual contexts.

The development of the fifth group of connectives, listed in (25) E. *nevertheless* ... from expressions originally asserting remarkable co-occurrence is based on pragmatic principles of interpretative enrichment and the conventionalization of an originally pragmatic inference. Even though essentially the same principle of enrichment seems to be involved in all cases, it is easier to illustrate its operation separately for the different subgroups of this fifth type. The basic principle seems to be that an emphatic assertion of co-occurrence of two eventualities is taken to be in some way remarkable and thus to be in conflict with what is generally known about the compatibility of the two eventualities in question.

Being pragmatic and perhaps also conversational in nature, these principles of informational enrichment can also be observed in the synchrony of a language. In the following English examples a basically temporal meaning ('simultaneity') is augmented to a concessive one:

(31) a. It is not easy to find examples of social services that are of general social benefit and, at the same time, not costly.
    b. Even as it admits of a serious pollution problem, East Germany is substituting cheap brown coal for imported oil.

A wide variety of such pragmatic inference patterns that go from a weaker to a stronger, informationally richer, proposition are described in the relevant literature (cf. Atlas and Levinson 1981, Horn 1985a and Levinson 1983 for more detailed discussion). Among the better known examples we find the classical fallacy *post hoc ergo propter hoc* (p and then q > q because p) and the principle called 'conditional perfection' by Geis and Zwicky (1971), according to which the assertion of a conditional 'if p then q' typically invites the inference 'if ~p, ~q' or equivalently 'only if p, q'. It has often been assumed in such discussions that it is not possible to give a Gricean account of such principles of informational enrichment in terms of conversational implicatures, and therefore labels like 'invited inferences' or 'bridging inferences' have been proposed. The reason is that such interpretative augmentation seems to be in conflict with the other well-established cases of conversational implicatures and the maxims they are based on, in particular with the so-called scalar or clausal implicatures derived from the first maxim of quantity. This maxim requires the speaker to be as informative as s/he possibly can and thus gives rise to the following standard implicatures: If a speaker asserts a proposition W that can be paired with a stronger proposition S such that S entails W, then the use of W implicates the denial of the applicability of S. Thus *Some of my friends are Arabs* would normally be taken to implicate *Not all of my friends are Arabs*.

In their discussion of this conflict and the apparent impossibility of basing principles of informational enrichment on any of the Gricean maxims, Atlas and Levinson (1981) suggested adding a 'principle of informativeness' to those maxims, which roughly says that the 'best' interpretation of an utterance is the most informative one consistent with what is not controversial. Their 'convention of non-controversiality' furthermore includes the assumption that referents and situations have stereotypical properties. Building on this discussion, L. Horn (1985a) has recently proposed a fundamental reassessment of Grice's conversational maxims and the schema of pragmatic inferences derived from them. Horn suggests that these maxims should be seen as one manifestation of an overarching Principle of Least Effort as formulated by Zipf (1949). This principle has different consequences for the two basic roles in communication (that is, speaker and hearer), which are in extreme conflict: seen from a hearer's perspective this principle requires that a speaker should say as much as s/he can. This is essentially Grice's first maxim of Quantity, which Horn dubs the 'Q Principle'. Seen from the speaker's perspective, least effort means that s/he should say no more than s/he must. This speaker-based 'R Principle', which according to Horn summarizes all of the other maxims except Quality, induces lower-bounding implicata and gives rise to informational enrichment such as we find in (31) and also in the development of the connectives listed in (25). Thus conversational implicatures are seen as the result of the interaction of two basic and competing principles: the Q Principle and the R Principle.[14]

Having established that the inference patterns relevant for the development of the connectives in (25) can be based on conversational principles, we can briefly return to the question of how these interferences are actually derived. As was already briefly mentioned, an assertion of co-occurrence of two eventualities is not highly informative or relevant in most cases unless this co-occurrence is in some way remarkable due to a general incompatibility between the two eventualities in question. That is, there are many co-existing eventualities which are just not worth pointing out. So it is quite plausible that on hearing an assertion of this sort, the hearer will look for an enriched interpretation that is consistent with background knowledge. And at this point stereotypical properties of situations, specifically assumptions about their general compatibility or incompatibility will enter the picture.

The affinity between simultaneity and concessivity can perhaps be regarded as one manifestation of an even more general connection between an assertion of identity and concessivity. Focus particles or adverbs that emphatically assert the identity of an argument in two different propositions, like G. *eben*, *gerade*, Finn. *juuri* or D. *net* frequently acquire a concessive interpretation. Such an inference can also be observed in the following sentence with adjectival *very*, where the use of this adjective points to the conflict between the two propositions:

(32) It is generally known that the seeds of the Shah's destruction were sown in the very phenomenon which he appears to have thought would save him.

Note also that E. *even* has changed its meaning from an element basically asserting identity (cf. (33a)) into an expression characterizing its focus value as an extreme, highly unlikely value for a given propositional schema (cf. (33b)):

(33) a. What you will have it named, even that it is. (Shakespeare, *Shrew*, III, iv)
     b. Fred reads even Chaucer.

Finally, the formal identity of emphatic reflexives and scalar focus particles like E. *even* in many languages (e.g. G. *selbst*, Ir. *féin*, Fr. *même*) points in the same direction (cf. Plank 1979).

Concerning the development of the fifth subgroup of connectives, listed in (25), that is, the connectives that assert remarkable co-occurrence by denying a damaging influence of one fact on another, it must also be assumed that the pragmatics of negation played an important role in their development. Several linguists, notably Givón (1978), have drawn attention to the marked character of negative sentences as opposed to the corresponding affirmative ones. According to Givón, negative sentences typically presuppose a context in which the corresponding affirmative proposition has been asserted or at least entertained. Although this formulation might be somewhat too strong (cf. Fretheim 1984), some condition of this kind seems to play a role in the use of the connectives with a negative affix in (25). An assertion of the type 'p nevertheless q' suggests that the contradictory assumption ('if p then normally ~q') has been entertained and functions as backdrop to this assertion. The effect of this principle is clearly noticeable in sentences of type (10a):

(10) a. This house is no less comfortable because it dispenses with air-conditioning.

That conversational implicatures become part of the conventional meaning of an expression or construction is again a very widespread and general phenomenon. It is a well-known fact that causal connectives frequently develop from temporal ones denoting a temporal sequence (cf. Horn 1973 or Abraham 1976 for examples). An example of a

Q-based, scalar implicature that has become conventionalized is provided by the expression *not* p *until* t_1 or *not* p *for* t_1 in English and their counterparts in other languages (e.g. Spanish). If we assume, as is generally done, that *until* t_1 takes wide scope over the negation in such constructions (cf. Mittwoch 1977) and that *until* is used in an 'exclusive' sense much like *before* (cf. Karttunen 1974), the original meaning of this construction can simply be paraphrased by '(not p) before t_1'. In other words, a sentence like (34) asserts that a state of not being awake obtained up to (but excluding) a point-in-time t_1.

(34) The princess didn't wake up until 8 o'clock.

Now, contexts like these define a Horn scale for points-in-time <8.10, 8.09, ... 8.01, 8.00>, that is, a scale that is ordered according to strength of information, in which later times rank higher than earlier ones. This ranking is a consequence of the fact that a sentence like (35a) clearly entails (35b):

(35) a. The princess did not wake up until 8.10 a.m.
      b. The princess did not wake up until 8.00 a.m.

Given such a scale, the usual upper bounding implicatures came into play: The assertion of (34) implicates that the state in question did not continue up to a higher value than the one given (cf. Levinson 1983: 132ff):

(36) It is not true of a later time than eight that the princess did not wake up until then.

And this implicature together with the entailments of (34) and the exclusive sense of *until* ultimately implies that there was a change of state at 8 o'clock. This originally conversational implicature is now part of the meaning of *not ... until* in English, which can no longer be cancelled as in the parallel construction of German.

  Finally, a few words have to be said about the fourth group of connectives, listed in (23) E. *true* etc. Again, it seems possible to give a Gricean analysis for the development of this group of connectives. As a consequence of the R Principle ('Say no more than you must') there is no point in emphasizing the truth of an 'antecedent' proposition unless this truth or the significance of this proposition as an argument is somehow called into question. An emphatic assertion of the truth of some proposition 'p' may be called for because of a principled dissonance between 'p' and a following 'q'.

  Seen from another perspective, concessive connectives of type (23) can be regarded as instances where the typical use that is made of such connectives in discourse has left a clear mark on their form. If such sentences are typically used in situations of partial agreement (S accepts premise and warrant) and partial disagreement (S rejects conclusion), then it is not surprising that the agreement part is asserted with great emphasis. In situations of this kind principles of politeness and preference ordering or, more generally, principles of maintaining equity play an important role. Disagreement is typically preceded by token agreement (cf. Levinson 1983: 334) and the same principle that provides the basis for this sequencing can be assumed to have played a role in the development of the connectives listed in (23).

6 Conclusion

Concessive connectives exhibit a high degree of similarity across languages in their formal make-up, their historical origins and development, and the affinities they show with respect to other notional domains. These common properties, which provide the basis for a classification into five different types, are motivated by the meaning of concessive sentences and the functions they fulfill in discourse. The earlier meanings from which concessive connectives typically derive express one of the essential ingredients of concessivity: the concomitance of two facts, the general incompatibility of the relevant eventualities and the truth of the two clauses linked by the connective. The development of a genuine concessive meaning and its differentiation from related meanings is motivated by general principles of language use and interpretative augmentation. The complex formal make-up of concessive connectives, their late acquisition and late development as well as the inability of the sentences they introduce to undergo further processes of interpretative augmentation reflects the derived character of concessive meaning, which is based on a prior experience of correlations between eventualities.

Notes

The research that this paper is based on was carried out while the author was a fellow at the Netherlands Institute for Advanced Study (September–December 1983 and August 1984–January 1985). The support of this institute is gratefully acknowledged. I am grateful to Thorstein Fretheim, John Hawkins, Heather Holmback and Sandra Thompson for criticisms of an early version of this paper. Furthermore, I would like to thank all of those who provided me with interesting data on their native language, notably A. Kärnä (Finnish), T. Fretheim (Norwegian), T. K. Zee (Mandarin), C. S. Philipose (Malayalam), M. Dobrenov (Hungarian), S. Dee (Bengali), D. Kunene (Sesotho) and D. Coşkontuna (Turkish).
1 The following languages are included in this sample: Arabic,Abkhaz, Acehnese, Acoma, Bengali, Cambodian, Cahuila, Danish, Dutch, Diyari, Duala, English, Ewe, Estonian, Finnish, French, Fore, Farsi, Guarani, German, Greek, Hebrew, Hindi, Hungarian, Bahasa Indonesian, Indonesian, Irish, Japanese,

Jacaltec, Korean, Kannada, Kiryawanda, !Kung, Latvian, Lahu, Latin, Manam, Mongolian, Malayalam, Margi, Maasai, Mundari, Nahuatl, Norwegian, Polish, Portuguese, Quechua, Quileute, Russian, Romanian, Sanskrit, Spanish, Sesotho, Susu, Sérère, Sierra Miwok, Swedish, Serbo-Croat, Swahili, Tamil, Toba Batak, Tagalog, Tibetan, Turkana, Tarascan, Thai, Turkish, Usan, Vietnamese, Yoruba, Zulu.

2 'Eventuality' is here used as a cover term for events, processes and states (cf. Bach 1986).

3 This analysis is meant to capture the traditional insight that concessive relations are in some kind of opposition to causal ones. According to Burnham (1911: 2), to give only one example, concessive connectives are used 'when the reason, the circumstance is admitted, but the opposite of its natural consequence is asserted' and thus express 'blocked or inoperative cause'. Hermodsson (1978: 59ff) has even suggested that the traditional term 'concessive' should be replaced by 'incausal'. This view, however, can only be justified for certain, perhaps prototypical, uses of concessive connectives. The adverb *normally* in (5) is to play the same role as the 'G' operator postulated for generic sentences in Stump (1985).

4 Concessive conditionals of type (6a) are closely related to polar interrogatives, just as those of type (6b) are closely related to wh-interrogatives, a relatedness that is often reflected in the form that these sentences take (cf. König 1986 for a more detailed discussion of concessive conditionals).

5 As far as sentences of type (6c) are concerned, this is only the case under certain conditions (cf. Bennett 1982).

6 This function is typically fulfilled in English by the conjunctional adverb *though*, by expressions like *mind you*, *but then*, *I hasten to add*, etc.

7 Members of this group are, of course, difficult to identify in languages where little or no historical and etymological information is available.

8 Cf. Haiman (1974); Haiman was the first to draw attention to this connection between 'volition' and concessivity.

9 There is good evidence for the assumption that the category of focus particles ('focusing adjuncts') is a universal one. The distinction between 'addition' or 'inclusion' of alternative values for a given propositional schema (E. *also*, *too*, *even*) vs. 'restriction' or 'exclusion' of such values (E. *only*, *merely*) seems to be expressible in all languages. Focus particles may either be realized as independent words, as in most European languages, or as affixes, as in Dravidian. The particles that play a role in the formation of concessive conjuncts are the 'additive' ones. The restrictive particles, on the other hand, may exhibit a marked .affinity with adversative conjunctions. 'But' and 'only' can be expressed by the same lexical element in many languages (cf. E. *but*; D. *maar*; Nahuatl *zan*; Thai *téɛ*).

10 This affinity is so noticeable and pervasive that analytical philosophers like Strawson tried to explicate the notion of truth with the help of concessive sentences (David Holdcroft, personal communication).

11 Concessive connectives that are derived from causal ones through the addition of a focus particle (e.g. Mundari *te-o* 'because – even'; Indonesian *sementang* 'because' *sementang-pun* 'although' ('because – even')) can also be assigned to this type. Concessives of this make-up give overt expression to (i) the factual character that concessive sentences share with causal ones and (ii) the principled incompatibility between the two relevant propositions.

12 Concessive conditionals of type (4a) (whether p or ~p, q) do of course entail their antecedent 'p or ~p', but this construction does not play any role for the development of concessive sentences.

13   From P. Highsmith, *A Suspension of Mercy* (Harmondsworth: Penguin, 1978), p. 6.

14   This distinction is analogous to that drawn by von der Gabelentz (*Die Sprachwissenschaft*) between two competing forces in the historical development of languages: the tendency towards ease of articulation and the tendency towards distinctness (cf. Lehmann 1982: 3ff).

References

Abraham, W. (1976) 'Die Rolle der Trueschlüsse in der Diachronie van Satzkonnektoren'. In H. D. Pohl and N. Salnikow (eds) *Opuscula Slavica et Linguistica*. Festschrift für A. Issatschenko, Klapenfurt.

Akatsuka. N. (1986) 'Conditionals are discourse-bound'. In Traugott et al. (1986).

Atlas, J. D. and S. C. Levinson (1981) 'If-clefts, informativeness and logical form: radical pragmatics'. In: P. Cole (ed.), *Radical Pragmatics*. New York: Academic Press.

Bach, E. (1986) 'The algebra of events'. *Linguistics and Philosophy*, 9, 5–16.

Bennett, J. (1982) 'Even if'. Linguistics and Philosophy, 5, 403–18.

Borkin, A. (1980) 'On some conjuncts signalling dissonance in written expository English'. *Studia Anglica Posnanensia*, 12, 47–59.

Bowerman, M. (1986) 'First steps in acquiring conditionals'. In Traugott et al. (1986).

Braunwald, S. R. (1985) 'The development of connectives'. *Journal of Pragmatics*, 9, 513–25.

Burnham, J. M. (1911) *Concessive Constructions in OE Prose*. New York: Yale Studies in English.

Fretheim, T. (1984) 'Denials and other negatives'. In Brendemoen et al. (eds), *Riepmočala. Essays in Honour of Knut Bergsland*. Oslo: Novus.

Funk, W.-P. (1985) 'On the semantic typology of conditional sentences'. *Folia Linguistica*, 19, 365–414.

Geis, M. L. and A. M. Zwicky (1971) 'On invited inferences'. *Linguistic Inquiry*, 11, 361–6.

Givón, T. (1978) 'Negation in language: pragmatics, functions, ontology'. In P. Cole (ed.), *Syntax and Semantics*, vol. 9. New York: Academic Press.

Haiman, J. (1974) 'Concessives, conditionals, and verbs of volition'. *Foundations of Language*, 11, 341–60.

Haiman, J. (1978) 'Conditionals are topics'. *Language*, 54, 564–89.

—— and S. Thompson (eds) (forthcoming) *Clause Combining in Grammar and Discourse*. Amsterdam: John Benjamins.

Halliday, M. A. K. and R. Hasan (1976) *Cohesion in English*. London: Longman.

Harris, M. (forthcoming) 'Concessive clauses in English and Romance'. To appear in Haiman and Thompson.

Herman, J. (1963) *La Formation du Système Roman de Conjonctions de Subordination*. Berlin: Akademie Verlag.

Hermodsson, L. (1978) *Semantische Strukturen der Satzgefüge im kausalen und konditionalen Bereich*. Uppsala: Almquist & Wiksell.

Horn, L. R. (1985a) 'Toward a new taxonomy for pragmatic inference: Q-based and R-based implicature'. In D. Schiffrin (ed.), *Meaning. Form and Use in Context*. Washington, DC: Georgetown University Press.

—— (1985b) 'Metalinguistic negation and pragmatic ambiguity'. *Language*, 61, 121–74.

Kähler, H. (1965) *Grammatik der Bahasa Indonésia*. Wiesbaden: Otto Harrowitz.

Karttunen, L. (1974) 'Until'. *Proceedings of the Chicago Linguistic Society 10*, University of Chicago, 10, 284–97.

and S. Peters (1979) 'Conventional implicature'. In C. Oh. and D. A. Dinneen (eds), *Syntax and Semantics*, vol. 11, *Presupposition*. New York: Academic Press.

Klare, J. (1958) *Entstehung and Entwicklung der Konzessiven Konjunktion im Französischen*. Berlin: Akademie Verlag.

Klein, J. (1980) 'Die Konzessivrelation als argumentations-theoretisches Problem. *Zeithschrift für Germanistische Linguistik*, 8, 154–69.

König, E. (1985a) 'On the history of concessive connectives in English. Diachronic and synchronic evidence'. *Lingua*, 66, 1–19.

(1985b) 'Konzessive Konjunktionen'. To appear in A. v. Stechow and D. Wunderlich (eds), *Handbuch der Semantik*. Königstein: Athenäum.

(1985c) 'Where do concessives come from?' In J. Fisiak (ed.), *Historical Semantics, Historical Word Formation*. Berlin: Mouton.

(1986) 'Conditionals, concessive conditionals and concessives: areas of contrast, overlap and neutralization'. In Traugott et al. (1986).

and P. Eisenberg (1984) 'Zur Pragmatik von Konzessivsätzen'. In G. Stickel (ed.), *Pragmatik in der Grammatik*. Düsseldorf: Schwann.

and J. Van der Auwera (forthcoming) 'Clause integration in German and Dutch conditionals, concessive conditionals, and concessives'. To appear in Haiman and Thompson.

Kronasser, H. (1952) *Handbuch der Semasiologie*. Heidelberg: Carl Winter.

Lehmann, C. (1982) *Thoughts on Grammaticalization*. Cologne: Arbeiten des Kölner Universalien Projekts, 48.

Lerch, E. (1929) *Historische Französische Syntax* II. Leipzig: Reisland.

Levinson, S. (1983) *Pragmatics*. Cambridge: Cambridge University Press.

Lyons, J. (1967) 'A note on possessive, existential and locative sentences'. *Foundations of Language*, 3, 390–6.

Mensing, O. (1981) 'Untersuchungen über die Syntax der Concessivsätze im Alt- und Mittelhochdeutschen'. Doctoral diss., Kiel.

Mittwoch, A. (1977) 'Negative sentences with *until*'. *CLS*, 13, 410–17.

Plank, F. (1979) 'Exklusivierung, Identifizierung, relationale Auszeichnung. Variationen zu einem semantisch-pragmatischen Thema'. In J. Rosengren (ed.), *Sprache und Pragmatik*. Lunder germanische Forschungen 48. Lund: Gleerup.

Quirk, R. (1954) *The Concessive Relation in OE Poetry*. New Haven, Conn.: Yale University Press.

Reichenbach, H. (1947) *Elements of Symbolic Logic*. New York: The Free Press.

Saebø K. (1986) 'Causal and purposive clauses'. In A. v. Stechow and D. Wunderlich (eds). *Handbuch der Semantik*. Königstein: Athenäum.

Stump, G. T. (1985) *The Semantic Variability of Absolute Constructions*. Dordrecht: Reidel.

Toulmin, S. (1958) *The Uses of Argument*. Cambridge: Cambridge University Press.

Traugott, E. C. ter Meulen, A., Reilly, J. S. and Ferguson C. A. (eds) (1986) *On Conditionals* Cambridge: Cambridge University Press.

Zipf, G. K. (1949) *Human Behavior and the Principle of Least Effort*. Cambridge, Mass.: Addison-Wesley.

CHAPTER 7

A Discourse Approach to the Cross-Linguistic Category 'Adjective'

Sandra A. Thompson

1 Introduction

Hopper and Thompson (1984) addressed the problem of a possible discourse explanation for the way in which the linguistic categories of Noun and Verb manifest themselves in actual language use. In this paper I will be concerned with the question of categorization of 'property concepts', that is, those concepts referring to properties, qualities or characteristics of referents.

In English, there is a fairly close correspondence between this set of concepts and the linguistic category of 'adjective', but it is well known that this is by no means the case for many other languages. In his justifiably celebrated 1970 paper, published in 1977, Dixon explores the question 'how does it [that is, a language with either no Adjective class at all or only a small non-productive minor class of Adjective] express concepts that are expressed through adjectives in languages, like English, which do have this major class' (p. 20)?

What I would like to do in this paper is to take a close look at Dixon's answer to this question, and supplement it with some findings of my own. I will then propose a discourse explanation for these findings. This research can be thus be seen as a contribution to the study of 'natural grammar', the study of what communicative factors are responsible for the design of grammars.

2 Dixon's Survey

Dixon introduces the notion of 'semantic type', suggesting that 'the lexical items of a language fall into a number of "semantic types" (each item belonging to just one type) ... Each semantic type has, in a particular language, certain "norm" syntactic and morphological properties. *Each* member of the type exhibits the norm properties. In addition, there will be a number of "extensional" properties, each applying only to *certain* members of the type' (p. 25, emphasis original). (Today such a description might be discussed in terms of the notion of 'prototype'.)

Dixon relates the notion of 'semantic type' to linguistic categories in the following way: he assumes that each 'semantic type' has a basic or 'norm' connection with a single part of speech (p. 27), and that since

> all languages appear to have Noun and Verb but some lack a major class Adjective, ... some semantic types must be associated with different parts of speech in different languages ... MOTION, AFFECT, GIVING, CORPOREAL [e.g. *laugh*, *sneeze*], and other types seem almost always to be classed together – this is the class that is in all languages called Verb. OBJECTS, KIN, and other types are almost always classed together – this is the class that is in all languages called Noun. (p. 28).[1]

Later he suggests 'what it means to say that a language has "a class of adjectives". This is a set of lexical items, distinguished on morphological and syntactic grounds from the universal classes Noun and Verb' (pp. 62–3).

Because Dixon assumes that each semantic type has, in a given language, its own 'normal' grammatical properties, he proposes to isolate the universal Adjective types by looking at the 'basic members' of the Adjective class just in English, and then to investigate their linguistic category affiliations in Adjective-deficient languages. The types which emerge, based on semantic, syntactic and morphological criteria, are these:

1 DIMENSION – *big*, *little*, *long*, *wide*, ...
2 PHYSICAL PROPERTY – *hard*, *heavy*, *smooth*, ...
3 COLOUR
4 HUMAN PROPENSITY – *jealous*, *happy*, *clever*, *generous*, *proud*, ...
5 AGE – *new*, *young*, *old*, ...
6 VALUE – *good*, *bad*, *pure*, *delicious*, ...
7 SPEED – *fast*, *slow*, *quick*, ...

For the remainder of this paper, I will take these seven types of concepts, which express properties of entities, as definitional for the term 'Property Concept'. That is, if a word expresses one of these types of properties in a language, I will call it a Property Concept Word.

Dixon's findings, based on a non-random sample of seventeen languages,[2] are summarized in (1):

(1) Languages may have a category of Adjectives which can be identified on language-internal morpho-syntactic grounds. No matter how small or restricted this category is, it is likely to include at least these four

types of Property Concepts in Dixon's list above: DIMENSION, COLOR, AGE, and VALUE.

(2) Whether or not there is a category of Adjectives, the words expressing Property Concepts tend to fall into categories which either share many properties with the class of Nouns, or many properties with the class of Verbs.

My own research, based on a further sampling (again not random) of some forty languages, has confirmed these findings.

The problem, then, is this: It seems to be a fact that the distinction between *Nouns* and *Verbs* itself is a language universal, where largely the same set of concepts are found in each of these categories from language to language (see Givón 1979, 1984), Hopper and Thompson 1984, Jacobsen 1979, Schachter 1985 and references cited in these works for discussion). Independently of whether or not there is an identifiable class of Adjective, the question which then arises is:

Why should a given set of concepts, namely Property Concepts, be distributed across these two quite distinct lexical categories, namely Noun and Verb, in the world's languages (as opposed, say, to being *exclusively* treated by grammars of languages as a subclass of either Noun or Verb, or as a separate class of Adjective)?

Before considering the discourse proposal, let us briefly consider some of the sorts of evidence that lead to these conclusions.

First, there are languages in which Property Concepts form a semantic subclass of the category Verb. For example, in Acehnese (northern Sumatra) (Durie 1985), there are a number of pieces of evidence showing that Property Concepts do not form a separate lexical category from Verbs. First, they may take optional Undergoer cross-referencing just as other non-controlled Verbs do:

(2) gopnyan sakêt =geuh
    3   sick =UNDGOER
    's/he's sick'

(3) gopnyan rhët =geuh
    3   fall=UNDGOER
    's/he is falling'

Second, they may occur with inchoative *ka*, just as verbs do:

(4) gopnyan   ka   sakêt =geuh
    3   INCHO sick =UNDGOER
    's/he's gotten sick'

(5) gopnyan ka   geu=woe
     3   INCHO AG=return
     's/he has already returned'

Third, any Verb can be used attributively with no morpho-syntactic ado:

(6) aneuk muda nyan
     child   young that
     'that young child'

(7) ureueng pula padè nyan
     person   plant rice   that
     'that person planting rice'

Finally, many non-controlled Verbs may take *that* 'very':

(8) ureueng nyan caröng that
     person   that clever very
     'that person is very clever'

(9) lôn galak that keu   jih
     1   like   very DAT 3
     'I like him/her very much'

     Other languages in my sample for which similar arguments can be made include:

Aghem (Bantoid) (Hyman 1979)
Chinese (Chao 1968, Li and Thompson 1981)
Lakhota (Buechel 1939)
Noni (Cameroon, Beboid Bantu) (Hyman 1981)
Thai (Noss 1964)
Turkana (E. Nilotic) (Dimmendaal 1983)
W. Makian (Papuan) (Voorhoeve 1982)
Wappo (California)
the Austronesian languages: Samoan (Marsack 1962), Indonesian (Mac-
     Donald 1976), Mokilese (Harrison 1976), Palauan (Josephs 1975),
     Ulithian (Sohn and Bender 1973), Woleaian (Sohn 1975), Kusaiean
     (Lee 1975) and Wolio (Indonesia) (Anceaux 1952).[3]

That is, in each of these languages, whether or not a class of Adjectives can be identified on language-internal distributional grounds, Property Concept Words share many features with verbs.
     Second, it is also well-known that there are a number of languages in which Property Concept Words pattern very similarly to Nouns. For example, in Finnish, Nouns and Property Concept Words have much in common: they are inflected in the same way, for number and case, and

they take the same possessive suffixes and enclitic pragmatic particles (Karlsson 1983: 22). Thus, in the sentence:

(10) Auto   on   sininen
     car:NOM COP blue:NOM
     'the car is blue'

the form *sininen* 'blue' inflects for case and takes the copula, just as a Noun would:

(11) iso–ssa   auto–ssa
     big–INESS car –INESS
     'in the big car'

(12) Pekka   on   mies
     P.:NOM COP man:NOM
     'Pekka is a man'

   Similarly, in a language with gender or noun class, such as Diyari (Austin 1981), spoken in South Australia, as well as a number of Indo-European and African languages, there is a class 'nominal', which can be said to subsume 'Nouns' and 'Adjectives' as subcategories, with common morpho-syntactic categories, such as case, number and gender or noun class, though of course Noun and Adjective will always be kept distinct by the fact that only Nouns, but never Adjectives, are subcategorized for inherent gender.
   Other languages in my sample for which analogous arguments can be made include:

Arabic
Asmat (Papuan) (Voorhoeve 1965)
Bantu languages
the Chadic languages Hausa (Cowan and Schuh 1976) and Margi
   (Hoffman 1963)
Dyirbal (Dixon 1972)
the Dravidian languages Kannada (M. Nadkarni, personal communica-
   tion) and Malayalam (George 1971)
Fore (E. New Guinea) (Scott 1978)
Israeli Hebrew (Rosen 1977)
the Indo-European languages Persian (Elwell-Sutton 1979), Polish
   (Laskowski 1979), Icelandic (Glendening 1961), Latin, Dutch
   (Donaldson 1981) and German (Schulz and Griesbach 1960)
Kalkatungu (Pama-Nyungan, Australia) (Blake 1979)
Quechua (Adelaar 1977)
Tagalog (Schachter and Otanes 1972).

However, while both of these patterns exist, that is, Property Concepts sharing many features with Verbs and with Nouns, they do not necessarily characterize languages, since it also happens, as in some West African languages (for example, Kusaal (Gur) (Ladusaw 1985) and Yoruba (Kwa) (F. Serzisco, personal communication)) or Japanese (Y. Koide, personal communication), for example, that within a given language some Property Concepts will be categorized with features shared with Nouns, while others will have features shared with Verbs.

Finally, of course, there are languages, such as English, Fula (Arnott 1970), Jacaltec (Craig 1977), Cherokee (Lindsey and Scancarelli 1985) and Manam (Austronesian) (Lichtenberk 1983), in which a class of Adjective can be identified which shares few or no obvious properties with either Nouns or Verbs.

The fact remains, however, that cross-linguistically, Property Concepts may show up as either Nouns or Verbs (see Dixon 1977 and Schachter 1985 for further discussion).

But why should this be so? This is the question which I will try to answer in the rest of this paper.

3 Time Stability

Givón (1979, 1984) has suggested a semantic factor underlying the categorization of cognitive 'percepts', namely, time stability. 'Experiences ... which stay relatively *stable* over time ... tend to be lexicalized in human language as nouns ... At the other extreme of the lexical-phenomenological scale, one finds experiential clusters denoting *rapid changes* in the state of the universe ... languages tend to lexicalize them as verbs' [1984: 51–2, emphasis original). According to Givón, the class Adjective, for languages which have it, occupies 'the middle of the time-stability scale' (1984: 52). But there are two problems with this explanation.

First, while time stability may be involved in distinguishing prototypical exemplars of the categories Noun and Verb in the world's languages, I question its relevance for the category Adjective, since, as Givón admits, the 'prototypical adjectival qualities' are 'those of *stable* physical qualities such as size, shape, texture, color, taste, or smell' (1984: 53, emphasis mine). In fact, all of Dixon's seven 'semantic types' which characterize the class of Adjectives in English, except possibly SPEED, denote relative stable characteristics. Thus, it does not appear to be true that 'adjectives occupy the middle of the time-stability scale'.

The second problem with the time-stability explanation for the categorization of Property Concepts is that it makes the wrong prediction about a particular set of morphosyntactic facts. That is, if 'Adjectives' indeed occupied the 'middle of the time-stability scale', then we would predict that in languages where 'Adjectives' are a subclass of Verbs, they should exhibit features related to the fact that they are more time-stable than Verbs; similarly, we would also predict that in languages where 'Adjectives' are a subclass of Nouns, they should exhibit features related to the fact that they are less time-stable than Nouns. Now, while support for the former prediction is abundant, support for the latter prediction is not.

Thus, as a subclass of Verbs, Property Concepts often exhibit morphosyntactic evidence of their *stativity*, their greater time-stability when compared to prototypical Verbs; they are often constrained not to occur with certain tense-aspect morphemes, for example.

But the primary way in which Property Concepts can be identified as a subclass of Nouns different from prototypical Nouns is, as mentioned above, that their gender categories are derived, while those of Nouns are typically inherent. I do not see a way to relate this fact to the lower degree of time-stability of Property Concepts as compared to Nouns. Rather, it has to do with the use to which Property Concepts are put by speakers.

Givón's semantic explanation in terms of time-stability, then, does not help me to explain the facts given in (1). In fact, while I believe that such semantic features as the stativity of verb-like Property Concepts have significant morphosyntactic consequences, I think that the explanation for the specific cross-linguistic facts in (1) may not be found in *semantics* at all. I suggest instead that a satisfying account of the lexical categorization of Property Concepts in the world's languages can only be stated in terms of the *use* of Property Concepts in actual *discourse*.[4]

4 A Discourse Explanation

To support this claim, I have taken a first step by investigating the use of Property Concept Words in two languages: English and Mandarin Chinese. In English, of course, it is a straightforward matter to argue for a class of Adjectives to which Property Concepts belong. In Mandarin, on the other hand, there is an extremely restricted category of Adjective, but most Property Concept Words are indistinguishable from Verbs (for discussion, see Li and Thompson 1981 and Schachter 1985).

So far, these are the only two languages whose discourse use of Property Concept Words I have investigated in any depth. However, the results are similar enough in these two genetically and areally unrelated languages to suggest that investigations of similar data in other languages will yield similar results.[5]

For English, since Property Concepts correlate largely with the category of Adjectives, I will describe my findings for this language in terms of the shorter term 'adjective' rather than 'Property Concept'.

I have looked at more than 100 pages of transcribed natural spontaneous conversational discourse with 308 Property Concept words, or adjectives. I did not count Nouns used as modifiers, such as *steak place* or *broccoli pie*, nor did I count adjective–Noun combinations which I took to be single lexical items, such as *blind date*.

I found that English adjectives are used in essentially two ways: see table 7.1. Let us look at some examples.[6] Examples of adjectives playing a predicate role fell into two syntactic categories, having to do with peculiarities of English grammar. First, there were those in which the adjective appeared as a predicate adjective with a copular verb, as in:

(13) and her parents apprently weren't even that *wealthy* (C1)

(14) I was getting kind of *good* at playing in the rain, really (Frie19)

(15) that got me so *mad* (HG35)

(16) aren't some chapters of Understanding Media *appropriate*? (Frie35)

Most of my examples of adjectives functioning as predicates (209, or 86 percent of the 242 instances of predicate function) were of this predicate adjective type.

Table 7.1 Discourse functions of 308 adjectives in English conversation

Predicating a property of an established discourse referent:	79% ($N = 242$)
Introducing a new discourse referent	21% ($N = 66$)
Total:	100% ($N = 308$)

The other, minority (14 percent), syntactic context in which I found adjectives functioning predicatively was that in which the adjective was an attribute to a predicate nominal head noun which is relatively 'non-new-information-bearing', that is, a relatively empty or an anaphoric head noun in predicate nominal position. Let us look carefully at one such example:

(17) (talking about a potential date)
      The last time she saw him which was three years ago he was pretty good looking, and um, you know she says he's a very *nice guy*, he's a real *good person* (HG21)

In (17), the predicate nominals *guy* and *person* are anaphoric (that is, they are interpreted as co-referential with a nominal earlier in the discourse) and, hence, non-new-information-bearing, since their referent has already been introduced much earlier in the conversation. Thus, while it is clearly the case that *nice* and *good* are *attributive* adjectives *grammatically*, they are counted here as *predicates functionally*. Here are two further examples of this situation:

(18) But I did have lots of fun up at Lehigh. That was a *good school* (C14)

(19) (talking about apartments)
      H: Well, theirs is a *nice apartment* really. (Frie25)

(17–19) show instances of an attributive adjective functioning as a predicate because its predicate nominal head is anaphoric. But there are also cases where an attributive adjective functions predicatively because its predicate nominal head is (relatively) *empty*. Here is an example of such a case:

(20) She and I are gonna go out and get drunk at four o'clock in the afternoon. It's a *religious thing* we're gonna have (Fra9)

In (20), a grammatically attributive adjective (*religious*) is functioning as the predicate of its clause, because its predicate nominal head is non-new-information-bearing. The difference between (20) and (17)–(19), however, is that this time the non-new-information-bearing head is an *empty noun* (*thing*).

Here is another example of this type of situation:

(21) (talking about wedding gifts)
      I said why don't you pack it away, and save it to give away to other people for wedding gifts, and she said, 'Hey, that's a *great idea*' (C19)

In each of these examples, the attributive adjective is functioning predicatively, since it modifies a non-informative predicate nominal head noun. Paraphrases in which the adjective figures as the sole element after the copula would often be appropriate ('their apartment is *nice* really'), for example.[7]

If English weren't so inclined to express predicative notions in the form of noun phrases with empty or anaphoric heads, these clauses could appear with predicate adjectives, and translations into other languages could easily find them coded as predicates rather than as noun phrases.

What I have shown, then, is that the primary function of adjectives in English, accounting for 79 percent of the adjective usage in my data, is as the predicate of their clause, whether they are the sole predicate word or an attribute to a non-informative predicate noun.

The second discourse function of adjectives, according to table 7.1, is to introduce new participants into the discourse. As expected, the adjectives serving this function are all attributive.

Let us consider an example.

(22) (talking about how to find something in the bookstore)
      S: Hey, you got a *funny baggie*.
      H: (It all wraps up.)

S: Your baggie is better than mine
H: Sure is (Frie2)

Here S brings up the participant *funny baggie*, which has not been mentioned before, and which figures in the successive discourse, at least for one turn.

In (22), it is clear that both the adjective and the noun in the phrase *funny baggie* are functioning to introduce the new referent. That is, both the item *baggie* and its property of being funny are new. Here is another example of the same type:

(23) (talking about apartments)
Aren't those fabulous; Tom Smith used to live there. And he had *black-and-white-striped sheets* in his bedroom (Frie21)

However, the *majority* of the instances in which the adjective is functioning to introduce a new discourse referent in my data are cases where the head noun is, again, *non*-information-bearing, that is, either empty or anaphoric. For example, consider (24):

(24) (talking about a movie)
and there's *something* really *sad* that happens (HG13)

In (24), the new referent is something unspecified except for its property of being sad. In the successive discourse, the speaker goes on to describe the sad thing, so it is clear that it is being introduced as a new referent in the discourse – the point is that it is the *adjective* which is carrying the burden of tagging this new referent for subsequent use in the later discourse, namely by identifying it as *sad*. This, then, is an example of the new referent being introduced by an adjective plus an *empty* head noun.

Here is a similar example:

(25) We used to do some *awful things* though (C5)

In (26) you can see an example of the other situation in which an adjective plays the major role in the introducing of the new referent: that in which the new referent is introduced by an adjective plus an *anaphoric* head noun:

(26) *H*: We've got to get umbrellas.
S: Why don't we get two, since there are two of us, good, that means I can get a *pretty fancy feminine one* (Frie18–19)

In (26), we see that the new referent, a pretty fancy feminine umbrella, is distinguished from other referents in this discourse only by the properties conveyed by the adjectives. This new referent, then, is contrasted with other similar referents. Once again, the new referent is being introduced by the adjective(s), not by the head noun, which is anaphoric (or what Halliday and Hasan 1976 call 'replacive'), and hence, non-new-information-bearing.

Here is another example to illustrate the case of an adjective introducing a new referent with an anaphoric head noun:

(27) (talking about apartments)
      I don't know, I think we're made more for *ethnic apartments* than *Danish modern apartments* (Frie25)

Example (28) is a particularly interesting illustration; the head noun *food* is not, strictly speaking, an anaphoric noun, since there had been no earlier mention of food in the conversation. But it is non-new-information-bearing in just the same way, given the verb *eat* just a few words earlier.

(28) (talking about acne)
      Yeah, but what you eat . . . if you eat *greasy food* . . . (HG5)[8]

In all of these examples, the adjectives are playing the role of introducing a new participant into the discourse.

Now, if adjectives are heavily involved in the introduction of new participants into the discourse, then we would expect two corollaries: (1) we would expect the noun phrases in which these referent-introducing adjectives are found to be grammatically indefinite or non-referential; (2) we would expect that the nominal positions in which these referent-introducing adjectives occur will be just those recorded independently for new participants.

Both of these predictions are borne out by the data. First, these referent-introducing adjective phrases are all grammatically indefinite or non-referential, with one exception. What I found hardly any examples of, interestingly enough, were *definite* noun phrases with adjectives in them. In fact, only *once* among all the 308 adjectives in my corpus did I find an instance of an adjective *re-identifying* or *distinguishing* an already introduced referent. This one example is shown in (29):

(29) (describing a movie)
      and this boy is Jewish
      (several turns later)
      There's this one part between *this Jewish guy* and the girl (HG13)

Clearly the adjective in the phrase *this Jewish guy* in (29) is functioning to *re-identify*, and not to *introduce*, a discourse referent. The fact that these cases, while perfectly easy to produce as examples, are so rare in these data, though, serves to underscore my claim that the two major functions of adjectives are their referent-introducing function and their predicating function. The referent-*distinguishing* function turns out to be an extremely rare function in actual conversational language, a fact which is contrary to expectation and which could not have been arrived at by examining one's intuitions.

The second prediction of my hypothesis is also borne out by the data: the nominal positions in which these attributive adjectives occur are in just those recorded independently for the introduction of new participants, and in roughly the same proportions (Du Bois, 1987): that is, patient (45 percent), oblique (19 per cent) and the S of an intransitive clause (36 percent), but never the A position of a transitive clause.

The discovery of this referent-introducing function of adjectives, then, is intriguing in two respects. First, it is intriguing because it is unexpected. Simply knowing that adjectives can function 'attributively' does not allow us to predict that *they*, and not their 'head nouns', do the majority of the work of introducing new referents in the noun phrases in which they occur. Thus an examination of how people talk has uncovered a hitherto underestimated use of adjectives, which is not the one usually discussed in treatments of context-free artificial examples. Second, this discovery is intriguing because of the finding that the noun in such constructions is so often superfluous. It is reasonable, then, to describe adjectives as referent-introducing.

So far, then, we have seen that adjectives in English function in spontaneous, natural conversation to predicate a property of a referent and to introduce a new referent into the discourse.

Implicit in my discussion so far is a claim which I can now make explicit: these two functions may also be viewed as differing in the discourse status of the referent to which a given Property Concept is being ascribed. That is, a predicating Property Concept ascribes a property to a referent already *established* in the discourse, while a referent-introducing Property Concept ascribes a property to a *new* referent, one which has not been established in the discourse. Semantically, of course, one could say that in both functions the Property Concept serves as a predicate (as implied in analyses of attributive adjectives as being semantically related to relative clauses); however, the data reported here clearly suggest that grammars reflect the discourse status of the referent to whom the property is being ascribed rather than the semantic function of predication.

For Mandarin, I have looked at similar data again of natural spontaneous language. The results, for 340 Property Concept Words, are strikingly similar to those found in English, as shown in table 7.2. From the table it is clear, then, that the same two functions as I found for English adjectives can be seen with Mandarin Property Concepts, and with roughly the same frequency in the data. This time, there were *no* instances of a Property Concept serving to *re-identify* an already established referent. That is, there were no analogues to the English case of (29).

Table 7.2   Discourse functions of 340 Mandarin property concept words

Predicating a property of an established discourse referent:	71% ($N = 243$)
Introducing a new discourse referent	29% ($N = 97$)
Total:	100% ($N = 340$)

Here is a Mandarin example of the predicating function for Property Concept Words:

(30) xue   yuwen fangmiande . . . suanshi   bijiao   *chixiang* yidian
study lang. aspect   can:be:considered relatively popular a:little
'studying languages could be considered relatively popular' (kh18)

In (31) and (32) you can see examples of the referent-introducing function for Mandarin Property Concept Words:

(31) (talking about Chinese children studying English in school)
zai hen *yukuaide qifen*   –zhong xue, na shi zui   haode
at very happy   atmosphere–in   learn, that be most good
'to learn in a very happy atmosphere, that's the best' (kh22)

Example (31) is parallel to the English (22) above: both the Property Concept word *yukuaide* 'happy' and the noun *qifen* 'atmosphere' are introducing the new referent, an atmosphere which has the property of being very happy.

Mandarin also exhibits the other type of situation, in which the Property Concept Word is taking most of the burden of introducing the new referent: (32) shows a Property Concept Word with an *anaphoric* head noun:

(32) (talking about entrance examinations)
suoyi women zhende shi xiwang nenggou you yige hen geng
so   we   really be hope   able   have a very more
'so we really hope that we can have a much more ideal exam'
lixiangde kaoshi
ideal   exam
(kh25)

In (32), the noun *kaoshi* 'exam' has already been introduced into the discourse; the whole discussion at this point is about the entrance examinations. As we saw with the analogous English examples, the new referent is contrasted with similar referents; what is *new* here is an examination which has the property of being *ideal*.

Analogous to the English cases described above in which the Property

Concept Word was attributive to an empty head noun are instances in Mandarin of a Property Concept word standing alone, that is, with a zero head noun. About 3 percent of the referent-introducing Property Concept Words in my data are of this type, of which (33) is an example:

(33) (talking about the grading of exams)
  ...geng *zhongyao*–de shi women yao tigao xuesheng
   even:more important–NOM COP we want raise student
 '... [the] even more important [thing] is that we want to raise the

  xuexi Yingyu –de nengli
  learn English–GEN ability
  ability of our students to learn English'

So far, what I have shown, then, is that in ordinary conversational language, Property Concept Words, or adjectives if we're talking about English, have exactly two functions, as listed in tables 7.1 and 7.2: one, to predicate a property of an established discourse referent, and two, to introduce a new discourse referent.

As I mentioned earlier, I think that these same discourse functions for Property Concept Words will be found in any language; if this is so, they provide the basis for an explanation of the facts about how languages categorize Property Concepts given in (1):

1 Property Concept Words (as exemplified in English and Mandarin) function in spontaneous, natural conversational discourse (i) to predicate a property of an established discourse referent or (ii) to introduce a new discourse referent. I note that these two functions were not decided upon in advance of my investigation; rather they emerged from examination of the data.[9]

2 Property Concept Words share the *predicating* function with *Verbs*, and the *referent-introducing* function with *Nouns* (see Hopper and Thompson 1984).[10]

3 This sharing of both Verbal and Nominal *functions in discourse* provides an explanation for the fact that Property Concepts will sometimes be categorized with morpho-syntactic properties similar to those of Verbs, and sometimes with morpho-syntactic properties similar to those of Nouns, while sometimes, since they are neither prototypical Nouns nor prototypical Verbs, they are categorized as a separate lexical category of Adjective.[11]

5 Conclusions

In this paper I have tried to suggest a discourse explanation for the way in which languages tend to categorize Property Concepts. I have taken Dixon's semantic study of Property Concepts as a starting-point, and shown that Property Concept Words tend to share features with both Nouns and Verbs cross-linguistically. I rejected a semantic explanation for this fact, since semantically, Property Concept Words tend to denote stable precepts like Nouns do, so that the widespread tendency to categorize Property Concepts as Verbs remains unaccounted for. Instead I have suggested that a consideration of the *function* of Property Concept Words in discourse might shed some light on the patterns we find in the way they are categorized in many languages. That is, given that Property Concept Words share the *predicating* function with *Verbs*, and the *referent-introducing* function with *Nouns*, this sharing of both verbal and nominal *functions in discourse* provides an explanation for the fact that Property Concepts will sometimes be categorized with morpho-syntactic properties similar to those of Verbs, and sometimes with morpho-syntactic properties similar to those of Nouns, while sometimes, since they are neither prototypical Nouns nor prototypical Verbs, they are categorized as a separate lexical category of Adjective.

Appendix

Criteria for determining noun-like or verb-like tendencies for property concept words

1 Do PCs have nominal inflection as predicates or as attributes?
2 In the predicate role, how are PC's different from Nouns?
3 In the predicate role, how are PC's different from Verbs?
4 In the attributive role, how is the PC attached to the Noun?
5 Can the PC be used anaphorically?

PCs more like Nouns

1 yes
2 few or no differences
3 not similar
4 as Nouns are
5 yes

PCs more like Verbs

1 no
2 not similar
3 Few or no differences
4 as Verbs are
5 not without a Noun, Pronoun
   or Relative Marker

Notes

I wish to thank Henning Andersen, Johan van der Auwera, Joan Bybee, Jack Du Bois, Mark Durie, Matthew Dryer, Aryeh Faltz, Mike Hannay, Teun Hoekstra,

Paul Hopper, Ekkehard König, Christian Lehmann, Lachlan MacKenzie, Hans-Jürgen Sasse, Hansjakob Seiler, Leon Stassen and Harrie Wetzer for helpful comments on the ideas in this paper and Manny Schegloff for sharing some of his conversational data with me. None of these people is responsible for the use I have made of their advice. I am also grateful to the Netherlands Institute for Advanced Study for the fellowship year during which this paper was written.

1 Interestingly, in some languages, such as those in the Yuman family, 'KIN' concepts may in fact be best analyzed as Verbs (Halpern 1942).

2 See Perkins (1980) and Bybee (1985) for a discussion of the importance of random sampling in cross-linguistic research. I acknowledge the points made by these authors, and regret that both Dixon's sample and the sample I collected for the present study could not be random.

3 The criteria which I used to determine whether Property Concept Words shared features with Nouns or Verbs are listed in the Appendix.

4 This is not to deny Givón's insightful remarks (p. 55ff) on the likelihood that more and less time-stable adjectives, in a language with this category, may be realized as more noun-like and more verb-like respectively. Nor do I wish to deny the likelihood of a semantic distinction underlying Nouns and Verbs along the lines Givón suggests (though, as A. Faltz points out (personal communication) it is quite possible that the notion of 'time stability' will turn out to be derived from a more primitive distinction between events and entities).

5 Clearly, much more work needs to be done on this question. It is conceivable, for example, that the similarities that I report here between English and Mandarin reflect a similar 'industrialized urban' cultural outlook, and that data from a non-industrialized non-urban speech community would yield different results.

6 Codes after each example refer to locations in my transcripts.

7 Thus the semantic distinction which is the focus of Siegel (1980), between 'intersective' and 'non-intersective' adjective readings, turns out, according to my data, not to be exploited by ordinary users of conversational English; in actual conversation the distinction between examples such as her 'That lutist is good' / 'That is a good lutist' (p. 55) is essentially neutralized. For an attested example of such a paraphrase, see Du Bois (1980: 213, ex. (23)).

8 In the transcription used here, three dots signal a pause and does not indicate material omitted.

9 I emphasize the necessity of basing claims about the discourse basis for lexical and grammatical categories on conversational discourse data; it is well known that the use of adjectives in written English, for example, is radically different from that in conversational (see, for example, Chafe 1982), but I hypothesize that it is conversational, and not written, language which has determined grammatical and lexical regularities.

10 Nouns (or nominal roots) can function as predicates too, but, as discussed in Hopper and Thompson (1984), there is abundant grammatical evidence that this is a marginal function for Nouns.

11 I acknowledge that the statistical predominance of the predicate function in my data suggests that more languages should have Property Concepts categorized like Verbs than like Nouns. Verification of this hypothesis must await a further study.

References

Adelaar, W. F. H. (1977) *Tarma Quechua: Grammar, Texts, Dictionary*. Lisse: The Peter de Ridder Press.

Anceaux, J. C. (1952) *The Wolio Language*. The Hague: N. V. de Nederlandse Boek- en Steendrukkerij.

Arnott, D. W. (1970) *The Nominal and Verbal Systems of Fula*. Oxford: Oxford University Press.

Austin P. (1981) *A Grammar of Diyari, South Australia*. Cambridge: Cambridge University Press.

Blake, B. J. (1979) *A Kalkatungu Grammar*. Pacific Linguistics B-57. Australian National University.

Buechel, E., S. J. (1939) *A Grammar of Lakhota*. St Francis, S. Dak. Rosebud Educational Society.

Bybee, J. (1985) *Morphology: A Study of the Relationship between Form and Meaning*. Amsterdam: John Benjamins.

Chafe, W. (ed.) (1980) *The Pear Stories*. Norwood, NJ: Ablex.

(1982) 'Integration and involvement in speaking, writing, and oral literature'. In Tannen (1982).

Chao, Y. R. (1968) *A Grammar of Spoken Chinese*. Berkeley and Los Angeles: University of California Press.

Cowan, R. and R. Schuh (1976) *Spoken Hausa*. Ithaca, NY: Spoken Languages Services.

Craig, C. G. (1977) *The Structure of Jacaltec*. Austin, Tex.: University of Texas Press.

Dimmendaal, G. J. (1983) *The Turkana Language*. Dordrecht: Foris.

Dixon, R. M. W. (1972) *The Dyirbal Language of North Queensland*. Cambridge: Cambridge University Press.

(1977) 'Where have all the adjectives gone?' *Studies in Language*, 1.1, 1–80.

Donaldson, B. C. (1981) *Dutch Reference Grammar*. The Hague: Nijhoff.

Du Bois, J. (1980) 'Beyond definiteness: the trace of identity in discourse'. In Chafe (1980).

(1985) Competing motivations. In J. Haiman (1985).

(1987) 'The discourse basis of ergativity'. *Language* 63.4, 805–55.

Durie, M. (1985) *A Grammar of Acehnese*. Dordrecht: Foris.

Elwell-Sutton, L. P. (1979) *Colloquial Persian*. London: Routledge & Kegan Paul.

George, K. M. (1971) *Malayalam Grammar and Reader*. Kottayam: National Book Stall.

Givón, T. (1979) *Understanding Grammar*. New York: Academic Press.

(1984) *Syntax: A Functional and Typological Introduction*, vol. 1. Amsterdam: John Benjamins.

Glendening, P. J. T. *Icelandic*. Teach Yourself Books. London: St Paul's House.

Haiman, J. (ed.) (1985) *Iconicity in syntax*. Amsterdam: John Benjamins.

Halliday, M. A. K. and R. Hasan (1976) *Cohesion in English*. London: Longman.

Halpern, A. A. (1942) 'Yuma kinship terms'. *American Anthropologist*, 44, 425–41.

Harrison S. (1976) *Mokilese Reference Grammar*. Honolulu: University of Hawaii Press.

Hoffman, C. (1963) *A Grammar of the Margi Language*. Oxford: Oxford University Press.

Hopper, P. J. and S. A. Thompson (1984) 'The discourse basis for lexical categories in universal grammar'. *Language*, 60, 703–52.

Hyman, L. (ed.) (1979) *Aghem Grammatical Structure*. Southern California Occasional Papers in Linguistics 7. Los Angeles: University of Southern California.

—— (1981) *Noni Grammatical Structure*. Southern California Occasional Papers in Linguistics 9. Los Angeles: University of Southern California.

Jacobsen, W. H., Jr (1979) *Noun and Verb in Nootkan*. Heritage Record 4. Victoria: British Columbia Provincial Museum.

Josephs, L. (1975) *Palauan Reference Grammar*. Honolulu: University of Hawaii Press.

Karlsson, F. (1983) *Finnish Grammar*. Helsinki: Werner Soderstrom Osakeyhtio.

Ladusaw, W. A. (1985) 'The category structure of Kusaal'. *Proceedings of the Eleventh Annual Meeting of the Berkeley Linguistics Society*. Berkeley: Berkeley Linguistics Society.

Laskowski, R. (1979) *Polnische Grammatik*. Leipzig: Veb Verlag Enzyklopädie.

Lee, K. (1975) *Kusaiean Reference Grammar*. Hololulu: University of Hawaii Press.

Li, C. N. and S. A. Thompson (1981) *Mandarin Chinese: A Functional Reference Grammar*. Berkeley and Los Angeles: University of California Press.

Lichtenberk, F. (1983) *A Grammar of Manam*. Honolulu: University of Hawaii Press.

Lindsey, G. and J. Scancarelli (1985) 'Where have all the adjectives come from? the case of Cherokee'. *Proceedings of the Eleventh Annual Meeting of the Berkeley Linguistics Society*. Berkeley: Berkeley Linguistics Society.

MacDonald, R. R. (1976) *Indonesian Reference Grammar*. Georgetown, Washington, DC: Georgetown University Press.

Marsack, C. C. (1962) *Samoan*. Teach Yourself Books. London: St Paul's House.

Noss, R. B. (1964) *Thai Reference Grammar*. Washington, DC: Foreign Service Institute.

Perkins, R. (1980) 'The evolution of culture and grammar'. Ph.D. diss., SUNY at Buffalo.

Rosen, H. (1977) *Contemporary Hebrew*. The Hague: Mouton.

Schachter, P. (1985) 'Parts-of-speech systems'. In Shopen (1985).

—— and F. Otanes (1972) *Tagalog Reference Grammar*. Berkeley and Los Angeles: University of California Press.

Schulz, D. and H. Griesbach (1960) *Grammatik der Deutschen Sprache*. Ismaning: Max Hueber Verlag.

Scott, G. (1978) *The Fore Language of Papua New Guinea*. Pacific Linguistics B-47. Canberra: Australian National University.

Shopen, T. (ed.) (1985) *Language Typology and Syntactic Description*. Cambridge: Cambridge University Press.

Siegel, M. A. (1980) *Capturing the Adjective*. New York: Garland.

Sohn, H. (1975) *Woleaian Reference Grammar*. Honolulu: University of Hawaii Press.

—— and B. W. Bender (1973) *A Ulithian Grammar*. Pacific linguistics C-27. Canberra: Australian National University.

Tannen, D. (ed.) (1982) *Spoken and Written Language: Exploring Orality and Literacy*. Norwood, NJ: Ablex.

Voorhoeve, C. L. (1965) *The Flamingo Bay Dialect of the Asmat Language*. The Hague: H. L. Smits.

(1982a) 'The West Makian language, N. Molluccas, Indonesia: a fieldwork report'. In Voorhoeve (1982b).

(ed.) (1982b) *The Makian Languages and Their Neighbors*. Materials in Languages of Indonesia 12, Pacific Linguistics D-46. Canberra: Australian National University.

CHAPTER 8

Coreference and Conjunction Reduction in Grammar and Discourse

Bernard Comrie

1 Introduction: Coreference in Grammar and Discourse

In this introductory section, I wish to outline a general framework of the relationship between grammatical devices and discourse structure in the establishment of anaphoric relations. In subsequent sections, one particular phenomenon – conjunction reduction – will be investigated in terms of its interaction with this framework.

One aspect of a natural discourse that the hearer must be able to retrieve from that discourse is the set of anaphoric relations intended by the speaker. In other words, it must be clear to the hearer whether a given participant in the discourse is coreferential to some other participant or non-coreferential, whether a participant is a new participant being introduced into the text or whether this participant has already been referred to, etc. Where such clarity is not provided, the hearer will normally stop the speaker and request this clarification. Given this, there is an onus on the speaker to make the anaphoric relations clear in the text as it is produced.

In principle, one might imagine that the speaker could answer this charge by identifying the referent of each noun phrase explicitly at each occurrence of that noun phrase, for instance by providing a sufficiently elaborate description of the referent of the noun phrase to exclude all other possible referents: this might involve repetition of proper names, such as *Edward Sapir*, or of lengthy descriptions, such as *the man who first spotted the burglar*. Presumably, at the very least, this strategy would make communication unnecessarily longwinded, and in fact all languages have devices that enable the speaker to abbreviate referential descriptions without necessarily prejudicing the hearer's ability to retrieve the intended anaphoric relations.

In fact, the existence of such abbreviatory devices, especially those that imply interpretations involving coreference, may well force an interpretation of non-coreferentiality in certain instances where the abbreviatory device is not used.[1] In some cases the non-coreferential interpretation may actually be forced, as in many languages with reflexive pronouns: in the domain of reflexivity, use of a reflexive pronoun forces a coreferential interpretation (for example, *the man hit himself*), while use of any other noun phrase forces a non-coreferential interpretation (for example, *the man hit him*), leading to bizarre results where it is difficult to reconcile conflicting requirements (for example, ?**the man who first spotted the burglar hit the man who first spotted the burglar*, where the non-reflexive object suggests non-coreference, but the detailed description clearly identifies the same individual twice). At best, repeated detailed identification of detailed descriptions will lead to undesirable Gricean implicatures: since the normal way of constructing a text is to use the abbreviatory referential strategies of that language, the hearer will be led to suspect some ulterior motive if the speaker systematically violates the norms for using these strategies by being 'too explicit'.

In many instances, reliance can be placed on knowledge of possibilities and probabilities in the world, knowledge of social relations, etc., so that the whole onus is not invariably placed on the grammatical structure of the language. Consider sentences (1) and (2):

(1) The cat knocked the melon off the table; it ran away and hid.

(2) The cat knocked the melon off the table; it burst.

In principle, the pronoun *it* in both of these sentences could refer either to the cat or to the melon (or, indeed, to the table). However, since neither melons nor tables can run away and hide, in (1) the pronoun is in fact interpreted as coreferential with *the cat*. Since tables cannot burst, and cats burst only under exceptional circumstances, for which there is no evidence in (2), while melons are notoriously prone to burst, the pronoun in (2) is interpreted as coreferential with *the melon*.

As an instance of the relevance of knowledge of social expectations, we might consider the use of politeness devices in Japanese. Of the various verbs meaning 'be' and referring to an animate entity being in a certain location, the most neutral verb is *i-ru*; *irassy-aru* can only be used where the speaker shows respect to the referent of the subject of the clause: and *or-u* can only be used where the speaker wishes to humble the subject of the clause. Japanese society requires that one never show respect towards oneself (or to members of one's own ingroup in talking to outsiders), and that one never humble one's addressee (one can only humble oneself, and members of one's ingroup in talking to outsiders). Thus the range of possible referents for the omitted subject in (3) and (4) is actually quite narrowly restricted by the choice of verb:

(3) Doko ni irassyaimasu ka?

(4) Doko ni orimasu ka?
    where LOC be-NONPAST Q

Sentence (3) cannot be a question about one's own location, while sentence (4) cannot be a question about one's addressee's location; if no third person referents are present in the universe of discourse, (3) is unequivocally 'where are you?', while (4) is unequivocally 'where am I?' Japanese makes frequent use of the most abbreviatory device for indicating coreference – namely, zero anaphora, the omission of the noun phrase in question – and the above examples indicate one way in which the reference of such missing noun phrases can be established.

In addition to such extralinguistic cues to the establishment of anaphoric relations, languages may (and do) also have grammatical devices that are sensitive to anaphoric relations, and therefore permit the retrieval of anaphoric relations from a text. Some of these grammatical devices serve the basic function of indicating coreference (or, occasionally, noncoreference), while others only incidentally serve this function. We may now examine these two kinds of grammatical devices in turn.[2]

One grammatical device that specifically indicates coreference has already been introduced in passing, namely reflexivization. In English, for instance, the occurrence of a reflexive pronoun necessarily requires an interpretation of coreference, while in domains where coreference makes reflexivization obligatory, the absence of reflexivization will force an interpretation of noncoreference:

(5) The man hit himself.

(6) The man hit him.

However precisely reflexivization is to be formulated in the grammar of English, the domain of obligatory reflexivization must include the relation between subject and direct object of the same clause. In (5), then, the reflexive pronoun *himself* must be coreferential with its only possible antecedent, the subject *the man*. In (6), the non-reflexive pronoun *him* must be non-coreferential with *the man*.

A richer grammatical device for indicating coreference is switch reference (see, for instance, Haiman and Munro 1983). In a language with switch reference, a number of clauses can be combined together into a single sentence; only one of the clauses is independent (that is, could stand as a separate sentence in isolation), all the others are dependent. Each dependent clause is marked (usually on the verb) to indicate whether its subject is coreferential or non-coreferential with the subject of the clause on which it is dependent. The following simple examples from Usan (Haiman and Munro 1983: ix) will serve to indicate the basic nature of switch reference:

(7) Ye nam su-ab isomei.
    I tree cut-SS descend:1SG
    'I cut the tree and [I] went down.'

(8) Ye nam su-ine isorei.
    I tree cut-DS descend:3SG
    'I cut the tree and it fell down.'

In (7), the same subject marker is used, so the subjects of the two clauses must be coreferential. In (8), the different subject marker is used, so the subjects must be co-referential. Note, incidentally, that the different subject marker tells us no more than this – in principle, any participant other than the referent of the subject of the independent clause could be subject of the dependent clause; this is similar to reflexivization: the reflexive indicates coreference, the non-reflexive indicates non-coreference but does nothing further to identify the referent.

Another grammatical device that serves to distinguish coreferential and non-coreferential referents is obviation, found in the Algonquian languages. Under obviation, there is a two-way split in the third person, into proximate and obviative. Within a certain span of discourse, one third person participant is selected as proximate, and all other third person participants are obviatives. Within this span of discourse, all reference to the proximate participant (for example, pronouns, verb indexing markers) is by means of proximate morphology, while all reference to other participants is by means of obviative morphology. The use of proximate morphology therefore unequivocally means coreference with the initially established proximate participant; the use of obviative morphology forces an interpretation of non-coreference with this participant (though without specifying with which of the other participants coreference is to be established). The following example from Cree will illustrate the principle:[3]

(9) Naapeew atim-wa waapam-ee-w ee-sipwehtee-t
    man:PROX dog-OBV see-DIR-3PROX CNJ-leave-3PROX
    'The man saw the dog as he left.'

(10) Naapeew atim-wa waapam-ee-w ee-sipwehtee-yit.
     man:PROX dog-OBV see-DIR-3PROX CNJ—leave-3OBV
     'The man saw the dog as it left.'

One difference between switch reference and obviation is that switch reference is strictly local (the relation operates only between a dependent clause and the clause on which it is dependent), while obviation is in principle global: example (11), taken from a Cree text cited in Ellis (1983: 464), indicates the use of obviation across sentence boundaries:

(11) Kaa-ataaweet o-štees-a n-t-iteelim-imaawa.
     trader 3SG-elder:brother-OBV 1SG-think-3OBV
     Nihtaa-weemistikoošiimo-liwa kwayask.
     competent-speak:English-3OBV properly

'I think [him to be] the trader's son. He [= the son] speaks English well.'

Since *kaa-ataaweet* 'trader' is proximate, the other noun phrase, *o-štees-a* 'his son', must be obviative. The obviative morphology in the second sentence indicates that it is not the trader who speaks good English, but (since only two third person participants are involved) his son.

Among grammatical devices that can serve to indicate anaphoric relations even though this is not their main function, we may mention gender/class systems. If, in a language, different nouns are assigned to different genders or classes, and if different markers are used in referring to nouns of different genders/classes (for instance, different pronouns, or different verb indexing), then these gender/class-differentiated markers can serve as a basis for retrieval of anaphoric relations. Although the most spectacular examples of the operation of this device are in languages with rich gender/class systems (for example, Bantu languages), the same phenomenon can be seen even in English, with its limited natural-gender system in the third person singular, as in sentences (12)–(13):

(12)   John kissed Mary, and then he ran away.

(13)   John kissed Mary, and then she ran away.

If we assume that John and Mary are the only relevant participants, then the masculine pronoun in the second clause of (12) unequivocally refers to John, and the feminine pronoun in (13) unequivocally refers to Mary. Of course, gender/class systems can only operate at their maximum if all participants in the text belong to different classes. The English pronoun *he* instructs the hearer to find a male human referent, but does not enable the hearer to discriminate among several male human referents. In (14), for instance, the pronoun *he* could refer to either John or Bill:

(14)   John introduced Mary to Bill, and then he ran away.

Verb indexing is another related way in which anaphoric relations can be retrieved. In a language like Spanish, where the verb encodes the person and number of the subject, a subject pronoun can (and regularly is) omitted – what has come to be called the pro-drop phenomenon[4] – so that *canto* is unequivocally 'I sing' because of the first person singular ending *-o*, while *cantamos* is unequivocally 'we sing' because of the first person plural ending *-mos*. In languages with gender/class systems, verb indexing is often sensitive to gender/class distinctions, so that these two can work in tandem to delimit possible anaphoric interpretations. Thus, in Swahili both *nili-ki-leta* and *nili-u-leta* are translated into English as 'I saw it', but in *nilikileta*, with the class 7 object prefix *ki*, the 'it' in question is necessarily the referent of a noun of class 7, whereas in *niliuleta*, with the class 3 object prefix *u*, the 'it' in question is necessarily the referent of a noun of class 3.

In the body of this article, I will be considering yet another example of a grammatical device that can serve, incidentally, to assign anaphoric relations, namely conjunction reduction. If we compare English sentences (15) and (16), then it is clear that both receive the same interpretation, although the second conjunct of (16) (at least apparently) lacks an overt subject:

(15) The man kissed the woman and the man ran away.

(16) The man kissed the woman and ran away.

In particular, (16) cannot be interpreted to mean that the woman ran away. This is because of a grammatical constraint on conjunction reduction in English, as discussed in more detail in section 4 below.

In any given discourse in any given language, there is necessarily interplay between the strictly grammatical factors and the extralinguistic (world knowledge) factors that help in determining anaphoric relations. The upshot of all this is that the speaker, in constructing his text, must manipulate structural principles, on the one hand, and the appeal to world knowledge, on the other, to produce a discourse whose anaphoric relations are clear to the hearer, but without being overspecific. The aim of the body of this article is to show how this communicative charge, in interaction with the structure of languages of different types and with world knowledge, serves to delimit the ways in which coreference is indicated by the omission of noun phrase constituents in coordinate constructions.

2 Conjunction Reduction

The body of this article will be a detailed study of conjunction reduction as it relates to the establishment of anaphoric relations, in particular as it relates to grammatical versus other means of establishing anaphoric relations. Data from a number of different languages will be examined, all the data having the general form of English sentence (17):

(17) The man kissed the woman and ran away.

Let us assume that the sentence (17) has two main components, namely *the man kissed the woman* and *ran away*.[5] In the second of these components, there is a missing argument: English verbs (except in the imperative) require an overtly expressed subject, and *ran away* is neither an imperative nor does not have an overtly expressed subject. Indeed, as a separate sentence *ran away* would be ungrammatical (or, at best, highly elliptical). Nonetheless, the interpretation of the subject of the second component of (17) is quite unequivocal in English: it must be *the man*, that is, the sentence as a whole is interpreted to mean 'the man kissed the woman and the man ran away'.

In other languages, sentences that apparently parallel (17) receive different interpretations: in some languages, for instance, such a sentence would mean that the woman ran away; in yet other languages, it would be ambiguous, in principle, meaning either than the man ran away or that the woman ran away. One thing that follows from this, and will be the subject of the bulk of the ensuing investigation, is that some languages have strict grammatical (syntactic) constraints on the interpretation of such sentences, while other languages lack such grammatical constraints, but may require use of extragrammatical strategies (such as world knowledge) to resolve potential ambiguities.

My use of the term 'conjunction reduction' is relatively informal. In particular, I am making no claim as to how sentences like (17), or their parallels in other languages, are derived. Thus the term 'conjunction reduction' does not imply that sentence (17) has an underlying structure with specification of the overt subject of the second component, that component then being deleted transformationally, but is entirely consistent with an analysis whereby no syntactic level of analysis of sentence (17) contains constituents not present in the surface structure, the restitution of the 'omitted subject' being carried out entirely by semantic interpretation. Indeed, I do not even wish to exclude the possibility (which strikes me as actually rather plausible) that the syntactic structure of (17) is at all levels roughly that given in (18), such that in a sense *the man* is subject of the compound verb phrase *[[kissed the woman]$_{VP}$ and [ran away]$_{VP}]_{VP}$*:

(18) [[the man]$_{NP}$ [[kissed the woman]$_{VP}$ and [ran away]$_{VP}]_{VP}]_S$

Given languages where sentences with the same apparent structure as (17), but with the interpretation whereby the woman ran away, or with the availability of both interpretations (either the man or the woman ran away), the reader may question whether what I am calling conjunction reduction is indeed a homogeneous phenomenon across all these types of language. I consider this an extremely important question, but one which does not invalidate the methodology I intend to use. Indeed, one of the conclusions of the investigation will be that there is a significant difference among different kinds of languages here, in particular those with only one interpretation and those with more than one interpretation for sentences like (17), so that my final conclusion will be quite close to the reservation some readers may have in permitting me to consider a range of data whose homogeneity and parallelism is far from guaranteed in advance.

In section 3 I examine languages where the interpretation of the omitted noun phrases in sentences like (17) is determined by means of strict grammatical principles; the main languages discussed are English and Dyirbal. In section 4 I examine languages where discourse plays a much greater role; the main languages considered in this section are Kalaw Lagaw Ya (Western Torres Strait Language), Lenakel and Serbo-Croatian.

3 Grammatical Constraints on Conjunction Reduction

In English, the interpretation of sentences like (17), repeated here for convenience as (19), is strictly determined by syntactic principles:

(19) The man kissed the woman and ran away.

(20) The man kissed the woman and the man ran away.

(21) The man kissed the woman and the woman ran away.

Sentence (19) can receive the interpretation of sentence (20), and only this interpretation. In particular, it cannot receive the interpretation of sentence (21), even though the woman is referred to in the first component of the conjunction and is thus in some sense discourse-available, and even though (21) has a perfectly sensible interpretation given our knowledge of the world.

Indeed, this syntactic constraint is so strong in English that it overrides extralinguistic possibilities and probabilities. Let us take sentence (22), for instance:

(22) The man dropped the melon and burst.

Let us assume, moreover, that (22) is uttered by someone we know to be a competent speaker of English (that is, there are no grammatical mistakes in the sentence, and the verb *burst* is indeed intransitive). Knowledge of the world would suggest that, if a man drops a melon, the melon is extremely likely to burst, whereas it is almost impossible that the man should burst. Nonetheless, the only semantic interpretation allowed by English for sentence (22) is the nonsensical interpretation: 'the man dropped the melon and the man burst.' Thus the syntactic constraint in English is very strong indeed.

So far I have not stated what this syntactic constraint is, and indeed for present purposes the most important point is to note that there is a strict grammatical constraint, irrespective of what its precise nature is. The usual assumption in current syntactic work is that the constraint is something like (23), an intuition that goes back at least to Chomsky (1957: 36):

(23) If X-A-Y is a sentence and X-B-Y is a sentence, then X-A *and* B-Y is a sentence, where A and B are constituents of the same type and X, Y are (possibly null) variables.

We may consider (24)–(25) as the relevant structures:

(24) $[[\text{the man}]_{NP} [\text{kissed the woman}]_{VP}]_S$

(25) $[[\text{the man}]_{NP} [\text{ran away}]_{VP}]_S$

(26) $[[\text{the man}]_{NP} [[\text{kissed the woman}]_{VP} \text{ and } [\text{ran away}]_{VP}]_S$

In these examples, the verb phrase *kissed the woman* is A and the verb phrase *ran away* is B. Each of A and B is a constituent, moreover they are constituents of the same type (verb phrase), therefore they can be conjoined as in (26). Moreover, *the man* is covered by the variable X, while the variable Y is null.

This analysis presupposes the existence of the VP node, which dominates the verb and its objects to the exclusion of the subject. This assumption is far from being uncontroversial. One empirical problem is the existence of sentences like (27), which receives the interpretation of sentence (28):

(27) The man kissed and the dog bit the woman.

(28) The man kissed the woman and the dog bit the woman.

Here the conjoined strings are *the man kissed* and *the dog bit*, neither of which is a constituent under the VP analysis; indeed, there is no way of assigning a standard phrase structure analysis to *the man kissed the woman* such that both *the man kissed* and *kissed the woman* will be constituents. One suggestion in the literature is that (27) is not straight-forwardly the output of conjunction reduction, but rather involves a special rule of right node raising, whereby the object noun phrase (the 'right node') is raised out of the verb phrase to be made an immediate constituent of the S node, that is, to give a structure as in (29) (with question marks indicating nodes whose label is uncertain):

(29) $[[\text{the man kissed}]_? \text{ the woman}]_{NP}]_S$

(30) $[[\text{the dog bit}]_? \text{ the woman}]_{NP}]_S$

(31) $[[\text{the man kissed}]_? \text{ and } [\text{the dog bit}]_?]_? [\text{the woman}]_{NP}]_S$

One piece of evidence in favor of this analysis is the intonation pattern typically assigned to sentences like (27), with an intonation break before the direct object – in other sentences the position between verb and direct object is one of the least natural positions for an intonation break in English:

(32) The man kissed, and the dog bit, the woman.

More recently, a radical alternative has been proposed to this traditional view of conjunction reduction and constituent structure. Work by van Oirsouw (e.g. van Oirsouw 1983; 1987) suggests that the basic constraint on conjunction reduction does not require that A and B be constituents. Thus sentences of type (19) and of type (27) are both produced by the same process of conjunction reduction. Some other constraints are required to exclude certain ungrammatical coordinations, but overall the fit between van Oirsouw's predictions and the grammaticality judgments of native speakers of English is remarkable, and the overall analysis is certainly no more complex than that required by constraint (23) (which requires a separate rule of right node raising).

The question of whether conjunction reduction in English is sensitive to constituent structure or not need not detain us further, since our main goal was to establish that there is some syntactic constraint on conjunction reduction in English. Before leaving the English data, however, it is worth noting that, even if a derived structure like (26) is appropriate at some level of derivation for such sentences in English, when such sentences are pronounced it is often with an intonation break before the coordinating conjunction, as in (33):

(33) The man kissed the woman, and ran away.

Thus the structure which serves as input to the phonology may well have immediate constituents *the man kissed the woman* and *and ran away*, making it more similar to some of the conjoined structures to be treated in section 4.

The second language to be treated with a strict syntactic constraint on conjunction reduction is Dyirbal, an Australian Aboriginal language spoken in northern Queensland.[6] Let us consider Dyirbal sentence (34):

(34) Jugumbil yara-nggu balga-n, walma-nyu.
      woman:ABS man-ERG hit-NONFUT, jump-NONFUT

The first conjunct unequivocally has the meaning 'the man hit the woman'; 'the man' is identified as agent of 'hit' because it is in the ergative case, while 'the woman' is similarly identified as patient by being in the absolutive case. The second conjunct says overtly that (someone) jumped up. In English, *the man hit the woman and jumped up* would receive the interpretation that the man jumped up. Dyirbal sentence (24) just as unequivocally receives the interpretation that the woman jumped up, that is (34) is equivalent in interpretation to (35):

(35) Jugumbil yara-nggu balga-n, jugumbil walma-nyu.
      'The man hit the woman and the woman jumped up.'

Dyirbal, then, also has a strict syntactic constraint on the interpretation of sentences with conjunction reduction – as in English, it overrides possibilities and probabilities in the world – although the principle in Dyirbal happens to give an interpretation diametrically opposed to that given in English.

If we accept the VP analysis for English, then a similar analysis can be given for Dyirbal, except that whereas in English the VP includes the transitive verb and its patient, to the exclusion of the agent (which is syntactically the subject), in Dyirbal the VP would include the transitive verb (or, more theory-neutrally, the two-place predicate) and its agent, to the exclusion of the patient (which could be considered the subject). In other words, in English the term 'subject' would subsume intransitive subject and transitive agent, whereas in Dyirbal the term 'subject' would subsume intransitive subject and transitive patient ('ergative syntax'; see Comrie (1978).[7] Constraint (23) could then be applied to Dyirbal in exactly the same way as in English. The structures of the relevant sentences would be as in (36)–(38):

(36) $[[\text{jugumbil}]_{NP} [\text{yaranggu balgan}]_{VP}]_S$

(37) $[[\text{jugumbil}]_{NP} [\text{walmanyu}]_{VP}]_S$

(38) $[[\text{jugumbil}]_{NP} [[\text{yaranggu balgan}]_{VP} [\text{walmanyu}]_{VP}]_{VP}]_S$

As in the case of English, it is irrelevant to our present purposes whether or not these structures are accepted as part of the explanation for the Dyirbal data: the crucial point is that Dyirbal does have a grammatical constraint on the interpretation of conjunction reduction.

One piece of evidence in favor of this analysis is that it makes a correct prediction where one has coreferential patients across a conjunction boundary: on this analysis the remainder of a clause once the patient is disregarded is a constituent (the verb phrase), and this therefore predicts that such verb phrases should be conjoinable, as in (39):

(39) Jugumbil yara-nggu ngamba-n, (jugumbil) gubi-nggu balga-n.
      woman:ABS man-ERG heard-NONFUT, (woman:ABS) doctor-ERG hit-NONFUT
      'The man heard the woman and the doctor hit [the woman].'

But there are some pieces of evidence pointing against this structural analysis of Dyirbal. One is that Dyirbal word order is extremely free, so that in the surface structure of a sentence there is no need for the constituents of the putative VP to be adjacent, that is, at least by surface structure the VP is no longer a constituent. The second is that the prosodic structure of Dyirbal conjunction reduction clearly involves a main intonation break where the comma appears in the above examples, thus suggesting that at least in the input to the phonology the immediate constituents of (35) are *jugumbil yaranggu balgan* and *walmanyu*, rather than a subject *jugumbil* and a conjoined verb phrase *yaranggu balgan*, *walmanyu*.

There is another complication in the Dyirbal data that is not taken care of by the VP analysis, this time a complication that has no parallel in English. In Dyirbal, if the agent of the initial conjunct is coreferential with the intransitive subject or patient of the second conjunct, then it is possible to omit the coreferential noun phrase in the second conjunct; in this case, however, the violation of the normal anaphoric pattern is indicated explicitly by attaching the suffix *-ngurra* (which excludes tense suffixes) to the verb of the second conjunct, as in (40), which should be contrasted with (35), repeated below as (41):

(40) Jugumbil yara-nggu balga-n, walma-ngurra.
     'The man hit the woman and [the man] jumped up.'

(41) Jugumbil yara-nggu balga-n, walma-nyu.
     'The man hit the woman and [the woman] jumped up.'

In (41), we have the 'normal' configuration of coreferential noun phrases: neither is agent of its clause. In (40), by contrast, the coreferential noun phrase in the first clause is necessarily the agent; in the second clause, as under the normal configuration, the coreferential noun phrase is non-agent (it happens to be an intransitive subject, though it could equally well have been the patient of a transitive verb).

There is no way of accounting for *-ngurra* forms in terms of the VP analysis, especially insofar as *-ngurra* does not involve any change in grammatical relations; certainly English has nothing comparable in syntactic function to *-ngurra*. The use of *-ngurra* does enable Dyirbal to express in relatively direct manner one syntactic configuration of coreferential noun phrases that would not be possible using the usual constraint on conjunction reduction in Dyirbal; in this sense, we might say that conjunction reduction in Dyirbal is slightly more discourse-oriented than its closest English parallel. It should, however, be noted that even with *-ngurra*, the syntactic possibilities are heavily constrained: the coreferential noun phrase must be agent of the first clause, and must be either intransitive subject or patient (that is, 'subject', under the VP analysis) of the second clause.

Before leaving Dyirbal, I want to discuss briefly a set of examples that might seem to be counterexamples to the analysis of Dyirbal proposed above, that is, even to the informal analysis (whether or not one accepts the VP analysis specifically). In Dyirbal it is possible to find examples which seem to involve coreference of agents across coordination boundaries, with the verb in its basic form, as in (42)–(43):[8]

(42) Ngaja yara balga-n, jilwa-n.
     I:NOM man:ABS hit-NONFUT, kick-NONFUT
     'I hit the man and [I] kicked [the man].'

(43) Ngaja yugu yuba-n, jugumbil jilwa-n.
      I:NOM stick:ABS put:down-NONFUT, woman:ABS kick-
      NONFUT
      'I put down the stick and [I] kicked the woman.'

Example (42) is perhaps less of a problem: both conjuncts do share the
same patient, and therefore conjunction reduction is licensed. Moreover,
it might simply be that (42) involves conjunction of verbs, that is, that the
structure is as in (44), in which case the relations of the noun phrases to the
verbs do not come into play:

(44) [ngaja yara [[balgan]$_V$ [jilwan]$_V$]$_V$]$_S$

Example (43) is more disturbing, but a ready analysis, consistent with
what has gone before, is in fact available, one which moreover also
subsumes (42). In Dyirbal, it is possible in an isolated sentence for the
agent to be omitted, that is, one can say simply *jugumbil balgan*. Often this
will be translated into English as an agentless passive 'the woman was hit',
a construction which can be interpreted either as having an indefinite
agent or as having as agent some participant retrievable from the broader
context, outside of the immediate sentence. Effectively, this means that
agent phrases in Dyirbal are freely deletable (and therefore freely
interpretable), as opposed to subjects (intransitive subjects, patients),
which are deletable only under highly specific syntactic conditions (and
whose reference is therefore retrievable syntactically).

I would therefore claim that in the second conjunct of (43), the agent is
freely deleted, that is, a more accurate English translation would be
something like 'the stick was put down by me and the woman was kicked.'
In (42), the patient is deleted under the appropriate syntactic constraint,
whereas the agent is freely deleted, cf. English 'the man was hit by me and
was kicked.' Agents in the basic voice in Dyirbal thus behave much like
agents in the passive voice in English. In particular, both are freely
deletable. In many instances, a freely deleted agent may in fact most
naturally receive the interpretation of being coreferential with the agent of
a preceding clause, as in English sentence (45), and I would argue that
Dyirbal sentence (42) is in all essential respects parallel to English
sentence (45). Of course, this interpretation of agent coreference is
sometimes implausible, and is therefore not assigned, as in (46):

(45) The man was attacked by a bandit and beaten up.

(46) The man was kidnapped by a bandit and rescued the next day.

To validate this assumption, it would be necessary to establish whether
sentences like (46) are possible in Dyirbal, as my analysis predicts – as far
as I am aware, this has not yet been tested by those with access to native

speakers. It should be noted that although I allude to a parallel between English and Dyirbal, the English parallel is by no means an integral part of my argument: given that agents are freely deletable in Dyirbal, one would predict quite independently of English that sentences like (42)–(43) should be possible in Dyirbal.

4 Discourse Interpretation and Conjunction Reduction

In section 3, we examined two languages with strict grammatical constraints on the interpretation of sentences with conjunction reduction. In this section, I wish to discuss some languages which lack such strict grammatical constraints, to see how sentences involving conjunction reduction are interpreted. In such languages, in principle the relevant sentences are ambiguous, and this ambiguity is often realized in practice, as in sentence (47) from Chukchi, a member of the Chukotko-Kamchatkan family of languages which is spoken in the Chukotka peninsula in the far north-east of the USSR (Nedjalkov 1979: 242):

(47) ətləg-e talayvə-nen ekək ənk?am ekvet-g?i.
       father-ERG hit-PAST:3SG → 3SG son:ABS and leave-PAST:3SG

The first clause of (47) means 'the father hit the son', since 'father', with ergative inflection, must be the agent and 'son', with absolutive inflection, must be the patient (given that the verb is transitive); the suffix -*nen* (a vowel harmony variant of -*nin*) indicates both past tense and that a third person singular agent is acting on a third person singular patient. The verb of the second conjunct is third person singular (intransitive), so that in principle either 'father' or 'son' could be taken, morphologically, to be its subject.[9] In Chukchi, there is no syntactic constraint on the interpretation of such sentences, so that the sentence can mean either 'the father hit the son and the father left' or 'the father hit the son and the son left.' The preferred interpretation is the former, although this preference can be eliminated by topicalizing 'son' in the first clause (which involves preposing the patient noun phrase), as in (48):

(48) Ekək ətləge talayvənen ənk?am ekvetg?i.

The relevance of topicalization will become clearer towards the end of this section.

In order to develop further the consideration of languages of this type, I wish first to consider some data from Kalaw Lagaw Ya, which is genetically a member of the Australian language family (although its speakers are culturally Torres Strait Islanders, rather than Aboriginals) and is spoken on islands in the Torres Strait, between the mainlands of

Australia and New Guinea.[10] In Kalaw Lagaw Ya, sentences with conjunction reduction are, in principle, ambiguous, as in (49):

(49) Kala Gibuma-n mathaman a zilamiz.
      Kala:NOM Gibuma-ACC hit:SG and run:away:SG
      'Kala hit Gibuma and [Kala/Gibuma] ran away.'

The preferred interpretation is '... and Kala ran away', although the interpretation '... and Gibuma ran away' is also perfectly possible.

Kalaw Lagaw Ya has a fairly complex morphology, and in many instances this morphology may exclude one of the interpretations that is in principle available. In other words, for many sentences one interpretation will be excluded, not by a syntactic constraint on conjunction reduction, but rather by the possibilities for combining different morphological forms in a clause. For instance, Kalaw Lagaw verbs show agreement in number (singular, dual, plural); intransitive verbs agree with their subject, transitive verbs with their patient. Consider now sentences (50)–(51):

(50) Kala yoepkoez-il mathamoeyn a zilamiz.
      Kala:NOM woman-PL hit:PL and run:away:SG
      'Kala hit the women and [Kala] ran away.'

(51) Kala yoepkoez-il mathamoeyn a zilamemin.
      Kala:NOM woman-PL hit:PL and run:away:PL
      'Kala hit the women and [the women] ran away.'

In (50), since the verb *zilamiz* is singular, its subject must be singular; therefore of the two possible antecedents, 'the women' is excluded and only 'Kala' is possible. Conversely, in (51) the verb *zilamemin* is plural, so 'Kala' is excluded as a possible antecedent and only 'the women' is possible. It is still possible in principle for the coreferential noun phrase in the first conjunct to be either agent (as in (50)) or patient (as in (51)). In sentence (49) above, both 'Kala' and 'Gibuma' are singular, so either is possible as subject of the singular verb *zilamiz*.

Sometimes one interpretation permitted by conjunction reduction will be excluded by nominal morphology. Most (though not all) Kalaw Lagaw Ya noun phrases have different morphological forms as agent and as patient of a transitive verb: for instance, personal names stand in the nominative (the same as the citation form) as agent but in the accusative (suffix -*n*) as patients. Compare sentences (52)–(53):

(52) Kala ngapa a Peku-n mathaman.
      Kala:NOM come and Peku-ACC hit:SG.
      'Kala came and [Kala] hit Peku.'

(53) Kala ngapa a Peku mathaman.
      Kala:NOM come and Peku:NOM hit:SG
      'Kala came and Peku hit [Kala].'

In the second conjunct of (52), the noun phrase *Peku-n* is accusative, therefore patient of the transitive verb *mathaman*. Since the verb 'hit' already has an overt patient but also requires an agent, the missing argument is, by elimination, the agent, thus giving the interpretation '. . . and Kala hit Peku'. In the second conjunct of (53), the noun phrase *Peku* is nominative, therefore agent of the transitive verb, which thus has a missing patient, giving the interpretation '. . . and Peku hit Kala'. Notice that in (52) the missing noun phrase is agent, while in (53) it is patient, indicating no syntactic constraint on the possibilities for conjunction reduction.

In the examples just discussed, it is the morphology that excludes one syntactically permissible interpretation. In yet another set of examples, neither syntax nor morphology excludes an interpretation, but one interpretation is excluded in terms of knowledge of extralinguistic possibilities and probabilities. Compare sentences (54) and (55):

(54) Kala woerab woeriman a zilamiz.
      Kala:NOM coconut:ABS strike:SG and run:away:SG
      'Kala struck the coconut and [Kala] ran away.'

(55) Kala woerab woeriman a papalamiz.
      Kala:NOM coconut:ABS strike:SG and break:SG
      'Kala struck the coconut and [the coconut] broke.'

The verbs in the second conjuncts of (54) and (55) are both singular, and so are both 'Kala' and 'coconut'. Thus neither syntax nor morphology would exclude the interpretation for (54) '. . . and the coconut ran away', or the interpretation for (55) '. . . and Kala broke'. (Note that *papalamiz* in (55) is, in Kalaw Lagaw Ya, unequivocally intransitive.) However, our knowledge of the world tells us that while people can run away, coconuts cannot; and that while coconuts are quite likely to break as a result of being struck, it is highly unlikely that a person would break as the result of striking a coconut. Thus in fact the interpretations given above are assigned, and the Kalaw Lagaw Ya speaker uttering these sentences need not worry about his intentions being misunderstood, even though the sentences are in a sense ambiguous.

One way of analyzing the above data from Kalaw Lagaw Ya would be to say that Kalaw Lagaw Ya is a pro-drop language, that is, noun phrases can be freely omitted provided their referents are retrievable. The ways in which the reference of an omitted noun phrase may be retrieved are many, including knowledge of the world and other structural information (noun and verb morphology), but in the absence of any syntactic constraints on conjunction reduction such constraints cannot, as in English or Dyirbal, be used in order to retrieve anaphoric relations.

The second language I want to examine in detail in this section is Lenakel, a language of the Southern Vanuatuan branch of Austronesian and spoken in southern Vanuatu (formerly the New Hebrides).[11] In

Lenakel, unlike Kalaw Lagaw Ya, the relevant phenomenon is not simply omission of a noun phrase, but rather the use of the 'echo subject' prefix *m-* as a means of indexing in the verb. This echo subject prefix commutes with the other person-and-number prefixes, for example third person *r-*, that is, it is mutually exclusive with them. The echo subject prefix always indicates that the subject of its verb is coreferential with some noun phrase in the preceding context, and what we are interested in establishing is the precise nature of the relation between the echo subject prefix and its antecedent.

In the most straightforward examples, the antecedent of the echo subject prefix is also a subject (intransitive subject or transitive agent), so that we get constrasts as in (56)–(57):[12]

(56) I-ɨm-vɨn m-ɨm-apul.
ISG-PAST-go ES-PAST-sleep.
'I went and [I] slept.'

(57) I-ɨm-vɨn r-ɨm-apul.
ISG-PAST-go 3-PAST-sleep
'I went and he slept.'

Let us now consider examples where the participants are all third person, and therefore the functional role of the echo subject prefix is most clear, as in (58)–(59):

(58) Magau r-ɨm-ho Tom kani m-akɨmw.
Magau 3-PAST-hit Tom and ES-run:away

(59) Magau r-ɨm-ho Tom kani r-akɨmw.
Magau 3-PAST-hit Tom and 3-run:away

In (58), with the echo subject prefix, the most natural interpretation is '. . . and Magau ran away', that is, with coreferential subjects; however, it is also possible to get the interpretation '. . . and Tom ran away', especially if the broader context establishes that Tom is the more likely subject (for instance, if this sentence were to occur in answer to the question 'why did Tom run away?'). In (59), the only possible interpretations are where the two subjects are non-coreferential; if Tom is the only other participant under consideration, then the interpretation is '. . . and Tom ran away'. This is one difference between the Lenakel echo subject marker and conjunction reduction in the other languages examined: in these other languages, conjunction reduction is always optional (one can say *the man hit the woman and the man/he ran away*), whereas in Lenakel use of the echo subject prefix seems to be obligatory.

In example (58), both noun phrases in the first clause are third person singular, and both interpretations (with Magau or Tom running away) make sense. What happens if these factors are changed? Sentence (60) shows that if the first clause contains a singular agent and a dual patient and the verb of the second clause is dual, then the echo subject prefix can be used to indicate coreference of the subject of the second conjunct with the patient of the first.

(60) Magau r-im-ho perasuaas mil kani m-u-akimw.
Magau 3-PAST-hit girl two and ES-DU-run:away
'Magau hit two girls and [the two girls] ran away.'

Example (61) shows that if knowledge of the world excludes or disfavors the interpretation whereby the agent of the first conjunct is the antecedent of the echo subject prefix, then the patient of the first conjunct can readily be taken as its antecedent:

(61) I-im-alak-hiáav-in kesi m-pwalhepwalhe.
ISG-PAST-throw-down-TRANS papaw/papaya ES-splatter
'I threw down the pawpaw and [the pawpaw] splattered.'

(The verb *pwalhepwalhe* in Lenakel is, incidentally, intransitive.)

In many respects, then, Lenakel is just like Kalaw Lagaw Ya with respect to the operation of conjunction reduction. There is, however, one important difference: in Kalaw Lagaw Ya the coreferential noun phrase is simply omitted in the second conjunct; in Lenakel, however, this noun phrase must be indexed by the echo subject prefix *m-*. The existence of this echo subject prefix, equivalent paradigmatically to any other subject prefix, indicates a somewhat greater integration of this phenomenon into the grammar of the language in Lenakel than in Kalaw Lagaw Ya.

At various points in this section, I have noted the relevance of topic status to interpretations of sentences. Although sentences like Chukchi sentence (47), repeated below as (62), are in principle ambiguous in Chukchi, Kalaw Lagaw Ya and Lenakel, there is a strong tendency for them to be interpreted with coreferential subjects (intransitive subjects and agents):

(62) ətləg-e talayvə-nen ekək ənk?am ekvet-g?i.
'The father hit the son and [the father > the son] left.'

The arrowhead in this gloss indicates that the interpretation where 'the father' is antecedent is preferred over the one where 'the son' is antecedent. If, however, the context makes clear that 'the son' is the topic, then the alternative interpretation is readily obtained. Since subjects/ agents in general make better topics than other constituents of a clause, one might even try to generalize the claim to say that overall the preferred antecedent is the most topical one: if no other noun phrase is explicitly the topic, then the preferred topic will be the agent/subject.

In order to carry this idea somewhat further, I want to conclude this section by investigating conjunction reduction in a typical European/ Mediterranean pro-drop language, Serbo-Croatian, spoken in Yugoslavia.[13] Since Serbo-Croatian is a pro-drop language, we might expect clauses lacking an overt subject, when they appear as second conjunct, to have freely interpreted subjects, as in the three languages discussed earlier in this section. When such examples are presented out of context, however, native speakers of Serbo-Croatian allow only the interpretation with coreferential subjects, much as in English (a clear case of a non-pro-drop language), as in examples (63)–(66):

(63) Petar je udario Pavla i otrčao je.
Petar:NOM be:PRES:3SG hit:PAST:MASC:SG Pavle:ACC and run:away:PAST:MASC:SG be:PRES:3SG
'Petar hit Pavle and [Petar/*Pavle] ran away.'

(64) *Petar je poljubio Maru i otrčala je.
Petar:NOM be:PRES:3SG kiss:PAST:MASC:SG Mara:ACC and run:away:PAST:FEM:SG be:PRES:3SG
'Petar hit Mara and [Mara] ran away.'

(65) *Petar je poljubio Maru i otrčali su.
Petar:NOM be:PRES:3SG kiss:PAST:MASC:SG Mara:ACC and run:away:PAST:PL be:PRES:3PL
'Petar hit Mara and [Petar and Mara] ran away.'

(66) *Petar je ispustio lubenicu i raspala se.
Petar:NOM be:PRES:3SG drop:PAST:MASC:SG melon:ACC and burst:PAST:FEM:SG REFL
'Petar dropped the melon and [the melon] burst.'

(Note that in Serbo-Croatian the usual way of forming the past tense is with the present of the copula 'be' – omitted in collocation with certain clitics, such as reflexive *se* – together with the past participle of the main verb. The noun *lubenica* 'melon' is feminine. The reflexive clitic *se* in (66) serves to make the verb intransitive.)

In (63), it is not possible to get the interpretation '... and Pavle ran away', even though *otrčao je* is well-formed as a separate sentence with the meaning 'he ran away.' In (64), likewise, the patient of the first conjunct cannot be interpreted as antecedent of the omitted noun phrase; since the verb of the second clause is feminine, *Petar* cannot be its antecedent, so the sentence is simply ungrammatical – crucially, the morphology (the feminine ending on the verb of the second conjunct) is not sufficient to force coreference between the patient of the first conjunct and the omitted subject of the second conjunct, even though *otrčala je* is a perfectly wellformed sentence in isolation, meaning 'she ran away.' Similarly, in (65) the plural ending on the verb in the second conjunct is not sufficient to permit the combined referent of agent and patient as subject of the second conjunct. Even more strikingly, in (66) it is not possible to get the interpretation where the patient of the first conjunct is subject of the second conjunct, although this is here reinforced by world knowledge – of the participants in the first clause, only the melon is a potential intransitive burster.

If, however, the broader context clearly establishes some noun phrase as topic, then that noun phrase is a possible antecedent to the missing subject of a second conjunct (or, more generally, of any following sentence), even if it is not coreferential with the subject of the immediately preceding clause. This is shown by examples (67)–(68):

(67) – Da li je Pavle otrčao?
       – Jeste, Petar ga je udario, i otrčao je.
       PTCL Q be:PRES:3SG Pavle:NOM run:away:PAST:MASC:SG
       be:PRES:3SG Petar:NOM he:ACC be:PRES:3SG
       hit:PAST:MASC:SG and run-away:PAST:MASC:SG
       be:PRES:3SG
       – Did Pavle run away?
       – Yes, Petar hit him and [Pavle] ran away.'

(68) Petar i Mara su ispustili lubenicu. Raspala se, i otišli su ka kupe
       drugu.
       Petar:NOM and Mara:NOM be:PRES:3PL drop:PAST:PL
       melon:ACC •platter:PAST:FEM:SG REFL and go:off:PAST:PL
       be:PRES:3PL that buy:PRES:3PL other:FEM:SG:ACC
       'Petar and Mara dropped a melon. [The melon] burst and [Petar
       and Mara] went off to buy another one.'

In Serbo-Croatian, then, the requirement that the antecedent of a pro-dropped subject be identified as topic seems to be particularly strong – much more so than in the other languages investigated in this section. In fact, the Serbo-Croatian data seem to point in the direction of two processes at work. In sentences like (67)–(68), we are dealing with the general pro-drop phenomenon. In examples like (63), however – compare also the ungrammatical (64)–(66) – we seem to be dealing with a phenomenon much more like conjunction reduction in English, with a syntactic constraint of coreferential subjects. It remains a task for future research to determine whether these sets of Serbo-Croatian sentences do indeed differ in the way suggested here, and more generally to investigate languages that would seem to fit in with the discussion of this section, to see what extent conjunction reduction phenomena are handled by pro-drop alone or to what extent a distinct rule of conjunction reduction is required.

5 Conclusions

Towards the beginning of this paper, I noted that there is no reason a priori to assume that the range of phenomena covered in this paper is homogeneous. To a certain extent, the progress of the discussion has borne this out: what I am calling conjunction reduction in languages like English and Dyirbal, which requires a special rule with syntactic constraints, is very different from apparent conjunction reductions that arise from the regular operation of pro-drop in languages like Chukchi, Kalaw Lagaw Ya or Lenakel. However, it remains true that the phenomena are comparable from a functional perspective – how it is that speakers express and hearers retrieve anaphoric relations in discourse. Moreover, the interaction between the two sets of phenomena is more complex than one might at first have imagined, as was seen in the interplay between pro-drop and conjunction reduction in Serbo-Croatian. The investigation of coreference from both grammatical and discourse perspectives, constrained by the communicative charge that limits the range of cross-linguistic variation, remains a viable research endeavor, of which only the surface has been scratched here.

Notes

Versions of material included in this paper have been presented to my seminar Coreference in Grammar and Discourse at the University of Southern California (1983) and in lectures at the following institutes: Max Planck Institute for Psycholinguistics, Institute of Language and Literature of the Academy of Sciences of the Estonian SSR, Memorial University of Newfoundland, Catholic University of Leuven and Nagoya University. I am grateful to all those who participated in these discussions.

    The following abbreviations are used: ABS – absolutive, ACC – accusative, CNJ – conjunct, DIR – direct, DS – different subject, DU – dual, ERG – ergative, ES – echo subject, FEM – feminine, LOC – locative, MASC – masculine, NOM – nominative, NONFUT – nonfuture, NP – noun phrase, OBV – obviative, PL – plural, PRES – present, PROX – proximate, PTCL – particle, Q – question, REFL – reflexive, S – sentence, SG – singular, SS – same subject, TRANS – transitive, V – verb, VP – verb phrase.

    1 For a more detailed development of this idea, see Reinhart (1983).
    2 In systematizing grammatical devices for indicating coreference, I have benefited greatly from the discussion in Foley and Van Valin (1984: ch. 7); I have used some of their examples below.
    3 In Algonquian languages, the term 'conjunct' is used for certain dependent verb forms. Direct transitive verb forms are those where the agent is higher on the person hierarchy than the patient, where the person hierarchy is $2 > 1 > 3PROX > 3OBV$; inverse transitive forms are those where the patient is higher than the agent.
    4 See, for instance, Chomsky (1981: sections 4.3, 4.5). Pro-drop is frequently

used for a cluster of properties, of which dropping of unstressed pronouns is only one. For present purposes, however, it is the only relevant property.

5 We will see below that this is a relatively informal sense of 'two components'. On standard syntactic analyses of sentences like (17), the immediate constituents are the subject noun phrase *the man* and the coordinate verb phrase *kissed the woman and ran away*.

6 The Dyirbal examples are taken or adapted from Dixon (1972), as is the basic analysis. In Dyirbal, nouns are usually (though not obligatorily) accompanied by classifiers; to avoid irrelevant distractions, all examples are cited here without classifiers.

7 To avoid irrelevant complications, I use the terms 'intransitive subject', '(transitive) agent', '(transitive) patient' here, for what in Comrie (1978) are, respectively, S, A and P. The slight differences between A and agent, and between P and patient, though important in other respects, are not relevant to the present discussion.

8 Note that personal pronouns in Dyirbal have nominative–accusative morphology, unlike the ergative–absolutive morphology of nouns. Syntactically, however, all noun phrases behave alike – in particular, pronouns participate in ergative–absolutive syntax.

9 The importance of verb agreement will become clearer in the discussion of Kalaw Lagaw Ya below.

10 For further discussion of Kalaw Lagaw Ya, see Comrie (1982).

11 The data are taken from Lynch (1983), supplemented by further information provided to me by the author.

12 In Lenakel, conjoined clauses may either be simply juxtaposed or separated by the conjunction *kani* 'and'. Explicit marking of tense is often dropped from non-initial conjuncts.

13 I am grateful to Svenka Savić for providing judgments on the Serbo-Croatian data. Judgments similar to those for Serbo-Croatian seem to hold in a number of other Mediterranean pro-drop languages, for example, Italian, Spanish and Tunisian Arabic, although this requires more detailed investigation.

References

Chomsky, N. (1957) *Syntactic Structures*. (Janua Linguarum, 4.) The Hague: Mouton.

— (1981) *Lectures on Government and Binding: The Pisa Lectures*. Studies in Generative Grammar, 9. Dordrecht: Foris Publications.

Comrie, B. (1978) 'Ergativity'. In: W. P. Lehmann, ed., *Syntactic Typology: Studies in the Phenomenology of Language*. Austin, TX: University of Texas Press.

— (1982) 'Ergativity and grammatical relations in Kalaw Lagaw Ya (Saibai dialect)'. *Australian Journal of Linguistics*, 1, 1–42.

— (1984) 'Person distinctions in coreference marking systems: a functional explanation'. *Working Papers in Linguistics* (University of Melbourne, Linguistics Division), 10, 49–56.

Dixon, R. M. W. (1972) *The Dyirbal Language of North Queensland*. Cambridge Studies in Linguistics, 9. Cambridge: Cambridge University Press.

Ellis, C. D. (1983) *Spoken Cree; West Coast of James Bay*, 2nd edn. Edmonton, Alberta: Pica Pica Press.

Foley, W. A. and R. D. Van Valin, Jr (1984) *Functional Syntax and Universal Grammar*. Cambridge Studies in Linguistics 38. Cambridge: Cambridge University Press.

Haiman, J. and P. Munro (eds) (1983) *Switch-Reference and Universal Grammar*. Typological Studies in Language 2. Amsterdam: John Benjamins.

Lynch, J. (1983) 'Switch-reference in Lenakel'. In Haiman and Munro (1983).

Nedjalkov, V. P. (1979) 'Degrees of ergativity in Chukchee'. In F. Plank (ed.), *Ergativity: Towards a Theory of Grammatical Relations*. London: Academic Press.

Reinhart, T. (1983) *Anaphora and Semantic Interpretation*. London: Croom Helm.

van Oirsouw, R. R. (1983) 'Coordinate deletion and *n*-ary branching nodes'. *Journal of Linguistics*, 19, 305–20.

(1987) *The Syntax of Coordination*. London: Croom Helm.

PART IV

Cognitive, Perceptual and Processing Explanations

CHAPTER 9

Language, Perception and the World

Michael Lee

It is always of interest to determine the grammatical character of languages ... and to classify languages according to the procedures that they use for expressing thought. But even after we become acquainted with the structures of language and classify them, we can draw no accurate conclusions outside the domain of linguistics proper.... *The true and unique object of linguistics is language studied in and for itself.*

Ferdinand de Saussure

True to the spirit of Saussure, a majority of the explanations offered for linguistic universals are, in some sense or another, related to the nature of language as an independent system of communication. Most analyses of linguistic structure require only that humans are machines with a certain degree of computational ability which have developed a formal (or semi-formal) symbol system for encoding the objects, properties and relations in their logically structured universe. Even 'semantic' explanations frequently depend only on the fact that there *are* objects, properties and relations, and that they obey the laws of logic (cf. Keenan 1978). The commonalities among human languages are attributed to the principles governing formal systems and to the realities of the computational 'hardware' (for example, memory and processing constraints). The force of the man-as-computer metaphor is obvious here. All of these explanations would remain in force even if human beings were suddenly transported to a planet far different from the Earth, or if our bodies were more akin to those of dolphins rather than apes.

Clearly, though, the structure of our everyday experience is reflected in the structure of our languages. Although language is indeed a system of communication, it is a system working within the confines of the real world. Language is constrained not only by the limitations of the hardware, but also by the particularities (and peculiarities) of observable reality. We humans have much more in common with each other than the hardware of our brain. Despite the fact that I come into contact with quite a different set of objects than a Kalahari bushman, the possible divergence between our experiences in this world is circumscribed by a number of factors which are independent of us both, and even of our speech communities as a whole. For example, we can both feel the effects of gravity and enjoy the benefits of stereoscopic vision. These shared experiences exert a force on the languages of all cultures, giving rise to linguistic universals. As a result, linguistic analysis has the potential to reveal the ways in which the outside world influences our conceptual structure.

Some universals of language are not mandated by our linguistic competence, nor are they the result of language use. Rather, the universals I will discuss are due to an interaction between the linguistic system and accidental properties of our human experience on Earth. I mean accidental in the sense that there is no logical necessity for the facts to be as they are. The physical structure of our eyes, ears and bodies is independent from our linguistic ability, but nevertheless affects our language. Similarly, the fact that animals with beaks tend to also have wings is a fact about the world, not about our minds. Nevertheless, the existence of such correlations is central to certain aspects of linguistic structure.

Language is a communication sytem which we use in order to talk about our experiences. It should not be surprising, therefore, to find that the structure of language is influenced by the structure of our experiences. In the first part of this paper, I will show some of the ways in which human beings *impose* structure on an unstructured world, not through cognitive or linguistic processes, but rather due to the physical properties of our perceptual systems. Next I will consider some cases in which our linguistic and conceptual systems take advantage of structure that is inherent in the world. The influence of inherent structure on language is clearest in certain well-defined semantic domains, and I will discuss one such domain (body-part terminology) before moving on to an extended discussion of noun classifier systems. Classifiers are grammatical morphemes which derive from nouns, and the transition from noun to classifier provides an illustration of how lexical structure becomes relevant for the grammar. The major moral of this exploration is that our everyday experiences as humans on Earth exert more pressure on linguistic systems than has traditionally been recognized.

1 Counteracting Forces in Phonology

In no area of the grammar are the opposing constraints of the language system and the outside world more apparent than in phonology. Because the effects are relatively clear in this area, it can act as a model to help us understand the more opaque semantic extensions of the same principles.

As far as the language *system* is concerned, the sole purpose of the phonological component is to translate semantic content into sound. From this point of view, the only requirement of a language's phonology is that it provide some set of perceptually distinctive units which can be combined into unique lexical items, that is, provide a different sound unit for each 'concept'. To perform this function most efficiently, each syllable in a language is ideally maximally contrastive. Lack of ambiguity between words and ease of identification are the goals of a communication system.

What is remarkable, say Lindblom, MacNeilage and Studdert-Kennedy (1984), is that all languages use the same method to achieve the goal of contrastiveness, namely via phonemic coding and distinctive features.

> Although by definition semantically irreducible, [language's] smallest meaningful elements – the lexical and grammatical morphemes – can be further analyzed phonologically into a limited number of phonemes and allophones, i.e. vowels and consonants . . . Rather than use (the logically equally possible alternative of) gestalt coding – one holistic phonetic signal per morpheme – languages uniformly favor phonemic coding. (Lindblom et al. 1984)

One plausible explanation is that phonemic coding is simply more efficient than holistic coding. 'Holistic coding tends to rapidly crowd the phonetic space and is therefore incompatible with communicative demands for sufficiently distinct signals' (Lindblom et al. 1984). This explanation is what I have characterized as system-internal, since it is based on the idea that language must serve as an effective communication device.

Actually, though, the explanation is not entirely divorced from real-world considerations. As I've already noted, the language system is embedded within a real-world context, and it is the real world which establishes its parameters. Holistic coding would not be appreciably less efficient (than phonemic coding) if we had an unlimited range of phonetic signals. We need to avoid crowding only because of the limited range of possible articulations. The range is limited not by linguistic competence, but rather by the nature of our articulatory and auditory mechanisms. We can only contort our tongues into a certain number of different positions, and can only hear signals within a certain frequency range.

Simplistically, we can think of two counteracting forces at work on a developing phonemic system. Language, with a capital L, is an error-correcting code, and would like distinct semantic notions to have maximally distinct phonetic realizations. Articulatory considerations, on the other hand, tend to favor syllables which require less manipulation of the oral tract. If a language (with a small L) wants the most efficient system overall, it will code its morphemes using a set of syllables that display 'sufficient perceptual differences at acceptable articulatory costs'.

Lindblom et al. (1984) set out to determine whether the interaction of these counteracting forces is sufficient to account for the universal development of distinctive features and for the 'favored systems of stops and vowels in the languages of the world'. In general, they wanted to test whether the most common phonemic inventories could be explained on the basis of a 'self-organizing process'.

Toward this end, they developed a series of computational simulations which assigned phonetic shape to a predetermined number of distinct semantic notions. That is, their program was designed to generate the set of k syllables which best fulfilled both semantic and articulatory needs, where k was a number decided upon in advance by the experimenter. The simulations had access to a universal specification of 'possible articulations' as well as a 'perceptual space'. To model the opposing constraints on the system, the program was instructed to show a preference for maximally distinct signals in the perceptual space and for 'less extreme' articulation in the phonetic space. They found that the interaction of performance constraints with the needs of the system automatically gives rise to preferences for certain syllables over others, and that minimal pairs arise spontaneously. That is, when the simulation chooses the most distinctive set of syllables, this set always includes syllables with the same vowel nucleus which differ only in their consonantal onset. Since these syllables are identical except for their initial segment, they form minimal pairs – the basis for phonemic coding.

The important point about the results of Lindblom et al. (1984) is that although the unstructured phonetic and perceptual spaces are inherently continuous, certain aspects of human perceptual and motor mechanisms impose discontinuities,[1] that is, prominence to certain aspects of the relevant domain, and the result is a set of language universals.

Random sampling of the possibilities offered by the universal phonetic space should make all such possibilities equally probable. However, in the presence of certain constraints, nonuniform preferences for certain syllables over others arise ... They are both performance constraints and the 'system'. (Lindblom et al. 1984)

The preference for a particular syllable is a result partially of the way it is produced, and partially of the way it is perceived. In both cases, non-linguistic aspects of human anatomy are relevant. The mechanics of articulation causes certain feature combinations to be easier to produce, making choices in the phonetic space non-random. Also, contrastiveness in the perceptual (acoustic) space is not a function of simple distance. In addition to setting the upper and lower bounds of the perceptual space, our sense of hearing imposes certain discontinuities. The shape of our ears, for instance, reinforces certain frequencies, thereby making formants at those frequencies more perceptible, and differences in those frequency ranges more contrastive. The length of the auditory canal causes it to have resonance properties which create an *equal loudness contour* (Scharf 1978): sounds at 1,000 Hz need reach our ears with only half the pressure (in dBs) of sounds at 500 Hz to be perceived as equally loud.

The importance of the equal loudness contour for linguistics is that it reaches its minimum (that is, fewer dBs for equal loudness) in the frequency range between 1,000 and 2,000 Hz, the average position of the second and third formant in speech. Carlson, Fant and Granstrom (1975) built an electronic model of auditory analysis which incorporated the resonance properties of the ear, and this model was found to produce two major peaks in the output spectrum near the positions of F2 and F3. As a result, vowels are more contrastive when they differ in their F2 and F3 frequencies than F1 or F4 frequencies.

A fair number of the non-random properties of phonemic systems can be explained as the result of the interaction between contrastiveness and ease of articulation. What I have particularly in mind are properties of markedness and redundancy. For every distinctive feature, there is an unmarked value which appears more frequently cross-linguistically and which is the only value for the feature when a language does not make a contrast. It has often been noted that the unmarked value for a feature tends to be the value with the least articulatory cost, that is, the value most easily articulated. Voiceless consonants, for instance, are more common than voiced consonants since voicing requires subglottal air pressure to be greater than supraglottal pressure while non-voicing imposes no such restriction. However, perceptual considerations come into play as well, particularly in explaining certain dependencies beween features. For many distinctive features, the unmarked value is dependent on the value of another feature. For example, the unmarked value of the feature [voice] is [−voice] for consonants, but [+voice] for vowels and nasals ([+son] segments).

The dependency between voice and sonority can be explained by reference to the opposing constraints on the system. In the case of consonants, there is no significant difference in perceptibility between voiced and voiceless consonants. However, voiceless consonants are easier to produce. Articulation of a voiced consonant has conflicting aerodynamic requirements. To preserve voicing, air pressure in the oral cavity must be lower than the subglottal pressure. To produce a consonant, the air pressure in front of the blockage (by the tongue) has to be greater than the pressure behind the blockage. For a voiced consonant, both conditions must be met (subglottal pressure > oral pressure > ambient air pressure).[2]

The articulation of vowels, on the other hand, requires no oral blockage, so there is no conflict. Furthermore, vowels contrast only with respect to the shape of the (resonating) oral cavity. The resonating properties of the oral tract are much more perceptible when there is glottal vibration. The frequent dependency between the features [nasal] and [voice] has a similar motivation. Nasalization is simply the addition of a resonating cavity – the nasal passage – and addition of the cavity has a more contrastive effect when there is greater vibration. The increase in contrastiveness offsets the increase in articulatory effort.

The resonance properties of the ear play a role as well. As I noted above, distinctions between the F2 and F3 positions of different vowels are more contrastive than differences in other formants due to reinforcement within the auditory canal. As a result, languages favor vowels which maximally contrast in the mid-frequency ranges. The fact that back vowels are frequently [+round] (and front vowels [−round]) finds its explanation here. The primary acoustic difference between front and back vowels is the frequency of F2 – front vowels have a high F2 frequency relative to the corresponding back vowel. Labial constrictions have the effect of lowering all formant frequencies (Pickett 1980). Rounding a back vowel, therefore, lowers its already low F2, as well as its F3 frequency. An unrounded front vowel, meanwhile, retains high frequencies for both formants. In this way rounding reinforces the contrastiveness of the feature [back] with a minimum of articulatory effort.

Non-linguistic factors, then, play a crucial role in the development of phonemic contrasts. If future generations of human beings develop substantially longer (or shorter) auditory tracks, this minor anatomical variation will change the dynamics of the self-organizing processes, with a resulting change in phonetic inventories. The universal phonetic inventory and the preferred types of phonological systems are in large part determined by contingent facts about the human body, not by any aspect of linguistic competence.

2 Imposed Discontinuities in Semantics

The model of these phonological explanations can be found in certain semantic domains as well. Bierwisch (1967) speculated that the ultimate semantic features, like phonetic distinctive features, would have a biological basis: 'There are good reasons to believe that the semantic markers in an adequate description of a natural language . . . represent . . . certain deep seated, innate properties of the human organism and the perceptual apparatus.' In the phonological domain we have seen how our sense of hearing shows preference for certain stimuli as opposed to others in the objectively continuous auditory space. When we look to 'semantic space', we find our other senses (particularly vision) selecting certain stimuli as prominent.

Probably the most famous example of this type of explanation comes from color term research. Investigation into the lexical domain of color originally arose as an attempt to prove a strong version of the Whorfian hypothesis. According to the hypothesis (which can be seen as the antithesis of the search for universals), languages can vary without restraint.[3] The color spectrum is a continuous domain, and one which presumably every culture has equivalent contact with, so its division into discrete lexical items should be completely arbitrary.

Early research tended to support the hypothesis. Languages varied in the number of lexical items they used to subdivide the color spectrum, with anywhere from two to eleven basic terms. Experimenters, armed with a complete set of Munsell color chips, went into the field and asked speakers to pick out all of the chips which were *red*. Consistent with the hypothesis, speakers of different languages picked out different sets of chips, suggesting that their concept of *red* was different.

There was a problem, however. Not only did speakers of different languages disagree about what constituted *red*, so did different speakers of the *same* language. If the point was to show that a language can arbitrarily divide the spectrum (and impose this division upon its speakers' conceptual system), then all speakers of the same language should make the same judgment.

The breakthrough was provided by Brent Berlin and Paul Kay (1969). They noticed that there was a certain subset of the chips which all the speakers of a language could agree on. So instead of asking for the range of chips that the speaker would label *red* or *blue*, they asked for 'the best example' of each color. On this task they found a high degree of agreement between speakers. And when they applied the same technique to speakers of many languages, they found that the focal point for the different color terms showed remarkable consistency cross-culturally. If a language had a term corresponding to *red*, then speakers of that language would choose the same focal point as, for example, an English speaker. Far from being arbitrary, the choice of focal point was completely predictable!

Berlin and Kay's (1969) research revealed that of the 2,048 possible combinations of eleven basic color terms, only twenty-two combinations are actually attested. Languages sharing the same number of color terms always code the same colors, and there is a non-arbitrary order in which focal points are added into a language's lexicon (see figure below). If a language has only three color terms, they are always centered on black, white and red. If such a language adds a fourth term, it will always be either green or yellow. And so on.

```
white           green
      > red >            > blue > brown
black           yellow
```

The explanation for these striking facts (Kay and McDaniel 1978) is that the focal points for color terms are in fact determined by the neural anatomy of our color vision. Different wavelengths of light (corresponding to different colors) cause different responses in the visual nervous system. In the neural pathway between the eye and the visual cortex, these responses are 'transformed into a set of opponent neural responses'.

Two properties distinguish a cell as an opponent response cell. First, an opponent response cell has a spontaneous rate of firing – a basal response rate that it maintains without external stimulation. Second, the cell shows an increased rate of firing in the presence of lights whose dominant wavelengths are from certain regions of the visual spectrum, while lights from the complementary spectral regions will decrease its rate of firing below its basal rate. (Kay and McDaniel 1978)

In the human visual system, there are four types of opponent cells. The first kind is excited by light from the red (far long) part of the spectrum and inhibited by light which is predominantly green (near short). The second kind is the mirror image of the first: these cells are excited by green and depressed by red. The third increases its firing rate when exposed to yellow light and decreases when exposed to blue light, and the fourth does the opposite.

These oppositions provide the basis for establishing four distinct color categories. The first and second cell types provide the same information, as do the third and fourth types. When exposed to the color red, for instance, the first type of neuron *increases* its rate while the second kind *decreases* its rate. Pure red, as far as the visual cortex is concerned, is that wavelength which maximally excites type 1 neurons and maximally inhibits type 2 neurons (while leaving types 3 and 4 at their basal rate).

As it turns out, the color chip chosen by all speakers of the various languages as the 'best example' of *red* corresponds to the wavelength which maximizes the rate difference between types 1 and 2. McDaniel has experimentally shown that 'the particular wavelengths at which the neural response functions reach their maxima . . . coincide with the wavelengths at which the semantic [color] categories reach their maxima, i.e. have their foci' (Kay and McDaniel 1978).

Focal colors correspond to the points in the spectrum which produce the most distinctive response in the neurons of our eyes. As in other areas of the grammar (for example, vowel systems), languages code the most contrastive stimuli first. The order in which color foci are differentiated in a language shows the pressure of the system just as the order of distinctive feature contrasts does in Lindblom et al. (1984). *Green* is added immediately after *red* because it is the most distinct from *red* (that is, more distinct than *blue* or *brown*). Only when the semantic component of the language system requires greater codability will finer distinctions be made.[4]

But the lexicalization of color is sensitive to real-world factors as well. The results of the color term research are comparable to the results of Lindblom et al. (1984) for phonemic systems: 'A particular structure is inherent in the human perception of color, a structure which is not deducible from the physical properties of light alone' (Kay and McDaniel 1978). Once again our sensory mechanisms are treating certain stimuli as special when the objective sensory space gives no basis for the distinction. The universals of lexical structure (and lexical development) in this domain are the result of processes completely outside of linguistic competence.

3 Iconicity

Another whole class of universals results from structure which is actually present in the objective data. Rather than creating distinctions which do not exist (as with color terminology), languages simply pick up on prominent features of the item(s) being labeled. The simplest way that language can reflect real-world distinctions is through iconicity, where the linguistic code is a direct model of the world it is describing.

The myriad ways in which language is iconic have received more and more attention in recent years, and at least one whole volume has been devoted to the subject (Haiman 1985). Iconicity is apparent in all areas of the grammar, from intonation to word order to lexical semantics. In a great many cases, however, the linguistic code is not directly isomorphic with the outside world, but rather with some other part of the grammar. This brand of iconicity is known as *automorphism*, and is amenable to system-internal explanation. A simple example is X-bar theory in syntax, which claims that there is a one-to-one correspondence between the structures of all phrasal nodes (Jackendoff 1977). The structure of the Noun Phrase is iconic with that of the Verb Phrase. Such relationships make the grammar of a language simpler, by making possible a more general statement of Phrase Structure rules. As a result, languages tend to display what Hawkins (1983) calls *cross-categorial harmony*: the modifiers of all syntactic head categories occur on the same side of that head. Hawkins (1983) is one of the many attempts to generalize the list of word order universals in Greenberg (1966) into an automorphic generalization.

Automorphism is not limited to formal properties of the grammar. Greenberg (1985) discusses the fact that time, space and discourse deixis are commonly mapped onto the same set of demonstrative pronouns as an instance of automorphism. The same pronominal form may signal, for example, first person, closeness to the speaker and the immediate future because the three domains have parallel (that is, iconic) structures. In this case, the inconicity is due to metaphorical extension of the spatial domain to the more abstract domains of time and 'discourse space'.

A particular conception of space derived from the speech situation as structured by human physiology and psychology underlies a series of iconic mappings from space into real time and discourse time. The term 'icon' has in relation to language diverse aspects . . . the mapping [in this case is from] . . . a set of linguistic terms . . . into yet another set of linguistic terms. (Greenberg 1985)

Greenberg's analysis shows that even when the iconicity is not a formal property of the grammar (as it is with X-bar theory), it may still show isomorphism with human conceptual structure rather than the world. Two of the most far-reaching claims of inconicity can serve to illustrate my point. Bybee (1985) argues that the relative order of verbal inflections in a language can be derived from a very general principle.

> The proximity of elements in a clause follows some natural (iconic) principle whose result is that elements that go together semantically tend to occur close together . . . The more relevant a morphological category is to the verb, the closer its marker will occur with respect to the verb stem. (Bybee 1985)

The iconic principle involved here is very robust, not just in morphology but in syntax as well. However, linguistic form is not mirroring the objective world. 'Elements that go together semantically' is not a notion which can be characterized by reference to inherent properties of the individual elements. It is defined by the human conceptual system. The principle follows from the conceptual metaphor CLOSENESS IS STRENGTH OF EFFECT (cf. Lakoff and Johnson 1980). This metaphor certainly has an experiential basis, but that basis is not strictly iconic.

The same caveat has been made by Givón (1985) in his discussion of iconicity in topic accessibility. The fact Givón sets out to explain is that 'one may rank various topic-coding devices along the continuum of degree of continuity/predictability/accessibility of the topic NP.'

most accessible/predictable

  ▲ zero anaphora
  │ unstressed pronouns/verb agreement
  │ stressed pronouns
  │ full NPs
  ▼ modified full NPs
least accessible/predictable

The principle which Givón suggests to account for the continuum is that 'the more mental effort is expended in processing a topic NP . . . , the more coding material is used to represent it in language.' This, he claims, is an iconic principle, but notes that 'the coding relation here is *not* between language/thought and some experience, but rather between language/thought and some abstract mental process' (Givón 1985).

My aim is not to diminish the importance or relevance of the work on iconicity in these areas. The main goal of that research has been to show that language is less purely symbolic than has previously been assumed, and I do not dispute this claim. My only point is that these explanations depend mostly on the nature of the human conceptual system, not directly on properties of the external world. Iconicity is a relation 'between a sign system and the *concepts* it denotes' (Haiman 1985; my emphasis), and so linguistic form only models the world to the extent that our conceptual system reflects properties of the world.

Most of the work which has established a clear link between the structure of the world and linguistic form has been in lexical semantics. It may be, in fact, that the source of all iconicity with the real world is ultimately lexical. The structure of semantic domains acts as the link between our conceptual system and the outside world. As we saw with Greenberg (1985), iconic elements in abstract domains frequently find their roots in metaphorical extension from a more concrete semantic domain. Temporal and discourse deixis are rooted in spatial deixis. This point, with many examples, is discussed in detail by Lakoff and Johnson (1980).

As a representative example of an iconically structured lexical domain, consider the human body. Because our bodies are so integrated with everything we do, the human body is a semantic domain which every language necessarily lexicalizes. Their means of dividing the body up into labeled parts is not arbitrary, however. Unlike the color domain, the human body is not continuous or unstructured. Its shape and functional structure provide the basis for treating certain parts as more important and as fundamentally different from other parts.

Andersen (1978) examined the lexical structure of this semantic field in over fifty languages and found a relatively small number of recurring patterns. First of all, every language treats the body as a partonomy.

> As in other fields, ... there is a hierarchical organization to body-part domains in all languages. However, the organization is somewhat different from that of other domains and is best described as a *partonomy* (consisting of 'part of' relationships) as opposed to the more typical *taxonomy* (consisting of 'kind of' relationships).

A finger is part of a hand which is part of an arm, and so on. This structure is presumably chosen because of the physical nature of the domain. Fillmore (1978) discusses the idea that different semantic domains have different lexical structure because of the inherent structure of the domains in the real world.

> Some of the [lexical] categorizations we find have only linguistic explanations: people do it that way because that's how their language evolved, and it could have evolved in a number of other ways. Others have, at least in part, explanations that depend crucially on such matters as how human beings perceive things in the world around them. (Fillmore 1978)

Andersen (1978) found that partonomies of body-part terms 'rarely exceed five levels of depth, and never exceed six'. There are two possible explanations for this limit. Cognitively, six levels of structure may simply be a limit on the human ability to classify. Berlin (1972) found the same depth as the limiting number for taxonomies of ethnobiological domains (cf. below). This explanation receives some backing from the fact that body-part partonomies *are* characterized by other properties which apply to taxonomies (for example, basic level structure). But nonetheless, the structure of the human body itself plays a role in determining the number of partonomic levels. At the very least, if our bodies were less differentiated, like those of fish for instance, then partonomic depth would presumably be less.

The interesting question about the body-part lexical field is which parts are given a unique label. 'While all languages may recognize and label the head, the trunk, and the upper and lower limbs, they often divide these parts differently' (Andersen 1978).

> In examining this domain in other languages . . . one is struck by two general phenomena: (1) certain types of polysemous relationships appear over and over again in unrelated languages; (2) a number of categories are (almost) universally given the least complex expression, with other categories often derived from them in fairly predictable ways. The categories . . . that are usually given morphologically simple expression include . . . HEAD, ARM, LEG, FACE, EYE, MOUTH, and EAR. (Andersen 1978)

The terms which are most frequently basic are clearly the structurally and/ or functionally most prominent parts of the body.

The effects of the mechanical implementation of our perceptual systems show that various features of our human bodies can shape our language. Just as the neural anatomy of our eyes determines our perception of the world, and therefore its coding in linguistic terms, so their position in the front of our heads affects perception. Most obviously, it determines what we can and cannot see. This effect, which at first seems innocuous, can have important ramifications for language. It means, for example, that we can more easily see the upper front portion of our bodies. As a result, in polysemous relationships it is always the terms for the upper limbs which are extended to cover the lower limbs, not vice versa. 'Thus, languages frequently refer to toes as "fingers of the foot", but never to fingers as "toes of the hand"' (Andersen 1978). Similarly, *elbow* can refer to both the elbow and the knee, but *knee* can never be extended to include the elbow.

Also, languages have more terms to differentiate the features of the anterior region of our bodies than the posterior. None of the frequent basic terms which Andersen lists refer to our back side. There is, of course, another reason for this asymmetry. Not only are our backs unavailable for inspection, but they are not as differentiated (or functional) as our 'fronts'. One consequence of this difference is that many languages have a general term for the posterior of the body, but not for the anterior.

> Hence an English-speaking person can say *My nose itches* or *My stomach itches*, but not *My front itches*. By way of contrast, the posterior part of the body is relatively undifferentiated and so . . . a

Hausa speaker can say *Bayata ta yi zufi* 'My back itches', as well as *Yana bayata* 'It's in back of me', just as an English speaker can comfortably say either of the two sentences that serve as glosses. (Hill 1982).

The importance of the placement of our sensory organs can be seen in other semantic domains as well. Clark and Clark (1977) have suggested that spatial terms which refer to areas 'upward' and 'forward' (for example, *in front of*, *ahead*, *above*) are conceptually simpler than those for the corresponding 'negative' directions (*in back of* , *behind*, *below*), and are also easier to process. The positive terms 'cover the optimally perceptible space' (Andersen 1978). Clark and Clark (1977) present evidence from language acquisition which shows that young children show an attentional bias for the upper portions of vertically oriented designs. Furthermore, when children are presented with pictures of figures in random configurations, they tend to orient the picture so that the center of attention is at the top. 'For instance, presented with a picture of a line with a circle at one end, they orient the picture so that the line is vertical with the circle at the top' (Andersen 1978). The influence of canonical human position is obvious.

These data show one way in which the structural asymmetries of our body have effects outside the lexical structure of the body-part domain. The effects, in fact, extend outside the linguistic system to influence performance on non-linguistic tasks. Children orient the center of attention at the top of a figure because they perceive this orientation as the natural one, as a result of interaction with human beings. Adults, too, perceive some objects in the world as having an inherent orientation on the vertical and horizontal axes. Hill (1982) demonstrates that the basis for determining the inherent orientation of an object is (metaphorical) projection of the human body onto the object. Our bodies have inherent asymmetries which can be used to define three axes of spatial orientation: up/down, front/back, left/right.

> In all languages there appear to be pairs of lexical items that name asymmetrical axes of spatial orientation: the up/down, the front/back, and the left/right. The referential functions for these lexical polarities may be compared across languages, for they are ultimately anchored in the human body itself. (Hill 1982)

Hill shows that the degree to which these three axes are differentiated on the human body is paralleled by the degree to which we impute intrinsic orientation to other objects.

> Bodily asymmetries do not differentiate the three axes to the same degree: the up/down has the most differentiation, then the front/ back and, finally, the left/right. This order is also reflected in the

degree to which each axis is viewed as belonging to other entities in the physical world. In effect, we view more entities as possessing up/down orientation than front/back or left/right . . . An entity is viewed as possessing an orientational axis if it is characterized by asymmetries . . . which are perceived as analogous to those which reflect the corresponding axis in our own bodies. (Hill 1982)

Gravity provides an intrinsic vertical axis to most objects, regardless of their shape. With the possible exception of balls, all objects are viewed as having a vertical orientation. In most cases, this orientation agrees with that dictated by gravity, that is, the *top* of the object is its higher side. However, this default assignment can be overridden by other considerations. Bodily asymmetries in humans are functional as well as formal, so in certain cases an object might have a functional area near its base which is perceived as a 'head', so that the object is treated as if it were upside-down. It is cases like these which show the influence of human anatomy.

Our bodies also have a fairly salient differentiation between front and back. The front is the most important functionally, since it contains all of the sense organs and is the side which faces the direction of travel when we walk. Front/back orientation is intrinsically assigned to objects which have a formal or functional differentiation between the two sides. 'We ascribe a front/back axis to a telephone. Like our bodies, it is characterized by a stable upright position, but it also reflects a horizontally oriented asymmetry – it possesses one side, which we call its front, more differentiated than the others' (Hill 1982).

In all cases, the *front* is the side which is functional and is therefore 'characteristically oriented toward the human user' (Hill 1982). The only reason for this side to be considered the front is the structure of the human body. If we really had eyes in the back of our head, or if we always walked backwards (or on our hands), then the facts would be different. An important point here is that it is human interaction with the object that defines its functional surface. In all examples where the inherent structure of the world is reflected in language, there is an element of functional interaction (cf. discussion of the basic level below).

The lexical universals of body-part terminology are a result of iconicity between language and the concepts it denotes. The difference between this semantic field and the examples of automorphism is that here our conceptualization of the domain is modeled on the real world. If a human brain were transplanted into the body of a dolphin, the dolphin might still use X-bar syntax, but would conceptualize the spatial domain quite differently. (And consequently also the temporal domain, which is metaphorically structured by the spatial domain.)

4 Classifiers: An Exercise in Explanation

Up to this point we have seen how real-world properties can influence the structure of particular lexical fields such as body-part terminology, color and orientational terms. In these areas, the real-world structure of the semantic domain is reflected in the conceptual structure of the corresponding linguistic domain. In addition to these domain-specific influences, there are also some more general ways in which facts about the world influence lexical and grammatical development. That is, there are some properties of the world which have ramifications beyond single well-defined semantic domains and apply 'across the board'. These properties of overall lexical structure gain particular importance for grammar when we consider that many grammatical terms derive historically from open-class lexical terms.

In order to illustrate some of these more general principles and the effect they may have on grammatical particles, I will discuss some of my own work on noun classifier systems. Classifiers occupy a unique position in the grammar. Although they are clearly grammatical morphemes, in most languages their origin from nouns is still transparent. Frequently, in fact, a language's classifiers are homophonous with nouns which are still in use. In Lee (1987b) I show that classifiers arise in a language as a result of the general process of lexical expansion discussed by Berlin (1972) for taxonomic domains. Because they originate in lexical domains which are subject to the influence of the outside world, classifier systems show how this influence can begin to invade the grammar.

A noun classifier is an independent morpheme which 'denotes some salient perceived or imputed characteristic of the entity to which the associated noun refers' (Allan 1977). The most common type of classifier is the numeral classifier, so named because it occurs obligatorily, between the number and the noun, in counting constructions. The closest thing that English has to classifiers occurs in measure phrases such as:

8 *head* of cattle
5 *sheets* of paper
9 *gallons* of gas

The word which immediately follows the numeral picks out some characteristic of the noun that is being counted. *Sheet* tells us that *paper* is flat, two dimensional: it can only occur with nouns having this property. In a classifier language, this type of construction is generalized to include what would be count nouns in English. A prototypical example is Mandarin Chinese.

liang *zhi* qianbi   'two (long-thing) pencils'
yi *ben* shu   'one (volume) book'

Since the distinction of classifier systems (as opposed to 'gender' or 'noun class' systems, cf. Dixon 1986) is their semantic coherence, most research has been directed toward describing their semantic properties. Interest in classifiers is primarily motivated by their being an instance of overt linguistic categorization, which makes them important in the context of recent work on the nature of human categorization in general (e.g. Rosch et al. 1976; Lakoff 1987). 'In their completely overt arrangement of objects into classes, classifier systems may indeed expose how the process of categorization works in more graphic ways than lexical taxonomies' (Craig 1986a). Because of this motivation, two main questions have been asked about classifiers: (i) to what extent do they establish semantically coherent categories?, and (ii) what does this coherence (or lack thereof) tell us about the cognitive processes which lie behind language?

A survey of the classifier studies made from a synchronic typological viewpoint reveals inconclusive, even contradictory, answers to these questions. Research has revealed that the same semantic notions are encoded by classifiers in widely disparate languages, and the nature of these notions appears to indicate the operation of cognitive principles. However, the realities of the systems which have been studied in detail have made any straightforward statement of cognitive principles impossible. Most languages have a set of noun classes which fall somewhere between a fully semantically based system and an arbitrary gender system. In Lee (1987b) I argue that the contradictory findings can only be resolved by looking at the historical development of classifier systems, and that it is in the mapping between diachronic states that the underlying cognitive principles most clearly reveal themselves. My primary concern here is with the ultimate origin of classifier morphemes, which I believe to be the result of an interaction between cognitive principles of organization and the contingent structure of the world.

The clues which lead to the origin of noun classifiers can be found in the *nature* of their semantic coherence. There have been two general hypotheses about the composition of noun classes in a classifier system. Works such as Allan (1977) and Adams and Conklin (1973) focus on the inherent properties which all (or at least most) of the members of a class share and try to provide an exhaustive list of the semantic features which serve as the basis for classification in natural language. They explain the recurrence of particular features in different languages on the basis of human perceptual faculties, explicitly treating noun classes as *cognitively* based categories. Denny (1976), on the other hand, sees classifiers as a means of partitioning the world into a set of functional classes. 'Nouns have more to do with what is out there in the world, and classifiers more to do with how humans interact with the world' (Denny 1976). Rather than reflecting cognitively salient properties, noun classes are *socially* determined categories. Class assignment is made on the basis of an object's primary social function.

As we will see below, each of these perspectives accounts for a certain range of the known facts about classifier systems. In particular, a cognitive approach provides the clearest explanation for the frequent similarities between the (inanimate) noun classes in widely varied languages, while a social/functional approach more effectively deals with classifiers of social rank, which are based on status rather than 'inherent' characteristics. However, some of the predictions made by a strong version of each claim are incompatible with the other view. The first step in uncovering the origin of the classes is to show that the two views of classifier categories are not incompatible, but complementary.

The most comprehensive cross-linguistic examination of classifier systems was made by Allan (1977). Allan looked at the noun classes in more than fifty languages and compared the kinds of things that were grouped together by classifiers. He found a small set of features which appeared again and again as the 'defining criteria' for noun classes. These features are listed in table 9.1.

Allan notes that, with a few exceptions, these properties are 'inherent' properties of an object rather than contingent ones.[5] These results suggest that the distinguishing feature of a classifier language is possession of a grammatical system which groups nouns according to their inherent characteristics.

Table 9.1 Semantic features of noun classification
(Allan 1977)

1 Material
   a. animacy
   b. abstract nouns
   c. material
2 Shape
   a. saliently one-dimensional
   b. two-dimensional
   c. three-dimensional
3 Consistency
   a. flexible
   b. hard or rigid
   c. non-discrete
4 Size
5 Location
   a. inherent location
   b. contingent location
6 Arrangement
   a. objects in specific, non-inherent configuration
   b. position
   c. objects in non-inherent distribution
7 Quanta

On the basis of Allan's results we can make a much stronger, more cognitively based, claim than simply that classifiers group nouns by inherent properties. His very specific list of features (table 9.1) limits the range of possible noun classes fairly radically. Most interesting is that a majority of the properties are either *visual* or *tactile*, to the exclusion of *smell*, *taste* and *sound*. The shape of an (inanimate) object is by far the most common basis for its classification. Nearly every classifier language has a classifier for long thin objects (that is, objects which are extended in one dimension), and classifiers for flat (two-dimensional) and round (three-dimensional) objects are also very common. Adams and Conklin (1973) go so far as to say that (besides animacy) extension in one, two, or three dimensions is the only 'primary' basis for noun classes, the other features being 'secondary' parameters which are used in combination with shape to increase the number of classes.[6] They quip, 'the semantics [of classifiers] . . . are observable to those who have eyes to see (the nose to smell is not necessary).'

Even within the two prominent sense domains not every possible criterion is used. For instance, color is not an attribute upon which classification is ever based. Therefore, we should not find a language which has a noun class consisting only of green things.[7] Allan points out that the properties on his list are not coincidentally those which Locke identified as the 'primary qualities of bodies'. Joseph Greenberg has also pointed out that you rarely find color in the dictionary definition of an object, but always a description of its shape (cited in Clark 1976).

Lending further support to a strictly cognitive explanation is the fact that the properties in table 9.1 have been independently verified as cognitively salient. For instance, Eve Clark (1976) has shown that these same features serve as the basis for children's over-extension of lexical items during acquisition. 'The basis for categorization discernible in the child's early uses of words often bears a strong resemblance to that found in actual classifier sytems. In both, visual perception appears to play a major role in determining category membership' (Clark 1976). The most frequent over-extensions are based on shape, for example, the word *moon* to all round objects, or *stick* to all long objects. And 'one notable absentee from the kinds of over-extension found in children's speech is color' (Clark 1976). Andersen et al. (1984) found the same reliance on tactile and visual information in blind children. Despite their deficit in visual perception, the children never used auditory information in over-extension or classification of any kind. Rather, they are 'slow to extend words and rarely overextended any'.

All of these findings support an explanation for classifier semantics which resides in the perceptual apparatus of the human species. 'The properties chosen as criterial for category membership . . . are presumably those that are most salient . . . These natural categories may be universal precisely because they have a common cognitive basis' (Clark 1976). This perceptual basis of classification negates the extreme cultural relativism which might be construed from the superficial diversity of attested systems (cf. Craig 1986a). Classifier systems around the world differ only in which perceptual data they choose to pick out. As Brown and Lenneberg (1954) put it: 'In general it looks as if there is a potential for sensory discrimination characteristic of the whole human species. Language communities do not differ in this potential but rather in their manner of categorizing potentially discriminable experience.'

The most problematic area for a cognitive/perceptual approach which claims that noun classes are based on perceptually salient properties is animacy classes. Every classifier language has an animacy distinction, often with more than one animacy class. Even English has a residual animacy distinction in words like *someone* vs. *something* or *everyone* vs. *everything* (Allan 1977). But as Allan (1977) points out, animacy is not an inherent characteristic of an object but an 'imputed' one, and is furthermore highly culture specific. Animacy hierarchies frequently extend into the social order. In many societies, different classifiers are assigned to people in different social classes. The basis for the distinctions within a society are most often age, occupation and kinship. It is interesting, and most damaging for the theory so far, that sex is never used as a primary distinction between classes. Clearly, a person's social class is not an inherent feature which is apparent by either visual or tactile means.[8]

A satisfying treatment of animacy classes is given in Denny (1976). Denny suggests that the motivation behind all classifier systems is primarily a functional one. Classifiers 'communicate a few especially important classes that objects fall into by virtue of the way we interact with them' (Denny 1976). The animacy distinctions within the society, he claims, are made because members of the society must *act* differently according to the social class (or kinship relation) of the person with whom they are interacting. Classifying people differently picks out this distinction.[9] His idea receives some support from the fact that languages which have classifiers based on social rank are typically spoken in highly stratified societies (for example, Vietnamese, Burmese).

Denny (1976) points out that even inanimate classes are ultimately grounded in our interaction with the objects. Claiming that classifier categories have internal consistency is not the same as claiming that the class of an object is predictable. 'The relationship between noun and classifier ... is typically explicable, but not always predictable' (Allan 1977). Every object has a large number of discernible characteristics, and languages can differ in their choice of which features are important for classificatory purposes. For example, the word for 'table' might be put into the class of three-dimensional objects (as it is in Malay), but is more often classed as two-dimensional since the flat functional surface is its important characteristic (for example in Mandarin).

In some cases, a language does *not* make a conventional decision about which feature is most salient, and the choice is left to the speaker. And since different features are salient in different situations, a given noun can

take more than one classsifier in these languages, depending on which
feature the speaker wishes to highlight. 'Whereas "a river is a river is a
river", one can by changing classifier convey some particular kind of
interaction with a river [cf. table 9.2]' (Denny 1976). A functional
perspective not only explains what classifiers are 'good for', but also the
motivation for which feature a language (conventionally) chooses as
salient for classification.

Table 9.2 Burmese (Becker 1965)

myi?te ya?	'river one place' (e.g. destination)
myi? te tan	'river one line' (e.g. on a map)
myi? te hmwa	'river one section' (e.g. a fishing area)
myi?te 'sin	'river one distant arc' (e.g. a path)
myi? te owe	'river one connection' (e.g. tying two villages)
myi? te 'pa	'river one sacred object' (e.g. in myth)
myi? te myi?	'river one river' (the unmarked cace)

The weakness of Denny's functional approach is the stronghold of a
cognitive analysis, just as his theory succeeds where the cognitive analysis
is weakest. Allan (1977) restricts the set of possible systems, but Denny
(1976) brings back cultural relativity in full force. As far as I can tell, there
is in principle no restriction on functional classes, since there is no
restriction on the possible function of an object in a culture.[10] Look, for
instance, at the range of functions which the tribe in the film *The Gods
Must Be Crazy* find for a Coke bottle.

In essence, we have a kind of complementary distribution between the
domains which each explanation straightforwardly handles. Cognitive
salience determines classes of inanimate objects, functional similarity
determines classes of humans. As in phonology, I believe that complementary distribution here indicates that we have two surface manifestations of the same underlying explanation. In order to integrate the two
different views of classifiers, and gain the advantages of both, we have to
explain why the properties on table 9.1 are (at least frequently) associated
with functional interaction. The most straightforward suggestion is that
table 9.1 properties are the only ones which determine how we interact
with objects.

Actually, this solution does not seem totally unreasonable. The shape
and material consistency of an object are obviously important to the use(s)
to which it is put (cf. again *The Gods Must be Crazy*). On the other hand,
there are no cases where our interaction with an object is different
depending on its color (except perhaps stoplights), so there are no
classifiers based on that feature. The idea is not without precedent, either.
The interdependence of shape and function has been discussed in the

child acquisition literature as a resolution of some conflicting findings in acquisition data very similar to those discussed above for classifier systems (cf. Bowerman 1978). Another indication that this idea may be on the right track is given by Plank (1980), who claims that the properties relevant for classification are also the only semantic features on the basis of which verbs can select their objects. For example, the English verbs *eat* and *drink* differ only in the consistency of the object consumed – and consistency is on table 9.1. If the inventory of verbs reflects our sense of what counts as a different interaction, then Plank's claim is significant.[11]

Craig (1986b) provides an important clue to the link between cognition and functional interaction in her analysis of the classifier system in Jacaltec, a Mayan language. Craig explored the quite reasonable idea that two different modes of classification – a classifier system and a folk taxonomy – might be related. She found that classifiers in Jacaltec serve to create 'a magnifying glass effect' on important sections of the folk taxonomy. The biological domains which are functionally important to the community are singled out by their own noun classifiers. The important features of the Jacaltec system can be seen in table 9.3.

Table 9.3 Jacaltec inanimate classifiers (Craig 1986b)

no?	animal	metx'	dog
te?	plant	ixim	corn
		tx'al	thread
		tx'an	twine
		k'ap	cloth
ch'en	rock	atz'am	salt
ha?	water		
ka?	fire		

The set of 'physical interaction'[12] classifiers in Jacaltec can be divided into two types: general and specific, corresponding to the left- and right-hand columns of table 9.3 respectively. 'A specific classifier can . . . be said to correspond to an object which is naturally in a relation of inclusion . . . to one of the general classifiers, but has come to function as head of a class of its own' (Craig 1986b). So while a single classifier covers most plants (*te?*), corn, in all its varieties, has a distinct classifier (*ixim*, homophonous with the noun 'corn'). Similarly, in the animal kingdom Jacaltec has a general animate classifier (*no?*), but dogs are classed separately (*metx'*). Craig provides ethnographic evidence that dogs and corn are important cultural commodities for the Jacaltec. The classifier for each noun refers to the category which is superordinate (that is, one level up the taxonomy) to the category of the classified object. For me, the most interesting and significant fact about the Jacaltec system is not just that the number of classifiers increases in culturally important areas, but also that the most functional, most frequently occurring classifiers – the specific ones – correspond to the *basic level* of the taxonomy.

To see the significance of this fact we need to consider the work on folk taxonomies and on basic level objects in general. Brent Berlin and his colleagues (e.g. Berlin et al. 1966; Berlin 1972) have studied the ways in which different cultures view the biological order of the world. Their main method of study is to look at the lexicon of the languages spoken by these cultures to see how they named the species, orders and sub-species of life around them. They found that languages always develop (single morpheme) words first for the genus[13] level, and that it was also at this level where the folk taxonomy was most similar to the accepted scientific one.

The explanation for these findings offered by Berlin (1972) is essentially a cognitive one, but one which relies crucially on the structure of the world. The level of the genus, he speculated, was the level at which a person could most easily identify a member of the category by visual cues. Real-world attributes do not occur independently of each other. Feathers, for instance, are usually found on animals which also have wings. At the level of genus, these basic discontinuities of nature are most easily perceived. Differentiation into species often requires a closer look, and at higher levels of the taxonomy, the similarities between members are less marked.

Later work by the psychologist Eleanor Rosch and others has confirmed that there is a *basic level* of classification in several domains at which the number of co-occurring features is maximized: 'In taxonomies of concrete objects, there is one level of abstraction at which the most basic category cuts are made. Basic categories are those which carry the most information, possess the highest category cue validity, and are, thus, the most differentiated from one another' (Rosch et al. 1976). The cognitive importance of the basic level is due to a clustering of logically independent properties in categories at this level of taxonomic structure. It is a fact about the world that animals which have wings are almost invariably birds and have other properties of birds (feathers, two short legs, beak, etc.). In this sense, the property *has wings* has a high 'cue validity', that is, it is a good predictor of other properties. The same is true of other typical bird properties like *has a beak*. Because of these (imperfect) correlations, we need only identify one of these properties when we want to know what kind of animal we are dealing with. *Bird*, for the urban English speaker, is therefore a basic level category.[14]

Members of categories at higher levels of structure than the basic level share fewer properties overall, and those properties which are shared have low cue validity. Think, for instance, how few properties are shared by all mammals as opposed to those shared by all (domestic) dogs. Finding that an animal *has fur* tells us very little else about it (only that it *bears live young*), unlike the properties of birds discussed above which correlate with any number of other properties. In particular, the mammalian properties tell us nothing about an animal's size, shape or whether it is dangerous.

Members of subordinate categories, on the other hand, share even more features than basic level categories, and would therefore seem to be better candidates for cognitive salience. However, despite the fact that the class of Doberman pinschers is less varied than the larger class of dogs, most of the properties we could list for Dobermans are also shared by Lhasa Apsos or any other breed of dog. That is, the set of properties *unique* to Dobermans is about as small as the set unique to mammals (cf. Tversky and Hemenway 1983 for actual property lists). The properties of Dobermans which have high cue validity are in large measure those common to all dogs. The overall moral is that basic level categories are categories which have a high degree of internal coherence (unlike superordinate categories) and whose members share many more properties with each other than with members of other categories (unlike subordinate categories).

One of the main consequences of this property-clustering is that basic level categories are 'the most inclusive categories for which a concrete image of the category as a whole can be formed' (Rosch et al. 1976). Also, there tends to be a generalized motor program associated with interacting with the class as a whole. 'Inseparable from the perceived attributes of objects are the ways in which humans habitually use or interact with those objects' (Rosch 1978). So, for example, *chair* is a basic level category while *furniture* is superordinate. Rosch's experiments have shown that it is hard to create and to identify a generalized image for pieces of furniture, but easy for chairs. Furthermore, we know how to interact with any sort of chair, but we need to know what kind of furniture we are dealing with before knowing whether to sit on it or store our clothes in its drawers. At the basic level, in other words, form and function are tightly integrated.

The existence of a basic level is perhaps the clearest example of objective fact influencing language, and it applies across all taxonomically structured lexical domains. The basic level results from a real-world correlation between logically independent properties, for example having a beak, having wings and having feathers. These properties *can* occur separately (and do, for example bats have wings, platypuses have beaks), but as an objective fact, they tend to occur together. Languages pick up on this correlation. The number of co-occurring properties is maximized at the generic level, so lexicalization of this taxonomic level creates the greatest degree of contrastiveness (and identifiability) between categories, which is the goal of the language system. Clearly, the primacy of basic level nouns in language is a result of *interaction* between the language system and the real world.

The interesting thing about Jacaltec is that 'specific' classifiers refer to the basic level while the associated noun refers to a subordinate category. The classifier *ixim*, for example, occurs with a noun referring to a species of corn. The classifier reinforces (by a kind of 'semantic reduplication') those properties which most unambiguously set corn apart from other plants, that is, those with high cue validity. As a result, the classifier focuses on the imagistic (shape) properties of the basic level which permit a generalized program for interaction with the items in the class. This is precisely the function which Denny (1976) suggested as the motivation for classifiers in general, that is, to set up classes of objects (or persons) with which we interact similarly. Table 9.1, meanwhile, shows that the basis for these functional classes is primarily shape. The psychological research into basic level objects provides the link between these two different perspectives – it is the schematic shape properties, characterizing the class as a whole, which permit us to develop a generalized interaction with the class.[15] In other words, Jacaltec 'specific' classifier categories are both function *and* shape-based.

My interpretation of the Jacaltec facts (which is the opposite of Craig's) is that specific classifiers developed *before* the general ones, in those semantic domains which have a high degree of lexical differentiation. In fact, I claim that the first (inanimate) classifiers in all languages arise as the result of lexical expansion. This expansion is caused by two simultaneous processes. First of all, close contact with certain parts of a taxonomy makes it possible for members of the culture to identify different species (rather than different genera) through a gestalt image (that is, an image which differentiates it from surrounding categories). The cultural contact also results in a functional differentiation between species. The interactive motor program associated with the different species may begin to diverge, in essence shifting the basic level from the generic to the specific in that part of the taxonomy. As a result, members of the society frequently have to linguistically differentiate the species. Again, we can see that this shift is due to the combined forces of function and property correlations – both non-linguistic facts about the world.

Berlin (1972) found that languages respond to this need in a very consistent way, and gives a detailed picture of the resulting lexical expansion.

> Situations of social intercourse may arise whereby one must be able to linguistically differentiate the type-specific category from its contrasting neighbor(s). The linguistic process by which this contrast comes to be indicated is quite general. Invariably, the type-specific will be modified with an attributive-like expression. (Berlin 1972)

In other words, specific (that is, subordinate) level nouns will contain the generic (that is, basic) level term, plus some modifier.

As a concrete example, consider the classification of juniper bushes in Navaho. At an earlier stage, Navaho had a single word for all species of juniper (*kat*). Speakers, however, often needed to distinguish between three types of juniper in the area, and the language developed a lexical distinction.

Navaho (Berlin 1972)

kat
The genus 'Juniperus'

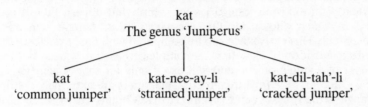

kat   kat-nee-ay-li   kat-dil-tah'-li
'common juniper'   'strained juniper'   'cracked juniper'

Like the English glosses, each specific term has the generic level term as its root. Berlin (1972) contains countless examples of parallel structure. Because the morpheme *kat* occurs in all of the specific terms, it may be reanalyzed as a classifier, as *ixim* has been in Jacaltec. The lexical structure of Navaho juniper terms is parallel to that of Jacaltec corn, except that the genus level term in Jacaltec has become a classifier. The other classifiers presumably came about in the same way. Of the twenty-four classifiers in Jacaltec, twelve are still homophonous with nouns that are still in use, two are shortened forms of nouns and six are compounds. Only four classifiers are 'not associated with any free nominal form' (Craig 1986b).

In Lee (1987b) I discuss a number of facts which lead me to believe that this basic level analysis can be extended to other languages as well. I will mention just a few of these. As I have already noted, classifiers are frequently homophonous with the central member of their class, and in fact it is not always easy to distinguish classifiers from nouns in the early stages of development (cf. Downing 1984 on early Japanese classifiers). Also, Adams and Conklin (1973) found that very few languages have classifiers at the level of biological kingdom (that is, one which classifies all and only plants or animals). Berlin (1972) discovered that lexical nouns for these superordinate levels of the taxonomy are rare as well, appearing only after a language has developed an extensive system at both basic and subordinate levels. This distribution of classifiers at various taxonomic levels mirrors the distribution of nouns, presumably due to the same process of lexical expansion. The most convincing evidence, perhaps, is that wherever the etymology of a classifier can be traced to its source, that source is invariably a basic level noun. For instance, the Ojibway classifier *onak*, used for modes of transportation, derives from the word 'boat (canoe)'. All of these points are discussed at more length in Lee (1987b).

My basic position is that the functional and shape-based coherence which we find in the world's classifier language is a result of the origin of noun classes in basic level categorization. The major question raised by this analysis is how (and why) these basic categories develop into the 'sketchier' shape-based noun classes which Allan (1977) found to be so frequent. The answer lies in the processes underlying extension of the classes to new nouns.

One of the major differences between an early system like that in

Jacaltec and a more fully developed system like the one in Mandarin is that Jacaltec classifiers are not grammatically obligatory. Objects which do not fit clearly into existing categories are simply left unclassified. It is this freedom which allows Jacaltec noun classes to remain semantically transparent. This early stage can be compared with the 'lexical' stage in a child's acquisition of classifiers. A child learns each new classifier in the context of a single object, and will use it only for that object (Erbaugh 1986). Similarly the (historically) first classifiers are extremely restricted in range, in many cases being confined to a few nouns. However, as further classifiers arise in other semantic domains the developing system begins to exert its own pressures towards regularization. Since many nouns require an additional morpheme in counting constructions there is pressure to make its occurrence mandatory for all nouns.

The next historical stage parallels the second stage in acquisition. 'Prototypical use develops after lexical use . . . The children's classifiers broadened to include potentially larger and more heterogeneous sets' (Erbaugh 1986). The initial members of the noun class serve as the prototype for the class, which is extended to new referents. When classifiers become obligatory, unclear cases must nonetheless be assigned to one of the classes. The decision about which class an object is assigned to is made on the basis of perceived similarity with objects already in the class. As Eve Clark and Elaine Andersen found in children's over-extensions, perceived similarity is most often based on the cognitively salient properties of the objects, that is, on their shape.[16]

Classifying objects which do not clearly fit into the system by shape is part of an overall tendency of humans to 'describe unfamiliar objects by shape' (Erbaugh 1984). The utility of shape descriptions is reinforced by their informativeness. 'The function of an object may be unknown, or variable over time' (Erbaugh 1984), but as we have seen, shape properties have high cue validity. Contrastiveness, after all, is a major goal of classification. Thus we have another reason why color is never the basis of a classifier category: 'Color is a relatively useless attribute for classifications of objects since it is little predictive of other attributes' (Rosch 1978). An interesting point which has not been frequently recognized is that *cognitively salient properties tend to be those with high cue validity*.[17]

Shape-based noun classes result when the classifier system is extended to new nouns on the basis of their shape. Over time the classes lose their functional homogeneity, but retain important parts of the schematic image. The process is clearest for two-dimensional classes. The Malay classifier *batang* etymologically derives from a noun meaning 'bamboo'. At the earliest stage, *batang* is only used with nouns which refer to species of bamboo. When nominal classification is made obligatory, however, speakers are faced with the task of deciding to which class all other objects belong. They make this decision on the basis of perceived similarity between the object to be classified and the prototypical member(s) of an existing class.[18] There are two kinds of objects which are quite naturally assigned to the *batang* class: products made from bamboo and long skinny objects which look like bamboo. As time passes, and perhaps the etymology of the classifier is obscured, the class can no longer be characterized as 'bamboo', but rather as the class of long rigid objects.

Eventually noun classes can lose almost all semantic coherence as a result of indeterminacy in classification. While the most salient similarity between objects is usually shape or function, it by no means always is. Furthermore, the shape of an object is not entirely immutable over time. Neither Denny nor Allan acknowledge that often the decision of which class an object will go into is based on a *conventional image* that the culture has of the object in question. In Mandarin, for instance, *yizi* 'chair' is classified with objects that have handles (*ba*) – because traditional Chinese chairs have handles on them. The role of functional metonomy[19] and conventional imagery creates a situation in which classes can (and almost invariably will) lose their semantic transparency. Once Chinese speakers become familiar with handleless chairs, the *ba* class is not limited to objects with handles. And if the cultural image is lost over time, the class becomes even more opaque.

A good example is given by the classifier *hon* in Japanese. The most common use of *hon* is for long, thin, rigid objects: sticks, canes, pencils, candles, trees, etc. Given this characterization, *hon* easily fits into Allan's (1977) survey (cf. table 9.1). However, in modern Japanese *hon* also classifies objects which less obviously fit this description: for example, 'martial arts contests, with staffs and swords . . . , Judo matches (a martial arts contest, but without a staff or sword) . . . , telephone calls . . . , letters . . . , medical injections . . .' (Lakoff 1986).

Each of these things is included in the *hon* class on the basis of a similarity with some object(s) already in the class. So, for instance, the staffs and swords used in martial arts contests are long rigid objects, clearly belonging to the *hon* category. Since martial arts contests are associated with these staffs (and do not have a shape of their own), they are put into the *hon* class. And once one type of martial arts match is included, Judo matches can be assigned to *hon* on the basis of similarity with staff matches.

Letters were originally included in the *hon* class by conventional imagery. In traditional Japan, letters were written on scrolls which were long and stick-like. Although this image has been lost, the assignment of letters to *hon* had already been conventionalized, and this assignment motivated the inclusion of other forms of communication, such as phone calls, into this class. Medical injections, of course, are associated with needles, which are prototypical members of the *hon* class.

'What are taken to be the central cases for the application of *hon* appear to be concrete basic-level objects: sticks, pencils, bamboo staffs, baseball bats, etc.' (Lakoff 1986). However, the actual range of nouns in the *hon* class is not so easily characterizable. Although the basis on which each object is assigned to the class of explicable, the 'perceived similarity' is different in each case, and intransitive chains of association lead to semantic opacity (staff → martial arts match → Judo match; but Judo matches are not related directly to staffs). Nonetheless, 'the direction of extension appears to go from concrete basic-level objects to other things' (Lakoff 1986).

It is easy to see that such processes can make the original semantic motivation for a class fairly opaque. What gets classified where is subject to highly idiosyncratic social pressures having to do with myths, beliefs and folklore. But although noun classes often look quite daunting and unintuitive, they become so only through well motivated semantic principles. The category *hon* is clearly a conventionalized class of objects, and for many people 'conventionalized' is equated with 'arbitrary'. However, just as a collection of phonetically motivated sound changes can result in the seemingly wild discrepancies between Proto-Indo-European and Modern English, so can a set of cognitively motivated principles lead from a Jacaltec-type system to German gender. Each change in the system might be perfectly natural, but their combination can lead to 'unnatural', rather odd-looking results.

5 Into the Grammar

On the basis of what I have said so far one might be tempted to conclude that the world infringes on linguistic structure only at its periphery, in particular the lexicon, that well-known repository of idiosyncracy. The structure of various lexical fields has certainly been the area in which researchers have most often appealed to cognitive or perceptual principles. As we have seen, properties of the real world impinge on lexical structure in ways both particular to certain lexical fields and general to lexical expansion. However, the effects of lexical structure extend far beyond the lexicon itself, into the grammar. Classifiers, for instance, are grammatical morphemes which owe their existence to lexical expansion. In many other areas (for example, deixis) various lexical domains are metaphorically projected on to others, accounting for a great deal of the iconicity between different grammatical domains. And in recent years all of the major syntactic theories have begun to recognize the important role of lexical projections as well (cf. Sells 1985).

Certain types of grammatical morphemes derive from open-class lexical items with fair regularity. Adpositional phrases in particular are frequently nominal in origin. In Mixtec, for instance, 'words for body parts are used for the purpose of referring to locational, and sometimes more abstract, relationships between an object or an event and an area of location' (Brugman 1984). English has examples like *at the foot of the mountain*, but the distinction of Mixtec is that 'such relational concepts are expressed purely through this system, with no system of grammatical devices resembling the Indo-European ones of case-marking, prepositions or postpositions' (Brugman 1984). The same type of system can be found in other American languages, notably Cora (Casad and Langacker 1982). Furthermore, Hill (1982) discusses the fact that even languages with more familiar deictic systems (English and Hausa) need to make a metaphorical transfer of human characteristics to decide which side is the *front* of an object with no inherent orientation. As a result, the universals of body-part terminology have a direct effect on certain types of ad-positional and deictic systems.

In fact, the influence of our bodily experiences extends very far into our conceptual system. In a forthcoming book, Mark Johnson discusses the ways in which our conceptual world is grounded in our kinesthetic experience of moving our bodies through space. Some of our most fundamental concepts, such as causality, force and motion, are ultimately projected from more mundane everyday encounters with such notions through bodily action. These notions are central to all aspects of linguistic structure as well, touching such issues as transitivity (Hopper and Thompson 1980), causatives (Shibatani 1976) and modals (Sweetser 1982). Talmy (1985) displays the pervasiveness of force-dynamic concepts throughout the grammar. Our understanding of the conceptual machinery on which linguistic form is based is deeply rooted in our experience of life of Earth.

6 Conclusion

Ever since Chomsky (1957) there has been an increasing tendency to think of linguistics as a branch of psychology. The goal of defining the 'competence' of an adult speaker presupposes that language is an entity which is contained within the mind of each speaker, as opposed to the structuralist notion of language as a social entity. The result of this perspective is that most linguists search for their explanations and their analyses within the workings of the speaker's brain. For those who believe in the autonomy hypothesis, only system-internal explanations will do, but even those who would rather see linguistic principles reduced to more general cognitive principles typically limit themselves to the human mind. My contention in this paper is that details of the external world have an important role in shaping both language and conceptualization.

The existence of a basic level in categorization is important to linguists because the generic level is the taxonomic level which has the highest cognitive salience, and this salience explains a great deal of (linguistic) data concerning lexical development, word choice and prototype effects. The basic level explains that data. If we wish to go further, however, and explain the cognitive salience of this level, then we must look outside the mind to the world in which we live.

I began this paper by looking out at the world, and by asking about the influence of non-psychological facts on the way we think and talk. The range of influences which I've found is remarkably large, from minor details in the construction of the human perceptual apparatus to the overall structure of a world shaped by evolution. The neural anatomy of our eyes and the 'baffle-and-tub' architecture of our ears have important ramifications for language structure. They set limits on our experience and automatically (perhaps even accidentally) pick out certain stimuli for special treatment. The structure of the human body has a particularly important effect on linguistic structure. As the physical object with which we have the most daily contact, its shape and functional structure form the basis on which we judge other objects. I have a head and a back, and so I expect other objects to have them too. These expectations are codified in our language when we say that the ball is *in front of* the car, or (even more strongly) in Mixtec where imagining that an object has a human body is an indispensable part of locating objects close to it. And if I do not see a head or a front, then I impose one by projecting my own body.

For a great many researchers, properties of the world are to be discounted as explanations because they are not part of our 'linguistic knowledge', defined as those abilities which allow us to learn and use a language, but nothing more. The rationale for dismissal is that the goal of linguistic theory is to define the set of 'possible human languages' (Chomsky 1957). This enterprise consists of the search for a list of the necessary and sufficient conditions that delimit the set 'human language' in *every possible world*. As Aristotle will tell you, this search requires that you look for the 'essence' of language – that set of features without which a language would cease to be a human language.

At first blush it would seem that the typologist's search for universal properties of language has a goal similar to the 'Aristotelian' approach. The preference for universals which are exceptionless, as opposed to simply statistical, finds its defense in this view. When I say that a particular property holds of all languages in a universal study, I am claiming that every 'possible human language' will possess the property in question. However, this is *not* the same as claiming that the property is a defining characteristic of the set.

As an analogy, consider the set of objects which English speakers label *cat*. All cats are animals, all cats have fur and all cats have razor-sharp claws and teeth. These three properties are 'universals' of the set of cats, but they are not all equal. The first two are *necessarily* true – any object which did not possess these properties would not and could not be a cat. This is not true of the third, however. If we found an animal that differed from other cats only in a congenital lack of claws, we would (or could) still label it a *cat* without being judged an incompetent speaker of English. The first two properties tell us what a *cat* is, while the latter tells us something interesting about the set.

Suppose we replace the word *cat* with the word *language*. The self-proclaimed goal of linguistic theory is to define the set of 'possible human languages'. For what I have termed the Aristotelian approach 'possible' means 'logically possible', and therefore only properties of the first type are relevant. A cat without claws is still a possible cat, and a language with a word for *blue* without a word for *red* is still a (logically) possible human language. The difference between the two types of property can be thought of as a difference in the conditions under which they must be true. One of the hallmarks of a typological approach to language is the *implicational universal*. Rather than indicating a property which all languages have, implicational universals 'take the form, given *x* in a particular language we always find *y*' (Greenberg 1966). In general, implicational universals have been considered to be of quite a different sort from 'absolute' universals, particularly by generative grammarians, but Keenan (1978) argues that 'properties which all languages have are a special kind of zero variation.' That is, absolute universals are simply those universals whose antecedent property is the definition of *language*: 'If *x* is a *language*, then we always find *y*.' This type of statement is equivalent to saying that *y* is a true of all languages by definition. The universals which I have discussed in this paper, on the other hand, have as their antecedent property contingent properties of life on Earth. But because all speakers of human languages live on the same planet and have roughly the same physical and mental characteristics, this antecedent property is always satisfied. If we all moved to Venus, however, only 'universals' of the first type may survive.

It seems to me that a more reasonable interpretation of the notion 'possible human language' is that 'no human community will develop a language without these properties under normal circumstances, for principled reasons.' The answer to the question of why all cats have razor-sharp claws might be just as revealing as the answers to the other questions. In addition to being closer to the actual practice of linguists, I believe that this broader perspective recognizes that Saussure was wrong, and that linguistic analysis *can* tell us something about human beings and the world we live in.

Notes

1 Throughout this paper I will use the term *continuous* with its meaning of 'internal seamlessness' rather than (the perhaps more usual) 'boundlessness'. Therefore, when I say that some domain is *continuous* I mean that no part of its internal composition is inherently more prominent (cf. Talmy 1987: n. 15). When I say that human perception *imposes discontinuities* I mean that perception creates prominence in certain parts of the domain.

2 These conflicting aerodynamic requirements also explain why voiced consonants are universally shorter than voiceless ones. In order to maintain voicing, air must continue to pass through the glottis. As it does so the pressure in the oral cavity increases while subglottal pressure decreases. The result is a rapid equalization of pressure across the glottis, and a corresponding loss of voicing. Only by releasing the tongue blockage can voicing be maintained.

3 The popular conception of the (Sapir–)Whorf hypothesis simply says that

language influences thought. However, Kay and Kempton (1984) point out that 'Whorf's interpreters have imbued his doctrine with an additional tacit premise. If the differences in world view . . . are to be interesting, they must be sizeable . . . Hence [the hypothesis] appears to have induced the tacit postulation of III on the part of Whorf's followers . . . [III] must be tacitly assumed, because otherwise the claim . . . is undramatic.'

III   The semantic systems of different languages may vary without constraint.

By no means do I claim that Sapir or Whorf actually espoused this view. 'As some careful commentators . . . have pointed out, they couldn't really have believed the absolute linguistic relativity they sometimes appear to profess and at the same time believed that they could explain in English what, for example, the Hopi view of time is' (Kay and Kempton 1984).

4   Paul Kay (personal communication) has suggested that a language is put under pressure to make more distinctions when the color of an object becomes less predictable. In non-technological cultures, the color of an object can usually be predicted simply by knowing what kind of object it is (for example, grass is green, pottery is red). If a language has a color term *grue*, covering *green* and *blue*, both the sky and the forest are *grue*. Given the predictability of the shades of these items, there is no communication problem. Once technologically produced items are introduced, however, the same object might appear in both *green* and *blue*. At this point, the distinction is either made by a circumlocution ('*grue* like the sky') or by differentiation of a new focal point.

The idea that a given object always has the same color while the same color is found on numerous objects will take on more significance below.

5   The exceptions (5b, 6 and 7 on table 9.1) serve as the basis of quantifier phrases in non-classifier languages as well, while categories based on the first five properties are found only in classifier languages. Some examples of non-inherent English 'classifiers' are given below.

> two loops of rope   three bundles of string
> a piece of paper   a kind of mammal

The 'classifier' in each case refers to a temporary state of the associated noun. The fact that exceptions to the generalization (that classifiers refer to inherent properties) are not peculiar to classifier languages strengthens the idea that this is a defining property of such languages. For further discussion, see Allan (1977).

6   That is, for example, consistency is never the sole criterion for class membership. However, two 'round' classes might be distinguished from one another by consistency. In the terminology of Adams and Conklin (1973), this makes consistency a secondary distinction.

7   Actually, finding a class whose members all HAPPEN to be green would not be a counterexample. The claim is that the greenness of the items would not be the basis for inclusion in the class. We might, for example, find a class of copper things (based on feature 1c) all of which are green.

8   One suggestion is that people in different social classes do in fact look different, that is, they wear different clothes or are typically seen performing different actions. The extent to which this is universally true is an empirical question, but in any case I don't think it can really provide an explanation. The importance of kinship and age is left unexplained.

9 However, this does not account for the fact that sex is never used as a primary discrimination. Very few societies lack a difference in the social roles of men and women.

10 At least Denny (1976) does not discuss any.

11 When I say that people 'interact similarly' with a set of objects or that two objects 'have the same function', I really mean that people 'feel they interact similarly' and that objects are 'perceived as having the same function'. In actuality, of course, we act somewhat differently toward every person (and every object) we meet. I do not mean to deny that the notion of functional equivalence is ultimately cognitive. The distinction between what I call cognitive and functional classes can be thought of as a difference in whether the perceived similarity is between the objects themselves or our actions toward them.

12 In her paper Craig draws a distinction between 'physical interaction' classifiers and 'social interaction' classifiers which is essentially equivalent to mine between inanimate and animate classes. The fact that the two types are often analyzed separately reinforces my impression that the appropriate account for the two is different, although ultimately grounded in the same process.

13 The genus level is the level of taxonomic structure between species and life form. For example, *oak* is the name of a genus – it subsumes a number of species (*white oak*, *red oak*, *bur oak*, *English oak*, etc.) but is less inclusive than the life form term *tree*.

14 The basic level status of this category is an exception to the generalization that basic level categories are found at the levels of genera in taxonomic structure (*bird* is a life form category). Rosch (1978) notes that the basic level can shift away from the generic in cases where a culture has either very little or very intense contact with some part of the taxonomy. I will exploit this fact below.

15 A good explanation of why shape is a good predictor of function in basic level nouns can be found in Tversky (1986).

16 Actually, while shape is usually the most salient property of an inanimate object, as acquisition studies and psychological experiments have frequently shown, in some cases the most salient similarity between two objects will be *function* rather than *shape*. Functional extensions, I expect, are common only in semantic domains where the function of an object is the feature which most particularly distinguishes it from other (similar) objects – that is, where function has higher cue validity than shape. Clearly, social class is such a domain. The distinction between socially based animacy classes must be functional, since there is, in fact, no other basis to go on – all humans have basically the same shape. In the case of inanimate objects, however, functional extensions are less common and only appear late, after shape-based classifiers are well established (Erbaugh 1984).

17 Now that I have made such a strong statement, let me hedge it. I do not claim that cognitively salient properties are salient *because* they are predictive of other properties. The salience of dimensionality, for instance, is surely an innate endowment – blind children, for whom shape is hard to identify, nevertheless use such visual criteria to extend words to new referents (Andersen et al. 1984). As Jackendoff (1983) says, 'The best we can say is that our evolutionary history luckily has provided us with a source of useful hypotheses about the world ... But the individual's behavior does not explicitly take into account his evolutionary history, and is certainly not explained by invoking it.'

18 It is important to note that the perceived similarity between two objects need not be objective similarity. For instance, time may be considered similar to a wheel

(both being circular), but this similarity is not inherent in nature, but is an imputed one.

19 That is, letting the functional part of an object stand for the whole object (for example, 'We need a *good glove* at third base' = 'We need *a person who can catch* at third base'). This is the principle which allows tables to be classified as two-dimensional.

References

Adams, K. and N. Conklin (1973) 'Toward a theory of natural classification'. In *Papers from the Ninth Regional Meeting, Chicago Linguistic Society*.

Allan, K. (1977) 'Classifiers'. *Language*, 53.2, 284–310.

Andersen, E. (1978) 'Lexical universals of body-part terminology'. In J. Greenberg (ed.), *Universals of Human Language*, vol. 3. Stanford, Calif.: Stanford University Press.

A. Dunlea and L. Kekelis (1984) 'Blind children's language: resolving some differences'. *Journal of Child Language*, 11, 645–64.

Becker, A. (1975) 'A linguistic image of nature: the Burmese numeral classifier system'. *Linguistics*, whole no. 165, 109–21.

Berlin, B. (1972) 'Speculations on the growth of ethnobotanical nomenclature'. Language in Society, 1, 51–86.

D. E. Breedlove and P. H. Raven (1966) 'Folk taxonomies and biological classification'. *Science*, 154, 273–5.

and P. Kay (1969) *Basic Color Terms: Their Universality and Evolution*. Berkeley and Los Angeles: University of California Press.

Bierwisch, M. (1967) 'Some semantic universals of German adjectivals'. *Foundations of Language*, 3, 1–36.

Bowerman, M. (1978) 'The acquisition of word meaning: an investigation into some current conflicts'. In N. Waterson and C. Snow (eds), *The Development of Communication*. New York: John Wiley.

Brown, R. and Lenneberg, E. (1954) 'A study in language and cognition'. *Journal of Abnormal and Social Psychology*, 49.

Brugman, C. (1984) 'Conceptual metaphor in the elaboration of the grammatical system of Mixtec'. Unpub. MS, University of California, Berkeley.

Bybee, J. (1985) 'Diagrammatic iconicity in stem-inflection relations'. In Haiman (1985).

Carlson, R., G. Fant and B. Granstrom (1975) 'Two-formant models, pitch, and vowel perception'. In G. Fant and M. Tatham (eds), *Auditory Analysis and Perception of Speech*. New York: Academic Press.

Casad, E. and R. Langacker (1982) 'Inside and outside in Cora grammar'. *IJAL*.

Chomsky, N. (1957) *Syntactic Structures*. The Hague: Mouton.

Clark, E. (1976) 'Universal categories: on the semantics of classifiers and children's early word meanings'. In A. Juilland (ed.), *Linguistic Studies offered to Joseph Greenberg*, vol. 3, Saratoga, Calif.: Anma Libri.

Clark, H. H. and E. Clark (1977) *Psychology and Language*. New York: Harcourt Brace Jovanovich.

Craig, C. (1986a) *Noun Classes and Categorization*. Philadelphia, Pa.: John Benjamins.

(1986b) 'Jacaltec noun classifiers: a study in language and culture'. In Craig (1986a).

Denny, J. P. (1976) 'What are noun classifiers good for?' In *Proceedings of the Twelfth Regional Meeting of the Chicago Linguistic Society*.

Dixon, R. (1986) 'Noun classes and noun classification in typological perspective'. In Craig (1986a).

Downing, P. (1984) 'Japanese numeral classifiers'. Unpub. Ph.D diss., University of California, Berkeley.

Erbaugh, M. (1984) 'Scissors, paper, stones: perceptual foundations of noun classifier systems'. *Papers and Reports on Child Language Development*, vol. 23, Stanford University, Department of Linguistics.

(1986) 'Taking stock: the development of Chinese noun classifiers historically and in young children'. In Craig (1986a).

Fillmore, C. (1978) 'The organization of semantic information in the lexicon'. In *Chicago Linguistic Society Parasession on the Lexicon*, University of Chicago.

Givón, T. (1985) 'Iconicity, isomorphism, and non-arbitrary coding in syntax'. In Haiman (1985).

Greenberg, J. (1966) 'Some univerals of grammar with particular reference to the order of meaningful elements'. In J. Greenberg (ed.), *Universals of Language*. Cambridge, Mass.: MIT Press.

(1985) 'Some iconic relationships among place, time and discourse deixis', In Haiman (1985).

Haiman, J. (ed.) (1985) *Iconicity in Syntax*. Typological Studies in Languge, vol. 6. Philadelphia, Pa: John Benjamins.

Hawkins, J. (1983) *Word Order Universals*. New York: Academic Press.

Hill, C. (1982) 'Up/down, front/back, left/right: a contrastive study of Hausa and English'. In J. Weissenborn and W. Klein (eds), *Here and There: Cross-linguistic Studies on Deixis and Demonstration*. Philadelphia, Pa: John Benjamins.

Hopper, P. and S. Thompson (1980) 'Transitivity in grammar and discourse'. *Language*, 56, 251–99.

Jackendoff, R. (1977) *X-Bar Syntax: A Study of Phrase Structure*. Cambridge, Mass.: MIT Press.

(1983) *Semantics and Cognition*. Cambridge, Mass.: MIT Press.

Johnson, M. (in press) *The Body in the Mind: The Bodily Basis of Reason and Imagination*. Chicago: University of Chicago Press.

Kay, P. and W. Kempton (1984) 'What is the Sapir–Whorf hypothesis?' *American Anthropologist*, 86, 65–79.

and C. McDaniel (1978) 'The linguistic significance of the meanings of basic color terms'. *Language*, 54, 610–46.

Keenan, E. (1978) 'Language variation and the logical structure of Universal Grammar'. In H. Seiler (ed.), *Language Univerals*. Tübingen: Gunter Narr.

Lakoff, G. (1986) 'Classifiers as a reflection of mind: the experiential, imaginative, and ecological aspects'. In Craig (1986a).

(1987) *Women, Fire, and Dangerous Things*. Chicago: University of Chicago Press.

and M. Johnson (1980) *Metaphors We Live By*. Chicago: University of Chicago Press.

Lee, M. (1985) 'Functional and cognitive explanations in the universals of classifiers: integrating the conflicting claims'. Unpub. MS, University of Southern California.

(1987a) 'The cognitive basis of classifier systems'. *Proceedings of the Thirteenth Annual Meeting of the Berkeley Linguistics Society*.

(1987b) 'The cognitive history of classifier systems'. Unpub. MS, University of Southern California.

Lindblom, B., P. MacNeilage and M. Studdert-Kennedy (1984) 'Self-organizing processes and the explanation of phonological universals'. In B. Butterworth, B. Comrie, and O. Dahl (eds), *Explanations for Language Universals*. New York: Mouton.

Locke, J. (1689) *Essay Concerning Human Understanding*. London.

Pickett, J. M. (1980) *The Sounds of Speech Communication*. Perspectives in Audiology Series. Baltimore, Md: University Park Press.

Plank, F. (1980) 'Verbs and objects in semantic agreement: minor differences between languages that might suggest a major one'. Unpub. MS, Technische Universität, Hannover.

Rosch, E. (1978) 'Principles of categorization'. In *Cognition and Categorization*. Hillsdale, NJ: Erlbaum.

C. B. Mervis, W. D. Gray, D. M. Johnson and P. Boyes-Braem (1976) 'Basic objects in natural categories'. *Cognitive Psychology*, 8, 382–439.

Saussure, F. de. (1959) *Course in General Linguistics*. New York: McGraw-Hill.

Scharf, B. (1978) 'Loudness'. In E. C. Carterette and M. P. Friedman (eds), *Handbook of Perception*, vol. 4: *Hearing*. New York: Academic Press.

Sells, P. (1985) *Lectures on Contemporary Syntactic Theories*. Stanford, Calif.: CSLI.

Shibatani, M. (ed.) (1976) *The Grammar of Causative Constructions*. Syntax and Semantics, vol. 6. New York: Academic Press.

Sweetser, E. (1982) 'Root and epistemic modals: causality in two worlds'. In *Proceedings of the Eighth Annual Meeting of the Berkeley Linguistics Society*.

Talmy, L. (1985) 'Force dynamics in language and thought'. In *Parasession on Causatives and Agentivity*. Twenty-First Regional Meeting of the Chicago Linguistic Society.

(1987) 'The relation of grammar to cognition'. To appear in B. Rudzka-Ostyn (ed.), *Topics in Cognitive Linguistics*. Philadelphia, Pa: John Benjamins.

Tversky, B. (1986) 'Components and categories'. In Craig (1986a).

and K. Hemenway (1983) 'Objects, parts, and categories. *Journal of Experimental Psychology*.

CHAPTER 10

Parameterizing the Language Processing System: Left- vs. Right-Branching within and across Languages

Lyn Frazier and Keith Rayner

We will address two issues in this paper. The first is the validity of the common belief that left-branching sentences are difficult to comprehend (Yngve 1960: Levin et al. 1972; Wanat 1971; Forster 1966, 1968) and the nature of the phenomena that underlie that belief. In particular, we want to determine whether the complexity of left-branching is of sufficient magnitude that explanations may appeal to it (or to the avoidance of left-branching) as a significant determinant of language structure. The second issue concerns the development of a theory of human language comprehension, specifying the architecture and principles of a language processing system that can account both for the uniformity and the variability in how users of different languages process sentences. The two issues are closely related because the fact that a great many languages exhibit left-branching constructions renders some accounts of the apparent difficulty of left-branching constructions in English quite implausible.[1]

1 Branching Patterns in English

Intuitive judgments of processing complexity indicate that the left-branching structure in (1a) is more difficult to understand than its right-branching counterpart in (1b), where the sentential subject has been extraposed (though see Koster 1978 for an alternative analysis of structures like (a)). In a fascinating paper, Yngve (1960) argued that it is better for complex constituents to occur on right branches (where there will be fewer predicted nodes to be held in memory) than on left branches, where all predicted sister nodes must be held in memory while the complex constituent is produced or parsed.[2] In (1a) but not (1b), the predicted matrix VP node must be held in memory while the sentential subject is processed. It has been shown that (left-branching) sentences with a relative clause in subject position are more difficult to process than (right-branching) sentences with a relative clause in object position (Levin

(1) a.   b.

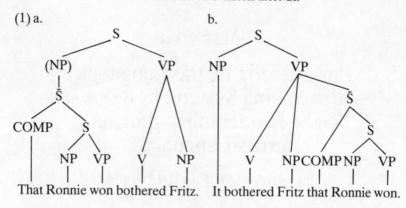

That Ronnie won bothered Fritz.   It bothered Fritz that Ronnie won.

et al., 1972; Wanat 1971). This finding could be attributed to the need to hold a predicted VP-node in memory during the processing of a clause in subject position. The complexity of sentences with an initial subordinate clause (see Bever 1970; Bever and Townsend 1979) might also be subsumed under this generalization since the predicted occurrence of an obligatory main clause must be held in memory during the processing of the initial clause.

If it is true that left-branching constructions are difficult to process, then we must explain why so many languages (perhaps a majority) preserve this branching pattern. The frequency of left-branching languages suggests that perhaps it is not left-branching per se that is responsible for processing complexity, but rather the interaction of left-branching with other processes found in a predominantly right-branching language like English. For example, the apparent complexity of sentences with initial subordinate clauses might arise because of operations involving the assignment of anaphoric relations between pronouns and their antecedents, rather than any operation related directly to the branching pattern per se. If the subordinate clause contains a pronoun whose antecedent appears in the main clause, interpretation of the pronoun may occur earlier if the subordinate follows rather than precedes the main clause. Thus, the question we are interested in is whether the left-branching structure in (2a) is more complex than its right-branching counterpart in (2b) when no pronoun-antecedent relation must be established.

(2) a.   S   b.   S

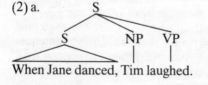
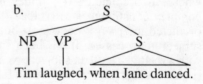

When Jane danced, Tim laughed.   Tim laughed, when Jane danced.

If it should turn out that the (left-branching) a-forms of sentences (1) and (2) are more difficult to process than the (right-branching) b-forms, we would like to know whether the degree of complexity associated with left-branching is substantial or whether it is really quite minor. For instance, is the complexity associated with left-branching sufficient to offset the complexity of processing a discontinuous constituent that has the effect of reducing the amount of left-branching? We may illustrate this concretely with sentences like those in (3).

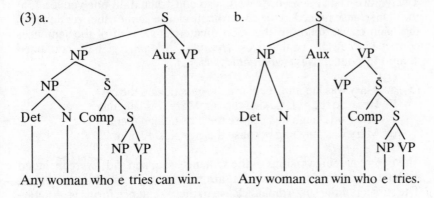

(3) a. Any woman who e tries can win.   b. Any woman can win who e tries.

The presence of a relative clause in subject position in (3a) creates a left-branching structure; as noted earlier, the predicted matrix VP node may have to be held in memory while the relative clause is processed. By contrast, in (3b) the relative clause has been extraposed and thus does not need to be parsed until after the matrix VP has been processed. However, the relative clause must be related to its head noun phrase *any woman*. Thus even though extraposing the relative clause in (3b) reduces the amount of left-branching in the sentence, it does so at the cost of creating a discontinuous constituent which might itself contribute to the processing complexity of the sentence. (See Frazier et al. 1984 for evidence that another gap-filler dependency, due to Heavy NP Shift, does increase the complexity of processing sentences.) In short, though it is difficult to quantify the notion of 'substantial processing complexity' we may at least compare the complexity contributed by left-branching to the complexity contributed by dependencies between non-adjacent items. In fact, this sort of comparison is crucial for evaluating the explanation Yngve (1960) offered for the existence of discontinuous constituents in natural languages.

To elucidate the source of the complexity associated with left-branching constructions in English, we recorded subjects' eye movements as they read sentences like those in (1)–(3). Eight sentences with sentential subjects were constructed, with two versions of each, as illustrated in (4). In one version (cf. (4a)) the sentential subject occurred in sentence-initial position; in the other version (4b) the subject was extraposed and pleonastic *it* occurred as the surface subject.

(4) a. That both of the Siamese twins survived the operation is remarkable.
   b. It is remarkable that both of the Siamese twins survived the operation.

Twelve two-clause sentences were also constructed. In one version (5a) the main clause preceded the subordinate clause; in the other version (5b) the main clause followed the subordinate clause. Half of the sentences contained 'causal' connectives (*because*, *although*); half contained 'temporal' connectives (*when*, *after*, *before*).

(5) a. Mary was laughing because the girls tickled the cat.
   b. Because the girls tickled the cat, Mary was laughing.
   c. Mary was laughing because the girls tickled them.
   d. Mary was laughing because the girls tickled him.

The two remaining versions of the sentence, (5c) and (5d), were included in the experiment for reasons that are not directly related to this paper. The subject of the subordinate clause in these sentence forms is structurally prohibited from serving as the antecedent of the pronoun in object position; however, in (5c), but not (5d), the subject is morphologically appropriate as an antecedent of the pronoun. (This contrast was included to determine whether a morphologically appropriate but syntactically impermissible antecedent would decoy the sentence processor. There was absolutely no difference between the reading times for these two sentence forms and thus they will not be discussed further here. See Frazier 1984 for discussion.) We must emphasize, however, that all pronoun versions (c and d) contained an initial main clause and thus, if anything, including these sentences in the experiment biased our results in favor of a preference for initial main clauses over initial subordinate clauses.

Twelve sentences with relative clauses modifying the subject noun phrase were also constructed, with four versions of each. In two versions (6a) and (6b) the relative clause occurred in subject position; in two (6c) and (6d) it was extraposed to the end of the sentence. To explore whether the complexity of processing a discontinuous constituent is influenced by the sheer amount of material intervening, we included sentences with a relatively short matrix predicate (6a) and (6c), and sentences with a slightly longer matrix predicate (6b) and (6d).

(6) a. Any girl who takes karate lessons could break the table easily.
   b. Any girl who takes karate lessons could break the mahogany dining table easily.
   c. Any girl could break the table easily who takes karate lessons.

d. Any girl could break the mahogany dining table easily who takes karate lessons.

Experiment 1

Method

Subjects   Twenty members of the University of Massachusetts community were paid to participate in the experiment. All of the subjects had normal uncorrected vision and they were all naïve with respect to the purpose of the experiment.

Apparatus and Materials   Eye movements were recorded by a Stanford Research Institute Dual Purkinje Eyetracker. The eyetracker, which has a resolution of 10 minutes of arc, was interfaced with a Hewlett-Packard 2100 computer that controlled the experiment. Eye movements were monitored from the right eye and viewing was binocular. The signal from the eyetracker was sampled every millisecond and a complete record of the sequence of eye movements and the location and duration of the eye fixations was obtained for every sentence.

The sentences were presented on a Hewlett-Packard 1300A Cathode Ray Tube (CRT) which was also interfaced with the computer. Luminance on the CRT was adjusted to a comfortable level for each subject and held constant throughout the experiment. The letters making up the sentences were presented in lower case (except for the first letter of the sentence or the first letter of proper nouns) on the CRT. The subject's eye was 46 cm from the CRT and three characters equalled one degree of visual angle. A black theatre gel covered the CRT so that the letters appeared clear and sharp to the subjects.

The experimental sentences were divided into four sets. For the twelve two-clause sentences and the twelve sentences with relative clauses modifying the subject noun phrase, one version of each sentence (as exemplified in 5 and 6 above) appeared in each set. For the eight sentences with sentential subjects, one version appeared in two of the sets and the other version appeared in the other two sets. More than one version of the same sentence never appeared within a given set. The experimental sentences were embedded in forty filler sentences, which consisted of a wide variety of sentence types.

Procedure   When a subject arrived for the experiment, a bite bar was prepared that eliminated head movement during the experiment. Then the eyetracking system was calibrated for each subject. This initial calibration was usually accomplished within ten minutes. Before each sentence was presented, the experimenter checked the calibration of the eyetracking system to ensure that accurate records were being obtained. Each subject read ten warm-up sentences and then the set of experimental and filler sentences. They were told that the purpose of the experiment was to understand what people look at when they read and that they should read the sentences to comprehend them. They were further told that they would periodically be asked by the experimenter to report the sentence they had just read. If they were asked to report a sentence, they released the bite bar to do so. Otherwise, they moved their eyes to a fixation marker and the next sentence appeared. When they completed reading each sentence, subjects pressed a telegraph key which resulted in the sentence disappearing from the CRT.

Results   The primary results of the experiment will be presented via analyses of the reading time for the sentence. To equate for word length and sentence length difference, we divided the reading time by the number of characters in each target word. Thus, our primary unit of analysis was *reading time per character* for the total sentence. However, eye movement data provide a means of examining local processing complexity. One can determine precisely where in the sentence processing difficulties occur. Thus, when significant differences occured with respect to total reading time for the sentence, we divided the sentence into different regions and examined reading time per character and average gaze durations associated with each region. The gaze duration measure consisted of summing all fixations on a word prior to an eye movement out of that word for each word in a region.

As expected on the basis of intuitive evidence, sentences with sentential subjects took significantly longer (41.6 msec per character) to read than sentences with extraposed sentential subjects (34.5 msec), $F(1,19) = 7.13$, $p < .03$. Counter to the predictions of the branching hypothesis, subordinate-initial sentences did not take longer to read (35.4 msec) than main-initial sentences (38.6 msec) $F(1,19) = 1.5$, $p < .23$. In fact, they tended to be read more quickly than sentences with initial main clauses.

Sentences with extraposed relative clauses were clearly more difficult to process (43.7 msec) than their non-extraposed counterparts (37.3 msec) regardless of the length of the phrase intervening between the relative clause and its head. In a 2 (extraposed vs. non-extraposed) by 2 (long vs. short) ANOVA the position of the relative clause was clearly significant, $F(1,19) = 12.68$, $p < .01$, though length and the interaction of length and relative clause position were not, $F < 1$.

More fine-grained analyses of the locus of complexity were undertaken by dividing the sentences into different regions. It should be noted that a comparison of corresponding regions in the different sentence forms is difficult since critical regions (for example, the *that*-clause for sentential subjects sentences and the relative clause in the relative clause sentences) are necessarily confounded with serial position and thus exhibit any increase in reading times associated with the ends of sentences (Just and Carpenter 1980). Although precise interpretations of reading times for local regions of the sentences are precluded, we have nevertheless divided the sentences into different critical regions to examine the locus of processing difficulty.

For the comparison of the sentences with sentential subjects and sentences with extraposed sentential subjects, we divided the sentences into four regions, corresponding to: (1) *that* plus the immediately following noun phrase, (2) the main verb of the clause introduced by *that*, (3) the remainder of the verb phrase in the *that*-clause, and (4) the matrix predicate. These data are presented in table 10.1. The average gaze duration in each region is also presented in table 10.1.

A 2 (sentence type) × 4 (region) ANOVA conducted on the reading time per character data confirmed the result that sentential subject sentences took longer to read than sentences with extraposed sentential subjects $F(1,7) = 6.71$, $p < .05$. More importantly, the analysis revealed a highly significant interaction, $F(3,21) = 12.54$, $p < .001$. (Any difference between means greater than 10.4 msec is significant at the .05 level by a t-test.) The beginning of the *that*-clause (Regions 1 and 2) takes longer to process than the end of the clause in non-extraposed sentence forms, but not in extraposed sentence forms. In the extraposed forms, reading times gradually increase throughout the processing of the sentence. (Thus the matrix predicate, which precedes Regions 1–3 in this sentence form, has shorter reading times than any of the other regions, as may be seen in table 10.1). Finally, the sentence-final region was associated with the longest reading time in both extraposed and non-extraposed sentence forms. It should be pointed out that the data presented include both first pass fixations and regressions. When regressive fixations were eliminated, the pattern identical to that presented in table 10.1 remained.

A similar ANOVA on the gaze duration data yielded a marginally significant effect for sentence type, $F(1,7) = 4.08$, $p < .10$. However, there was a main effect of region, $F(3,21) = 3.78$, $p < .05$ and a significant interaction, $F(3,21) = 13.14$, $p < .001$. Both effects were primarily due to longer gaze durations at the end of the sentence region as can be seen in table 10.1.

For the relative clause sentences, we divided the sentences into three regions: (1) the begining of the sentence, (2) the relative clause and (3) the remainder of the sentence. The data are presented in table 10.2. An ANOVA confirmed that sentences with extraposed relative clauses were more difficult to process than non-extraposed sentences, $F(1,11) = 10.02$, $p < .01$. There was also a region effect, $F(2,22) = 7.71$, $p < .01$, and a Newman-Keuls analysis revealed that the relative clause was more difficult to read than the other two regions. More importantly, there was an interaction such that the relative clause was much more difficult to read when it was extraposed to the end of the sentence, $F(2,22) = 12.26$, $p < .001$. Again, the same pattern of results emerged when regressive fixations were eliminated. Analyses of the gaze duration data revealed a significant interaction, $F(2,22) = 8.77$, $p < .01$, due to

Table 10.1 Regions analysis for extraposed and non-extraposed sentential subject sentences[a]

| Sentence form | Matrix | Region | | | Matrix |
		1	2	3	
Extraposed sentential subject	(it is remarkable) 24 (213)	(that . . . twins) 29 (225)	(survived) 33 (246)	(the operation) 47 (296)	(is remarkable) 53 (407)
Sentential subject		(that . . . twins) 42 (264)	(survived) 52 (255)	(the operation) 28 (221)	

[a]Data are reading time per character (msec). Values in parentheses are gaze durations (msec).

Table 10.2   Regions analysis for relative clause sentences[a]

Sentence form	Region		
	Beginning	Relative clause	Remainder
Relative clause-subject	32 (230)	37 (244)	43 (247)
Relative clause-extraposed	33 (236)	61 (366)	39 (251)

[a]Data are reading time per character (msec). Values in parentheses are gaze durations (msec).

longer gazes in the relative clause region for sentences with extraposed relative clauses.

These results argue against the hypothesis that left-branching per se gives rise to processing complexity. Though sentences with sentential subjects are difficult to process relative to their right-branching counterparts, sentences with initial subordinate clauses were not more difficult than sentences with initial main clauses. Further, in sentences with initial subordinate clauses there are at least as many predicted nodes to be remembered (assuming the structure in (2) there are actually more predicted nodes to be remembered) and thus the left-branching hypothesis would lead us to expect the difference between initial-subordinate and initial-main clauses to be at least as great as the difference between extraposed and non-extraposed sentential subjects.[3] (Hence, the usual worry about interpreting a null effect does not really apply here.) The fact that extraposed relative clauses were actually harder to process than relative clauses in subject position shows that the complexity of processing discontinuous constituents is greater than the complexity of processing left-branching structure – which is not very surprising if left-branching is not very complex. This in turn shows that Yngve's explanation for the existence of discontinuous constituents (that they reduce the memory complexity caused by left-branching) cannot be correct *if* it is interpreted as a parsing explanation rather than as an explanation based on the complexity of sentence production (see note 1 and Frazier 1985).

One might argue that Experiment 1 did not provide a fair test of the branching hypothesis. After all, the predicted complexity of initial subordinate clauses might be offset by some independent source of complexity in processing final subordinate clauses, for example, the complexity of the operation required to attach the subordinate clause to the main clause. Indeed, if subordinate clauses have the structure indicated in (7b), rather than that illustrated in (2b), the addition of the Chomsky-adjoined node (circled in (7b)) may constitute a revision of the processor's initial analysis of the sentence.

(7) a.

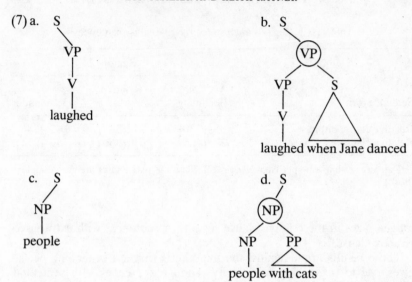

In general, however, the insertion of a Chomsky-adjoined node (that is, one of the same syntactic category as the node it dominates) does not seem to give rise to more than an extremely minor increase in processing complexity, especially when the postulation of that node is unambiguously required, as in (7b) or, say, (7d) where a subject noun phrase is followed by a prepositional phrase modifier which must be adjoined to the noun phrase. Thus, if the minor complexity required to postulate the circled VP node in subordinate-final sentences is sufficient to offset the complexity of the left-branching in subordinate-initial sentences, we may at the very least conclude that the complexity contributed by the left-branching is itself not substantial, but relatively minor. Further, recall that there was at least a tendency for initial subordinate sentences to be read more quickly than their right-branching counterparts, suggesting that the left-branching in intial subordinates is, if anything, even less complex than the postulation of a single Chomsky-adjoined node.

With respect to the extraposed relative clauses, one might argue that the correct structure is that in (8a), where 'e' stands for an empty category left by the extraposed relative clause. Assuming the structure in (8b) will be computed before the extraposed relative is encountered, one might assume that the complexity of constructing the structure (8a) will override any complexity due to the left branching of the non-extraposed relative clause sentences. Thus again one might claim that our test of Yngve's branching hypothesis is unfair, since we did not manipulate branching alone, keeping all other factors equal.

(8) a.

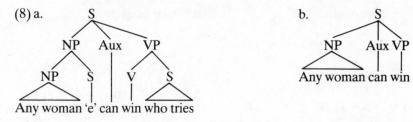

b.

Any woman can win

What the above arguments show is that we may not completely eliminate the possibility that left-branching contributes some minor complexity to sentence processing. However, what is crucial is that our major conclusion still holds. Yngve's intriguing explanation for the existence of discontinuous constituents and extraposition phenomena cannot be maintained. The reason should now be obvious: namely, the complexity of the only mechanisms which natural language grammars use to avoid the complexity of left-branching (according to Yngve's hypothesis) is as great or greater than the complexity they are claimed to alleviate, namely that due to left-branching. In short, it simply is not compelling to argue that constructions B and C exist because they permit us to avoid the complexity of contruction A, if the complexity of B and C is as great or greater than the complexity of A.

The conclusion that left-branching per se does not create substantial complexity leaves us without an explanation for the truly substantial complexity of sentences with sentential subjects. Frazier (1984) argued that the complexity of unambiguous sentences is a function of the number of (non-lexical) syntactic nodes that must be postulated at once (say, within a three-word window). This local non-terminal count is the sum of the value of all non-terminals introduced over three adjacent terminals. Because clausal nodes (S, S̄) seem to contribute more to complexity than do other nodes, Frazier (1984) argues that these nodes should be assigned a value of $1\frac{1}{2}$; all other non-lexical syntactic nodes are assigned a value of 1, as illustrated in (9). The Local Non-Terminal Count hypothesis simply claims that, other things being equal, a sentence with a higher local non-terminal count will be harder to process than one with a lower local count. The *Local Non-Terminal Count* will of course predict that sentences with sentential subjects should be difficult to process relative to their extraposed counterparts, owing to the high concentration of syntactic nodes warranted by the initial few words of the sentence, as illustrated in (9).

Alternative explanations are also available, on the assumption that the subject of a sentence typically establishes the topic of a discourse.[4] In an isolated sentence or the first sentence of a discourse, people must determine what the linguistic message is about. Hence, they may expect the subject of the sentence to relate to information which may be assumed to be shared by the producer (author or speaker) and the perceiver. Sentences with sentential subjects may violate this expectation. Further, in

(9) a. Sentential Subject   b. Extraposed Subject

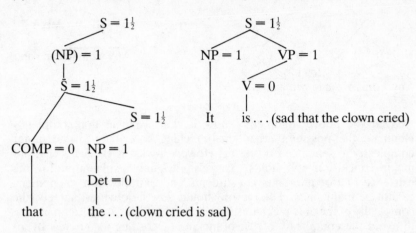

general, information may be processed more rapidly when it occurs in a position where the processor expects to allocate considerable resources or attention than when it occurs in some position where less attention is typically required. In the comprehension of speech, it has been argued that more attention is allocated to stressed positions (Cutler 1976), and to focused positions than unfocused positions (Cutler and Fodor 1979), and it has been shown in both speech and reading that asserted information is verified more quickly than presupposed information (Hornby 1974; Langford and Holmes, reported in Holmes 1979). In English the predicate of a sentence typically contains the nuclear stress of the sentence and it generally contains new asserted information. It may also be argued to define or correspond to the default focus of the sentence. Hence, if the processor typically devotes more attention to the predicate of the sentence than to its subject, a sentence with an extraposed sentential subject will conform more closely to the processor's expectations about where it should allocate its resources than will a sentence with a non-extraposed sentential subject. The 'topic effect' discussed earlier might conspire with general expectations about attention allocation to make sentences like (9a) more difficult to process than sentences like (9b) where new information is contained in the predicate. In context, however, the difference in the complexity of these sentence forms should be reduced or eliminated if a preceding context-paragraph has already established a discourse topic and presented some of the information conveyed by a sentential subject.

In sum, the Local Non-Terminal Count predicts that the relations between the complexity of sentences with extraposed vs. non-extraposed sentential subjects should be preserved even when the sentences are presented in context (though both forms may be expected to be processed more quickly in context than in isolation). By contrast, the *Discourse Hypothesis* predicts that the complexity of sentential subjects is due to their unnaturalness in isolation and to the violation of attention allocation expectations. Appropriate contexts should thus neutralize the differences in the complexity of extraposed vs. non-extraposed sentence forms. To test these predictions, we constructed contexts for the sentential subject sentences tested in Experiment 1. The contexts described an event, the consequences of which were later characterized by the sentential subject of the target sentence.

Experiment 2

Method

Subjects Twelve members of the University of Massachusetts community were paid to participate in the experiment. All of the subjects had normal uncorrected vision and they were naïve with respect to the purpose of the experiment. None of them had participated in Experiment 1.

Apparatus and procedure The same apparatus that was used in Experiment 1 was used in Experiment 2. The procedure was also identical except that subjects read short passages rather than single sentences. To ensure that subjects read for comprehension, the experimenter periodically asked the subjects comprehension questions about the paragraph they had just read.

Materials The eight sentential subject sentences and eight extraposed sentential subject sentences from Experiment 1 were used in the study. Appropriate contexts were written for each sentential subject sentence. For example, for sentences (4a) and (4b) the following context was written:

My friend Jennifer had Siamese twins last month, but they both had heart problems. Some doctors advised her against operating on them at such a young age. But she decided to go ahead with the operation.

(4) a. That both of the Siamese twins survived the operation is remarkable.
    b. It is remarkable that both of the Siamese twins survived the operation.

Sentence (4a) or (4b) then followed immediately after the context. Half of the subjects received the passage with the sentential subject in sentence initial position; half received the passage with the final sentence containing the extraposed sentential subject. Each subject read only one version of each passage and the eight passages were embedded in twenty other short passages.

Results

Reading times were significantly longer for sentences with sentential subjects (34.3 msec per character) than for sentences with extraposed sentential subjects (26.6 msec), $F(1,11) = 6.75$, $p < .05$. Though different subjects were tested, it is of some interest to note that the difference in the complexity of the two sentence forms was just as large as when the same sentences appeared in isolation, 41.6 msec per character versus 34.4 msec per character. This strongly supports the Local Non-Terminal Count Hypothesis over the other (discourse or attention allocation) hypotheses considered here.

A more fine-grained analysis of the locus of the complexity was also carried out using the same four regions as defined in Experiment 1. The data are presented in table 10.3. Like the overall reading time data, these data were also very similar to the data from Experiment 1. The ANOVA confirmed that sentential subject sentences took longer to read than sentences with extraposed sentential subjects, $F(1,7) = 21.036$, $p < .01$. Again, there was an interaction, $F(3,21) = 14.55$, $p < .001$ and the pattern was very similar to that obtained in Experiment 1. (Any differences between means greater than 9.7 msec is significant at the .05 level by a t-test.)

The gaze duration data yielded a significant interaction such that longer gazes were associated with the end of the sentence region, $F(3.21) = 11.89$, $p < .001$.

We have argued that left-branching per se does not substantially increase the difficulty of processing a sentence and we have presented evidence supporting the hypothesis that the complexity of sentences with sentential subjects is due (at least in part) to the need to postulate a large number of non-terminal nodes locally, at the beginning of the sentence. In short, our contention is that the complexity of left-branching constructions in English is due not to their branching pattern directly but to independent properties of specific constructions or to the interaction of branching patterns with other processes, such as assigning anaphoric relations and processes of semantic interpretation.

2 Parsing left- vs. right-branching languages

We turn now to the issue of developing a theory of the language processing system that can accommodate the processing of different language types. We take it to be an obvious fact that children acquiring a language do not receive any evidence or explicit training concerning what particular parsing strategies or routines would allow them to efficiently process the

Table 10.3 Regions analysis for extraposed and non-extraposed sentential subject sentences[a]

| Sentence form | Matrix | Region | | | Matrix |
		1	2	3	
Extraposed sentential subject	(it is remarkable) 20 (200)	(that . . . twins) 22 (216)	(survived) 27 (223)	(the operation) 30 (259)	(is remarkable) 46 (289)
Sentential subject		(that . . . twins) 36 (244)	(survived) 36 (242)	(the operation) 22 (209)	

[a]Data are reading time per character (msec). Values in parentheses are gaze durations (msec).

sentences of their language. Hence, given two languages L_1 and L_2, we expect any differences between the processing systems for these languages to be a direct consequence of the differences between the grammars of L_1 and L_2, or the interaction of the grammar with biologically encoded principles governing the language system. Minor idiosyncratic differences between languages might alter the output of the processing systems in a totally trivial fashion, without altering the specification of the processing system at all. This is particularly clear if one views the grammar of a language as a knowledge source consulted during processing. Changes in the specific content of some propositional knowledge that does not alter the format in which the information is mentally represented might affect the particular outcome of some processing operation (for example, the details of the representation constructed) but the change in the outcome might be a direct reflection of the change in the content of the knowledge source. More interesting is the case where a difference between two grammars interacts with the specification of the processing system. To take a hypothetical example, fixing S as a bounding node for L_1 (see discussion of Subjacency in Chomsky 1981) might in principle entail that S becomes a shunting unit in the language processing system, that is, that the representation of the syntactic structure of each complete S may be removed from immediate memory as soon as that S is complete. In other words, fixing the value of some parameter in the grammar being acquired might serve to fix or determine the value of some parameter in the specification of the processing system. If so, then we expect there to be uniformity across different perceivers of the language with respect to this aspect of the language processing system.[5]

X-theory (e.g. Jackendoff 1977) embodies the claim that major phrases are projections of lexical heads in all languages, for example NP is the projection of N. As a result of exposure to a language, the language learner must determine whether the heads of phrases precede (or follow) their complements in the language being acquired. In typologically consistent languages, if the head of one phrasal type precedes its complement, then the heads of all other phrases will also precede their complements. Since recursion typically occurs in the complements of phrases (for example, sentential complements embedded inside sentential complements), a language in which heads consistently precede their complements will be predominantly right-branching. Thus, we will refer to languages where heads consistently precede their complements as right-branching languages; languages with heads of phrases that uniformly follow their complements will be considered left-branching languages.[6] The question we wish to address is what consequences for the sentence processing system result from fixing the value of the parameter determining the linear order of heads with respect to their complements.

In several papers we have argued for a theory of sentence processing with the following properties. The sentence processing mechanism operates in an orderly fashion incorporating each word of the input into a constituent structure representation of the sentence (essentially) as the word is encountered (cf. Frazier and Rayner 1982 in particular). We might formulate this as the Left-to-Right Constraint.

Left-to-Right Constraint: Each item is incorporated into a constituent structure representation of a sentence (essentially) as the item is encountered.[7]

At points of (temporary) ambiguity the processor adopts the first syntactic analysis available to it, typically the structure that requires the postulation of the fewest syntactic nodes or permits a phrase to be associated with more recently presented material rather than more distant material (Frazier 1979; Frazier and Fodor 1978; Frazier and Rayner 1982; Rayner et al. 1983; Frazier et al. 1983).

First Analysis Constraint: At choice points the processor adopts the first syntactic analysis available (specifically the analysis that follows from Minimal Attachment, Late Closure and the Most Recent Filler Strategy) rather than pursuing multiple syntactic analyses or delaying analysis of the input.

Minimal Attachment: Postulate the fewest nodes consistent with the grammar.

Late Closure: Incorporate a new item into the phrase or clause currently being processed, rather than to an earlier (or subsequent) phrase or clause.

Most Recent Filler: When a gap is detected, assign the most recent potential filler to that gap.

Thus if the first word of a sentence is a determiner, for example, the minimal attachment of this item into a constituent structure representation of a sentence is as shown in (10a).

(10) a.

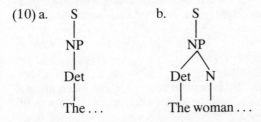

If the next word were *woman*, the minimal attachment of this item into the CPPM (Current Partial Phrase Marker) in (10a) would be as shown in (10b), since no analysis requiring the postulation of fewer syntactic nodes is permitted by the grammar of English. The requirement that the first word of a sentence be attached into 'S' has, to date, remained a mere stipulation, which we dub the Partial Top Down Constraint.[8]

Partial Top Down Constraint: The first word of a sentence must be (minimally) attached to the topmost 'S'; each subsequent item must be attached into the CPPM.

The Partial Top Down Constraint may itself be a consequence of another principle, formulated below as the Maximal Chunk Constraint.

Maximal Chunk Constraint: During processing, the human language processor forms the largest CPPMs possible given the inherent restrictions on its immediate memory and computational capacity and the grammar of the language being processed.

In Frazier and Fodor, one specific version of the Maximal Chunk Constraint was defended; specifically, it was suggested that the processor may form chunks (CPPMs) subsuming roughly six words of the input string. Here we will leave open questions concerning the precise restrictions on immediate memory capacity and assume only that there is some (universally fixed) restriction. Given the restriction on node-postulation provided by Minimal Attachment ('Don't postulate any potentially unnecessary nodes'), we may view the Partial Top Down Constraint as the consequence of the processor's attempt to satisfy the Maximal Chunk Constraint, that is, maximal chunking entails building warranted structure 'upwards' (to the top S) as well as 'sideways' (to incorporate additional items in the input word string). In short, maximal chunking entails that CPPMs grow as big as possible, with the proviso that potentially unnecessary structure is not postulated (due to Minimal Attachment).

We have suggested above (and in Frazier 1984) that a sentence is difficult to process if many syntactic nodes must be postulated all at once, over a few adjacent words of the input string, and impossible to parse in extreme cases (for example, multiply center embedded sentences of the form *Men women children dogs bit like marry hate pets*, multiply embedded sentential subjects of the form *That that that dogs bite upsets children bothers Fred surprised Mary*, etc.). We might formulate this as the Bounded Complexity Constraint.

Bounded Complexity Constraint: There is a (universally fixed) bound on the number of syntactic nodes that can be postulated over a few adjacent words in the input; if this upward bound is exceeded normal sentence processing routines will be disrupted or break down altogether.

For the purpose of our argument, what is crucial is only that there is some bound of the sort described by the Bounded Complexity Constraint (the details, but not the form, of the following argument depend on knowing the precise value of this bound). Though we in fact think that a precise and fully accurate statement of the complexity bound is not available at present, we will adopt Frazier's (1984) Local Non-Terminal Count Hypothesis as an approximation of this bound, assuming that a local count of more than nine will exceed the processor's normal capacity.[9] Thus, postulating more than nine (nonlexical) syntactic nodes over three adjacent lexical items will severely tax the processor's resources (assuming, as before, that S and $\bar{S}$ contribute the complexity of $1\frac{1}{2}$ nodes – see discussion of example (9) above and Frazier 1984: 164).

We must emphasize that the constraints proposed above clearly require refinement. It is, of course, important to know the exact restrictions on immediate memory and computational capacity, the precise conditions under which analysis of an input is delayed, the detailed interplay of the subcases of the First Analysis Strategy, etc. Recognizing that many of the details of this system have not yet been worked out even for English, we nevertheless wish to propose the following bold hypothesis: The Left-to-Right Constraint, the First Analysis Constraint, the Maximal Chunk Constraint and the Bounded Complexity Constraint are universal, that is, they constrain the structure and operation of the human sentence processor in general, regardless of the particular language being processed. What differs across languages, as a function of the grammar being processed, is the specific consequences of the Maximal Chunk Constraint. In a predominantly right-branching language like English (that is, a language where heads of phrases typically precede their complements) the Maximal Chunk Constraint results in a Partially Top Down Constraint; whereas, in a left-branching language like Japanese (that is, a language where the heads of phrases typically follow their complements) it does not.

The reason that Maximal Chunking cannot result in Partial Top Down parsing in left-branching languages is that this would prohibit the existence of parsable degree two-phrase markers (that is, a phrase marker with two embedded Ss, illustrated in (11), given the Bounded Complexity Constraint). The form of this argument is quite simple: (i) (we propose that) Universal Grammar prohibits human language systems from incorporating restrictions that would limit the availability of degree two phrase markers; (ii) given the Bounded Complexity Constraint, Partial

(11) a. S_0 b. right-branching   c. left-branching

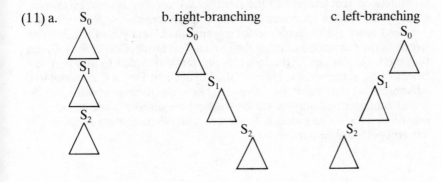

Top Down processing would violate this principle in a left-branching language; therefore (iii) though the Maximal Chunk Constraint is operative in left-branching languages, it cannot result in Partial Top Down processing. In short, we propose that the Maximal Chunk Constraint is 'parametrized'; its consequences depend on the type of grammar being processed.

We may now examine the consequences of the Partial Top Down Constraint in a left-branching language. This constraint specifically governs the parsing of the initial portion of a sentence and only indirectly constrains later processing, as a result of its influence on the shape of the CPPM. Degree two phrase markers may result from embedding in sentence-initial constituents either by self-embedding of sentential subjects, self-embedding of relative clauses or by relativizing a noun phrase in a sentential subject, for example. Since Japanese provides an example of a consistent left-branching language, we may illustrate the effect of Partial Top-Down processing by examining Japanese. If we assume Japanese structures comparable to those we have been assuming for English (apart from the order of phrases), the (simplified) English rules in (12a) will have the Japanese counterparts in (12b).[10]

$$(12) \text{ a. } \bar{S} \longrightarrow \text{COMP S} \qquad \text{b. } \bar{S} \longrightarrow \text{S} - \text{COMP}$$

$$\text{NP} \longrightarrow \text{NP } \bar{S} \qquad\qquad \text{NP} \longrightarrow \overset{(-)}{\text{S}} \text{ NP}$$

$$\text{VP} \longrightarrow \text{V} \left(\left\{ \begin{matrix} \text{NP} \\ \bar{S} \\ \text{Adj} \end{matrix} \right\} \right) \qquad \text{VP} \longrightarrow \left(\left\{ \begin{matrix} \text{NP} \\ \bar{S} \\ \text{Adj} \end{matrix} \right\} \right) \text{V}$$

Given these assumptions, the English structures in (13a)–(15a) would have the Japanese counterparts illustrated in the corresponding b-forms. The unboxed nodes in the b-example are the nodes required to grammatically parse the first few words of the sentence given the Partial Top Down Constraint and the above assumptions about Japanese. In the ultimately correct analysis of the sentences, these nodes must be dominated by the nodes in boxes. (In the English examples, all nodes are unboxed, since each is required for a grammatical analysis of the first few words of the sentence assuming the Partial Top Down Constraint). Given that the boxed nodes in the b-forms are not warranted by the first few words of the sentence, the effect of the Partial Top Down Constraint in a left-branching (left-recursive) language becomes obvious: it will serve no useful function but only cause the highest required S-node to be mis-identified as S_0 – the topmost S, thereby complicating the processing of left-embedded phrase markers.

(13) a.

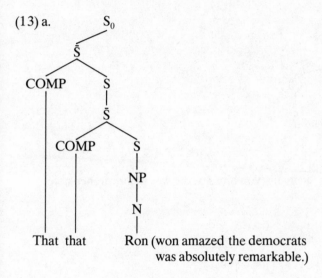

That that   Ron (won amazed the democrats
was absolutely remarkable.)

(13) b.

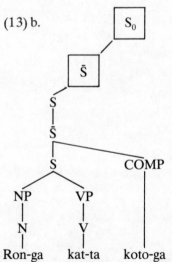

Ron-ga   kat-ta   koto-ga   (Minsyutooin-o odorokase-ta
    Nom   win-Past   Nom   democrats Acc amaze   Past
koto - wa   mattaku   tyunmokuni ataisuru   koto   data-ta)
COMP Top   absolutely attention   deserve-Pres thing   be - Past

(14) a.

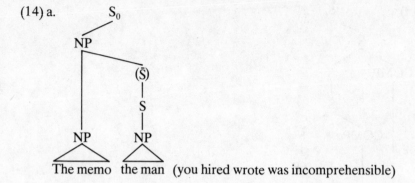

The memo the man (you hired wrote was incomprehensible)

(14) b.

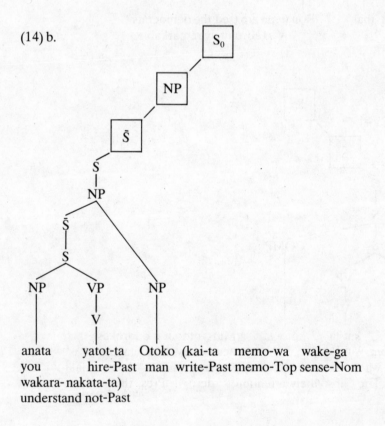

anata   yatot-ta Otoko (kai-ta   memo-wa   wake-ga
you   hire-Past man write-Past memo-Top sense-Nom
wakara-nakata-ta)
understand not-Past

(15) a.

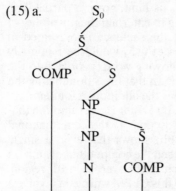

That people   who (don't vote complain about the country
upsets many traditional Americans)

(15) b.

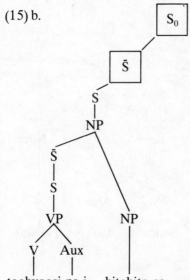

toohyoosi-na-i   hitobito-ga   (kuni-nituite-no   human — o   iw-
    vote   not-Pres people Nom country about Gen complaint Acc say-
u   koto-ga   ooku-no hosyutekina amerikaźin-o   toowakus- ase -
Pres COMP Nom many   conservative Americans Acc bewilder-cause-
te-i -ru)
Prog-Pres

If we look at some of the intermediate steps in processing the Japanese version of a sentence like (15), it is apparent that this sentence would tax the processor's computational capacity to its limit, given a partial Top Down Constraint. If the processor is willing to entertain the possibility of null arguments in Japanese (as it must if the sentence is presented in context, at least), then the first two words of (15) would be minimally analyzed as in (16a). Incorporating the following word, *people*, into the CPPM would require changing the assumption that the S dominating the VP is S_0, and deleting the empty subject, plus the addition of four entirely new syntactic nodes, as illustrated in (16b). If revising the assumption that the S dominating the VP is S_0 contributes anything to the computational cost of processing the sentence, then (16b) shows that even a single relative clause in subject position could exceed the computational limit on the number of nodes that may be postulated over a local region. Incorporating the following two words into this CPPM will again involve a revision of the hypothesis that the highest S in the old CPPM (16b) is S_0. Even without the computational cost of revising the S_0 hypothesis forced by the Partial Top Down Constraint, this will result in a cummulative node-to-word ration of 9:3, the proposed computational limit, for parsing the string *people complain that* in (16).

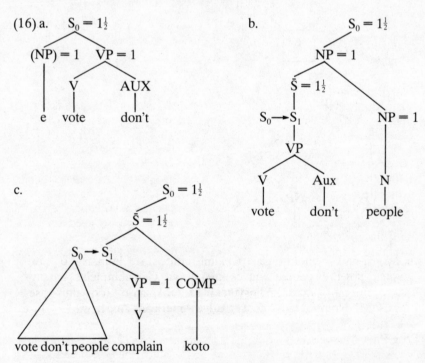

That people who don't vote complain upsets traditional Americans.

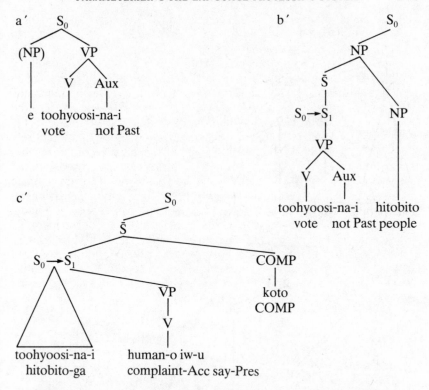

If the Maximal Chunking Constraint entailed a Partial Top Down Constraint in left-branching languages it would thus limit the availability of degree two phrase markers (including sentences with just a single relative clause in subject position, as illustrated in (16b)).[11] Further, if Maximal Chunking is itself a result of the fact that structuring material relieves the burden on immediate memory, an alternative (or additional) explanation of the absence of a Partial Top Down Constraint emerges, namely that the syntactic structure this constraint imposes in left-branching languages is irrelevant structure with respect to the material being remembered. As may be seen in the preceding examples, the relations between the words and phrases that have already been processed are not clarified by the structure imposed by this constraint. Moreover, unlike the English examples where the presence of S_0 provides potentially useful disambiguating information about the attachment of a later VP, as in (17), hypothesizing that some S is S_0 in Japanese provides no useful constraints on the analysis of subsequent material. In the English example (17a), the presence of S_0 provides an alternative grammatical attachment site for the verb *swim*; the corresponding Japanese example in (17b) is unambiguous since the head of the relative clause must follow the constituents of the relative.[12]

(17) a.

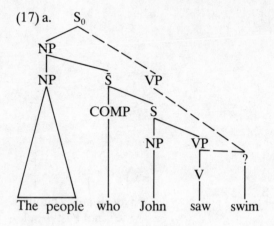

(17) b.

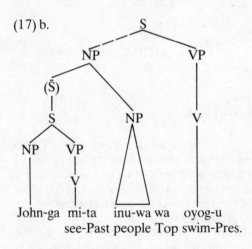

We turn now to some preliminary evidence, taken from Ueda (1984), suggesting that our conclusions are correct, at least for Japanese (that is, consistent with what is currently known). Ueda presents an initial analysis of the processing of Japanese. Working within the framework of Frazier and Fodor (1978) he suggests that one only needs to replace the grammar of English with the grammar of Japanese in the parsing system and ignore or relax the Partial Top Down Constraint to account for intuitions concerning the processing of Japanese. In support of this analysis, he presents the preference for low left attachment of *kinoo* ('yesterday') in sentences like (18), where this adverb is preferentially analyzed as a constituent of S_1 rather than as a constituent of the top S (S_0).

(18) Kinoo John-ga kekkonsi-ta to Mary-ga it-ta
     yesterday   Nom marry-Past COMP Nom say-Past
     'Mary said that John married yesterday'

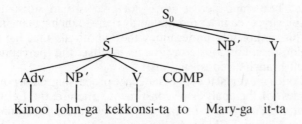

Note that this follows from Minimal Attachment if the requirement to attach the first word into the top S (that is, the Partial Top Down Constraint) is abandoned.

Ueda offers sentences like (19) as independent evidence for the operation of Minimal Attachment in Japanese. Here *Jane-ni* is preferentially attached to the S dominating *Tod-ga* (rather than correctly attached to an embedded S as illustrated in (19))

(19) Tod-ga Jane-ni Bill-ga hon -o atae-ta   to   sinzi-te   i-ru
       Nom   Dat   Nom book Acc give-Past COMP believe-Prog.-Past
     'Tod believes that Bill gave a book to Jane.'

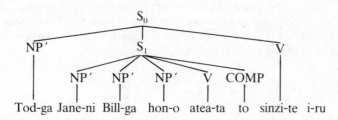

even though this attachment results in an ungrammatical sentence. On the account given here, this follows naturally. Structuring the first two NPs in (19) together requires the postulation of some higher node or nodes. Thus minimally structuring them into a CPPM will require postulating an S-node dominating them. When *Bill-ga* is encountered, a lower S-node must be postulated. It is to this lower S-node that *Jane-ni* must eventually be attached to arrive at a grammatical analysis of the sentence.

3 Conclusions

Section 1 presented experimental evidence and various arguments showing that left-branching per se does not give rise to substantial processing complexity, even in a predominantly right-branching language like English. This completely undermines the hypothesis that natural languages develop discontinuous constituents to offset the (perceptual) complexity of left-branching constructions.

Section 2 laid out a universal theory of language processing, incorporating four principles for the analysis of constituent structure: the Left-to-Right Constraint, the First Analysis Strategy (crucially including Minimal Attachment), the Maximal Chunk Constraint and the Bounded Complexity Constraint. We suggest that the only language-specific differences in the language processing system for left- vs. right-branching languages result from the particular consequences of the Maximal Chunk Constraint. Specifically, maximal chunking results in the 'partial top down constraint' only in right-branching languages: in left-branching languages, maximal chunking does not result in a partial top down constraint. Examples taken from Ueda (1984) provide initial evidence in support of these proposals.

Clearly more evidence is needed to evaluate this (or any) hypothesis about the universal properties of the language processing system, and the claimed absence of any differences in the actual specification of the processing system for left- vs. right-branching languages. Our hope is that the analysis offered here will help to uncover relevant evidence (confirming or disconfirming) and to prompt discussion of how a universal theory of human sentence processing can be parameterized to account for, and explain, the processing of different language types.

Notes

This paper develops the general framework for studying branching structure which was assumed in the investigation of Dutch (Frazier, submitted) carried out by the first author while she was at the Max-Planck-Institute in Spring 1985. The experimental research reported here was supported by grant HD 17246 from the National Institute of Child Health and Human Development and Grant BNS-8510177 from the National Science Foundation. We wish to thank Marcia Carlson and Bill Collins for help collecting the data, and Chuck Clifton, Matthew Dryer and several anonymous reviewers for comments on an earlier draft of this paper. We are especially grateful to Masa Ueda for comments and for providing Japanese translations of examples (13)–(19).

1 The structures considered below (e.g. (1a), (2a), (3a)) have traditionally been labeled 'left-branching' despite the fact that both left- and right-branches are further articulated. The reason for considering such constructions to be left-branching is simply that recursive nodes (e.g. S, NP) appear on left-branches.

2 Though Yngve's model was proposed as a model of sentence production it has often been interpreted and tested as a model of sentence comprehension (see Wright 1966; Martin and Roberts 1966, 1967, 1968; Perfetti 1969a, b; Perfetti and Goodman 1971).

3 Grosu and Thompson (1977) and Dryer (1980) point out that there is a clear cross-linguistic tendency to prefer structures like (1b) to structures like (1a) even in languages which otherwise tolerate extensive left-branching. Apparently there is no comparable cross-language preference for the b-forms of (2) and (3) (Dryer, personal communication).

4 One reviewer suggests yet another alternative explanation for the complexity of (1a), namely its lower frequency (see Dryer 1978). However, there are many problems which arise with frequency-based explanations. First, precisely *what* is more/less frequent (a terminal string, a sequence of major phrases, some 'construction type' in a particular 'type' of discourse, etc.)? Second, what mechanisms underlie the hypothesized frequency effect? Third, there is often circularity in frequency-based explanations where frequency is often taken to both cause and be caused by perceptual complexity. Fourth, until the mechanisms underlying frequency differences are understood, it is unclear whether frequency in the language at large is (i) relevant to the experimental setting where frequency is balanced or (ii) relevant to the processing of unambiguous structures (see discussion of perceptual set effects in Frazier et al. 1984).

5 In principle, it is possible that the specification of the human sentence processing mechanism has certain free or open parameters whose values are not determined by universal principles in conjunction with the type of grammar being acquired. If so, since all normal humans acquire a system adequate to process the sentences of their native language, we must assume either that all values for a free parameter are acceptable (result in an adequate processing system) or that the value of the parameters is set by some efficiency criterion which itself results from some biologically determined aspect of the human cognitive system.

6 At present we simply have no insights to offer concerning the processing of typologically mixed languages. We think it likely that work currently in progress on the processing of Dutch and German will help to elucidate the issues involved (see Bach et al 1986).

It should also be noted that 'right-branching' and 'head-initial' cannot always be identified with each other, that is, in a particular construction the two may diverge. But with respect to a language type, presumably it is the parameter governing the position of the head relative to its complement which underlies basic branching direction.

7 In Frazier and Rayner (1987) we argue that the syntactic processor delays assignment of structure to phrases with categorially ambiguous items until disambiguating information arrives.

8 Clearly this constraint does *not* impose strict Top Down Parsing where each mother node must be entered into the CPPM before any of its daughter nodes.

9 There is admittedly something very artificial about the numeric values exploited in this complexity measure. As noted in Frazier (1984) the Local Non-Terminal Count is only intended to capture the relative complexity of syntactic structures, and only the ordinal relations between the numeric values are intended to be taken seriously. Imposing a ceiling (e.g. 9/3) on the number of nodes that can be postulated in a local region should not be viewed as an absolute limit. Rather, the claim is that the processor may keep pace with the input string only operating within this limit. At higher values (e.g. above 9/3) the processor lags behind the

input, thus risking complete breakdown should any new processing difficulties arise in the analysis of immediately following material, since the processor is already operating at the limit of its capacity. Finally, we must emphasize that the Local Non-Terminal Count is computed in terms of the actual point in the string when the processor postulates nodes (as governed by Minimal Attachment), and thus cannot be determined simply by counting the nodes dominating some word in the final phase marker.

10 Hypothesizing the existence of a VP-node in Japanese is controversial. The existence of a VP-node is expected given most versions of X̄-theory (see Jackendoff 1977, for example) and some evidence for it is provided in Saito (1982); however, the freedom in the relative order of subjects and objects in Japanese is often taken as evidence against the existence of a VP-node in Japanese. For present purposes, the advantage of assuming a VP-node (even though it inflates a local non-terminal count if the VP-hypothesis is incorrect) is that it permits us to examine the consequences of processing comparable left-branching and right-branching structures.

11 Why should Universal Grammar prohibit restrictions excluding degree two phrase markers? Though one might appeal to the expressive needs of speakers to justify this principle, we suspect the explanation lies elsewhere. Possibly the answer is as simple as that natural language grammars permit recursion and do not have the counting properties needed to impose restrictions on the application of recursive rules (and the possibility of recursion on S is just one of the possibilities permitted by Universal Grammar). However, we know that the human parsing system cannot cope with unlimited recursion in many instances (e.g. in English, multiply center embedded structures, multiply embedded possessive phrases, etc.) so why should degree two phrase markers (just two levels of clausal embedding) be special?

Wexler and Culicover (1980) have shown that language is learnable in the limit given text presentation of the data. Further, they show that one does not need phrase markers more complex than degree two phrase markers assuming particular syntactic constraints (which look remarkably similar to those proposed by linguists on independent grounds). Their proof, of course, does not demonstrate that degree two phrase markers are required for a language to be learnable (in the limit). It only shows that one would need to assume additional syntactic constraints to prove learnability given only, say, degree one phrase markers. So it might turn out that the syntactic constraints needed to prove degree one learnability are in fact natural constraints that correspond to some (as yet unnoticed) constraints on natural language grammars. But we doubt it. If one looks, for example, at early classifications of rule types in generative grammar, three types of grammatical dependencies clearly emerge: those involving just a single clause; those involving two subjacent clauses (that is, one clause immediately dominating another); and dependencies that are in principle unbounded (in Ross's 1967 terms, those requiring essential variables). The special status of degree two phrase markers may thus be attributed to their role in distinguishing the latter two rule types. Unless Universal Grammar imposes such tight restrictions on these two types of rules that the language learner could never encounter a dependency in a degree one phrase marker that could be couched as either a two-clause or an unbounded dependency, degree two phrase markers will be needed to determine which type of dependency the grammar contains. Hence we think that the special status of degree two phrase markers is real and not merely a reflection of the current state of work in formal learnability proofs.

If, as we've suggested, degree two phrase markers can be crucial for sorting out the grammar of some natural languages, then it is not surprising that Universal Grammar should prohibit restrictions on the existence or availability of degree two phrase markers. Rather this general sort of restriction is just what we expect to constrain the principles of Universal Grammar, if Universal Grammar is supposed to characterize the properties that a grammar must have to be acquired by humans. The fact that some languages may not exhibit a distinction between two clause and unbounded dependencies is of course irrelevant, unless there is some way for a child to know in advance of successfully acquiring a grammar which type of language he or she is learning.

The Degree Two Principle is perhaps best viewed as an observation about Universal Grammar rather than as an explicit principle of (that is, statement in) Universal Grammar. The crucial substance of the principle is the restriction it places on the relation between universal parsing principles and universal grammatical principles. That is, taken jointly, these two sets of principles must permit grammars to be learnable.

12 Notice that this alternative explanation of the differential consequences of Maximal Chunking does not require the assumption that the VP-node exists in Japanese. Thus, the basic account of the different effects of our proposed parsing principles can, on this view, be stated in a fairly theory-neutral way, independent of one's assumption about the status of a VP-node in Japanese (and other left-branching languages) and independent of the Degree Two Principle that we propose.

References

Bach, E., C. Brown and W. Marslen-Wilson (1986) 'Crossed and nested dependencies in German and Dutch'. *Language and Cognitive Processes*, 1, 249–62.

Bever, T. G. (1970) 'The cognitive basis for linguistic structures'. In J. R. Hayes (ed.), *Cognition and the Development of Language*. New York: Wiley.

and D. J. Townsend (1979) 'Perceptual mechanisms and formal properties of main and subordinate clauses'. In W. E. Cooper and E. C. T. Walker (eds), *Sentence Processing*. Hillsdale, NJ: Erlbaum.

Chomsky, N. (1981) *Lectures on Government and Binding*. Dordrecht: Foris Publications.

Cutler, A. (1976) 'Phoneme-monitoring reaction time as a function of preceding intonation contour'. *Perception and Psychophysics*, 20, 55–60.

and J. A. Fodor (1979) 'Semantic focus and sentence comprehension'. *Cognition*, 7, 49–60.

Dryer, M. S. (1978) 'Sentence-initial complementizers and perceptual strategies'. Paper given at the 1978 meeting of the LSA.

(1980) 'The positional tendencies of sentential noun phrases in universal grammar'. *Canadian Journal of Linguistics*, 25, 123–95.

Forster, K. I. (1966) 'Left-to-right processes in the construction of sentence'. *Journal of Verbal Learning and Verbal Behavior*, 5, 285–291.

(1968) 'Sentence completion in left-and-right branching languages'. *Journal of Verbal Learning and Verbal Behavior*, 7, 296–99.

Frazier, L. (1979) 'On comprehending sentences: syntactic parsing strategies', Indiana University Linguistics Club, Bloomington, Indiana.

(1985) 'Syntactic complexity'. In D. Dowty, L. Karttuen and A. Zwicky (eds)

Syntactic Theory and How People Parse Sentences. Cambridge: Cambridge University Press.

(submitted) 'Syntactic processing: evidence from Dutch'.

and C. Clifton and J. Randall (1983) 'Filling gaps: decision principles and structure in sentence comprehension. *Cognition*, 13, 187–222.

and J. D. Fodor (1978) 'The sausage machine: a new two-stage parsing model'. *Cognition*, 6, 291–326.

and K. Rayner (1982) 'Making and correcting errors during sentence comprehension: eye movements in the analysis of structurally ambiguous sentences'. *Cognitive Psychology*, 14, 178–210.

and K. Rayner (1987) 'Resolution of syntactic category ambiguities: Eye movements in parving lexically ambiguous sentences'. *Journal of Memory and Language*, 26, 505–26.

L. Taft, T. Roeper, C. Clifton and K. Ehrlich (1984) 'Parallel structure'. *Memory and Cognition*, 12, 421–30.

Grosu, A. and S. Thompson (1977) 'Constraints on the distribution of NP clauses'. *Language*, 53, 104–51.

Holmes, V. M. (1979) 'Some hypotheses about syntactic processing in sentence comprehension'. In W. E. Cooper and E. C. T. Walker (eds) *Sentence Processing*. Hillsdale, NJ: Erlbaum.

Hornby, J. A. (1974) 'Surface structure and presupposition'. *Journal of Verbal Learning and Verbal Behavior*, 13, 530–8.

Jackendoff, R. (1977) *X̄-Syntax: A Study of Phrase Structure*. Cambridge: MIT Press.

Just, M. and P. Carpenter (1980) 'A theory of reading: from eye fixations to comprehension'. *Psychological Review*, 87, 329–54.

Koster, J. (1978) 'Why subject sentences don't exist'. In S. J. Keyser (ed.), *Recent Transformational Studies in European Languages*. Cambridge, Mass.: MIT Press.

Levin, H., J. Grossman, E. Kaplan and R. Yang (1972) 'Constraints on the eye-voice span in right and left embedded sentences'. *Language and Speech*, 15, 30–9.

Martin, E. and K. H. Roberts (1966) 'Grammatical factors in sentence retention'. *Journal of Verbal Learning and Verbal Behavior*, 5, 211–18.

(1967) 'Sentence length and sentence retention in the free learning situation'. *Psychonomic Science*, 8, 535.

Perfetti, C. A. (1969a) 'Sentence retention and the depth hypothesis'. *Journal of Verbal Learning and Verbal Behavior*, 8, 101–4.

(1969b) 'Lexical density and phrase structure depth as variables in sentence retention'. *Journal of Verbal Learning and Verbal Behavior*, 8, 719–24.

and D. Goodman (1971) 'Memory for sentences and noun phrases of extreme depth'. *Quarterly Journal of Experimental Psychology*, 23, 22–3.

Rayner, K. and L. Frazier (1987). Parsing temporarily ambiguous complements. *Quarterly Journal of Experimental Psychology*, 39A, 657–673.

Rayner, K., M. Carlson and L. Frazier (1983) 'The interaction of syntax and semantics during sentence processing: eye movements in the analysis of semantically biased sentences'. *Journal of Verbal Learning and Verbal Behavior*, 22, 358–74.

Ross, J. R. (1967) 'Constraints on variables in syntax'. Diss., MIT.

Saito, M. (1982) 'Case marking in Japanese'. MS, MIT.

Ueda, M. (1984) 'Notes on parsing in Japanese'. MS, University of Massachusetts.

Wanat, S. F. (1971) 'Linguistic structure and visual attention in reading'. Doctoral diss., Cornell University.

Wanner, E. (1980) 'The ATN and the sausage machine: which one is baloney?' *Cognition*, 8, 209–25.

Wexler, K. and P. Culicover (1980) *Formal Principles of Language Acquisition*. Cambridge, Mass.: MIT Press.

Wright, P. (1966) 'Two studies of the depth hypothesis'. *British Journal of Psychology*, 60, 63–9.

Yngve, V. H. A. (1960) 'A model and an hypothesis for language structure'. *Proceedings of the American Philosophical Society*, 104, 444–66.

CHAPTER 11

Psycholinguistic Factors in Morphological Asymmetry

John A. Hawkins and Anne Cutler

1 Introduction

Recent research on language universals has uncovered several cases of what we will call *left–right asymmetries*.[1] In these univerals, linguistic categories that are predicted by independently well-motivated principles to be, for example, leftward-occurring within their respective phrases will often show up on the right, whereas the converse fails: when these same independent principles predict a rightward occurrence in languages of the relevant type, there is no leftward skewing and the categories in question do occur to the right. In other examples, a leftward skewing may be favored. Most of the cases documented so far involve asymmetries within syntax, for which explanations of an extragrammatical nature have been proposed that make use of certain findings from psycholinguistics, particularly theories of language comprehension. The importance of such findings for the field of linguistics is that they provide suggestive explanatory hypotheses for left–right asymmetries across languages which may otherwise be unexplained. For psycholinguistics such work is important for theories of language processing, since what is being claimed is that principles of processing are reflected not just in the use of language but also in its structure. The need to readily comprehend and produce language joins other demands upon successful communication systems in constraining the variation space within which the set of possible human languages can be constructed (cf. Hawkins this volume). Asymmetries in linguistic structure may also provide evidence for one processing model over another.

The present paper will concentrate on some left–right asymmetries in morphology rather than in syntax, involving the cross-linguistic preference for suffixing over prefixing. Some explanatory hypotheses for the grammatically unpredicted asymmetries will be given that are strongly suggested by current psycholinguistic research on lexical access.

The order of presentation is as follows. The next section briefly summarizes the kinds of processing explanations advanced for some left–right asymmetries in syntax. Section 3 presents some morphological univerals and documents the suffixing preference. Sections 4 and 5 review the relevant processing literature on lexical access. Finally, section 6 presents our processing hypotheses for the suffixing preference.

2 Some Left–Right Asymmetries in Syntax

There are a number of syntactic left–right asymmetries across languages for which processing explanations have been offered. Hawkins (1988a) discusses several. Hawkins (1988b) argues, even more ambitiously, for a processing explanation both for such asymmetries *and* for basic grammatical regularities such as cross-categorial head ordering from which asymmetrically ordered categories depart (cf. also Frazier 1979, 1984).

Consider, for example, the positioning of relative clause and head noun. There is an asymmetry in their distribution across languages. The languages that are independently predicted to have the relative clause after the head noun (that is, head-initial languages such as English) do so; the languages that are independently predicted to have the relative clause before the head noun (that is, head-final languages) may (Japanese) or may not (Sumerian) do so, and in a significant number of cases have postnominal relatives as in English. The result is a rightward skewing in favor of postnominal relatives overall.

This skewing becomes significant when we consider that the ratios of head-initial to head-final languages are roughly equal across languages. In all current samples of which we are aware, the proportions of pre-positional (Pr + NP) to postpositional (NP + Po), and of verb–object (VO) to object–verb (OV) languages hover around the 50–50 mark, as shown in table 11.1. By contrast, between one-eighth (Lehmann 1984) and one-quarter (Hawkins 1983) of the world's languages have pre-nominal relatives in different samples, with the great majority of the remainder having postnominal (that is, head first) constructions in these noun phrases. And whereas head-initial languages have almost exclusively postnominal relative clauses, a significant proportion of otherwise head-final languages also have the postnominal relative clause order.

What could explain this preference? Antinucci et al. (1979) were the first to address this question. They argued that prenominal relatives cause perceptual problems that are avoided in their postnominal counterparts. They provide too many opportunities for misanalyzing subordinate clause constituents as matrix constituents in structures such as (1). Because the relative clause precedes its head, subordinate clause constituents such as NP_1 and V will often be integrated on-line into the matrix clause, producing a garden path effect, and forcing the parser to reconstruct the tree retrospectively by introducing the circled dominating nodes over the misrecognized constituents.

Table 11.1 Proportions of head-initial and head-final languages in current samples[a]

Sample	Sample size in lgs	Word order	% of sample
Hawkins (1983)	336	Pr + NP	44%
		NP + Po	56%
Greenberg (1966)	142	Pr + NP	44%
		NP + Po	56%
Stassen (cf. Hawkins and Gilligan 1988)	113	Pr + NP	50%
		NP + Po	50%
Ruhlen (1975)	427	VO (SVO, VSO, VOS)	48%
		OV (SOV)	52%
Tomlin (1986)	402	VO (SVO, VSO, VOS)	54%
		OV (SOV, OVS)	46%
Hawkins (1983)	336	VO (SVO, VSO, VOS)	48%
		OV (SOV)	52%
Greenberg (1966)	142	VO (SVO, VSO)	55%
		OV (SOV)	45%
Stassen (cf. Hawkins and Gilligan 1988)	113	VO (SVO, VSO)	54%
		OV (SOV)	46%
Mallinson and Blake (1981)	89	VO (SVO, VSO, VOS)	52%
		OV (SOV, OVS, OSV)	48%
Ultan (1978)	75	VO (SVO, VSO, VOS)	56%
		OV (SOV)	44%
Perkins (cf. Bybee 1985)	40	VO (SVO, VSO)	47%
		OV (SOV)	53%

This table gives the proportions of Pr + NP to NP + Po and of VO to OV languages in current samples. The samples are listed in descending order of sample size, first for adposition order, then for verb position. VO stands for SVO, VSO and also VOS, as shown. SVO typically outnumbers VSO in these samples by at least 2-to-1, with VOS being much rarer than VSO, cf. Pullum (1981), Tomlin (1986) and Hawkins (this volume). OV stands for SOV, but occasionally also for OVS and OSV, again as shown. We indicate in parentheses which particular subtypes of VO and OV are represented.

[a]The proportions hover around 50–50 in these different samples. The precise aggregates are: 46% Pr + NP to 54% NP + Po (three samples); and 52% VO to 48% OV (eight samples); which averages out at 49% head-initial to 51% head-final.

(1)
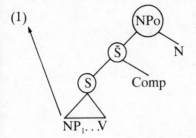

An illustrative example from Japanese is (2) (cf. Clancy et al. 1986):

(2) (Japanese)
Zoo-ga   ₙₚₒ(s̄(s(ₙₚ₁(kirin-o)   taoshi-ta))   shika-o) nade-ta.
'elephant-SU   giraffe-OBJ knocked-down deer-OBJ patted',
i.e.
The elephant patted the deer that knocked down the giraffe.

kirin-o and *taoshi-ta* can be parsed on-line as a matrix clause direct object and verb for the subject *zoo-ga* (by Frazier's 1978 principle of Minimal Attachment), and it is not until the head noun *shika-o* is encountered that the misanalysis will be recognized and the appropriate reanalysis can take place. The attendant processing difficulty associated with such structures in Japanese has been demonstrated experimentally, both for adults (cf. Frazier & Rayner this volume) and for children (in Japanese and Korean, cf. Clancy et al. 1986). But no comparable structural misanalysis arises in the corresponding postnominal relatives, in which the head noun serves to immediately indicate the leftmost boundary of the dominating NPo, whereupon the relative clause and its daughters will be attached under the domination of this NPo (cf. further Hawkins 1988b).[2]

Underlying this and other processing explanations for syntactic universals is the assumption that processing difficulty is a (quantifiably) gradient notion, with empirical consequences for language frequencies and implicationally defined co-occurrences of properties (cf. Hawkins, this volume, 1988b; Cutler and Hawkins 1987). The relevant implicational universal for relative clauses is set out in (3), together with exemplifying languages and quantitative data. With the exception of one or two languages like Chinese (which combine prepositions – but also postpositions – with prenominal relatives) a prenominal relative clause occurs only in fairly rigid head-final languages (those with both NP + Po and OV).

(3) If a language is head-initial (Pr + NP v VO), then it is NRel within NP; (i.e. if RelN, then −(Pr + NP v VO), i.e. NP + Po & OV).

Co-occurrences:

1   Pr & VO ⎫   English; Arabic; Swahili; Malagasy
2   Pr & OV ⎪   NRel   Persian; German
3   Po & VO ⎬   Finnish; Koyo
4a Po & OV ⎭   Galla; Sumerian; Lushei

4b Po & OV ⎬ RelN   Korean; Lahu; Basque

Quantitative data (from Hawkins 1983):

1% of Pr lgs   = RelN; 99% of Pr lgs = NRel;
61% of Po lgs = RelN; 39% of Po lgs = NRel
2% of VO lgs   = RelN; 98% of VO lgs = NRel;
56% of OV lgs = RelN; 44% of OV lgs = NRel

The proportion of languages whose relative clauses depart from the predicted prenominal order, coupled with the almost complete absence of the reverse skewing (head-initial languages with prenominal relatives), gives an indication of the degree of processing difficulty associated with the prenominal structure. The difficulty is clearly within the level of tolerance (in contrast to mirror-image transformations, cf. Hawkins this volume), but it is dispreferred nonetheless, and this dispreference is in opposition to the demands of consistent head ordering across categories (which is also argued to have a processing motivation in Hawkins (1988b, albeit of a different kind).[3] The resolution of such conflicts is played out in language variation and in the implicational universals that define it. The relative strengths of the competing principles are seen in the frequencies with which languages opt for one or the other solution.[4]

3 Left–Right Asymmetries in Morphology

Greenberg (1957, 1966) was the first to point out that suffixal morphology within a word is more frequent across languages than prefixing, and that both are considerably more frequent than infixing (whereby an affix is inserted into a lexical stem; for a detailed discussion of types of affixation processes, cf. Matthews 1974: ch. 7). The goal of Hawkins and Gilligan (1988) is to discover the cross-linguistic regularities in this area in greater detail. In the present paper we shall summarize these regularities, consider the grammatical principles that can be argued to underlie them and explore a possible psycholinguistic explanation for the suffixing preference.

The major pattern of interest that emerges from Hawkins and Gilligan's work can be summarized in (4):

(4)   *Prefixes*   *Suffixes*

$\left\{ \begin{array}{l} \text{VO} \\ \text{Pr} + \text{NP} \end{array} \right\}$ X   X

$\left\{ \begin{array}{l} \text{OV} \\ \text{NP} + \text{Po} \end{array} \right\}$ O   X

Languages with VO and/or Pr + NP word orders in their syntax regularly have prefixes and/or suffixes in their morphology. But in a suggestively large number of cases, languages with OV and/or NP + Po have suffixes only. This distribution strongly implies the need for two major principles at the explanatory level: one which explains why prefixes occur productively only in VO and Pr + NP languages, while similar functions in OV and NP + Po languages are performed by suffixes; and another that favors suffixing in both language types and that is partially opposed to the independent predictions of the first principle for VO and Pr + NP languages. It will be argued here that the first principle makes crucial reference to the notion 'head of phrase' in both syntax and morphology, and that heads are identically ordered relative to their modifiers at both levels (the Head Ordering Principle). The second principle, responsible for the postposing asymmetry, will be argued to be a psycholinguistic one. Its effects corroborate the Head Ordering Principle's prediction for suffixing in OV and NP + Po languages, and account for why suffixes occur at all in VO and Pr + NP languages.

Section 3.1 below summarizes the morphological univerals; section 3.2 motivates the Head Ordering Principle; section 3.3 sets out the need for a set of counterprinciples to the Head Ordering Principle and documents the suffixing asymmetry in morphological universals.

3.1 Some prefixing and suffixing universals

The correlations observed by Greenberg (1966) between basic word order and morpheme order in his thirty-language sample are summarized in table 11.2. These data establish clearly the greater frequency of suffixing over prefixing. Greenberg also points out that both are considerably more frequent than infixing. The data of table 11.2 show that suffixing is massively preferred in NP + Po and OV languages, and that if a language is prefixing only, the basic word order will be Pr + NP and VO . What is missing in Greenberg's discussion, however, is any indication of what the precise morphemes were (in terms of meaning and syntactic function) that he studied. Hawkins and Gilligan (1988) have accordingly set up a categorization of morphemes, and formulate implicational universals linking morpheme order within each category to verb and adposition order in the syntax. The languages consulted number around 200 and are drawn from three samples: a computerized typological sample of 113 languages collected by Leon Stassen, containing entries for many hundreds of

Table 11.2 Morpheme order correlations with verb and adposition order in
Greenberg's sample

	Overall morpheme order and verb position		
	Prefix only	Both	Suffix only
VO (i.e. VSO and SVO)	1	16	2
OV (i.e. SOV)	0	1	10

	Overall morpheme order and adposition order		
	Prefix only	Both	Suffix only
Pr + NP	1	15	0
NP + Po	0	2	12

linguistic properties including some morpheme orders; a forty-language
computerized sample of morphological properties provided to us by Joan
Bybee and originally collected by Revere Perkins; and a sample of fifty
languages compiled by Gary Gilligan. Only a handful of languages belong
to more than one of these samples.

The morpheme categories that have been documented within these
three samples are summarized in table 11.3. In addition, Stassen and
Gilligan provide syntactic information on adposition order (Pr + NP and
NP + Po) and verb position (VSO, VOS, SVO, SOV). Perkins–Bybee give
syntactic information on verb position only.

Below we list the eighteen implicational universals of Hawkins and
Gilligan (1988). Of these, six are exceptionless (numbers (5)–(9) and
(15)), and the remainder are statistical in Greenberg's sense, that is, they
hold with more than chance frequency.

(5)   If a language has CASE affixes on N, they are always suffixed.
(6)   If a language has NP + Po, GENDER affixes on N (if any) are
       suffixed.
(6) a. That is, if a language has prefixed GENDER affixes, it will have
       Pr + NP.
(7)   If a language has SOV, GENDER affixes on N (if any) are
       suffixed.
(7) a. That is, if a language has prefixed GENDER affixes, it will have
       VO (that is, not SOV).
(8)   If a language has NP + Po, INDEFINITENESS affixes on N (if
       any) are suffixed.
(9)   If a language has SOV, INDEFINITENESS affixes on N (if any)
       are suffixed.

Table 11.3 Morphological categories of this study[a]

Affixes on N
CASE (Stassen, Gilligan)
GENDER (Gilligan)
PLURAL (Gilligan)
NOMINALIZATION (Gilligan)
INDEFINITENESS (Stassen)
DEFINITENESS (Stassen, Gilligan)

POSSESSIVE (Gilligan)

Affixes on V
MOOD (Perkins–Bybee, Gilligan)
TENSE (Stassen, Perkins–Bybee, Gilligan)
ASPECT (Stassen, Perkins–Bybee, Gilligan)
VALENCE (Perkins–Bybee)
CAUSATIVE (Perkins–Bybee)

PERSON-MARKING (SUBJECT) (Stassen, Perkins–Bybee, Gilligan)
PERSON-MARKING (OBJECT) (Perkins–Bybee)
NEGATION (Stassen, Perkins–Bybee, Gilligan)
VOICE (Perkins–Bybee)

[a]The six nominal and five verbal affixes occurring above the line figure in universals (5)–(21). For the five affixes below the line,
no implicational universals linking affix order and syntactic order are possible.

(10)   If a language has NP + Po, NOMINALIZING affixes on N (if any) are suffixed with considerably greater than chance frequency.

(11)   If a language has SOV, NOMINALIZING affixes on N (if any) are suffixed with considerably greater than chance frequency.

(12)   If a language has SOV, DEFINITENESS affixes on N (if any) are suffixed with greater than chance frequency.

(13)   If a language has NP + Po, PLURAL affixes on N (if any) are suffixed with considerably greater than chance frequency.

(14)   If a language has SOV, PLURAL affixes on N (if any) are suffixed with overwhelmingly greater than chance frequency.

(15)   If a language has NP + Po, MOOD affixes on V (if any) are suffixed.

(16)   If a language has SOV, MOOD affixes on V (if any) are suffixed with greater than chance frequency.

(17)   If a language has NP + Po, TENSE affixes on V (if any) are suffixed with overwhelmingly greater than chance frequency.

(18)   If a language has SOV, TENSE affixes on V (if any) are suffixed with greater than chance frequency.

(19)   If a language has NP + Po, ASPECT affixes on V (if any) are suffixed with greater than chance frequency.

(20)   If a language has VALENCE affixes on V (that is, INTRANSITIVE/TRANSITIVE/DITRANSITIVE affixes), they are suffixed with more than chance frequency.

(21)   If a language has SOV, CAUSATIVE affixes on V (if any) are suffixed with more than chance frequency.

(22)   There is more prefixing on V than on N. If a language has any prefixes on N, then any affixes on V will include prefixes with more than chance frequency.

Most of these univerals are formulated with NP + Po or SOV as the antecedent of an implication whose consequent is suffixing within the morphology, as in (6): if a language has NP + Po, GENDER affixes on N (if any) are suffixed. It follows that if gender affixes are *not* suffixed in some language, that language cannot be NP + Po but must be Pr + NP. Thus (6) is logically equivalent to (6a) in which prefixes constitute the antecedent property and Pr + NP is the consequent, and similarly for (7) and all of the other implicational universals with NP + Po or SOV as antecedent and suffixing as consequent.

These universals result in the three-way distribution between affix order and syntactic order depicted in (4). NP + Po and OV imply the co-occurrence of suffixing, and prefixing implies Pr + NP and VO. Pr + NP and VO, on the other hand, imply nothing, since they co-occur with both prefixing and suffixing, and suffixing likewise co-occurs with both Pr + NP/VO and NP + Po/OV.

3.2   The Head Ordering Principle

These implicational universals point to the reality of a generalization linking morphology and syntax with respect to the notion 'head', as is assumed in fact in recent generative work on morphology (e.g. Aronoff 1976, Williams 1981). Within syntax, the categories N, V, P and Adj are the heads of their respective phrasal categories (NP, VP, PP, AdjP) and they preserve category constancy. That is, the categorial status of the most immediately dominating category is determined by the head of phrase, and not necessarily by any modifiers. The verb is the head of the verb phrase, the adposition (preposition or postposition) the head of the adposition phrase and the noun the head of the noun phrase, etc. Similarly, within morphology it is possible to argue that the component morphemes of whole words are divided into heads and modifiers, and that the morpheme which determines the categorial status of the word in question, more precisely of the immediately dominating lexical category, is the head. Thus, a derivational affix determines the category status of its immediately dominating lexical category, and may or may not change the category of the item to which it attaches. The suffix -*ess* when added to *lion* does not change the category of the latter: both *lion* and *lioness* are nouns. But the suffix -*ness* attached to *sad* converts an adjective to a noun, and here it is crucially the affix rather than the stem that determines the category of the resulting word *sadness*. Inflectional affixes, like -*s* in English (cf. *girl*/*girls*), pattern like *lion*/*lioness* and maintain the categorial status of the item to which they attach. Across languages inflectional affixes are generally unique to some particular category, cf., for example, the case inflections of the various noun paradigms in Latin, or the person and tense inflections of Latin verbs. And hence the nature of the dominating lexical category can be just as readily determined from the affix as from the stem in these cases. As a result of the categorial status of a word containing affixes can regularly be computed from the affix, whereas non-affixes or stems will very often have their categorial status changed through the addition of a (derivational) affix. It is therefore feasible to assume (for the sake of morphological simplicity and generality) that derivational and inflectional affixes are always the heads of their respective lexical categories.

On the other hand, in those cases where an affix does not actually change the category of the item to which it attaches, that is, inflectional and some derivational affixes, one could in principle argue that the non-affix is the head. For example, Williams (1981) argues that certain prefixes in English are not heads (for example, *un*- in *unable* and *undo*), and argues more generally for a right-hand head rule. But there are important exceptions to his approach involving prefixes which do change category status, for example, *a*- in *akin* (= Adj, *kin* = N). And the number of affixes like *un*- which appear not to determine higher categorial status is relatively small in number. In these cases we shall simply have to state that *un-* is homophonous between [+Adj] and [+Verb] values, etc. In this way we can preserve the morphological generalization that lexical category status can always be computed from affixes (both derivational and inflectional), whereas the same generalization cannot be made for stems. And we also gain a consistent generalization linking morphology and syntax with respect to the notion 'head': heads at both levels determine the status of their immediately dominating categories.

Further evidence for this head of phrase/head of word generalization comes from the very universals linking word order within the phrase to morpheme order within the word which we summarized in the last section. Head-final order in the syntax (NP + Po and SOV) guarantees head-final order in the word (suffixing); and head-initial ordering in the word (prefixing) guarantees head-initial ordering in the syntax (Pr + NP and VO). That is, these universals define a common ordering for a common (albeit abstract) entity at both levels, and in the simplest, unmarked case this is what we should expect. We can accordingly define a common Head Ordering Principle, as in (23):

(23) *The Head Ordering Principle (HOP)*
      The affixal head of a word is ordered on the same side of its subcategorized modifier(s) as P is ordered relative to NP within PP, and as V is ordered relative to a direct object NP.

The HOP therefore predicts prefixes in Pr + NP and VO languages, and suffixes in NP + Po and OV languages. Clearly, these predictions are not sufficient on their own. If they were, we would expect a perfect line-up between head categories in the syntax and in the word, and our implicational universals would be reversible: NP + Po would imply suffixing *and* suffixing would imply NP + Po; prefixing would imply Pr + NP *and* Pr + NP would imply prefixing. But there *is* still a need for the HOP as part of the descriptive and explanatory package. Let us review the evidence.

First, whenever we can set up implicational universals defined on basic word orders on the one hand and on suffixing or prefixing for individual morpheme categories on the other, the correlation is always in accordance with the HOP: NP + Po and/or SOV always implies suffixing, never prefixing; and prefixing implies Pr + NP and/or VO, never NP + Po and/or SOV.

Second, consider the languages that have exclusive prefixing or suffixing for all morpheme categories within each of our samples, as shown in table 11.4. The same implicational pattern emerges: if a language has exclusive prefixing, then it has Pr + NP and VO word orders, not NP + Po and SOV; if it has NP + Po or SOV, it can have exclusive suffixing, but not exclusive prefixing.

Third, the aggregated proportions of prefixing to suffixing in all the languages of our samples provide additional evidence for the HOP (cf.

Table 11.4 Exclusive prefixing and suffixing in the language samples (relative to sample properties)

	Exclusive prefixing %	Exclusive suffixing %
% of VO languages		
Greenberg sample	5	11
Stassen sample	8	44
Perkins–Bybee sample	18	0
Gilligan sample	10	13
	Avge 10	Avge 17
% of Pr + NP languages		
Greenberg sample	6	0
Stassen sample	8	46
Gilligan sample	7	17
	Avge 7	Avge 21
% of OV languages		
Greenberg sample	0	91
Stassen sample	0	61
Perkins–Bybee sample	0	39
Gilligan sample	0	58
	Avge 0	Avge 62
% of NP + Po languages		
Greenberg sample	0	86
Stassen sample	2	60
Gilligan sample	0	50
	Avge 0.7	Avge 65

Hawkins and Gilligan 1988): the average ratio of prefixing to suffixing in head-initial (Pr + NP/VO) languages is split roughly evenly, that is, there are significant numbers of prefixes; the average ratio for head-final (NP + Po/OV) languages shows a 4-to-1 to 7-to-1 skewing in favor of suffixes for different categories, that is, suffixes predominate.

3.3 The suffixing preference

The HOP cannot be the only principle determining affix order across the world's languages, on account of the suffixing preference. Before addressing the explanatory problem that this raises, let us describe and quantify the facts.

Hawkins and Gilligan (1988) set up the following counterprinciples to the HOP:

(24) GENDER affixes (on N) are suffixed.
(25) CASE affixes (on N) are suffixed.
(26) INDEFINITENESS affixes (on N) are suffixed.
(27) NOMINALIZING affixes (on N) are suffixed.
(28) DEFINITENESS affixes (on N) are suffixed.
(29) PLURAL affixes (on N) are suffixed.
(30) MOOD affixes (on V) are suffixed.
(31) TENSE affixes (on V) are suffixed.
(32) ASPECT affixes (on V) are suffixed.
(33) VALENCE affixes (on V) are suffixed.
(34) CAUSATIVE affixes (on V) are suffixed.

The HOP predicts prefixing in head-initial languages and suffixing in head-final languages. The above counterprinciples predict suffixing in both language types. That is, both sets of principles cooperate to predict the co-occurrence of suffixing with OV and NP + Po, and neither predicts prefixes with these word orders. But for VO and Pr + NP languages, the HOP predicts prefixing while the counterprinciples predict suffixing, and it is significant that both affix orders are productively attested. That is, both principles succeed in asserting themselves in VO and Pr + NP languages, and we see a reflection of their relative strength in the different proportions of languages involved.

The proportions of languages with prefixing versus suffixing for these categories across the globe (that is, proportions relative to the numbers of languages that do actually have morphological affixes) are shown in table 11.5. The relative strength of the HOP and the counterprinciples within head-initial languages can be read off the first line in each chart, and the residue of languages accounted for (if any), that is, head-final languages with prefixes, can be seen in the bottom left-hand corner of each. A random distribution in these correlations would assign 25 percent to each of the four cells. The lower the residue's percentage relative to 25 percent, the more insignificant it becomes.

The relationship between these counterprinciples operating in conjunction with the HOP, and the universals of section 3.1 can now be accounted for. Most of the universals are implicational statements formulated with NP + Po or SOV as the antecedent properties, and suffixing as the consequent (or alternatively with prefixing as the antecedent, and Pr + NP and VO as consequent properties). These statements result in the three-way distribution of affix orders set out in (4) that is documented in table 11.5. This distribution is a consequence of the fact that the above counterprinciples always reinforce the HOP's independent predictions for suffixing, and oppose its predictions for prefixing. It will always be possible to formulate implicational universals when counterprinciples and the HOP cooperate in this manner and when there is no residue of languages unaccounted for. If there is such a residue, a statistical universal can be formulated, as long as the size of the residue is not too large.

Table 11.5 Order correlations with head-initial and head-final word order

	GENDER		CASE		INDEFINITENESS	
	Prefixes	Suffixes	Prefixes	Suffixes	Prefixes	Suffixes
VO Pr + NP	20%	30%	0%	50%	25%	25%
OV NP + Po	0%	50%	0%	50%	0%	50%

	NOMINALIZING		DEFINITENESS		PLURAL	
	Prefixes	Suffixes	Prefixes	Suffixes	Prefixes	Suffixes
VO Pr + NP	7%	43%	22%	28%	14%	36%
OV NP + Po	3%	47%	8%	42%	2%	48%

	MOOD		TENSE		ASPECT	
	Prefixes	Suffixes	Prefixes	Suffixes	Prefixes	Suffixes
VO Pr + NP	24%	26%	26%	24%	27%	23%
OV NP + Po	2%	48%	1%	49%	9%	41%

	VALENCE		CAUSATIVE	
	Prefixes	Suffixes	Prefixes	Suffixes
VO Pr + NP	0%	50%	29%	21%
OV NP + Po	6%	44%	7%	43

The nature of the cross-linguistic morphological asymmetry in favor of suffixing can now be summarized. First, all the above counterprinciples to the HOP's predictions favor suffixing over prefixing, and never the other way round. As a result, suffixes are predicted either by both principles (in NP + Po and OV languages) or by the counterprinciples alone (in

Pr + NP and VO languages) and so end up being more frequent than prefixes overall, as Greenberg observed. There is even one set of affixes in our data that is exclusively suffixed (CASE (on N)), whereas there are no affixes that are exclusively prefixed.

Second, the suffixing preference emerges from the correlations between word order and exclusive prefixing and suffixing given in table 11.4. Exclusive suffixing occurs in both word order types (Pr + NP/VO and NP + Po/OV), whereas exclusive prefixing occurs only in the Pr + NP/VO type. In addition, the average number of languages with exclusive suffixing and NP + Po and OV (a co-occurrence predicted by the HOP) far exceeds the average number of languages with exclusive prefixing and Pr + NP and VO (which is equally predicted by the HOP): 65 and 62 percent of NP + Po and OV languages (respectively) are exclusively suffixing; 7 and 10 percent of Pr + NP and VO languages (respectively) are exclusively prefixing. There is therefore a skewing towards suffixing even in those co-occurrences that are predicted by the HOP.

Third, the aggregated proportions of prefixing to suffixing documented in Hawkins and Gilligan (1988) also reveal a suffixing skewing. There are roughly equal proportions of prefixes to suffixes in head-initial languages, and a 4-to-1 to 7-to-1 skewing to suffixes in head-final languages, making more suffixing overall.

Notice finally that the affixes that we have been concentrating on are primarily inflectional rather than derivational. There is a reason for this concentration. Inflectional categories are more constant across languages, and hence more amenable to cross-linguistic comparison, whereas derivational categories are more language-particular and idiosyncratic.

In the following section we shall consider a possible explanation for why suffixing should be so preferred cross-linguistically. We shall argue that this preference reflects characteristics of the process of lexical access in speech understanding, that is, it is the result of a putatively general property of linguistic performance. In brief, the process of word recognition involves using the sound of a word to access the lexical entry, as listed in a mental dictionary. Psycholinguistic evidence indicates both that the beginning of a word is its most salient part for this access process, and that lexical access separates the processing of lexical semantics from the processing of the kinds of phrasal syntactic and semantic information typically carried by the affixes whose cross-linguistic distribution we have been documenting. We will argue that for these reasons, and because the use of lexical information must at least largely precede the use of syntactic information in comprehension, it makes sense for affixes which do not aid lexical recognition and which are primarily relevant for the processing of larger syntactic and semantic units to be postposed rather than preposed in a word. Sections 4 and 5 summarize the psycholinguistic evidence bearing on these issues.

4 Psycholinguistic Evidence: Word Onsets

Studies of word recognition strongly suggest that the psychologically most salient part of any word is its beginning portion. The evidence is of two general kinds: beginning portions are the most effective cues for successful recall or recognition of a word (see section 4.1 below); and the effects of distorting the beginning of a word are much more severe than the effects of distorting later portions (section 4.2). Some further effects in word production argue for a co-operative principle in production and perception processes (section 4.3). The combined evidence suggests a view of the mental lexicon as a structure determined primarily by the exigencies of the temporal constraints operative in spoken word understanding (sections 4.4 and 4.5).

4.1 Onsets as retrieval cues

A number of recent studies have investigated listeners' recognition of spoken words when only fragments of the words are presented. Grosjean (1980, 1983) has explored the effects of context on the recognition of words presented in successively larger fragments from the onset on. However, only Nooteboom (1981) has compared the effectiveness of initial and final portions of spoken words as retrieval cues. Nooteboom chose Dutch words with unique initial and final portions; for instance, the word *kannibaal* has seven phonemes, and no other Dutch word has the same four initial phonemes, or the same four final phonemes. Listeners were presented with either the unique beginning portion or the unique final portion, and were asked to guess the word. The initial fragments provoked correct responses in 95 percent of presentations, but the correct response rate for final fragments (which determined the word no less unequivocally than the initial fragments) was significantly lower at 60 percent. Moreover, correct response latency was significantly faster for responses to initial fragments than for responses to final fragments.

An analogous result was found with visual presentation by Broerse and Zwaan (1966). These authors also chose words in which the informativeness of initial and final portions was precisely matched; again, presentation of initial fragments elicited faster and more accurate word recognition than presentation of final fragments.

Similarly, recall of a word from a previously presented list is prompted more effectively by giving the initial portion as a cue, while the middle portion is the least useful cue; again response latency is also faster with initial prompts (Horowitz et al. 1968; Horowitz et al. 1969).

In a 'tip-of-the-tongue' (TOT) state, the speaker quite often knows something about the word being sought; and the most common correctly known aspect of the word is its onset (Brown and McNeill 1966; Browman 1978). The most effective cue for bringing a person *out* of a

TOT state, that is, prompting correct recall of the partially remembered word, is also to provide or confirm the knowledge of the word's onset (Freedman and Landauer 1966).

4.2 The effects of onset distortion

The effects of distortion of parts of a word on recognition performance are greatest if the distortion occurs at the word onset. This was established for spoken words as early as 1900 by Bagley, who found that mispronouncing an initial consonant disrupted recognition far more than mispronouncing a final consonant. Similar effects occur with visual presentation; blurring the first few letters of a word interferes with recognition more than blurring the end (Oleron and Danset 1983), and the same is true for reversing the position of two adjacent letters (Bruner and O'Dowd 1958).

By contrast, distortions at the ends of words are so little disruptive that they can go unnoticed. Studies of shadowing (Marslen-Wilson 1975; Marlsen-Wilson and Welsh 1978), in which listeners are required to repeat back an auditorily presented text, have established that mispronunciations in the text are particularly likely to be replaced by the correct phoneme, without noticeable disruption of the speaker's fluency, if they occur towards the end of a word.

Cole (1973; Cole and Jakimik 1978, 1980) studied the detection of such deliberate mispronunciations. Explicit comparison of word-initial with word-final consonant mispronunciations in monosyllabic words showed that, as would be predicted, word-initial mispronunciations were more detectable (Cole and Jakimik 1978). Reaction time to respond to the mispronunciation was, on the other hand, consistently slower if the distorted segment was at the beginning of the word (Cole 1973; Cole and Jakimik 1980); thus the disruption of word identification acts simultaneously to increase the likelihood of the mispronunciation being noticed but to delay the response to it, since the response in mispronunciation detection depends on successful reconstruction of what the word ought to have been, a process which is more difficult the more recognition has been disrupted.

In correctly pronounced words the greater attention paid to word onsets has as a consequence a reduced likelihood of slips of the ear occurring on initial segments; the most likely part of the word for a hearing slip to occur is the middle (Browman 1978).

Evidence of the kind summarized in this section has led Marslen-Wilson (e.g. 1978, 1980; Marslen-Wilson and Welsh 1978) to propose a theory of auditory word recognition specifically based on left-to-right processes. According to this model the first segment of a spoken word activates the lexical elements corresponding to all words beginning with that segment; this set of words constitutes the 'initial cohort'. As subsequent segments are heard, they cause all words which do *not* contain them to drop out of the cohort. Eventually the cohort will contain only one word; this state constitutes word recognition. Obviously this state can be reached well before the end of the word, if the word in question has few lexical colleagues beginning in the same way. The point in the word at which all other members of the initial cohort have dropped out is called the word's *uniqueness point*. Where it is in a word depends entirely on the properties of the rest of the lexicon; thus the uniqueness point of *dwindle* is on the third segment, since no other word beginning with *dw-* has that vowel; but the uniqueness point of *intestine* does not occur until the final segment, where it parts company with *intestate*.

This model, it can be seen, amounts to a definition of what constitutes an onset with respect to the preceding discussion. It claims that those portions of the word preceding the uniqueness point will be unpredictable and hence of great importance for successful word recognition; segments which follow the uniqueness point will be redundant and tolerant of distortion. Thus the effective 'onset' of *intestine* is the entire word, of *dwindle* only the first three segments.

Although there is experimental evidence which indicates that the 'cohort model' may be too restrictive to cope with all aspects of word recognition (Nooteboom 1981; see also section 4.5 below), its concept of the word as divided into two parts, one more informative than the other, is potentially helpful in accounting for many of the effects discussed in this paper. The next section describes some word production processes, for example, in which the relative informativeness of word parts appears to be crucial.

4.3 Word onsets in production

Although relatively few phonological elision and assimilation processes apply specifically to word onsets, some such processes apply across word boundaries and hence have the effect of distorting the initial segment of the word following the boundary. Cooper (e.g. Cooper and Paccia-Cooper 1980) has studied in considerable detail the factors which determine whether or not this kind of (optional) phonological process is applied in speech production. For one such rule, palatalization (which produces an affricate from an alveolar stop followed by a palatal glide), Cooper explicitly investigated the effects of manipulating the information load of the word preceding the word boundary (which would be distorted at its end by the palatalization) and of the word following it (which would have its onset distorted). For instance, the high-frequency *rode* in 'rode your horse' was replaced by the low-frequency *goad*; 'had utensils' by 'had euglena'. Similarly, either the word before or the word after the critical boundary was assigned contrastive stress. The results were very clear. Manipulation of the word preceding the boundary had no effect on the likelihood of palatalization occurring across the boundary. When the word following the boundary was of low frequency, however, or when it was contrastively stressed, the frequency of palatalization fell from over 50 percent to almost zero.

This result indicates that speakers are aware of the importance for listeners of word onsets, and try not to distort them, especially if they are more than usually informative. The same principle appears to govern speakers' choice of neologistic word formations. Speakers frequently make up words, usually by adding endings to existing words; (35)–(37) are three examples from the second author's collection of spontaneous neologisms:

(35) idioticness, it's as good a word as any

(36) I can't morphologize that

(37) a pretty zombific lot

Analysis of this collection reveals that neologisms characteristically preserve the base form transparently within them; the word *idiotic* is pronounced identically in *idioticness* as it would be on its own, whereas *idiotic* would not have been perfectly preserved if the speaker had chosen instead to say *idioticity* (which by analogy to similar English words ought actually to have been the preferred form). Slips of the tongue show a similar effect – in general, errors of affixation (for example, saying 'professoral' instead of 'professorial') exhibit the base form more transparently than the real word would have (Cutler 1980a). This pattern reflects a real speaker preference for transparent derivations over opaque ones; when speakers are given a choice of alternative derived forms of the same base, they consistently prefer the transparent options (Cutler 1980a). Some apparent exceptions to this general rule prove not to be exceptions when Marslen-Wilson's distinction between informative and uninformative parts of the word is applied; derived words which do not preserve all of the base word, for instance, or which bear primary stress on a syllable different from the stressed syllable of the base word, prove to be quite acceptable *as long as they preserve the base word as far as its uniqueness point* (Cutler 1981).

In word formation as in the application of phonological rules, therefore, speakers behave in accord with listeners' priorities in word recognition. Onsets – defined as the first segment and as many subsequent segments as are necessary for identifying the word – receive special treatment in word production.

4.4 *Left-to-right lexical access*

Speech takes place in time; the onset of a spoken word arrives first at the listener's ear. The temporal constraints of understanding speech provide a compelling explanation for why word onsets should appear so over-whelmingly important. In fact, it would surely be very surprising if the lexicon used in speech comprehension were *not* organized in such a way as to accommodate optimally to the constraints on auditory word recognition.

Our view is that the evidence surveyed in this section argues persuasively for a lexicon in which the temporal structure of the listed words is of paramount importance. Moreover, we suggest that the pervasiveness of onset salience, expressing itself not only in auditory comprehension but in reading as well, and in parallel effects in speech production, argues that the importance of the temporal structure of words in their mental representation extends beyond the auditory access code. There are certainly further speech production effects which suggest that the lexicon used in production gives weight to left-to-right phonological structure. As mentioned above, speakers with a word on the tip of their tongue frequently are fairly sure of its onset; and their erroneous guesses most often coincide with the target word in the initial segments. Slips of the tongue in which the intended word is replaced by another word with no semantic relation to it of any kind (for example, *winter* for *window*) show a similar pattern; such slips tend to resemble the target word phonetically, with by far the greatest resemblance occurring in the initial segments (Fay and Cutler 1977).

In fact, Fay and Cutler used the evidence for these 'malapropisms' to argue that there is only one mental lexicon used in both speech production and speech perception, and that its primary organizational principle is left-to-right phonological structure (that is, it is arranged first and foremost for the convenience of the comprehension process). The semantic ordering demanded by the production process would be in some sense subsidiary. A word's nearest neighbour in the phonological ordering would be the word which sounded most like it left to right (*intestine* would be right next to *intestate*), and malapropisms would occur when an intended word's near neighbour was selected by mistake.

Giving greater consideration to the demands of the comprehension process rather than the production process makes perfect sense, Fay and Cutler argued, since the temporal limitations on speech understanding, and the often very imperfect signal which is presented to the listener, make the process of lexical access in comprehension vastly more difficult than the analogous process in production. Fay and Cutler's model of a single, phonologically ordered lexicon is admittedly controversial; many current models of lexical structure and access postulate separate listings for production and comprehension purposes, or an unordered central lexicon with separate access codes for listening, speaking, reading and writing (left-to-right phonological structure being of major importance only to the first). For the purpose of the present paper, it is unimportant how these current controversies are eventually resolved; it is only important that temporal phonological structure be represented in some significant part of the lexical system.

Our present argument concerns not the structure of the lexicon, but the structure of the language as a function of the processing regularities we have observed. Given that the human language processing system appears to have accommodated itself to the temporal constraints of speech understanding by assigning particular salience to word onsets, how might this adaptation in turn lead to further adaptation of the structure of words in the language, to ensure that words are optimally processed by such a system?

Nooteboom (1981) has suggested two ways in which one might expect phonological structure to accommodate to the characteristics of an onset-weighted processor: (i) word onsets should tend to be more phonologically variable than word endings, and (ii) phonological assimilation and coarticulation rules should tend to apply less to word onsets than to word endings. Here, however, we are concerned with *morphological* structure, which, we suggest, is no less affected by the properties of the processing system than is the phonology. In section 6 we will spell out how we think morphological effects have been brought about. First, however, we will conclude this section with a look at some apparent counter-evidence to the primacy of word onsets.

4.5 *The comparative salience of endings*

It is not the case that *only* word onsets are important in word recognition. The strictest form of, say, the cohort model, or any other model of lexical access which allowed only left-to-right word search, would hold that later parts of the word – segments following the uniqueness point – are entirely redundant. Yet the evidence shows clearly that although onsets are unquestionably the most salient word parts, *endings are more salient than middles*.

For example, endings are better recall prompts than middles in the experiments of Horowitz et al. (1968, 1969) described above; and reversal of letters at the end of a word disrupts recognition more than word-medial reversal (Bruner and O'Dowd 1958). Both of these are visual word recognition effects, and one might argue that in reading, where the entire word is presented simultaneously in space, the recognizer can afford to attend to other parts of the word. Recall, however, that slips of the ear happen less often on endings than on middles of words (Browman 1978). Consider further the fact that TOT guesses are more often correct about the final parts of the intended word than about medial parts; and that malapropism errors coincide with their intended targets more often in final segments than in medial segments (Hurford 1981; Cutler and Fay 1982). Both these latter effects in word production strongly suggest that a lexical explanation is called for: ends are more salient than middles of lexical representations.

Finally, consider also the fact that one can retrieve words successfully given only an ending (think of a word ending with -*vark*). This is true even in the auditory modality; Nooteboom's (1981) subjects still achieved 60 percent successful word recognition given only the latter parts of the words. This simply could not be done if words could only be accessed from the lexicon in left-to-right order. Moreover, in a more recent experiment van der Vlugt and Nooteboom (1986) presented listeners with the same word fragments as used in Nooteboom's earlier study, with the sole difference that the previously missing portion of the word was now present but masked by white noise. Under these conditions word recognition was not significantly different for initial versus final fragments. This suggests that some information about overall word length can usefully constrain lexical access even if word-initial portions are missing. Of course, measures of correct identification such as Nooteboom used show what the lexical access system is capable of when information is poor; but measures of relative *speed* of identification, as summarized above, still suggest that word onsets are disproportionately important in auditory word recognition.

5 Psycholinguistic Evidence: Affixes

There is abundant evidence from studies of lexical access and structure that, at the very least, morphological structure is lexically represented. Some psycholinguists have even argued that the evidence indicates that only bases appear in the lexicon, with complex forms being produced and comprehended via the application of morphological rules. Others have suggested that, while affixed forms may be lexically available, it is the stem which is the head of the lexical entry, and hence the basis for lexical access. The relevant psycholinguistic evidence is summarized below, separately for inflections, derivational suffixes and prefixes.

5.1 *Inflections*

The evidence for separate processing of stem and affix is strongest in the case of inflections, such as tense or number marking. There is abundant evidence that inflected words do not have lexical representation independent of their base form, and that base word and inflection are separated in language processing. In tachistoscopic presentation inflected words seem to be perceived as two units (Gibson and Guinet 1971). If a word is homographic between an uninflected and an inflected form (e.g. German *SAGE*), the uninflected form appears to be processed first, even when, as in this instance, the inflected form is of far higher frequency (Guenther 1988). Recall of adverbs ending in -*ly* is affected by the frequency of the base adjective rather than the frequency of the inflected adverb form (Rosenberg et al. 1966). Regular inflected forms (e.g. *pours*) show a repetition priming effect on their base words (e.g. *pour*) as strong as that of the base word itself (Stanners et al. 1979a; Fowler et al. 1985). Priming with irregular inflected forms (e.g. *hung*) is less effective than

priming with the base word itself (e.g. *hang*), though still significantly
better than no prime at all (Stanners et al. 1979a). Pretraining with an
inflectional variant (e.g. *sees*) significantly facilitates later learning of a
word (e.g. *seen*) in comparison with no pretraining, or with pretraining on
a word having as much visual similarity to the target word as the
morphological relative (e.g. *seed*; Murrell and Morton 1974). Only
regular inflections provide effective priming, however, when the dependent variable is accuracy of report of a degraded auditory signal
(Kempley and Morton 1982). Plural morphemes tend to get detached in
memory representations (van der Molen and Morton 1979), and inflectional suffixes of all kinds tend to be overlooked in script scanning
tasks (Drewnowski and Healy 1980; Smith and Sterling 1982). Lexical
decision reaction times are sensitive both to the frequency of occurrence
of the surface form and to the combined frequency of base plus inflectional variants (Taft 1979).

This body of evidence has led psycholinguists to suggest that inflectional affixes may be generated by rule in speech production, and
stripped prior to lexical access in speech perception. Speech errors in
which misplaced inflections accommodate to their erroneous rather than
their intended environments, as in (38):

(38) I'd hear one if I knew it.

have also been used to support such a model (Fromkin 1973; Garrett
1976; MacKay 1979; Butterworth 1980). Jarvella and Meijers (1983)
proposed a stem-based lexicon on the basis of an experiment in which they
primed target verbs with differently inflected forms of the same stem, or
with similarly inflected forms of different stems; subjects performed
same–different stem judgments significantly faster than same–different
inflection judgments. Similarly, MacKay (1976) based the same claim on
the finding that translating a present into a past tense form takes longer
and is more subject to error the more complex the relation between base
and inflected form.

Other authors have been more cautious, proposing models in which
inflected forms are represented but only as subsidiary entries to base or
stem forms (Stanners et al. 1979a; Cutler 1983; Henderson 1985). A
series of experiments by Lukatela and colleagues have investigated the
processing of inflected words in Serbo-Croation, using both visual
(Gurjanov et al. 1985; Gurjanov et al. 1987; Lukatela et al. 1980; Lukatela
et al. 1982; Lukatela et al. 1983) and auditory (Katz et al. 1987)
presentation. In brief, these studies find that lexical decision responses to
nominative forms are consistently faster than responses to genitive or
instrumental forms. Lukatela and his colleagues argue for a model of
lexical representation of inflected forms in which the nominative
comprises the nucleus of a cluster of separate entries, one for each form.
Fowler, Napps and Feldman (1985) argue even more conservatively that

inflected words are represented as a concatenation of their component morphemes. Even the most radical recent proposal for a model in which complex forms have their own separate lexical listings (Butterworth 1983) allows for the internal representation of morphological structure within the listing, and the grouping together of morphologically related forms in the lexicon.

5.2 Derivational suffixes

There is no indication that words with derivational suffixes are in any way more difficult to understand than monomorphemic words; the very few experimental studies which claim to have shown a processing cost for morphological complexity of this kind are seriously flawed (see Cutler 1983: 61). However, there is evidence that the morphological structure of derived words is computed as they are understood. For instance, Manelis and Tharp (1977) found that subjects took longer to decide whether two letter strings were both words if one was suffixed and the other not (*printer slander*) than if both were suffixed (*printer drifter*) or both simple (*slander blister*). Similarly, understanding a derived word produces facilitation for understanding its morphological relatives (Kintsch 1974; Stanners et al. 1979a). This suggests that lexical storage of words with derivational suffixes embodies close connections with other members of the same morphological family, as argued by Cutler (1983) and Henderson (1985). Production evidence showing slips of the tongue which confuse morphological relatives, such as (39):

(39) if you have a hierARCHy of frames . . .

in which *hierarchy* has been pronounced with the stress pattern of its relative *hierarchic*, suggest the same conclusion (Cutler 1980b). Similarly, the evidence from neologism formation (section 4.3 above) demonstrates that speakers have control over the morphological structure of their vocabulary.

5.3 Prefixes

The psycholinguistic evidence on the processing of prefixes is in some ways similar to the evidence on derivationally suffixed words. Simply recognizing prefixed words is no more difficult than recognizing monomorphemic words (Taft and Forster 1975; Fay 1980; Cutler 1983). But recognizing a prefixed word produces facilitation for its stem (Stanners et al. 1979b). However, the matching effect, reported above, which Manelis and Tharp found for suffixes does not hold for prefixes (Segui and Zubizarreta 1985). In general, prefixes have aroused much livelier debate than suffixes; this debate was begun by Taft and Forster (1975), who claimed that the process of recognizing a prefixed word necessarily required stripping the prefix from the stem, since lexical access could only proceed via a stem representation. This claim was based on experiments which measured the time to reject nonwords in a lexical decision task as a function of whether or not the nonwords were stems of existent prefixed words: for example, *juvenate* from *rejuvenate* versus *pertoire* from *repertoire*, which is not prefixed. The *juvenate* type of nonword took significantly longer to reject than the *pertoire* type. This response time difference also held when the items were presented bearing pseudo-prefixes (*dejuvenate* versus *depertoire*). Taft and Forster argued that *rejuvenate* is actually stored in the lexicon as *juvenate + re*. Taft and Forster's experiments have been criticized on methodological grounds (Cutler 1983; Henderson 1985) and have stimulated many subsequent studies (Rubin et al. 1979; Stanners et al. 1979b; Fay 1980; Taft 1981; Henderson et al. 1984). More recently, there have been results from eye-movement studies supporting the notion of prefix-stripping in reading (Lima 1987), and evidence for the same effect in auditory word recognition (Taft et al. 1986). However, Taft's most recent evidence (Taft 1988) suggests that the strong version of the prefix-stripping model (access via stem only) may not be warranted; instead, Taft now proposes (separate) representation of both prefix and stem in the input to the lexicon. Decomposition of prefixed words nonetheless appears to be a routinely available strategy in word recognition, with the main question still at issue being the content of lexical entries for prefixed words.

5.4 *Stem–affix separability*

The psycholinguistic literature on morphological complexity is in agreement that morphological structure is available to the language processing devices. There is considerable diversity as to how this might be achieved, from strict affix-stripping models at the strongest end of the continuum to, at the other, attempts to account for the experimental results via simple contiguity of morphological relatives in the lexicon. But even those who wish to argue that complex forms have separate lexical representations (e.g. Butterworth 1983; Segui and Zubizarreta 1985) admit that morphological boundaries are marked in these representations. For present purposes it is not necessary to subscribe to one or other model of the role of affixes in lexical access; the point that we wish to make is sufficiently general to be applicable, we feel, to any current model.

One line of psycholinguistic evidence, bearing on all affix types, has not yet been mentioned. If a nonword is present in a lexical decision task, it takes longer to reject if it bears a real affix, be this inflectional or derivational, prefix or suffix (Fay 1980; Lima and Pollatsek 1983; Henderson et al. 1984; Laudanna and Burani 1985). This strongly suggests that some separate processing of the affix is undertaken despite the nonexistence of the stem. Indeed, we will argue that this is the most basic conclusion to be drawn from psycholinguistic studies of affixation: at some level it is necessary to process stems and affixes separately. All the evidence is compatible with this very general claim; most processing models embody far stronger claims. Furthermore, the information carried by affixes is of a different nature from that carried by stems. Affixes constitute a closed class, with predictable syntactic effects; they are in this respect entirely equivalent to other closed class linguistic items, 'function words' such as articles and conjunctions. Stems on the other hand are open class items; a new stem, embodying an entirely new meaning, can in principle be created at any time (although in practice new stems – e.g. *byte* – are rarer than new meanings for old stems – e.g. *chip* – or new derivations – *debug*). Thus as long as lexical or syntactic processing are considered distinct operations in production and comprehension, stems and affixes must in some sense be processed separately.

Interestingly, certain patients with language disorders show systematic affixation errors – additions, deletions or substitutions – which parallel their errors with function words (Patterson 1980; Job and Sartori 1984). Most of these errors happen to involve suffixes, but this may reflect the fact that the reports deal mainly with Italian- and English-speaking patients, and both Italian and English contain more suffixes than prefixes.

Note that our main conclusion does not distinguish between prefixes and suffixes; and we have also not separated inflectional from derivational affixes. It is impossible to compare their separate effects in the current experimental evidence, because the evidence is confounded; nearly all the research in this area has been carried out on languages in which all inflectional affixes are suffixed. It is to be hoped that psycholinguists will soon turn their attention to those few languages with inflectional prefixes (for example, Welsh). Meanwhile, for our present purposes it is, again, unnecessary to distinguish between inflections and derivations; a detailed discussion of the psycholinguistic considerations involved in making this distinction may be found in Henderson (1985). The one consideration which may be relevant to our argument is the degree to which a particular affix has entirely syntactic function or exercises also some *semantic* effect; the more its function is entirely syntactic, the more its processing will be distinct from the way its stem is processed. (See Segui and Zubizarreta 1985 for further elaboration of this argument.)

Psycholinguistic studies of affixes, then, suggest that there is a processing distinction between stem and affix; both types of information are necessary but they must be separable. The implications of this in the light of the evidence reviewed earlier will be discussed in the next section.

6 Explaining the Suffixing Preference

In this section we bring together the linguistic evidence of cross-linguistic asymmetries in affix attachment, and the psycholinguistic evidence from studies of lexical access, summarized in the preceding sections, and argue that the two lines of evidence combine to provide an explanatory model with relevance to both linguistics and psycholinguistics.

For ease of exposition, we will base our reasoning on the simplest examples, that is, words consisting of just one stem and one affix. English examples are *walk* + *ing*, *walk* + *ed* or *girl* + *s*. Our argument is of relevance only to stem–affix ordering; it is neutral with respect to ordering of affixes in multiply affixed items, which may be determined by principles qualitatively different from the processing explanation proposed here.

In section 6.1, below, we will spell out our argument about computational order of stems and affixes. Section 6.2 contains some additional arguments based on relative redundancy of stems versus affixes. Before concluding, we will also show how the infrequency of infixing can be explained on processing grounds independently of the preference for suffixes over prefixes (section 6.3), and we will consider some facts about language change that are of relevance for the suffixing preference (section 6.4).

6.1 *Order of computation for stems and affixes*

The cross-linguistic evidence of implicational and distributional universals shows that languages prefer stems to precede affixes (section 3). The psycholinguistic evidence on word onsets indicates that speakers and listeners pay most attention to the beginnings of words, rather less attention to the ends and least attention of all to the middles (section 4). The psycholinguistic evidence on affixes suggests that stems and affixes must at some level be processed separately (section 5).

We maintain that the simplest explanation encompassing these three effects is: speakers and listeners process stems before affixes. That is, the stem favors the most salient initial position of a word, and the affix the less salient end position, because in the compositional process of determining the entire meaning of a word from its parts, the stem has computational priority over the affix. Thus the fact that languages exhibit a suffixing preference, that is stem + affix order on numerous occasions when their remaining structural characteristics would predict the reverse, reflects the order of computation of stem and affix in processing.

In a model of comprehension, this argument follows inevitably from the fact that affixes convey primarily syntactic information, stems primarily lexical-semantic information, if one assumes that lexical processing precedes syntactic and higher-level semantic processing (cf. below). Case affixes, for example, function to integrate a noun or noun phrase into the overall interpretation of a clause, and they are invariably suffixed. But even within the word itself and with affixes whose syntactic and semantic functions are not primarily clausal in nature, stems typically have computational priority over affixes. Consider, for example, *sad* + *ness*. We can paraphrase the meaning of *sad* as 'having an unhappy state of mind', and that of -*ness* as 'the abstract quality of X', where X is the thing that -*ness* combines with, much as a function category applies to an argument category within a categorial grammar to make a derived expression. The effect of the suffix cannot be determined without knowing what stem it has combined with.

In fact, all current psychological models of comprehension are based on the tacitly accepted general ordering of lexical before syntactic before higher-level semantic processing. But models differ fundamentally in the way they describe the relationship between these levels of processing. Briefly, there is a major controversy concerning the autonomy versus interdependence of levels; at one end of a continuum in this regard stand models which view the various levels of processing as strictly serially ordered and autonomous, at the other end models which allow interaction or feedback between any and all levels. (Of course, there are many intermediate models, which allow feedback only between adjacent levels, or only between certain levels, or only under certain conditions, that is, which mix features of the serial autonomous and interactive positions.) With respect to the two levels we are considering, the lexical and syntactic levels, a serial model would require all lexical processing to be complete before syntactic processing was begun on the same items; irresoluble ambiguities would have to be passed on to higher levels for resolution. Lexical processing would be wholly independent of prior syntactic context. An interactive model, on the other hand, would allow for prior syntactic processing to be fed back to constrain decisions – for example, the choice between noun and verb form of a syntactically ambiguous word – at the lexical level.

While the present argument makes no general claim about the structure of a model of comprehension, it does suggest that in respect to lexical processing, and syntactic processing of the particular kind in which affixes are involved, a serial autonomous model might provide the best description. That is, if the preferred order of computation is, as we have argued, stems first, affixes second, it does not appear that feedback from the kind of syntactic information provided by affixes is of value in constraining lexical access. If it were, we would expect more prefixing. This limited conclusion, of course, says nothing about other kinds of syntactic information, for example, word order information. Our argument does, however, amount to a claim for non-interactive serial ordering of lexical and affixal processing in comprehension.

We would also argue that stem–affix computational order should apply in production. We see no principled reason why affix distribution across languages should be determined by processing considerations from comprehension alone. The ordering of lexical processing and syntactic processing in psycholinguistic models of production is a matter of dispute; although it has been claimed that speech error evidence suggests that much syntactic processing precedes lexical processing in production (e.g. Fromkin 1971, 1980), the justification for this claim has been questioned (Cutler and Isard 1980; Butterworth 1982), and other models have either ordered lexical selection strictly before syntactic specification (e.g. Garrett 1976) or postulated two separate but parallel processes (e.g. Butterworth 1980). Again, our argument is most consistent with a model such as Garrett's: lexical selection strictly preceding affixal processing.

6.2 Redundancy of stems versus affixes

There are two further processing considerations which argue in favor of a stem–affix sequencing in languages, although neither seems to us either as simple or as compelling as the computational order argument. Both rely on the assumption of greater redundancy for affixes in comparison with stems; phonological redundancy in the first case, syntactic/semantic in the second.

As pointed out in section 5, affixes comprise a closed class, a very much smaller set than the set of stems. They are also all short. Thus, of necessity, they exhibit vastly less phonological diversity than do stems. In any left-to-right comprehension model, therefore, prefixed words will be less informative in the most salient initial portions than will equivalent words carrying the same information in a suffix. In the cohort model, for example (see section 4.2 above), the initial cohort for any prefixed word will contain all other words with the same prefix; the uniqueness point will occur later in an affix–stem ordering than in a stem–affix ordering. This will effectively delay lexical access for prefixed words in comparison with suffixed words,

This consideration seems to us less satisfactory than the computational order argument for two reasons. First, it refers exclusively to comprehension, whereas the computational order claim applies equally to comprehension and production. Second, if pushed to its logical conclusion, it is forced to assume the computational order argument. What is delayed by prefix redundancy is access to the lexical semantics. Access to the affix information itself, on the other hand, is speeded in prefixed as opposed to suffixed words. Given our assumption, based on the psycholinguistic evidence, that both stems and affixes need to be processed separately, early processing of either one should be equally useful *unless there is a preferred processing order*. That is, delay in accessing the stem should only matter if stems are preferably dealt with before affixes. Early access to the affix should be helpful unless affixes are preferably dealt with after stems.

The second kind of redundancy concerns the considerable predictability, in context, of the syntactic and/or semantic properties of some affixes (particularly the more inflectional ones). It might be argued that presence of the affix is not at all necessary for comprehension. Consider the English sentence *yesterday I walked to the store*. The past tense meaning of the *-ed* suffix is already implied by the adverb and the suffix can be masked or deleted without serious consequences. Similarly, many verb agreement affixes, or nominal and adjectival inflections, may be redundant in many environments. Lexical stems, by contrast, are predictable to a much lesser degree. There are many more lexical stems than grammatical affixes that the speaker could use on any one occasion, and context does not guarantee the same degree of predictability (or at least does not reduce the range of options so severely) as it does for affixes. It therefore makes sense that lexical stems should be given greater prominence by being regularly assigned a more salient position in the word, namely initial position.

Unfortunately, the force of this argument is also weak. Most affixes are not predictable most of the time. The most suffixed morphemes of all are case affixes, and the information they convey is typically vital for sentence understanding and is unpredictable on account of word order freedom. (Recall that affixes regularly receive the second position on the saliency hierarchy, final position, rather than the least salient medial position.)

Although both of these considerations may have a partial role to play in explaining the suffixing preference, we feel that the computational order argument is the most convincing, as well as being, in its application to both production and comprehension, and in its implications for psycholinguistic models as well as linguistic explanations, the most powerful.

6.3 The infrequency of infixing

Infixing – the insertion of an affix into the middle of a word – is the rarest form of affixation. (An example is *fikas* in Bontoc (a Philippine language), which means 'strong', while *fumikas*, into which *um* has been infixed after the initial consonant, means 'he is becoming strong.') We believe that the infrequency of infixing is also motivated by a general processing consideration, namely: languages are reluctant to break up structural units. This applies not only to morphemes but also to phrasal units: witness the relative infrequency of discontinuous constituents in syntax both within and across languages. It appears highly likely that the adjacency of immediate constituents, both in morphology and syntax, facilitates processing, whereas discontinuities and crossed branching complicate it. By this explanation either prefixing or suffixing should be vastly preferable to infixing, as indeed the distributional facts attest that they are.

Of course, if a stem has been effectively recognized by the time its uniqueness point has been processed, one might argue that infixing a morpheme between the uniqueness point and the end would provide all the continuity necessary (since the end should be irrelevant), *and* get the important affixed information in at the earliest possible useful point, that is, just when the word has been recognized. There is yet another processing reason for avoiding this, however: the relative insalience of middle positions in a word. The evidence summarized in section 4.5 suggested that the middle of a word is its least salient part. It may be that affixes are simply too informative to be inserted into the *least* salient position in a word, that is, into the kind of position that can be distorted with minimal consequences for word recognition and recall. For example, languages with rich case suffixing regularly permit considerable word order freedom and scrambling of major constituents in the clause. As a result, the case affix becomes crucial in identifying the grammatical function of each NP within the clause, and there could be real communicative disadvantages to relegating such affixes to the least salient position in a word. Communicative disadvantage would result from infixing, then, wherever a morpheme was informative, that is, not predictable.

6.4 The suffixing preference and language change

Notice finally that there are some relevant considerations of a historical nature that need to be taken into account in connection with the suffixing preference (cf. Hall this volume for detailed discussion).

Givón (1979) makes three interesting observations: (i) affixes typically derive historically from independent words, for example, verbal affixes from independent auxiliaries and modals; (ii) affix orders are frozen relics of earlier syntactic orders, for example, auxiliaries regularly occur to the right of the (non-finite) verb in SOV languages, SOVAux, resulting in a suffix when the auxiliary becomes morphologically bound, that is, SOV_{af}; and (iii) all current language families were originally SOV in their syntax. It is tempting to infer from these observations that the true explanation for the suffixing preference is a historical one. Given assumption (iii), coupled with rightward positioning of auxiliaries and modals relative to the verb in SOV languages and the diachronic drifts of (i) and (ii), the suffixing preference would appear to be explained.

Unfortunately, the crucial SOV assumption (iii) is quite unsupported. The proportion of OV to VO languages and of NP + Po to Pr + NP languages is currently 50–50, as was shown in table 11.1 above, and this random distribution provides no foundation for the assumption of a 100 percent skewing in favor of OV in the past. Even for the Indo-European family, whose western branches provide the best attested evidence for the progression from SOV to VO, it has been argued (Hawkins 1982, 1983) that the syntactic reconstruction for Proto-Indo-European most consistent with language universals is VO and Pr + NP, rather than the reverse.

Assumptions (i) and (ii), however, are both reasonable and well supported (though there are some counterexamples to both, cf. Comrie 1981: 209–11). And Hall (this volume) develops an interesting account of the suffixing preference which integrates the processing considerations that we have developed here with these diachronic facts. Specifically, he argues that our order of computation consideration facilitated the drift from adjacent words to stem and affix when a suffix would result, and opposed it when a prefix would have resulted, and this produced the synchronic suffixing preference as well as a retention of independent words corresponding to the bound morphemes of suffixing languages (for example, prepositions in head-initial languages are generally independent words; postpositions in head-final languages are suffixed as often as they are independent words).

We welcome this integration of psycholinguistics and diachrony, and this view of processing as a facilitator of certain changes and a check on others. The diachronic dimension, however, does not provide any explanation for the Head Ordering Principle linking syntax and morphology, since affixes (the heads of words) do not always derive historically from head categories in the syntax (cf., for example, definiteness, indefiniteness, gender and plural affixes on nouns, which generally derive from various modifiers on the nominal head, cf. Greenberg 1978). And if one prefers some other account of the prefixing/head-initial and suffixing/head-final correlation that the HOP defines, there will be no ready historical explanation for it either (contrary to what Hall this volume suggests), since the relevant syntactic heads and modifiers from which prefixes and suffixes derive are not positioned with sufficient consistency in relation to the future stem to guarantee the prefixing/head-initial and suffixing/head-final correlation (for example, the kinds of syntactic determiners and deictic elements from which definiteness, indefiniteness and gender affixes derive may regularly precede or follow the head noun in both head-initial and head-final languages, cf. Hawkins 1983).

6.5 Conclusions

This paper has attempted to bring together linguistic and psycholinguistic evidence in such a way that the resulting explanatory synthesis is of value to both disciplines. We have shown how cross-linguistic studies of morphology have revealed an asymmetry in favor of suffixing over prefixing. Two separate lines of psycholinguistic research have been drawn upon in providing an explanation: studies of word recognition and production indicate that word onsets are accorded more attention than other parts of the word; and studies of morphological processing indicate that stems and affixes are processed separately. We have argued that the linguistic and psycholinguistic evidence together suggest that language structure reflects the preference of language users to process stems before affixes, in that the component preferred for prior processing receives the most salient (initial) position in the word, the component to be processed second a less salient position. That is, the suffixing preference results in stems generally being ordered before affixes because language users prefer to process stems before affixes.

Notes

This paper is a much revised and updated version of a paper that was originally published in *Linguistics*, 23 (1985), 723–58, under the title 'The suffixing preference: a processing explanation'. The original paper was co-authored with

Gary Gilligan. The most recent version of our prefixing and suffixing universals in relation to basic word order across languages can be found in Hawkins and Gilligan (1988).

1 Throughout this paper we will use *left* and *right* in their standard metaphorical sense of a temporal ordering. Thus in discussing how some elements tend to precede others in syntax and morphology, we will refer to 'left–right asymmetries' (sections 2 and 3); in discussing lexical access beginning with word onsets, we will refer to 'left-to-right word recognition processes' (section 4). However, we recognize that the *left–right* metaphor is based on a left-to-right orthography; in a right-to-left orthography, prefixes still precede suffixes and words are still read beginning to end! The terms *left* and *right* should therefore be taken as having temporal reference only; our conclusions apply to language, not to its various spatial representations.

2 Japanese is rare among prenominal relative clause languages in not having any subordination (Š) indicators within the relative clause. Generally, these languages employ either a clause-final complementizer (Basque, Lahu, Chinese) or a distinctive participial verb form, again in clause-final position (Dravidian languages, Turkish). These devices will, of course, enable the parser to construct Š prior to encountering the head noun of NPo and will (in the case of participial verbs) avoid a misanalysis of the subordinate verb as a matrix verb. For an explanation of why Š indicators cannot be clause-initial in prenominal relatives (even though they can be both clause-initial and clause-final in postnominal relatives), cf. Hawkins (1988b).

3 Notice that most processing explanations for syntactic universals are given in terms of comprehension rather than production strategies. Ultimately it is likely that the explanation for these cross-linguistic facts will involve a complex interplay of both comprehension and production strategies. But since relatively little is known about production at the moment, the findings from comprehension experiments are being used as an index of processing ease or difficulty in general (cf. further Hawkins 1988b).

4 The evidence we have presented in this section suggests (contra Frazier and Rayner this volume) that left-branching relative clauses *are* more difficult for processing, though not for the 'depth' reasons advanced in Yngve (1960). Our primary evidence is the striking asymmetry in their distribution across languages compared with the word orders of table 11.1, coupled with the kinds of Minimal Attachment that they so regularly invite (cf. further Hawkins 1988a, b).

References

Antinucci, F., A. Duranti and L. Gebert (1979) 'Relative clause structure, relative clause perception, and the change from SOV to SVO'. *Cognition*, 7, 145–76.

Aronoff, M. (1976) *Word Formation in Generative Grammar*. Cambridge, Mass.: MIT Press.

Bagley, W. A. (1900) 'The apperception of the spoken sentence: a study in the psychology of language'. *American Journal of Psychology*, 12, 80–130.

Broerse, A. C. and E. J. Zwaan (1966) 'The information value of initial letters in the identification of words'. *Journal of Verbal Learning and Verbal Behavior*, 5, 441–6.

Browman, C. P. (1978) 'Tip of the tongue and slip of the ear: implications for language processing'. *UCLA Working Papers in Phonetics*, 42.

Brown, R. and D. McNeill (1966) 'The "tip-of-the-tongue" phenomenon'. *Journal of Verbal Learning and Verbal Behavior*, 5, 325–37.

Bruner, J. S. and D. O'Dowd (1958) 'A note on the informativeness of words'. *Language and Speech*, 1, 98–101.

Butterworth, B. (1980) 'Introduction'. In B. Butterworth (ed.), *Language Production*, vol. 1. London: Academic Press.

(1982) 'Speech errors: old data in search of new theories'. In A. Cutler (ed.), *Slips of the Tongue and Language Production*. The Hague: Mouton.

(1983) 'Lexical representation'. In B. Butterworth (ed.), *Language Production*, vol. 2. London: Academic Press.

Bybee, J. L. (1985) *Morphology: A Study of the Relation between Meaning and Form*. Amsterdam: John Benjamins.

Clancy, P. M., H. Lee and M. Zoh (1986) 'Processing strategies in the acquisition of relative clauses: universal principles and language-specific realizations'. *Cognition*, 24, 225–62.

Cole, R. A. (1973) 'Listening for mispronunciations: a measure of what we hear during speech'. *Perception and Psychophysics*, 11, 153–6.

and J. Jakimik (1978) 'Understanding speech: how words are heard'. In G. Underwood (ed.), *Strategies of Information Processing*. London: Academic Press.

and J. Jakimik (1980) 'A model of speech perception'. In R. A. Cole (ed.), *Perception and Production of Fluent Speech*. Hillsdale, NJ: Erlbaum.

Comrie, B. (1981) *Language Universals and Linguistic Typology: Syntax and Morphology*. Oxford: Basil Blackwell.

Cooper, W. E. and J. Paccia-Cooper (1980) *Syntax and Speech*. Cambridge, Mass.: Harvard University Press.

Cutler, A. (1980a) 'Productivity in word formation'. *Papers from the Sixteenth Regional Meeting of the Chicago Linguistic Society*, 45–51.

(1980b) 'Errors of stress and intonation'. In V. A. Fromkin (ed.), *Errors in Linguistic Performance: Slips of the Tongue, Ear, Pen and Hand*. New York: Academic Press.

(1981) 'Degrees of transparency in word formation'. *Canadian Journal of Linguistics*, 26, 73–7.

(1983) 'Lexical complexity and sentence processing'. In R. Jarvella and G. B. Flores d'Arcais (eds), *The Process of Language Understanding*. Chichester: John Wiley.

and D. A. Fay (1982) 'One mental lexicon, phonologically arranged: comments on Hurford's comments'. *Linguistic Inquiry*, 13, 107–13.

and J. A. Hawkins (1987) 'Computational order as a motivation for word order'. Paper presented at the XIVth International Congress of Linguists, East Berlin.

J. A. Hawkins and G. Gilligan (1985) 'The suffixing preference: a processing explanation'. *Linguistics*, 23, 723–58.

and S. D. Isard (1980) 'The production of prosody'. In B. Butterworth (ed.), *Language Production*. London: Academic Press.

Drewnowski, A. and A. F. Healy (1980) 'Missing -ing in reading: letter detection errors on word endings'. *Journal of Verbal Learning and Verbal Behavior*, 19, 247–62.

Fay, D. A. (1980) *Morphology and Stress in the Mental Lexicon*. Report to the National Institute of Mental Health, NIMH Grant no. R03MH32912.

and A. Cutler (1977) 'Malapropisms and the structure of the mental lexicon'. *Linguistic Inquiry*, 8, 505–20.

Fowler, C. A., S. Napps and L. Feldman (1985) 'Relations among regular and irregular morphologically related words in the lexicon as revealed by repetition priming'. *Memory and Cognition*, 13, 241–55.

Frazier, L. (1978) 'On comprehending sentences: syntactic parsing strategies'. Ph.D. diss., University of Connecticut.

—— (1979) 'Parsing and constraints on word order'. In J. Lowenstamm (ed.), *University of Massachussetts Occasional Papers in Linguistics*, 5, 177–98.

—— (1984) 'Syntactic complexity'. In D. Dowty, L. Karttunen and A. M. Zwicky (eds), *Syntactic Theory and How People Parse Sentences*. Cambridge: Cambridge University Press.

—— and K. Rayner (this volume) 'Parameterizing the language processing system: left- vs. right-branching within and across languages'.

Freedman, J. L. and T. K. Landauer (1966) 'Retrieval of long-term memory: 'tip-of-the-tongue' phenomenon'. *Psychonomic Science*, 4, 309–10.

Fromkin, V. A. (1971) 'The non-anomalous nature of anomalous utterances'. *Language*, 47, 27–52.

—— (1973) 'Introduction'. In V. A. Fromkin (ed.), *Speech Errors as Linguistic Evidence*. The Hague: Mouton.

—— (1980) 'Introduction'. In V. A. Fromkin (ed.), *Errors in Linguistic Performance: Slips of the Tongue, Ear, Pen and Hand*. New York: Academic Press.

Garrett, M. F. (1976) 'Syntactic processes in sentence production'. In R. J. Wales and E. C. T. Walker (eds), *New Approaches to Language Mechanisms*. Amsterdam: North Holland.

Gibson, E. J. and L. Guinet (1971) 'Perception of inflections in brief visual presentations of words'. *Journal of Verbal Learning and Verbal Behavior*, 10, 182–9.

Givón, T. (1979) *On Understanding Grammar*. New York: Academic Press.

Greenberg, J. H. (1957) *Essays in Linguistics*. Chicago: Chicago University Press.

—— (1966) 'Some universals of grammar with particular reference to the order of meaningful elements'. In J. H. Greenberg (ed), *Universals of Language*, 2nd edn. Cambridge, Mass.: MIT Press.

—— (1978) 'How does a language acquire gender markers?' In J. H. Greenberg, C. A. Ferguson and E. A. Moravcsik (eds), *Universals of Human Language*, vol. 3, *Word Structure*. Stanford, Calif.: Stanford University Press.

Grosjean, F. (1980) 'Spoken word recognition and the gating paradigm'. *Perception and Psychophysics*, 28, 267–83.

—— (1983) 'How long is the sentence? Prediction and prosody in the on-line processing of language'. *Linguistics*, 21, 501–29.

Guenther, H. (1988) 'Oblique word forms in visual word recognition'. *Linguistics*, 26.

Gurjanov, M., G. Lukatela, K. Lukatela, M. Savic and M. T. Turvey (1987) 'Grammatical priming of inflected nouns by the gender of possessive adjectives'. *Journal of Experimental Psychology: Learning, Memory and Cognition*, 11, 692–701.

—— G. Lukatela, J. Moskovljevic, M. Savic and M. T. Turvey (1985) 'Grammatical priming of inflected nouns by inflected adjectives'. *Cognition*, 19, 55–71.

Hall, C. J. (this volume) 'Integrating diachronic and processing principles in explaining the suffixing preference'.

Hawkins, J. A. (1982) 'Language universals and the logic of historical reconstruction'. *Linguistics*, 20, 367–90.

(1983) *Word Order Universals*. New York: Academic Press.

(1988a) 'On explaining some left–right asymmetries in syntactic and morphological universals'. In M. Hammond, E. Moravcsik and J. Wirth (eds), *Studies in Syntactic Typology*. Amsterdam: John Benjamins.

(1988b) 'Some processing motivations for linear order universals'. MS, USC Dept of Linguistics.

(this volume) 'Explaining language universals'.

and G. Gilligan (1988) 'Prefixing and suffixing universals in relation to basic word order'. In J. A. Hawkins and H. K. Holmback (eds), *Papers in Universal Grammar: Generative and Typological Approaches*, *Lingua* Special Issue, 74, 2/3.

Henderson, L. (1985) 'Toward a psychology of morphemes'. In A. W. Ellis (ed.), *Progress in the Psychology of Language*, vol. 1. London: Erlbaum.

J. Wallis and D. Knight (1984) 'Morphemic structure and lexical access'. In H. Bouma and D. G. Bouwhuis (eds), *Attention and Performance X*. Hillsdale, NJ: Erlbaum.

Horowitz, L. M., P. C. Chilian and K. P. Dunnigan (1969) 'Word fragments and their redintegrative powers'. *Journal of Experimental Psychology*, 80, 392–4.

M. A. White and D. W. Atwood (1968) 'Word fragments as aids to recall: the organization of a word'. *Journal of Experimental Psychology*, 76, 219–26.

Hurford, J. (1981) 'Malapropisms, left-to-right listing and lexicalism'. *Linguistic Inquiry*, 12, 419–23.

Jarvella, R. J. and G. Meijers (1983) 'Recognizing morphemes in spoken words: some evidence for a stem-organized mental lexicon'. In R. J. Jarvella and G. B. Flores d'Arcais (eds), *The Process of Language Understanding*. Chichester: John Wiley.

Job, R. and G. Sartori (1984) 'Morphological decomposition: evidence from crossed phonological dyslexia'. *Quarterly Journal of Experimental Psychology*, 36A, 435–58.

Katz, L., S. Boyce, L. Goldstein and G. Lukatela (1987) 'Grammatical information effects in auditory word recognition'. *Cognition*, 25, 235–63.

Kempley, S. T. and J. Morton (1982) 'The effects of priming with regularly and irregularly related words in auditory word recognition'. *British Journal of Psychology*, 73, 441–54.

Kintsch, W. (1974) *The Representation of Meaning in Memory*. Hillsdale, NJ: Erlbaum.

Laudanna, A. and C. Burani (1985) 'Address mechanisms to decomposed lexical entries'. *Linguistics*, 23, 775–92.

Lehmann, C. (1984) *Der Relativsatz*. Tübingen: Gunter Narr.

Lima, S. D. (1987) 'Morphological analysis in sentence reading'. *Journal of Memory and Language*, 26, 84–99.

and A. Pollatsek (1983) 'Lexical access via an orthographic code? The basic orthographic syllable structure reconsidered'. *Journal of Verbal Learning and Verbal Behavior*, 22, 310–32.

Lukatela, G., B. Gligorijevic, A. Kostic and M. T. Turvey (1980) 'Representation of inflected nouns in the internal lexicon'. *Memory and Cognition*, 8, 415–23.

A. Kostic, L. Feldman and M. T. Turvey (1983) 'Grammatical priming of inflected nouns'. *Memory and Cognition*, 11, 59–63.

J. Moraca, D. Stojnov, M. Savic, L. Katz and M. T. Turvey (1982) 'Grammatical priming effects between pronouns and inflected verb forms'. *Psychological Research*, 44, 297–311.

MacKay, D. G. (1976) 'On the retrieval and lexical structure of verbs'. *Journal of Verbal Learning and Verbal Behavior*, 15, 169–82.

——— (1979) 'Lexical insertion, inflection and derivation: creative processes in word production'. *Journal of Psycholinguistic Research*, 8, 477–98.

Mallinson, G. and B. J. Blake (1981) *Language Typology: Cross-Linguistic Studies in Syntax*. Amsterdam: North Holland.

Manelis, L. and D. A. Tharp (1977) 'The processing of affixed words'. *Memory and Cognition*, 5, 690–5.

Marslen-Wilson, W. D. (1975) 'Sentence perception as an interactive parallel process'. *Science*, 189, 226–8.

——— (1978) 'Sequential decision processes during spoken word recognition'. Paper presented to the Psychonomic Society, San Antonio.

——— (1980) 'Speech understanding as a psychological process'. In J. C. Simon (ed.), *Spoken Language Generation and Understanding*. Dordrecht: Reidel.

——— and A. Welsh (1978) 'Processing interactions and lexical access during word recogniton in continuous speech'. *Cognitive Psychology*, 10, 29–63.

Matthews, P. H. (1974) *Morphology: An Introduction to the Theory of Word Structure*. Cambridge: Cambridge University Press.

Murrell, G. A. and J. Morton (1974) 'Word recognition and morphemic structure'. *Journal of Experimental Psychology*, 102, 963–8.

Nooteboom, S. G. (1981) 'Lexical retrieval from fragments of spoken words: beginnings versus endings'. *Journal of Phonetics*, 9, 407–24.

Oleron, P. and A. Danset (1983) 'Données sur l'appréhension des mots'. *Psychologie Française*, 8, 28–35.

Patterson, K. E. (1980) 'Derivational errors'. In M. Coltheart, K. E. Patterson and J. C. Marshall (eds), *Deep Dyslexia*. London: Routledge & Kegan Paul.

Pullum, G. K. (1981) 'Languages with object before subject: a comment and a catalogue'. *Linguistics*, 19, 147–55.

Rosenberg, S., P. J. Coyle and W. L. Porter (1966) 'Recall of adverbs as a function of the frequency of their adjective roots'. *Journal of Verbal Learning and Verbal Behavior*, 5, 75–6.

Rubin, G. S., C. A. Becker and R. H. Freedman (1979) 'Morphological structure and its effects on visual word recognition'. *Journal of Verbal Learning and Verbal Behavior*, 18, 757–67.

Ruhlen, M. (1975) *A Guide to the Languages of the World*. Stanford University: Language Universals Project.

Segui, J. and M. Zubizarreta (1985) 'Mental representation of morphologically complex words and lexical access'. *Linguistics*, 23, 759–74.

Smith, P. T. and C. M. Sterling (1982) 'Factors affecting the perceived morphological structure of written words'. *Journal of Verbal Learning and Verbal Behavior*, 21, 704–21.

Stanners, R. F., J. J. Neiser, W. P. Hernon and R. Hall (1979a) 'Memory representation for morphologically related words'. *Journal of Verbal Learning and Verbal Behavior*, 18, 399–412.

——— J. J. Neiser and S. Painton (1979b) 'Memory representation for prefixed words'. *Journal of Verbal Learning and Verbal Behavior*, 18, 733–43.

Taft, M. (1979) 'Recognition of affixed words and the word frequency effect'. *Memory and Cognition*, 7, 263–72.

(1981) 'Prefix stripping revisited'. *Journal of Verbal Learning and Verbal Behavior*, 20, 289–97.

(1988) 'A morphological decomposition model of lexical representation'. *Linguistics*, 26.

and K. I. Forster (1975) 'Lexical storage and retrieval of prefixed words'. *Journal of Verbal Learning and Verbal Behavior*, 14, 638–47.

G. Hambly and S. Kinoshita (1986) 'Visual and auditory recognition of prefixed words'. *Quarterly Journal of Experimental Psychology*, 38A, 357–66.

Tomlin, R. S. (1986) *Basic Word Order: Functional Principles*. London: Croom Helm.

Ultan, R. (1978) 'Some general characteristics of interrogative systems'. In J. H. Greenberg, C. A. Ferguson and E. A. Moravcsik (eds), *Universals of Human Language*, vol. 4, *Syntax*. Stanford, Calif.: Stanford University Press.

van der Molen, H. and J. Morton (1979) 'Remembering plurals: unit of coding and form of coding during serial recall'. *Cognition*, 7, 35–47.

van der Vlugt, M. J. and S. G. Nooteboom (1986) 'Auditory word recognition is not more sensitive to word-initial than to word-final stimulus information'. *IPO Annual Progress Report*, 21, 41–9.

Williams, E. (1981) 'On the notions "lexically related" and "head of a word"'. *Linguistic Inquiry*, 12, 245–74.

Yngve, V. H. A. (1960) 'A model and an hypothesis for language structure'. *Proceedings of the American Philosophical Society*, 104, 444–66.

PART V

The Diachronic Dimension

CHAPTER 12

Integrating Diachronic and Processing Principles in Explaining the Suffixing Preference

Christopher J. Hall

1 Introduction

Across languages it has been observed (Greenberg 1966; Hawkins and Gilligan 1988) that there is a distinct preference for suffixing over prefixing and for both over discontinuous morphology.[1] In addition, there is a correlation between exclusive prefixing and head-initial languages on the one hand, and exclusive suffixing and head-final languages on the other. The pattern of the data from Hawkins and Gilligan's sample of some 200 languages[2] may be summarized as follows (cf. Hawkins and Cutler, this volume, table 11.4):

(1) | | Pref only | Both P & S | Suff only |
|---|---|---|---|
| Head-initial languages | 08.5% | 72.5% | 19% |
| Head-final languages | 00% | 36.5% | 63.5% |
| All languages | 04% | 54.5% | 41% |

Two apparently distinct explanations for this suffixing preference have been offered in the literature: one appeals to principles of language change (Givón 1971b, 1975, 1979); the other invokes principles of lexical processing (Cutler et al. 1985; Hawkins and Cutler this volume; Hall 1987). In this paper I wish to suggest that these accounts are not incompatible, and indeed that the diachronic and psycholinguistic facts are two aspects of a single, more complete explanation. I advocate that an approach which draws on the various linguistic sub-disciplines and other disciplines should be adopted in all attempts to seek explanation for cross-linguistic regularities in natural language.

The particular concern of the present discussion is with the diachronic account of the suffixing preference and how it serves to define a link between processing constraints and morphological structure. I consider Givón's diachronic claims that the languages of the world all share a common ancestral or current SOV word order, and that 'today's morphology is yesterday's syntax'; I argue that while the former is unfounded and, in any case, inadequate as an explanation, the latter is largely correct and, indeed, allows us to state more fully and clearly how processing principles could be responsible for the skew in affix positioning. I pursue the postulation that the diachronic processes which instantiate Givón's 'syntax → morphology' transition (cf. e.g. Givón 1979) involve the semantic reduction or generalization of lexical items, typically syntactic heads, and a consequent reduction of phonological form and (ultimately) fusion with other lexical items, giving affixes.

A full account of the suffixing preference must examine diachronic semantic and phonological change within words in order to understand the exact way in which lexical processing might be responsible for this morphological regularity, that is, to specify the 'link' between psychological explanation and structural regularity (cf. Clark and Malt 1984). Previous accounts have been satisfied with less than the full story. Givón, as linguistic archaeologist, does not dig deep enough and seems to suggest (albeit only implicitly) that a diachronic study of word order will provide a sufficient explanation of the distribution of the data, whereas the first major proponents of the processing explanation, Cutler, Hawkins and Gilligan (henceforth, C, H & G) do not examine the diachronic facts in any detail, because they arise from what C, H & G perceive as a competing explanatory model. Adopting a rather broader perspective, Greenberg, in a short essay on 'general linguistics', the name he gives to that branch of linguistics which seeks the identification and explanation of universal properties of language, conjectured about the relationship between psychological constraints on comprehension and universal regularities of language structure, with specific reference to the suffixing preference (Greenberg 1957). Here he anticipated the approach taken by C, H & G, by sketching an explanation for the preference in terms of information processing. It is within the spirit of the multidisciplinary approach advocated in that essay and with due acknowledgement to the suggestions contained there that the present paper is written.

2 Explanation in Linguistics

Givón (1979) suggests that explanations for language structure lie along a number of 'parameters' of which at least the major ones are essentially either psychological or functional in nature. These are: *propositional contents* (referring to clause-level notions such as subject, object and action); *discourse pragmatics* (topic-comment, presupposition, etc.); *world-view pragmatics* (the importance of 'a constructed view of the universe'); *the processor* (production and comprehension constraints); *ontogenetic development* (acquisition constraints); and *cognitive structure* (more general, non-linguistic cognitive and perceptual apparatus).

In addition to these functional or psychological principles he includes the phenomena of *phylogenetic evolution* and *diachronic change*. Both these principles I would view not as explanatory parameters but rather as mediating mechanisms between explanandum and explanans. Chomsky's biological explanation (e.g. 1965, 1981) is, I would claim, of this order. In all likelihood it is true that certain universal properties of language are innately specified, that is, that there *is* a specifically linguistic cognitive component, as he claims; but the recognition of this can still not rank as a full explanation. We must consider the question of why these particular properties have become innate rather than others. What is it about these properties that has led them to be favored through natural selection over other potential properties? The emergence of some of the properties may be arbitrary, but it is also likely that many of the properties become set because they afford advantages of the type appealed to by Givón, above. Of course, we are a long way from having the kind of sophisticated research technology necessary to be able to categorically determine the sources of innate properties. However, this does not mean that we should ignore potentially relevant functional or psychological evidence from our knowledge of the current state of human development and, instead, be guilty of complacency in viewing the biological explanation as complete.

In fully explaining consistent regularities of structure across languages, therefore, the scholar (or, more realisically, interdisciplinary *team* of scholars) must (i) rigorously describe the data in the most general and insightful manner (as do the generativists), but also (ii) examine all levels of analysis to determine potential underlying principles, probably of a psychological or functional nature, rather than allowing description to count as explanation (as, unfortunately this time, do the generativists). In addition, we must (iii) attempt to establish the mechanism by which the underlying pressure or pressures actually instantiate in language the structural pattern under investigation. This latter requirement will involve the investigation of diachronic change for some properties and of phylogenetic evolution for others.

In this paper I examine the preference for suffixing across languages, observed principally by Greenberg (1966) and Hawkins and Gilligan (1988), and seek an explanation for it. I assess the accounts offered by C, H & G (cf. also Hawkins and Cutler this volume) and Givón (1979) in the light of the above assumptions, and bring them together to produce a unified account. This is then refined and supported with the help of apparently independent principles from various levels of linguistic analysis, themselves identified as *derived* from the account offered. I demonstrate that some of the diachronic facts are themselves motivated by processing principles which also motivate independently formulated principles governing certain phonological and semantic regularities. The processing principles themselves are shown to be an instantiation of the mediation between two higher level communicative principles, namely those of *economy* (speaker-oriented) and *clarity* (hearer-oriented) (Slobin 1977).

3 The Cutler, Hawkins and Gilligan Account

3.1 *The data and universals*

Greenberg originally observed a correlation between word order and affix/stem order. This led him to make the claim that exclusively suffixing languages were postpositional, and that exclusively prefixing languages were prepositional (Universal 27, 1966: 93). He also noted that 'there is a distinct predominance of suffixing. Exclusively suffixing languages are fairly common, while exclusively prefixing languages are quite rare (p. 92).' These observations were based on a sample of thirty languages, rather modest by current standards. Current work by John Hawkins and Gary Gilligan (Hawkins and Gilligan 1988, henceforth, H & G), using a considerably expanded sample, has yielded observations which weaken Greenberg's original claims but still reveal significant cross-linguistic tendencies. Based on examination of mostly inflections on nouns and verbs in their extensive sample, H & G came up with the following universal observations:

(2) 1a. Languages which are exclusively suffixing are considerably more frequent than those which are exclusively prefixing.
   b. Across languages, suffixal morphology is more frequent than prefixing and infixing.[3]
   2a. If a language is exclusively prefixing, it is prepositional.
   b. About half of postpositional languages are exclusively suffixing; the majority of prepositional languages are both prefixing and suffixing.

They also draw up a list of eighteen universal statements correlating particular affix types (according to function, for example number or person marking) with word order indicators (that is, verb and adposition orders). The universals are all of the implicational type with prefixing or head-final as implicans and head-first or suffixing as implicandum, respectively. What these universals amount to is an observation that affix position tends to correlate with syntactic head position; but, in opposition to this tendency, there is a significant skew towards suffixing across the number of languages which employ exclusive affix positions (within languages which utilize both positions, suffixing still predominates, but not as significantly). The figures are given in Hawkins and Cutler this volume, table 11.4.

3.2 *Explanations*

3.2.1 *The HOP*   H & G claim that the syntactic head/affix correlation may be accounted for if we adopt the (rather controversial) assumption that an affix always constitutes the 'head' of the word. Such an assumption allows them to formulate a principle which, they claim, is 'part of the explanatory package':

(3) Head Ordering Principle (HOP)
The affixal head of a word is ordered on the same side of its subcategorized modifier(s) as P is ordered relative to NP within PP, and as V is ordered relative to a direct object NP.

As I have argued elsewhere (Hall 1987, ch. 2), however, the affix is not always the head of the word, and indeed, inflections are *never* heads (recall that H & G's data base consists mainly of inflections). In any case, to truly *explain* the correlation, we must ask *why* affixes tend to correlate with heads in the syntax – that is, we must attempt to identify an underlying motivation for such a pattern. In Hall (1987) I address this matter and conclude that, in fact, the correlation is a historical 'accident', but is *derived* from a head ordering principle operating in the syntax. The HOP as it stands merely records an observation; it does not explain the facts.

3.2.2 The processing account   C, H & G address the specific observation that there is a definite skewing in favor of suffixation away from the head-initial/prefixing prediction of the HOP. They offer a processing explanation which is based on the fact that words, like sentences, are processed from 'left to right' in real time, that is, that the first part of the word is received before the last part and that processing occurs 'on-line', from the very first milliseconds of acoustic input. This observation is perhaps most strikingly documented in the reports of experiments carried out by Marslen-Wilson and his associates (e.g. Marslen-Wilson and Welsh 1978; Marslen-Wilson and Tyler 1980; Marslen-Wilson 1983) which suggest that word recognition (isolation of an item in the lexicon) is typically achieved after only the first 200–250 msec stretch of English stem-initial words of over 400 msec duration. They have also been able to show that context effects (for example, semantic cuing with words in the same lexical field) operate to shift the recognition point further to the beginning of the word than its location when the word is presented in a neutral context (for example, in the carrier phrase, 'The following word is ——').
That the lexical processor operates from the very first moment and attempts to gain lexical access as early as possible, using any information it has available to do so, is evidence of the optimal efficiency of the language processing mechanism, the primary goal of which is, in comprehension, to decode the acoustic signal and build semantic representations as rapidly and as accurately as possible. The need for such rapidity and the success of the processor in achieving it is attested by the fact that we *do* communicate with ease (and seemingly instantaneously) at a rate of 2–3 words per second in less than perfect input conditions.
C, H & G argue that, since lexical access is typically achieved on the basis of the initial part of the word, then this will be the location in which the

most 'salient' information will be placed. They review a good deal of experimental evidence in the literature which supports this view, and also a range of results on the perception of affixed words, from which they draw the general conclusions that affixes are recognized as such *at some point* in the comprehension process, but that the lexicon is, essentially, stem-based. On the basis of this evidence they argue that the suffixing preference may be explained because the stem is the most 'salient' element of the word, has 'computational priority' over the affix and therefore favors initial position (cf. Greenberg 1957: 91). The precise details of the psychological account remain to be fully worked out, and it is not clear that C, H & G have presented the correct formulation of it (cf. Hall 1987, ch. 3); however, the major claim here is clear: optimally efficient processing is served by having the stem at the beginning of the word, so as to facilitate the earliest possible meaningful interpretation of the input.

4 The Diachronic Approach

4.1 *Today's morphology: the origin of affixes*

A reasonable question to ask is where affixes come from. C, H & G offer no opinion as to the origin of the structures they seek to explain. The only reference they make to the issue is in a refutation of a potential diachronic explanation of the suffixing preference (see below) – it is not thought to be a crucial element of the explanatory hypothesis. Indeed, it is as though affixes are first 'introduced' (or 'evolve') in a language as a category, and the HOP, tempered by the preferences of the lexical processor, then decides where to put them. This viewpoint ignores a wealth of evidence which points to a less ethereal source: namely processes of semantic generalization and phonological attrition and fusion which result in the boundedness of previously free-standing lexical morphemes (see, for example, Meillet 1958: 130–48 for an early statement of this, and Bybee and Pagliuca 1985 for a more recent, detailed analysis of such processes).

Givón's explanation of the suffixing preference crucially refers to this process of affixation, which he has discussed in some detail, principally in Givón (1971b). There he cites evidence from Amharic and various Romance, Germanic and Bantu languages, some of it speculatory, but most of it very convincing. His assumptions and conclusions are strong ones, and if true, have important consequences for linguistic theory:

> If it is true that bound morphemes, derivational as well as inflectional, arise historically from erstwhile free 'lexical' morphemes, and if it is further true that the syntax of the language, at some point of the derivation, determines the order of the free 'lexical' morphemes, then the syntax of the language ultimately also determines the morphotactics of the morphology which ultimately evolves. (1971b: 409)

As illustration, consider his account of the genesis of prefixed modality markers and suffixed verb-derivational markers on Bantu verbs. According to Givón (1971a) both affixes are derived from main verbs dominating sentential complements (and so may be construed as heads – cf. section 5 below). He maintains that their differential positioning as prefixes and suffixes is a result of the dominant syntactic word order in Bantu at the time that they fused with the verb of the sentential complement ('comp'): there was a historical change from comp:verb to verb:comp with derivational markers arising during the former stage and modal markers during the latter:

(4) a.   comp:verb (syntax)   suffixation (morphology)

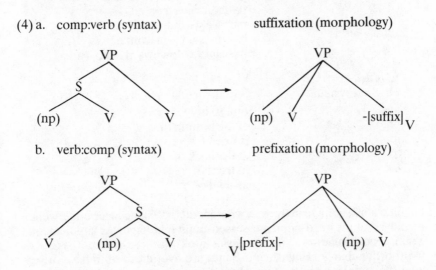

b.   verb:comp (syntax)   prefixation (morphology)

In support of this hypothesized word order change and its morphological consequences, Givón appeals to the positioning of the object pronoun affix, which appears as a verbal prefix. He reasons that the current word order (verb:comp) would predict suffixes, and so the object pronoun must have become fused at an earlier stage of Bantu when the word order was comp:verb. Syntactic change affects free lexical morpheme order but leaves bound morphemes '"stranded" or frozen in [their] earlier syntactic position'. Although the Bantu object pronoun case supports Givón's hypothesis only by virtue of its consistency with the hypothesis (and therefore is no 'independent support' as he claims), his data from other languages (Amharic, Spanish) do strengthen the empirical basis of the model.

Further evidence is offered from noun affixes, for example in Amharic where some locatives appear as suffixes whereas others are prepositional. The suffixed class are the supplemental forms derived from head nouns, paralleling the English and Bantu systems:

(5) AMHARIC
    Original system   Supplemental system
    l- 'to, for'   ba-lay-u 'at the top'
    b- 'at, in, on'   ba-tac-u 'at the bottom'
    k- 'from'   ba-layu lay 'at the top'

    BANTU (ChiBemba)
    Original system   Supplemental system
    pa- 'at, on'   pa-isamba lya 'underneath of'
    ku- 'to, from, at'   ku-muulu wa 'on top of'
    mu- 'in'   pa-kati ka 'in the middle of'
                           pa-nnuma ya 'behind'
                           mu-nse ya 'outside of'
                           pa-ntanshi ya 'in front of'
                           ku-nshi ya 'downward from'

    ENGLISH
    Original system   Supplemental system
    at   on top of
    on   at the bottom of
    in   inside of
    to   at the back of
    for   in front of
    from   instead of

Givón claims, convincingly, that whereas all three languages underwent a reanalysis of the head-noun:possessed-noun relation in the supplemental genitive constructions, this reanalysis took place at different stages of word order change. English and Bantu are hypothesized to have originated the supplemental system when their syntax was noun:pos, and to have been reanalyzed as follows:[4]

(6) [noun [of-noun]   ]   → [[noun-of]   noun]
               mod np   prep   pp

On the other hand, Amharic is claimed to have had pos:noun order when the supplemental system developed, and therefore was reanalyzed as in (7):

(7) [[of-noun]   noun]   → [of-noun [noun]   ]
          mod   np   postp pp

The original prepositional systems in all three languages also arose from head nouns at an earlier time when all three languages had noun:pos order in their noun phrases.

    Although Givón's account of the genesis of affixes is based almost entirely on hypothesized recontructions in a less than representative sample of languages, it provides a very logical explanatory model which is generally consistent with broader diachronic facts (for example, word order reconstructions, cognate forms). The process of attrition from free lexical item to bound morpheme is a natural phonological process (see section 5 below), and as such is apparently the *only* major candidate process which can explain the introduction of affixes into a language.[5] Given that the diachronic account is accurate, though, how do we explain the skewing in favor of suffixation? Givón (1979) is again the source of an apparent answer to this question, although here his arguments are less convincing.

4.2 *Yesterday's syntax: SOV as universal word order*

Although never offered explicitly as an explanation of the suffixing preference, Givón's claim that all human languages exhibit, either currently or at some stage in their history, SOV word order, can be construed as such (cf. Zirmunskij 1966: 86 for a brief but explicit suggestion of support for such a theory). In the light of the assumptions presented in the previous section, we can see that for Givón the problem of the suffixing preference can be solved by identifying a skewing in earlier syntactic word order. He notes in a section of his 1979 book:

> Greenberg [1966] ... observed that many VO languages, with English being a representative sample, do not abide by this correlation [OV/suffixation and VO/prefixation] very consistently, and exhibit mostly suffixal morphology. As I pointed out [Givón 1971b], such inconsistencies arise because of a sequence of natural diachronic changes:
> 1. A layer of morphology arises and at that time 'conforms' to the prevailing syntactic typology of the language.
> 2. Due to highly natural processes the syntax of the language changes, while the old morphology – being bound – remains as a frozen relic.

Thus, if we can identify a skewing in 'the prevailing syntacic typology of the language[s]', then we can account for the consequent skewing in the morphology which arose from it. Such a skewing is postulated by Givón – a skewing of *all* languages, in one direction: SOV. He claims that *all* languages were or are SOV, summarizing the facts as follows:

> 1. It seems that the majority of language families known to us exhibit SUBJECT–OBJECT–VERB (SOV) syntax, and so far as one can tell they were always SOV (Altaic, Turkic, Caucasian, Dravidian, Sino-Tibetan, all Papua-New-Guinea philums, Kushitic, Khoi-San, Athabascan, Uto-Aztecan, Hokan, and many others).

2. The overwhelming majority of languages and language families which do not show actual SOV syntax currently, can be nevertheless reconstructed via internal and comparative methods back to an earlier SOV stage. In other words, either their syntax or – at the very least – their bound morphology exhibit coherent relics of the earlier SOV stage (Indo-European, Semitic, Finno-Ugric, Mandarin, Niger-Congo, Nilo-Saharan, Afro-Asiatic, Iroquois, Mayan, and in fact all currently non-SOV Amerindian languages with perhaps one exception).

3. Only very few language families seem to show no solid evidence for an earlier SOV stage (Austronesian, Salish (?)). Even in those the evidence is by no means conclusive.

4. The most common natural drive in word-order change seems to be SOV > VSO > SVO, with a much more restricted drift of SOV > VSO > VOS also attested in a number of cases. The drift *toward* SOV from any other typology is relatively rare.

The argument runs as follows. The elements that morphologize into affixes (perhaps via cliticization) are heads (cf. Givón 1971b: 412ff) – in verb phrases it is a higher verb such as an auxiliary which will develop into an affixal marker of, for example, tense. In SOV languages, auxiliaries always follow the main verb (cf. Greenberg 1966: 85) and therefore when they lose free lexical status they will become *suffixes*. It is hypothesized that affixation, if it occurred mostly during the SOV stage of most languages, would therefore result in more suffixing than prefixing on the verb cross-linguistically.

4.3 *Problems with the SOV account*

There are two major criticisms of the SOV account: (i) that the underlying premise of primitive SOV word order in all human languages is inaccurate, thereby annulling the explanatory power of any account derived from it; and (ii) that the SOV account, if accurate, is only a partial one, covering only a minimal portion of the data.

In support of the claim for a universal primitive word order of SOV, Givón produces very little hard evidence, and, indeed, evidence for such a grand claim *can* only be speculative in nature, considering the dimensions of its breadth and depth. Hawkins (1983) offers, on the other hand, a controversial though convincing rebuttal of the claim. He demonstrates that Proto-Indo-European (PIE), at least, is more likely to have been VO than OV. His demonstration is based on the assumption that reconstructions in proto-languages and all intermediate stages be consistent with universal variants observed in daughter languages (the 'Logic of Competing Variants'). The universal variants of the current and earliest daughter languages are therefore the key to the proto-language. Hawkins' universals are multi-clausal implicational statements which determine permissible and non-permissible co-occurrence restrictions, using 'typological indicators' such as adpositions (postp, prep), verb positions (OV, VO) and N-modifier positions (e.g. NGen, GenN). Hawkins shows that the earliest IE daughter languages exhibited the following N-modifier co-occurrence sets (as defined by the Prepositional Noun Modifier Hierarchy (p. 75), that is, using Prep as the typological indicator):

(8) Subtype 1   (Prep)   NAdj & NGen & NRel
    Subtype 2   (Prep)   AdjN & NGen & NRel
    Subtype 3   (Prep)   AdjN & GenN & NRel
    Subtype 4   (Prep)   AdjN & GenN & RelN

Although all IE daughters have *only* the N-modifier orders shown in (8) above, they do not all have prepositions; however, no early IE languages exhibit co-occurrence sets attestable in other postpositional languages (as shown in Hawkins' Postpositional Noun Modifier Hierarchy (p. 86)). For example, no postpositional IE language has the following co-occurrence sets:

(9) (Postp)   NAdj & GenN & RelN
    (Postp)   NAdj & GenN & NRel

This, then, is very strong motivation for reconstructing Prep rather than Postp for PIE. Hawkins also offers an argument for PIE prepositions from synchronic distributional evidence (p. 268ff), which suggests that the likelihood of IE innovating postpositions is far greater than of it innovating prepositions. Postpositions in IE daughters are attested in only the universal word order co-occurrences where they would be expected; however, IE prepositions are found in large numbers in word orders where they are not favored in current synchronic samples. Thus, Hawkins argues,

> The reconstruction of postpositions for Proto-Indo-European necessarily leads to the unfortunate conclusion that prepositions were innovated not only in the majority of IE daughters, but in numerous co-occurrences for which all other languages of the world demonstrate an overwhelming preference for, or strong tolerance of, postpositions rather than prepositions. (p. 271)

It follows from this that PIE is far more likely to have been VSO or SVO, since prepositions and SOV is a highly marked co-occurrence. Hawkins demonstrates this by examining compatibility with other universal co-occurrence sets and with the current distributional facts (cf. pp. 271ff).

The importance of Hawkins' conclusions for PIE is that they considerably weaken Givón's claim for pan-proto-language SOV. Furthermore, many of the reconstructions Givón cites for earlier SOV stages, for

example the Afro-Asiatic group (cf. 1979: 275, n. 6), are based on an
analysis of the bound morphology of current family members. The
explanation for the suffixing preference then becomes circular: there is
more suffixing because all languages are or were SOV; we know that all
languages are or were SOV in part because they exhibit more suffixing.
The current distributional evidence also speaks against Givón's thesis: at
present the ratio of OV to VO languages is roughly 50–50 (according to
Hawkins' expanded sample of 336 languages, 162 have V before O and
174 have O before V (Hawkins 1983: 288)).

Even if we accept Givón's claim, we may only exploit it to a limited
degree, namely to account for a preference for suffixing in verbs; however,
in H & G's sample there is a greater tendency for suffixes in *nominal*
morphology (81.6% versus 60.7% for suffixes in verbal morphology):

(10)   AFFIXES ON VERBS AND NOUNS: QUANTITIES

	Pref only		Both P & S		Suff only		Total	
	N	%	N	%	N	%	N	%
Verbal	157	30.7	44	8.6	310	60.7	511	100
Nominal	36	14.7	9	3.7	200	81.6	245	100
Total	193	25.5	53	7.0	510	67.5	756	100

If, then, the SOV account is to cover the data adequately, it would need to
be demonstrated that affixed nominal elements also typically appeared
after rather than before the noun to which they subsequently attached.
Although tendencies of head serialization are observed across languages
and through language change (cf. e.g. Vennemann's Natural Serialization
Principle (1974) and Hawkins' more tenable principle of Cross-Category
Harmony (1983: 133ff)), there is no simple guarantee that head position
in the VP will correlate with head position in the NP, that is, that, in our
case, SOV in proto-languages will imply modifier-N order in the NP. Note
the co-occurrences counted in Hawkins' expanded sample (1983: 166):

(11) SOV & Postp & AN & GN : 96 languages
      SOV & Postp & NA & GN : 55 languages
      SOV & Postp & NA & NG : 11 languages
      SOV & Prep & AN & GN : 3 languages
      SOV & Prep & AN & NG : 0 languages
      SOV & Prep & NA & NG : 10 languages

Although the majority of languages obey a strict serialization principle (96
out of a total of 175), it can be seen that in 76 cases SOV does *not* predict
that all modifiers precede the noun.[6]

4.4 Interim assessment of the diachronic approach

The explanation for the suffixing preference offered in C, H & G is, I would argue, fundamentally correct in its appeal to processing principles; however, it is substantially incomplete: it provides no mechanism which can link explanans and explanandum (that is, a model of processing combined with grammatical principles on the one hand, and the attested predominance of suffixing across languages on the other), and so it is impossible to conclude whether it does, in fact, constitute the *correct* explanation. Hawkins emphasizes (1988) that when we are faced with a choice between competing motivations for some linguistic regularity, we must be as rigorous as possible in our criteria for choosing between them. This condition of rigor can only be met, I would argue, if the path from structure to explanation is clearly specified.

In C, H & G it is as if the processing model influences a choice of whether to 'place' a particular category as a suffix or prefix, that is, by innovation. The mechanism by which a language may spontaneously create new substantive categories of the grammar like affixes is not specified – nor is it likely to become specifiable, especially once the diachronic facts are given due attention. A much more tenable claim is that the processor influences the diachronic process of fusion of the morpheme with subsequent stem, according to whether the erstwhile free lexical item stands before or after the element with which it fuses. Hence, the explanandum is the observation that fusion takes place most typically *after* the stem rather than before, and the postulated explanans is that although fusion is freely allowed post-stem, it is resisted in pre-stem position, because greater comprehension problems arise in the latter case than in the former.

I submit that (i) Givón's account of the genesis of affixes provides the processing hypothesis with the necessary degree of thoroughness by detailing a mechanism which explicitly links cause with result in a linguistically plausible manner; (ii) that the adoption of Givón's account thereby changes the nature of both explanans and explanandum (as shown above), giving us a clearer insight into the nature of the problem than hitherto attained, without jeopardizing the force or correctness of the processing explanation ultimately appealed to; but (iii) that the SOV extension of Givón's diachronic account must be rejected on account of its own inadequacies and the superiority of the psycholinguistic explanatory model.

It should be noted here that although I adopt Givón's claim for the origin of affixes, it is not necessary to accept his further claim that current morpheme order allows us always to reconstruct previous syntactic order. There are a number of counterexamples to this strong prediction (cf. e.g. Comrie 1981: 209ff), yet these do not weaken the model described here, since the predominant word order at the time of affixation is immaterial to whether the word reduces to affixal status or not. So, where there are problems with Givón's strict historical account, the account presented here *generalizes* to these problems.

One prediction of the claim that fusion is resisted in pre-stem position is that we may expect to find cross-linguistically a greater number of *free* grammatical morphemes in pre-stem position. H & G only examine bound morpheme distribution and so cannot help here; however, Matthew Dryer (personal communication) suggests on the basis of his extensive sample that this prediction is largely confirmed, pointing specifically to the example of negation, which languages typically express by a free morpheme in preverbal position, but by a bound morpheme postverbally. There is, in addition, the observation that prepositions are almost always realized as free morphemes, whereas postpositions are equally likely to be realized as free or bound (as suffixes in the latter case).

In the next section we will examine natural phonological processes of attrition and fusion and show that they reflect this asymmetry between word-initial and word-final positions. If this is correct, then it constitutes a further argument against the SOV extension of the diachronic approach by providing a broader and more empirically verifiable basis for the phenomena to be explained: I maintain that the reason we have more suffixing is not because it is the natural consequence of SOV word order but because free lexical morphemes are demonstrably less likely to fuse in pre-stem position for reasons of optimally efficient lexical processing.

Before continuing, however, I should point out that it is not guaranteed that the processing factors appealed to here will account for *all* of the data. Bybee (this volume) suggests that in addition to the sort of explanation dealt with here, there are at least two other possibilities. The first is that it might be that grammatical material tends to be postposed, whether it is bound or not, leading to more suffixation, since it is grammatical (lexically empty) material which tends to undergo affixation. This hypothesis is unmotivated and, at present, untestable, and if correct would not, in any case, 'explain' the data, but rather shift the need for explanation elsewhere (conceivably to the level of syntactic as opposed to lexical processing). The second possibility is that morphemes cannot become fused with free lexical neighbors unless they enjoy exclusive adjacency, for instance it could be that adverbs and the possibility of Subj–Aux inversion are blocking the fusion of English auxiliaries with following verbs. Kahr (1976) has proposed that, at least for a limited number of languages and for only one grammatical function (case), preposed morphemes, in her examples prepositions, do not reduce to prefix status because other elements intervene between preposition and noun. However, the crucial cross-linguistic evidence needed to establish whether this explanation generalizes to a significant number of languages and morpheme functions is not yet available, and again, the need for explanation would only be shifted, this time to account for the asymmetry in adjacency between preposed and postposed morphemes and the potential stems to which they become bound. Nevertheless, it may well be that such factors are involved in the suffixing preference, and it is to be hoped that the extent of their potential involvement will soon be measurable. The possibility of their involvement is not, however, a motivation for abandoning the investigation of processing factors which, in the absence of counter-evidence, constitute the only major convincing account of the phenomenon.

5 Phonological Decay and Semantic Redundancy

5.1 *Phonological decay*

Processes of phonological weakening, attrition and loss are very natural diachronic and synchronic processes, attestable in probably all human languages. Such decay of phonological substance has its roots in the articulations of individual speakers of a language, particularly in rapid speech, where often drastic simplification of form occurs, as a way of transmitting the same message in a shorter time and with the least muscular effort.

It seems that, in general, processes of phonological attrition take place typically at the *end* of words rather than at the beginning. This tendency has been explicitly recognized in Natural Phonology (cf. e.g. Stampe 1973; Hooper 1976), and in the work of Foley (e.g. 1977) we see a model of phonology in which the sounds of natural language are classified according to their 'strength' or 'weakness' on certain phonological parameters (for example, resonance, spirantization, lenition, etc.). Rules in his model refer not to phonetic classifications but to the strength or weakness of elements, determined by their degree of susceptibility to various phonological processes. In addition to this inherent paradigmatic determination of strength, he describes syntagmatic distinctions – that is, the 'positional potentiation' of an element according to his 'inertial development principle' (1977: 107):

(12) Inertial Development Principle (IDP)

    (i) Strong elements strengthen first and most extensively and preferentially in strong environments.

    (ii) Weak elements weaken first and most extensively and preferentially in weak environments.

Of particular interest to the present study is his classification of word initial position as a strong environment and word final as a weak environment. An example (p. 109):

> Since the beginning of a word is a strong position, we expect either simple maintenance, as in Lt *dictus* → It *detto*, with retention of *d*, or strengthening, as in Lt **rete* → Sp *red* [rred], with prolongation of initial *r*. Since the end of a word is a weak position, we expect either

simple maintenance, as in Lt *amica* → Sp *amiga*, with retention of *a*, or weakening, as in Lt *dictus* → It *detto*, with loss of final *s*.

The basis for deciding which elements are strong and which weak is not made explicit in Foley's theory. He states categorically that 'relative phonological strength refers not to the absolute phonetic strength of elements, but to the relation of the elements to one another in a phonological system' (p. 29) and that 'phonological elements are ... properly defined not in terms of their acoustic or articulatory properties, but in terms of the rules they participate in.' These rules reflect processes of strengthening and weakening familiar in other phonological frameworks. Hyman (1975: 165) defines strengthening and weakening as follows: '[A] segment X is said to be weaker than a segment Y if Y goes through an X stage on its way to zero. Strengthening, on the other hand, refers to the reinforcement of a segment, as when a nongeminate [p] becomes geminate or double [pp].'

The particular mechanics of Foley's theory are not important to us (and it is certainly not necessary to adopt his assumption of a non-phonetic base for phonology). What is interesting for the present discussion is the identification of word endings as weak, and word beginnings as strong environments. Hyman notes (1975: 168) an example of this from Chinese (Chen 1973) and also, a similar phenomenon in Burmese (cf. Maran 1971). The set of Middle Chinese word final elements *m*, *n*, *ŋ* and *p*, *t*, *k* are currently being merged and neutralized in certain dialects:

(13)   Nasal endings   Stop endings

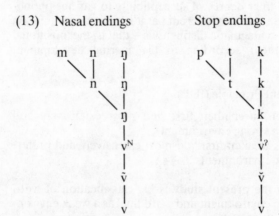

In addition, experimental work by Cooper (e.g. Cooper and Paccia-Cooper 1980) has shown that assimilation across word boundaries in fluent speech is considerably reduced when the second of two adjacent words is of low frequency in word counts, or when it is contrastively stressed, but *not* when the first word is rare or stressed. This suggests that when assimilation between two words is possible in fluent speech, it is the phonological integrity of the word-initial portion of the second word, rather than the word-final portion of the first, which is maintained when one of the words requires special processing attention from the hearer.

Instead of viewing the ends of words as particularly vulnerable to weakening processes (whether these be neutralization or attrition or loss) it might inform our discussion more to look at the *beginnings* of words as particularly *robust* and able to 'resist' such processes, maintaining (or even strengthening) their phonological integrity. So, for example, when we observe that in Chinese compounds, tone is neutralized only in the second constituent (the first determining tonal contrasts) and that in English it is the penultimate morpheme which typically carries primary stress in compounds, we can view this as evidence that word-initial position constitutes an informationally more important site than word final position, for which there seem very few examples of this sort.

Some particularly pertinent data is to be found in Williamson's (n.d.) study of Ịjọ, which is considered in some detail here. In Ịjọ, words contain a maximum of three stem consonants C1, C2 and C3. Williamson observes also that consonant types can be divided into three sets, according to their 'strength' (p. 6):

(14) Obstruents
  voiceless

non-stop	f	s			STRONG
stop	p	t	k	kp	

  voiced

non-implosive	b	d	g	gb	MEDIUM
implosive	ɓ	ɗ			

  Sonorants

non-approximant	m	l	ɣ	WEAK
approximant	w	r	y	

The division of the consonants into these three sets is apparently motivated by the same criterion that Hyman gives (above): stronger elements weaken to weak elements, and weak elements weaken to zero. In addition, weaker elements are subject to more phonological processes than strong ones, indicating their greater vulnerability.

In Williamson's corpus of 450 reconstructed Proto-Ịjọ words, the vast majority of C2 and C3 consonants are either weaker than or of equal strength to the preceding consonant, i.e. $C1 \geqslant C2 \geqslant C3$. The figures in (15) show that the majority of combinations are stronger consonant–weaker consonant (61.1 percent):

(15)

C_{n-1}	C_n	N	%
S	S	19	01.5
S	M	15	06.0
S	W	78	30.9
M	S	07	02.8
M	M	39	15.5
M	W	61	24.2
W	S	04	01.6
W	M	09	03.6
W	W	20	07.9
		252	100.0

Key: n = position in word (1, 2 or 3)
N = number of combinations in corpus
S = strong; M = medium; W = weak

Unfortunately, a breakdown of words according to syllable number is not given, so we cannot be absolutely sure that the C_{n-1} in (15) is always stem initial. In addition, there are sometimes vowel prefixes before C1 and vowel suffix enclitics after C#. I assume, however, that most words are bisyllabic (of a subset of twenty-six given in Williamson's paper, only three are monosyllabic and two trisyllabic). Williamson's reconstructions and synchronic studies of the various Ịjọ dialects lead her to conclude that

> If a consonant weakens in C1 position, it will also weaken at C2 and C3; but a consonant can weaken at C2 or C3 without any corresponding change at C1. The result of this is that consonants at C2 and C3 will, over periods of time, be considerably more weakened than those at C1, as they are affected by more changes. (p. 14)

She speculates further that phonetics might provide us with an explanation for this tendency, in that 'more breath force is available to articulate earlier in an utterance and that therefore a greater variety of articulations is easier to produce at an earlier stage than at a later.' This explanation is not adequate, however, since it refers to whole *utterances* rather than individual words, and so predicts in fact that the ends of words at the beginning of utterances will be articulated more fully than the beginnings of words at the ends of utterances, which patently does not inform our quest for an explanation of the data. The answer, I contend, lies in the demand of the *hearer* for clarity of expression, at least at the *beginnings* of words.

Recall that in the psycholinguistic account of the suffixing preference offered in C, H & G a crucial assumption is that lexical processing operates on-line from left to right according to some model such as that expounded by Marslen-Wilson and Tyler (e.g. 1980). This processing model, independently of any consideration of morphological processing or structure, provides a rather transparent explanation of the resistance of word beginnings to any processes which result in a diminishing of their phonological integrity: the processor is assumed to access lexical entries by receiving only enough acoustic information necessary to distinguish the word from all others in the mental lexicon. Hence, less redundancy word initially will result in more optimally efficient processing, by cutting down the size of word initial 'cohorts' (to use Marslen-Wilson's term), that is, the set of words which match the initial stretch of the input word (its left to right acoustic neighbors), and which are therefore competing candidates, at that point, for recognition.[7]

The observations cited above from the phonological level about the strength of word-initial position have been made independently from consideration of morpho-phonological processes leading to the reduction of lexical items and their fusion with others as affixes. When placed in the context of fusion, however, the independently attested robustness of word beginnings as opposed to endings is confirmed, at least in English. Consider, for example, the following pairs of stem/stem + suffix in English: *catholic/catholicism*, *democrat/democracy*, *cycle/cyclist*, *usher/usherette*, *predict/prediction*. All involve alternation at the end of the stem, whereas in the following *prefixed* forms, the *prefix* alternates, and the stem beginning remains constant: *illegitimate/inhospitable/ irregular*, *compassion/condense/colloquium/correspond*, *entitle/ empower*, *subdivide/suffix/suspect*. As far as I am aware, counterexamples to this trend, that is, prefixes which provoke assimilation in the stem, are very rare (the only examples I can think of are of stem-initial /s/ → /z/, for example *resume* (cf. *consume*), etc., and these are only with bound stems). Assimilation is not the only weakening process that occurs at word endings upon suffixation: consonant loss, in order to maintain preferred syllable structure, is also attested, for example in Korean (cf. Hyman 1975: 162):

(16) /əps # ta/ → [əp + ta] 'there is no'
/nəks # to/ → [nək + to] 'the soul also'
/anč # kəra/ → [an + kəra] 'sit!'

This maintenance of the stem-initial position in prefixed words is a natural consequence of the predominance of progressive over regressive assimilation processes in language, which reflects the drive toward anticipatory economy in the articulation of spoken language. The asymmetry between progressive and regressive assimilatory processes is matched by a cross-linguistic asymmetry in the reduction of unstressed vowels: those in initial syllables do not reduce to the extent that those in final syllables do.

So the effect on affixation of the asymmetries in these natural phonological processes is that prefixes tend not to promote modification of the stem, whereas suffixes typically do induce stem alternations. Consequently, in the ongoing diachronic process of isolation, prefixed words typically become lexicalized (that is, reanalyzed as monomorphemes) more slowly than suffixed words, since the integrity of the stem is maintained in the former but not in the latter. In Bybee and Brewer's (1980) terms, suffixed forms will tend towards a greater degree of 'autonomy' (that is, representation as a single, independent unit in a speaker's lexicon) than will prefixed forms, at least on the morphophonemic opacity measure of this notion. If we recall, also, that prefixes are themselves the admittedly decimated remains of formerly independent lexical items, we can see that *their* initial portions will also resist reduction, and in so doing will constitute unwanted, phonologically redundant material before the stem, whereas this same material will be incorporated into the stem in suffixation. This interplay between (i) the asymmetry of natural non-morphophonemic processes of phonological change stemming from economy of articulation in rapid speech and (ii) the reduction and fusion processes whereby free lexical items become bound to either a left-hand or right-hand neighbor, results in a processing preference for suffixes over prefixes, at least as far as accessing of lexical *form* in the stem-based lexicon is concerned.

In the next section we shall address the problem from the point of view of semantic content, and see how the process of *semantic* reduction or generalization tempers the phonological processes of fusion discussed above. It will be argued, again, that psychological factors of comprehension and production underlie the types of diachronic change observed, and that all these factors again conspire in the direction of suffixation rather than prefixation.

5.2 Semantic redundancy

It is the differential degree of semantic content in pairs of words subject to fusion which determines which one of them reduces and becomes bound on the other. The item which reduces phonologically is the member of the pair which is communicatively the less important because (i) it is relatively 'empty' of semantic content (Greenberg (1957) notes that the Chinese refer to affixes as 'empty words'); and (ii) what content it retains is relatively redundant and predictable in context. We have already observed that it seems to be heads which becomes affixes on elements which modify them in the syntax. Why should this be so? Givón claims that 'in the combination NOUN:MODIFIER NOUN and VERB:COMPLEMENT VERB, the head of the construction is the *more generic* semantic item, it is the *classifier*, the *type marker*. While the modifier or complement is the *more specific* item, the classified.' He offers as examples (i) the English noun *kingdom* where -*dom* (= 'domain' < OE *dom* = 'fate, destiny' (OED)) is head of an NP which is modified by a sentential phrase 'the king rules NP'; (ii) the verb *purify* where -*fy* (= 'make' < Fr -*fier* < Lt *facere* = 'make' (OED)) is head of a VP with sentential complement 'NP be pure'. It seems incorrect to call the head a 'classifier' and the modifier the 'classified'; however, the terminology used is a (presumably inadvertent) red herring on Givón's part: he simply misleads us by using the terms in a way opposite to conventional usage. As the examples show, he is, in fact, employing a standard semantic notion of head, where the classifier is the more specific item which picks out a subset of the set specified by the type-marker (the head) (cf. Jespersen 1924: 96): a *kingdom* picks out a subset of the set of places (*domains*), so *king* classifies (in this standard sense) the type of domain; *purify* picks out from the set of processes by which some object X is changed from state A to state B (X_A is *made* X_B), the particular process of making *pure* – the process (*make*) is classified by the particular end result (the classifier *pure*). It is not at all clear that we can equate here the syntactic and semantic notions of head (cf. Zwicky 1985 and Hall 1987, ch. 2, for discussion of the problems involved here), although it is clear that there is a significant overlap between them. In any case, it is not necesary to claim that it is *always* the syntactic head which reduces; however, it is probably typically the case, since the syntactic head *is* the more general in a head/modifier relationship.

That semantic reduction is accompanied by and actually is a prerequisite for phonological reduction is well attested. Zirmunskij (1966: 83) states, for instance, that

> The grammaticalization of the word combination is connected with a greater or lesser weakening of the lexical meaning of one of its components, its consistent transformation from a lexically meaningful ... word into a semi-relational or relational word, and the transformation of a whole group of words as an entity into a grammatical form of the word.

The 'grammaticalization' referred to here is the reduction of two lexical items into a single morphologically complex item consisting of stem + inflectional/derivational affix. Zirmunskij claims that this morphophonological reduction is a consequence of the *semantic* reduction of one of the original free items. This word loses its 'lexical meaningfulness' and becomes 'relational' or 'semi-relational'. Examples of such semantic reduction from a wide variety of language families are documented in Kahr (1976) and Bybee and Pagliuca (1985). In the latter, for instance, they discuss the generalization of habitual or continuous aspect markers into imperfective markers with consequently extended ranges of meaning (cf. Comrie 1976), and show that this correlates with the degree of fusion of the morphemes with the verb stems to which they are bound. In the Perkins sample (cf. note 2) they found that stem changes conditioned by the imperfective marker significantly outnumbered those conditioned by habitual or continuous markers.

Perhaps one specific example from English will serve to illustrate more concretely the type of semantic generalization process which renders a free lexical item susceptible to phonological reduction. One of the main sources for verbal morphology is the auxiliary verb (as noted by Givón, who, as we have seen, attempts to construct a controversial theory of word order evolution from this one observation). The original source of these auxiliaries is typically a full lexical verb with quite restricted and specific meaning. For instance, the future auxiliaries in English, German, Old Church Slavonic, Modern Greek, Romanian, Arabic, Somali and Tagalog have developed from verbs of volition (Ultan 1978), and desiderative markers in Siberian and Sierra Miwok have developed future tense readings (Bybee and Pagliuca 1985). Bybee and Pagliuca chronicle in detail the development of the English verb *have* from full lexical possessive verb to past tense auxiliary and modal of obligation and prediction (pp. 71ff). The original meaning (OED) was 'to hold in hand'; this generalized as follows, they argue, by means of metaphorical extension:

(17) a. 'to hold in one's hand' →
      b. 'to have in one's immediate personal possession (physically present)' →
      c. 'to have or own as a possession (not physically present)' →
      d. 'to have as an abstract possession, such as time, an idea, an education, a debt'

The possibility of 'having' an abstract NP object allows even further abstraction and consequent generalization, so that the next stages of development are:

(18) a. 'to have (in a very general sense) a non-completed activity' (expressed by an infinitive verb), i.e. still having it to do (obligation, necessity)
      b. 'to have a completed activity' (expressed by a past participle), i.e. recently done

The modal meaning in (18a) is then further extended/generalized from uniquely 'agent-oriented' modality, involving a willful agent, to an epistemic sense of prediction. In (19) following, (a) is an example of the former, and (b) of the latter:

(19) a. John has to do the washing up (because it's his turn).
      b. John has to be home by now (because he set off over an hour ago).

The possibility of reduction of the auxiliary *have* to bound morpheme status can be seen in the contractions -*s*, -*ve* used in ordinary speech:

(20) a. The children've come home for Christmas.
     b. The author's written at least twenty books.

Hand in hand with this semantic generalization and loss of specific lexical meaning is a certain degree of redundancy and predictability, pointed out in the work of Kiparsky (1982), who notes two semantic motivations for the diachronic reduction of phonological form in morphemes:

(21) a. Morphological material which is predictable on the surface tends to be more susceptible to loss than morphological material which is not predictable on the surface. (p. 67)
     b. There is a tendency for semantically relevant information to be retained in surface structure. (p. 87)

This redundancy/predictability factor is most important in the consideration of the numerical asymmetry between prefixation and suffixation in the world's languages. Greenberg, noting the typical modification of the stem form in suffixation as opposed to prefixation, argues that

this results, from the point of view of information processing, in the reduction of the amount of information given by the suffix, since the choice of a particular root modification narrows down the choice of possible suffixes. This is typical for many suffixing languages, with their numerous and irregular declensional and conjugational classes. As the suffixes give less information, they in turn become largely superfluous and are reduced or lost, the difference in function now being carried by alternations of the root. (1957: 93)

In prefixation, as we have seen, fusion and isolation are likely to be much delayed, although Greenberg does point out that modification of the prefix *will* reduce the number of potential candidates for the following word. However, it is clear that the closed set of bound morphemes will be far more predictable than the open set of free stems, and so the semantic generalization and reduction of morphemes *following* the stem will lead to more predictability and redundancy, allowing, in consequence, a more forceful rationale for further phonological reduction, ultimately loss.

Hard psycholinguistic evidence for the redundancy of morphological information in post-stem position is yielded in recent experimentation by Tyler and Marslen-Wilson (1986). Using the gating method as a measure of the on-line point of lexical access, they demonstrate that subjects may predict suffixal morphology if the previous syntactic context is strong enough. So, for example, in the following sentences subjects were able to produce the '-ing' suffix on the verb CORRESPOND in (22) before they actually heard it, whereas their performance in sentences such as (23) was far more erratic:

(22) Peter and Janet were old friends. For many years they had been regularly CORRESPONDING/CORRESPONDENCE with each other.

(23) Alice was getting worried. The only news she had received was through CORRESPONDING/CORRESPONDENCE with her uncle.

Connecting all these strands together, we can extract the following account of the suffixing preference and how it could come about: As semantic information in lexical items becomes more general, less specific and hence more redundant, it succumbs to phonological attrition: in terms of Slobin's 'charges to language' (1977), the charge 'to be quick and easy', a speaker-oriented principle, instantiated in language through semantic and phonological reduction, is able to exert its influence without doing so at the expense of the charge 'to be clear', which is, conversely, hearer-oriented, and requires, therefore, that reduction in content and form not impinge too greatly on the efficacy of the hearer's comprehension mechanisms. Kiparsky suggests that the second of his two principles quoted above 'would appear to be motivated by the requirements of speech perception'; Ohlander (1976: 68) points out that the first principle 'can be regarded as the natural outcome of the clash between the two more fundamental principles of clarity and economy: the trend towards greater economy can be allowed only to an extent not threatening communicative function.'

The requirements made on language by the principle of clarity clearly militate against prefixation and in favor of suffixation, since in the former case access to the stem-based lexicon is disrupted by a morpheme which for a longer period than in suffixation resists complete fusion with the stem (due to the relative robustness of its initial elements) and is simultaneously 'rebuffed' by the stem (because of *its* maintenance of stem-initial position). In contrast, suffixes typically become more easily integrated phonologically with the stem, and as a consequence of this and the inherent semantic redundancy and predictability of affixes in both positions, do not constitute the same problem for the lexical processor.

6 Conclusion

The approach to linguistic explanation advanced here has as its goal the identification and explanation of regularities across significant numbers of languages, in the hopes of revealing important aspects of the fundamental nature of human language in the context of its actual manipulation by speakers, hearers and learners in a communicative setting. This approach differs, then, from both the dominant generative and universal-typological paradigms in linguistics by seeking to do more than specify the variation space of human language through parametrical or statistical description; this approach has as its primary goal the *explanation* of universal regularities or tendencies, where explanation is necessarily *external* to the descriptive theory within which the regularity is identified.

The approach adopted involves multidisciplinary investigation of linguistic phenomena. Of course, this type of research is not new. Stampe's Natural Phonology (e.g. 1973), Haiman's Natural Syntax (e.g. 1980, 1983) and Bresnan's Lexical Functional Grammar (e.g. 1982) are only a few examples of work done in this vein, and both Greenberg and Givón, whose investigations prompted in large part the writing of this paper, have championed this approach.

In taking the broader perspective it is possible to reveal the redundancy of many of the apparently independent principles advanced in the autonomous linguistic literature. In the present case I have shown how diachronic semantic and (morpho)phonological principles seem to be quite transparently derivable from processing and higher level communicative principles, whilst at the same time stressing the importance of identifying these surface reflexes of underlying principles in order to substantiate the dynamic explanation by tracking the link between explanans and explanandum.

In doing so, I hope to have gone some way towards identifying a 'strong' psychological constraint on language, as defined by Clark and Malt (1984) who propose four criteria for such constraints. These are (i) empirical grounding, (ii) structure independence, (iii) theoretical coherence and (iv) linkage. In the area of empirical grounding, all the facts are not yet in. C, H & G and Hawkins and Cutler this volume report a lot of suggestive evidence, but this must be followed up with more specific experimentation (a task which has been begun in Hall 1987) before we can be fully confident. However, the constraint on affixation advanced here *is* independent of the facts it seeks to explain, and is fully consistent with broader theoretical claims about language comprehension and diachronic change. A major purpose of this paper was to stress the importance of what Clark and Malt call 'linkage', the dynamic processes by which explanandum is linked to explanans, and it is this that constitutes the major development here on previous accounts of the suffixing preference. In particular, I have shown how the proposed processing motivation could actually be instantiated diachronically in a language, and in so doing I have also shown how the processing motivation is itself one part of a broader communicative rationale (i.e. the clarity/economy balance).

Given the enormous complexity of human language evolution and the many often conflicting pressures which influence it, it must be emphasized here that it would be unwise to claim categorically that the processing dispreference constitutes the exclusive factor underlying the observed regularity; it is quite feasible that other factors (such as those suggested by Bybee this volume and Kahr 1976) might contribute. It is, though, very likely, given the rationale expressed here, that an appeal to processing factors will take us a long way toward understanding the asymmetrical distribution of bound morphology in the languages of the world.

Notes

I am greatly indebted to the following who have contributed variously to the writing of this paper: Elaine Andersen, Pat Clancy, Jack Hawkins, Doug Pulleyblank, Gary Gilligan, Larry Hyman, Joan Bybee, Lolly Tyler, William Marslen-Wilson and Nigel Vincent. I am particularly grateful to Juan Galindo González for all his support.

1 We shall ignore the rare cases of discontinuous affixal morphemes such as (i) *intercalation*, e.g. in Semitic languages, where the value of the vowel slots of a word constitute a morpheme, and this is intercalated into a consonantal template which constitutes the stem; (ii) *ambifixing*, where the stem appears inside the affix – that is, elements of the affix precede and follow the stem; or (iii) *infixing*, where the affix appears inside the stem. The rarity of such structures has a ready psycholinguistic explanation, namely the processing dispreference for discontinuous elements (e.g. verbs and particles, sentences with center embedding, etc.) because of the necessity to pass over the first element without assigning an interpretation to it (and hence adding to memory load), or because the first element may be perceived as a complete entity, thus causing a 'garden path' analysis.

2 The corpus of 203 languages consists of three samples:
Leon Stassen (113 languages) recording for Ns: case, definiteness, indefiniteness; and for Vs: tense, aspect, person-marking, negation.
Revere Perkins (40 languages) recording only for Vs: tense, aspect, mood, person-marking, negation, voice, valence, causatives.
Gary Gilligan (50 languages) recording for Ns: case, gender, plural, possessive, definiteness, nominalizers; and for Vs: tense, aspect, mood, person-marking, negation, voice.

3 I take it that by this they mean that, within the grammatical functions observed, more are realized as suffixes than prefixes or infixes in the language sample taken as a whole.

4 Givón's original formulation (p. 401) of (6) and (7) confusingly labels the output of the reanalysis as 'np' rather than 'pp' (here pre- or postpositional phrase) and labels the postposition in (7) as 'prep'. I have corrected these labelings here.

5 According to Meillet (1958: 130–48) there is only one other source of affixation: 'innovations analogiques', or (cf. Bybee and Brewer 1980) *reanalysis*, whereby one affix is derived from another in the same grammatical paradigm. Presumably the 'basic' affix in the paradigm typically has its source in the reduction of a lexical morpheme. Back formation is another, much rarer type of reanalysis which occurs in derivational forms, in, for example, Eng. *peddler* where the pseudo-suffixal -*er*, an undifferentiated part of the stem, is reanalyzed as the agentive suffix.

6 Although the languages in the H & G corpus do maximally reflect the wide distribution of language families in the world, details of their genetic relations are not taken into account in this calculation, and so the quantification of languages here and in other parts of this paper can only give a rough approximation of actual genetic variation (it is possible, for example, that the seventy-six languages

appealed to here are all genetically related, although even if this were so (and it is most unlikely), they still as a body speak against the SOV/Mod-N claim).

7 The size of the word-initial cohort per se should not have an effect on word recognition point, since the determinant of isolation is the distribution of syntagmatic acoustic specifications rather than any paradigmatic quantification of alternative candidates; however, the probability of extended syntagmatic redundancy (and hence later recognition point) increases as the pool of candidates is enlarged. So, for example, although it is possible that a two-word initial cohort might lead to recognition at the *end* of the target word if the two only differ in, say, their final consonant, whereas a thirty-word cohort might be reduced to one after only the first CV sequence, it is clear that the greater the number of candidates, the more likely one or more of them is going to share acoustic features with the target for a longer stretch of the input string.

References

Bresnan, J. (1982) *The Mental Representation of Grammatical Relations.* Cambridge, Mass.: MIT Press.

Bybee, J. L. (this volume) 'The diachronic dimension in explanation'.

and M. A. Brewer (1980) 'Explanation in morphophonemics: changes in Provençal and preterite forms'. *Lingua*, 52, 201–42.

and W. Pagliuca (1985) 'Cross-linguistic comparison and the development of grammatical meaning'. In J. Fisiak (ed.), *Historical Semantics, Historical Word Formation.* The Hague: Mouton.

Chen, M. (1973) 'Cross-dialectal comparison: a case study and some theoretical considerations'. *J. Chinese Linguistics*, 1, 38–63.

Chomsky, N. (1965) *Aspects of the Theory of Syntax.* Cambridge, Mass.: MIT Press.

(1981) *Lectures on Government and Binding.* Dordrecht: Foris.

Clark, H. H. and B. C. Malt (1984) 'Psychological constraints on language: a commentary on Bresnan and Kaplan and on Givón', in W. Kintsch, J. R. Miller and P. G. Polson (eds), *Method and Tactics in Cognitive Science.* Hillsdale, NJ: Erlbaum.

Comrie, B. (1976) *Aspect.* Cambridge: Cambridge University Press.

(1981) *Language Universals and Linguistic Typology.* Chicago: University of Chicago Press, and Oxford: Basil Blackwell.

Cooper, W. E. and Paccia-Cooper, J. (1980) *Syntax and Speech.* Cambridge, Mass.: Harvard University Press.

Cutler, A., J. A. Hawkins and G. Gilligan (1985) [C, H & G] 'The suffixing preference: a processing explanation'. *Linguistics*, 23, 723–58.

Foley, J. (1977) *Foundations of Theoretical Phonology.* Cambridge: Cambridge University Press.

Givón, T. (1971a) 'On the verbal basis of the Bantu verb suffixes'. *Studies in African Linguistics*, 2.2, 145–63.

(1971b) 'Historical syntax and synchronic morphology: an archaeologist's field trip.' In *Papers from the 7th Regional Meeting of the Chicago Linguistic Society.* Chicago: CLS.

(1975) 'Serial verbs and syntactic change: Niger-Congo'. In C. Li (ed.), *Word Order and Word Order Change.* Austin, Tex.: University of Texas Press.

(1979) *On Understanding Grammar.* New York: Academic Press.

Greenberg, J. H. (1957) *Essays in Linguistics*. Chicago: University of Chicago Press.

—— (1966) 'Some universals of grammar with particular reference to the order of meaningful elements'. In J. H. Greenberg (ed.), *Universals of Language*. Cambridge, Mass.: MIT Press.

Haiman, J. (1980) 'The iconicity of grammar: isomorphism and motivation'. *Language*, 56, 515–40.

—— (1983) 'Iconic and economic motivation'. *Language*, 59, 781–819.

Hall, C. J. (1987) 'Language structure and explanation: a case from morphology'. Doctoral diss., University of Southern California.

Hawkins, J. A. (1983) *Word Order Universals*. New York: Academic Press.

—— (1988) 'On explaining some left–right asymmetries in syntactic and morphological universals'. In M. Hammond, E. Moravcsik and J. Wirth (eds), *Studies in Syntactic Typology*. Amsterdam: John Benjamins.

—— and A. Cutler (this volume) 'Psycholinguistic factors in morphological asymmetry'.

—— and G. Gilligan (1988) [H & G] 'Prefixing and suffixing universals in relation to basic word order'. In J. A. Hawkins and H. K. Holmback (eds) *Papers in Universal Grammar: Generative and Typological Approaches*, *Lingua* Special Issue, 74, 2/3.

Hooper, J. B. (1976) *Introduction to Natural Generative Phonology*. New York: Academic Press.

Hyman, L. M. (1975) *Phonology: Theory and Analysis*, New York: Holt, Rinehart and Winston.

Jespersen, O. (1924) *The Philosophy of Grammar*. London: Allen & Unwin.

Kahr, J. C. (1976) 'The renewal of case morphology: sources and constraints'. *Stanford Working Papers on Language Universals*, 20, 107–51.

Kiparsky, P. (1982) *Explanation in Phonology*. Dordrecht: Foris.

Maran, L. R. (1971) 'Burmese and Jinghpo: a study of tonal linguistic processes'. In F. K. Lehman (ed.), *Occasional Papers of the Wolfenden Society on Tibeto-Burman Linguistics*, vol. 4. Urbana, Ill.: University of Illinois.

Marslen-Wilson, W. D. (1983) 'Function and process in spoken word recognition'. In H. Bouma and D. Bouwhuis (eds), *Attention and Performance*, vol. 10. Hillsdale, NJ: Erlbaum.

—— and L. K. Tyler (1980) 'The temporal structure of spoken language understanding'. *Cognition*, 8, 1–71.

—— and A. Welsh (1978) 'Processing interactions and lexical access during word-recognition in continuous speech'. *Cognitive Psychology*, 10, 29–63.

Meillet, A. (1958) *Linguistique historique et linguistique générale*. Paris: Champion.

Ohlander, S. (1976) *Phonology, Meaning, Morphology. On the Role of Semantic and Morphological Criteria in Phonological Analysis*. Göteborg: Acta Universitatis Gothoburgensis.

Slobin, D. I. (1977) 'Language change in childhood and history'. In J. Macnamara (ed.), *Language Learning and Thought*. New York: Academic Press.

Stampe, D. (1973) 'A dissertation on natural phonology'. Doctoral diss., University of Chicago.

Tyler, L. K. and W. D. Marslen-Wilson (1986) 'The effects of context on the recognition of multi-morphemic words'. *J. Memory and Language*, 25.6, 741–52.

Ultan, R. (1978) 'The nature of future tenses'. In J. Greenberg et al. (eds), *Universals of Human Language* 3. Stanford, Calif.: Stanford University Press.

Vennemann, T. (1974) 'Topics, subjects and word order: from SXV to SVX via TVX'. In J. M. Anderson and C. Jones (eds), *Historical Linguistics* 1. Amsterdam: North Holland.

Williamson, K. (n.d.) 'Consonant distribution in Ịjọ'. Unpub. MS, University of Ibadan.

Zirmunskij, V. M. (1966) 'The word and its boundaries'. *J. Linguistics*, 27, 65–91.

Zwicky, A. (1985) 'Heads'. *J. Linguistics*, 21, 1–29.

CHAPTER 13

The Diachronic Dimension in Explanation

Joan L. Bybee

As a sign system that makes use primarily of symbols rather than icons, human language is underlaid by a large number of conventionalized elements and relations. These conventionalized aspects of language must be learned and are passed on from generation to generation with minimal alteration. The language user does exert some influence over these conventions, manipulating them for expressive purposes, but their apparent rigidity has attracted much attention and evoked the metaphor that language is a system, is governed by a set of rules, and so on. The sound–meaning correspondence of lexical items is a typical example of a conventional relation, as is the set of formal and semantic relations that constitute inflectional morphology. Some aspects of grammar are subject to varying degrees of conventionalization. For instance, word order and ellipsis may be freer at the sentence level but conventionalized at the level of discourse.

In principle, conventions may be of any sort, as long as they are understood by all relevant parties. One property of conventions that has been commented on particularly with regard to language is that they may be partially or wholly arbitrary. Of course, conventions are not by necessity arbitrary, but in language it appears that they are largely so, as evidenced by the fact that each language has its own set of arbitrary pairings of meaning and sound. This observation was made by Saussure, and the framework that grew up from the acceptance of this notion predicts that the similarities among languages are due entirely to the way linguistic systems are structured – for example, the existence of contrast, of complementary distribution, of phrase structure rules and transformations, or whatever structural devices one wants to propose – while the content of these structures is arbitrary. However, the steady flow of research on empirically based language universals over the last thirty years has revealed that language or grammar is not as arbitrary as the structuralist program would predict. Rather, many similarities obtain cross-linguistically which involve not just the structure of language, but also its substance.

The existence of similarities among languages that refer to the *substance* of grammar – categories and elements such as noun and verb, subject and object, singular and plural, constructions such as passive and causative, phonological processes such as palatalization and nasalization – all point to a much richer set of general principles governing language than one would expect of an arbitrary, conventional object. However, all of these elements are part of the *conventional* aspects of language. Their cross-linguistic similarity suggests that general principles govern the way in which conventions come to be established. This means that if we are to explain similarities across languages, then we must explain what factors govern the establishment of one set of grammatical conventions rather than another.

Greenberg (1957) made this point in outlining a new program for general linguistics, one that could deal with statements pertaining to all languages, by saying that whether a particular typological pattern was frequent or rare was 'the resultant of two factors, one of origin, the other of survival' (p. 89). This statement emphasizes that synchronic states must be understood in terms of the set of factors that create them. That is, we must look to the diachronic dimension to learn how the conventions of grammar arise if we are to know why they take the particular form that they do. Unfortunately, Greenberg's suggestion is not always followed: too often we find linguists stop short of this level of explanation, being instead satisfied with the formulation of general principles offering a summary of the cross-linguistic patterns without suggesting how they might come into existence. To see the place of diachronic considerations in the explanation of language universals, let us consider a typical strategy for progressing toward explanation, illustrated by work in word order studies.

1 Towards Explanation

Often the first step towards explanation in language universals research is the statement of an *empirical generalization*, such as those formulated by Greenberg (1963), on the basis of the examination of a large number of languages, for example:

> With overwhelmingly greater than chance frequency, languages with normal SOV order are postpositional.

Of course, such statements are descriptive only, and represent what needs to be explained.

The second step is to reach for a higher level of description by formulating a *principle* that ranges over several empirical generalizations. In formulating such principles, one must make some assumptions, which are theoretical in nature, about how and why the separate empirical generalizations are similar to one another. For instance, Greenberg noted that the orders of constituents in SOV and VSO languages were largely mirror images of one another, so that one could postulate some link or 'harmony' among co-occurring word orders. Vennemann (1973) suggested that this link may be found in the 'operator'–'operand' relation – that is, the linear order of modifier and modified elements is consistent in a language. Similarly, principles proposed by others, such as Hawkins (1979, 1983) and Dryer (1988), make use of this observation about grammatical relations between ordered constituents.

The formulation of such principles is an important step in theory building because it shows how a number of apparently diverse grammatical conventions are similar to one another. Many linguists seem content to have reached this stage in their theory building, because such general principles are capable of making predictions about new phenomena, for example the word orders in some language not yet studied. But it is important to point out, as Lass (1980) does, that prediction and explanation are in an asymmetrical relationship: the fact that we can predict some of the linear orders in a language if we know one does not necessarily mean that we can explain why these orders tend to correlate. On the other hand, if we can explain why the ordering of different constituents in a language tend to correlate, then we can also predict some ordering relations on the basis of others.

Vennemann (1972) proposes that an innate predisposition exists which allows the speaker/hearer to grasp the operator–operand relation and linearize pairs of elements in a consistent way in his or her language. Vennemann refers to this as an analogical process which can be represented as a single rule of linearization. Similarly, Hawkins argues that the explanation for his Cross-Category Harmony principle is that it allows the formulation of more consistent rules of ordering in a language and therefore results in a simpler grammar. These proposals are intended to answer the 'why' question.

My own intuitions about explanation are not satisfied by such principles, however, unless they provide answers to the 'how' question – how do such generalizations arise in language? What are the mechanisms that bring the state of affairs about? Perhaps seeking mechanisms or causes in language-specific synchronic studies may not be possible or interesting (Itkonen 1983), but in language universals causal factors are linguistic changes that create particular synchronic states, and the existence of massive cross-language similarity in synchronic states implies powerful parallels in linguistic change. Moreover, the identification of mechanisms that bring about synchronic states serves as a test of the principle formulated in that the validity of the principle as explanatory can only be maintained if it can be shown that the same principle that generalizes over the data also plays a role in the establishment of the conventions described by the generalization. In the current case, then, we would want to know how the analogical principles of harmony are manifested through linguistic changes.

Both Vennemann and Hawkins claim that the analogical principle (Vennemann's version is the Natural Serialization Principle, and Hawkins' the Cross-Category Harmony Principle) operates in linguistic change to create word order correlations. Hawkins puts it as follows: 'In the word order co-occurrence preferences defined by CCH [= Cross-Category Harmony], I see a strong internal motive for any language either to remain within, or to move toward, a preferred type' (p. 646). In fact, Hawkins quite explicitly claims that the existence of an implicational universal of the form 'if P, then Q' means that if a language develops a structure P, it implies the prior existence or simultaneous acquisition of Q. Of course, this follows logically, but it represents a prediction and not necessarily an explanation. The explanation must tell us what the relation is between P and Q and how the development of one influences the other. We still must seek the mechanism of change to see if these reveal a causal relationship between one structure and the other.

One might hope that the existence of the correlations is in itself proof enough that the orders of different constituents are related analogically. Unfortunately this is not so, since there are other possible explanations for at least some of the correlations. Consider the very strong correlation between the ordering of adpositions, as either prepositions or post-positions, and the ordering in a noun–genitive construction. One of the strongest correlations found by Greenberg (1963), confirmed in a larger sample by Hawkins, is stated in Greenberg's Universal 2:

In languages with prepositions, the genitive almost always follows the governing noun, while in languages with postpositions it almost always precedes.[1]

This correlation follows from both Vennemann's and Hawkins' principles, since the adposition in an adpositional phrase and the possessed noun in a genitive phrase are both the heads, or operands:

operand	*operator*
adposition	noun
noun	genitive

Now since the ordering in phrases such as these is usually fixed in a given language, that is, highly conventionalized, it is necessary to ask how these orders came to be fixed in such a way that these correlations obtain. That is, does the ordering in an adpositional phrase exert some influence over the ordering in a genitive phrase (or vice versa) and if so how is this manifested in the development of such constructions? To answer these questions, we must ask how these constructions arise in languages, and when we do, we see at least two types of strong relations between adpositional phrases and genitive phrases.

First, it often happens that adpositions develop out of genitive phrases (Greenberg 1963: 99; Vennemann 1973: 32). For instance, prepositional phrases in English such as *inside the house* and *outside the house* derive from the use of the nouns *inside* and *outside* in genitive constructions, that is, *inside of the house* and *outside of the house*. The preposition *of* is now optionally deleted, making *inside* and *outside* prepositions. Similar developments may be observed in other languages (for instance, Abkhaz, Basque, Bihari, Buriat and Kui) where a genitive marker remains in adpositional phrases. Consider the following example from Buriat (Poppe 1960).

> ger-ei   xazuu-da
> house-poss side-loc
> 'at the side of the house; by the house'

Note that in Buriat the order in a genitive phrase is GN, so the resulting adposition will be a postposition, unlike English, where the adpositions are prepositions. Thus if a language that has a productive order NG produces new adpositions through the genitive construction, it will produce prepositions, while a language with a productive order GN will produce postpositions.

Interestingly enough, we can find causality moving in the opposite direction as well. A frequent source of the genitive marker is an adposition, as in English where the more recently developed genitive *of* is a preposition. Given that the genitive marker appears between N and G if it is an adposition, a language with prepositions will development a new genitive construction in the order NG, while a language with postpositions will develop a new genitive with the order GN.

Both of these frequent diachronic developments contribute heavily to the correlation of adpositional and genitive phrase orders.[2] Yet in neither case do we find analogy in the form of rule simplification playing a role. One grammatical order is not established on analogy with or to harmonize with another order, rather a new grammatical construction develops in a language out of constructions that already exist and shows ordering consistent with the construction from which it developed.

Considering these diachronic sources for the correlation raises a whole new sheaf of questions, and impels us to ask how and why one construction is formed out of another. Ultimately, we are brought back to the synchronic plane where we must ask what cognitive processes are behind the development of genitive markers from other types of adpositions, and what motivates the development of new adpositional phrases from nouns in genitive constructions. Thus, having consulted the diachronic domain, we find that the questions we want to ask are very different from the ones we were considering when only synchronic cross-linguistic generalizations were being considered.

This example is meant to illustrate what I consider to be the necessary third step following the formulation of a *principle*: testing the principle to see if it can be shown to be actually involved in the diachronic processes that lead to the states described by the principle. I have given two examples that show developments leading to states describable by a principle that are the result of processes that are independent of the principle. This evidence does not falsify the principle, but it does diminish its explanatory power. I would suggest that further work on universals of word order take into account to a greater extent how the correlating structures develop historically if the goal of such work is the explanation of language universals.

2 Principles as Constraints on Change

Principles of the type we have just been discussing (that is, Cross-Category Harmony or Natural Serialization), which define syntactic typologies, have also been invoked as constraints on possible diachronic changes. For instance, Hawkins (1979, 1983) discusses this possibility: 'All languages in their evolution are constrained by implicational universals such as have been defined, and can change only relative to the co-occurrence possibilities which these permit' (Hawkins 1979: 647). That is, implicational universals may be used to predict linguistic change in the sense of setting the upper limits of such changes. However, such constraints cannot be invoked as explanations unless the mechanism by which the universals constrain change can be explicated.[3]

An unfortunate tendency exists nevertheless to invoke typological facts as *explanations* for particular historical changes. A very specific case is found in Fleischman (1982), where she discusses the question of why the Romance future formed from the Infinitive plus postposed *habeo* underwent fusion to produce a synthetic construction, while the Perfect from preposed *habeo* plus Past Participle did not fuse. She says that since *habeo* has person/number suffixes, fusion of preposed *habeo* would result in internal person/number inflection:

> With preposed *habeo*, fusion would have (a) phonetically reduced or obliterated altogether the person-number information, which was carried by the final syllable of *habe-o*, *-es*, *-et*, etc., and (b) created the anomalous situation, for languages such as Latin and its off-shoots, of having prefixed or infixed inflections. (p. 115)

Fleischman presumably believes that it is normal for the fusion of grammatical morphemes with stems to take place in the position in which they develop, unless otherwise blocked. The possibility of preventing the loss of information is often invoked as an explanatory factor in change, but this cannot be a very powerful force, if it is a force at all, since language change does in fact in so many instances bring about the loss of morphological information. The other potential preventive is more interesting in the present context, since it is an appeal to typological principles. Not only would it be anomalous for Latin and her daughters to have person/number markers closer to the verb stem than a tense/aspect marker, it is an extremely rare situation in any of the world's languages (although it does occur, for example in Athapaskan languages, such as Navaho Bybee 1985b). But this typological fact cannot explain why affixation did not occur in this particular case, for it is certainly not possible for the speakers who were tending toward this change to test out the results, compare them with existing typologies and decide against the change. Moreover, this type of 'explanation' has the relationship between diachrony and universals reversed. Since the order of grammatical morphemes, and particularly affixes, is a matter of convention, we must look to the manner in which such orders are established to explain cross-linguistic patterns. We cannot use cross-linguistic patterns to explain why a particular change is or is not implemented.[4]

Now consider a similar example from Comrie (1980). Comrie considers the problem of the development of subject agreement suffixes in an SOV language, where the pronouns from which they evolved could occur either before or after the verb. However, only the pronouns that occurred after the verb were affixed, not the preposed pronouns. Among the three potential explanations Comrie suggests is the following:

> Since the languages in question are already exclusively or over-whelmingly suffixing, preference is given, in deriving affixes, to that word order which produces further suffixes rather than introducing prefixes, i.e. in accordance with the existing patterns of the language.

This statement implies that speakers in some sense 'decide' on suffixes rather than prefixes, as more appropriate for their language. This would mean that the typology of a language is manifested in individual grammars in such a way that it may come into play during the creation of new structures. Is this what Sapir calls 'the structural "genius' of the language' (Sapir 1921: 120)? It may be, but exactly what it is, how it is manifested in the grammar and how it functions in language change has not been investigated.

Again I would argue that we must seek instead causal mechanisms. In this case, Comrie actually offers two other potential explanations which are causal in nature, given the assumption that grammatical material tends to reduce and fuse. The first is that the pronouns in postposed position are unstressed, while the pronouns that occur before the verb are stressed. Thus, as Comrie observes, the postposed pronouns are more likely to reduce and fuse. The second factor is that only the postposed pronouns are consistently adjacent to the verb. The subject pronouns in initial position are separated from the verb by an object or other complement in many cases. Both of these factors point to the greater likelihood of fusion for the postposed pronouns. Both contribute to the causal mechanism; neither refers to the resulting state.

These cases illustrate that typologists are well aware of the fact that cross-linguistic generalizations must be considered together with linguistic change, but they are not always consistent about the proposed relationship between the two. Causal and non-causal explanations are often invoked indiscriminately. My suggestion is that complete explanations must specify a causal mechanism; thus we cannot explain change with reference to preferred types, but we must explain common types by referring to the factors that create them.

3 Identifying Causal Mechanisms

Most of the attempts at explaining grammatical phenomena that are frequent cross-linguistically proceed by identifying certain factors that show the phenomena in question to be beneficial from the language user's point of view. These might be called synchronic explanations; they are explanations based on processing ease, on iconicity, on cognitive or semantic factors, or on typical discourse structure. In order for these factors to qualify as explanations, a causal connection between the factor and the grammatical phenomenon must be demonstrated: that is, it must be shown that the factor appealed to as explanation actually contributes to the creation of the particular grammatical convention. Let us consider several cases to see what this would entail.

3.1 *Processing*

Consider first a processing explanation proposed by Cutler, Hawkins and Gilligan (1985) for the greater frequency cross-linguistically of suffixes over prefixes. They cite psycholinguistic evidence that the beginnings of words are more salient than the ends, and that stems are processed before affixes. They propose the following: 'the stem favors the most salient beginning position of the word, and the affix the less salient end position, because in the compositional process of determining the entire meaning of a word from its parts, the stem has computational priority over the affix' (p. 748). As Hall (this volume) points out, this may well be true, but it does not qualify as an explanation until it can be shown that the computational process referred to actually contributes to the formation of suffixes, or impedes the formation of prefixes. It must be remembered that the actual process of forming affixes begins gradually as lexical material reduces and grammaticizes. This fact creates two problems for the proposed principle. First, since affixes can be demonstrated to begin as stems, this principle would seem to predict that affixes cannot develop at all, since their development entails the reduction of a stem. Second, grammatical morphemes (hereafter, *grams*) are usually fixed in their position long before they actually fuse with a noun or verb. Thus it is important to ask whether non-bound grams also tend towards postposing, and if so whether the processing principle described above contributes to this positioning. Another possibility is that postposed material tends to fuse more often than preposed material. In this case, the processing principle might act as a retardant to fusion, which is in itself a primarily phonological process. Alternatively, preposed grams may more often be separated from their semantic hosts by other lexical material (as in the case cited above from Comrie 1980), which prevents their fusion. If this is so, then processing order has nothing to do with affix order. The viability of a processing principle as an explanation depends upon a complete understanding of the factors involved in the creation of grammatical structures, and a demonstration that processing ease is one of those factors.

3.2 *Iconicity*

With the recent interest in universals and non-arbitrariness in grammar has come the suggestion that some grammatical and lexical structures are iconic. Haiman (1983) proposes the 'distance principle';[5]

> The linguistic distance between expressions corresponds to the conceptual distance between them.

The 'linguistic distance' has to do with expression units which range from most distant to least distant as follows:

> two separate words with the possibility of intervening material;
> two separate words, but always contiguous;
> a stem and affix;
> a single lexical unit.

Haiman proposes several ways of viewing conceptual distance. We will only consider one, that is, 'two concepts are close to the extent that they are perceived as inseparable' (p. 783). This principle makes very specific predictions with regard to the structure of causatives. To state the prediction informally: if a language has more than one way to express causation and these differ in their 'linguistic distance' or degree of fusion, 'then the conceptual distance between cause and result will correspond to the formal distance between cause and result' (p. 783).

This may be illustrated with the well-known 'kill' vs. 'cause to die' examples from English. The lexical expression of causative implies very strongly that the cause and result take place at the same time and place, with possible physical contact, while the periphrastic expression implies the opposite. Consider the following pairs that Haiman offers as examples:

(1) I caused the tree to fall.
    I felled the tree.

(2) I caused the chicken to die.
    I killed the chicken.

(3) I caused the cup to rise to my lips.
    I raised the cup to my lips.

Examples similar to these, as well as examples illustrating causatives that appear in other expression types, may be cited from many different languages.

Haiman's principle of distance in this manifestation is very similar to the 'relevance' principle that I propose in Bybee (1985a) and (1985b). My hypothesis is that the degree of fusion of grammatical material with lexical depends upon the semantic relevance of the grammatical morpheme to the lexical: the extent to which the grammatical meaning directly affects or modifies the semantic content of the lexical morpheme. With this principle even finer degrees of fusion or 'distance' between linguistic units, such as the ordering of affixes, the existence of allomorphy, irregularity, stem change and suppletion may be predicted.

As general principles concerning the relation of meaning to form, these principles are far-reaching and seem to grasp some essential quality in the structure of language. However, despite making correct predictions, they do not qualify as explanations. They certainly tell us what to expect in the expression of particular notions, but to the extent that these principles deal with conventionalized structures, such as affixes or lexical items, they would need also to explain how these structures become conventionalized, and in that respect these principles fail to be explanatory. Haiman does not claim that iconicity provides an 'explanation' for the structures he discusses; he prefers instead to use the term 'iconic motivation'. I argue in Bybee (1985a) and (1985b) that we need evidence that semantic relevance (or distance in Haiman's terms) actually influences the diachronic process of fusion that leads to the formation of affixes.

This argument is made in the following way: Two elements may become fused if they occur next to one another frequently. This means that at a stage in which the positioning of these elements is not yet conventionalized, if speakers nevertheless place them together very frequently, they are likely to become fused. The motivation for placing them together in the speech stream may very well be their semantic closeness to one another. If this is so, then the proposed principle, when coupled with other principles in a general theory of affix formation, may be said to be explanatory.

The argument might also be made that lexicalization, which is the formation of new autonomous lexical items, is influenced by relevance. Thus if two elements together form a semantic complex that can be taken to be unitary and discrete from other semantic complexes, the two elements might together comprise a single lexical item. Questions of categorization patterns in the lexicon relate to the general psychological issue of how categories are formed and structured (Berlin and Kay 1969; Rosch 1978). Research in this area indicates that the nature of linguistic categories depends a great deal upon how we perceive reality. If this is so, then it is not clear that the phenomenon actually belongs in the domain of iconicity.

Thus until we understand better the way that fusion occurs, how affixes are formed and what factors encourage or impede their formation, how new lexical items are formed and become autonomous, we cannot demonstrate that the relevance or distance principles are explanatory.

3.3 Economy

In the same article, Haiman (1983) also discusses 'economic motivation' which is the principle that the 'simplicity' of words or expressions is an index of their familiarity or frequency. He cites Zipf's 'principle of least effort' (Zipf 1935) which is intended to explain why the more frequently used words of a language tend to be shorter than the less frequently used words. He also cites work by Givón and Bolinger which suggests that the more familiar, predictable information is signalled in shorter units than the less familiar, less predictable information.

Haiman's discussion is largely ahistorical so no mechanism is proposed to explain why the more familiar or frequent expressions are generally shorter. Of course, where speakers have a choice – for instance, in how many lexical items to include in a phrase or clause – they are probably motivated by economy. However, in the conventional aspects of language, the speaker is limited by the established elements. If pronouns are shorter than full nouns, if auxiliary verbs are shorter than main verbs, if 'horse' is shorter than 'elephant', the speaker must use them all the same. So what is it that motivates the economy in grammar? The choice of the phrase 'economic motivation' suggests that familiar words grow shorter *in order to* make familiar conversation more economic. But this does not tell us what the mechanism behind the principle is.[6]

While one might expect that research into the implementation of such an obvious question would have progressed quite far, unfortunately the role of frequency of use in conditioning phonological change has been neglected while structural factors in change have received primary attention. However, the casual observation that frequent words and phrases undergo reductive change at a faster rate than infrequent ones (Schuchardt 1885) has been documented by numerous examples in the work of Mańczak (Mańczak 1978), and by comparison of frequency counts with differential reduction by Fidelholtz (1975), Hooper (1976) and Pagliuca (1976). If frequent words undergo phonetic reduction at a faster rate than infrequent ones, then Zipf's correlation is created. The question, then, is what *causes* reductive sound change to progress more quickly in frequent words? If reductive and assimilatory sound change is caused by a sort of physical economy of articulation, why isn't that economic motivation equally applicable in infrequent words and phrases? In the end we must admit that the 'principle of least effort' labels a correlation or at best describes the outcome of change, it does not provide an explanation for the facts of phonetic reduction.

3.4 *Discourse*

Discourse-based explanations for grammatical phenomena typically do involve a diachronoic dimension and do identify a causal mechanism, thus coming closer than the other principles we have discussed to constituting valid explanations. The structure of such explanations is as follows: A certain configuration of syntagmatic, grammatical or semantic elements is shown to be frequently occurring in discourse, due to the way that information flow is typically structured. These frequently chosen patterns, it is argued, become rigidified or frozen into syntactic rules in some languages. Thus what is optimal discourse structure in one language is grammatical rule in another.

A good example of this sort of explanation is found in Du Bois (1985), which treats the discourse basis of ergativity. Du Bois finds that natural discourse in Sacapultec is structured such that a clause, whether it be transitive or intransitive, rarely contains more than one full noun phrase.[7] In the intransitive clause this one noun phrase is the subject, while in the transitive clause it is the object. The subject of the transitive verb occurs very rarely in discourse. Du Bois argues that this strong discourse tendency gives rise to the 'absolutive' case – it is the case of the noun phrase most frequently occurring in discourse. The rare case – that of the subject of the transitive verb – is a category apart, that is, the ergative case.[8] Du Bois argues further that the 'preferred argument structure' derives from the general preferred information flow of Sacapultec discourse, in which new protagonists are introduced by intransitive (usually motion) verbs and thereafter referred to only by agreement morphology. Only the objects of the verbs to which they are agents receive full noun phrase coding.

The causal factor of this type of explanation is frequency in discourse. The mechanisms that must be understood are discourse structuring and the process of grammaticization, whereby a frequent grammatical structure changes from being preferred in a certain context, to being obligatory.[9] At our present state of knowledge, then, discourse explanations seem to involve fewer unknown factors than processing factors, iconicity or economy.

4 Diachrony in Explanation: the Semantics of Futurity

4.1 *The phenomenon*

In this section we take up an explanation for a much observed language 'universal' in which diachrony plays a very important role. The phenomenon in question is a largely semantic one, which makes it appear somewhat different from the universals involving structure which we have been discussing. However, I will argue in the conclusion that the role of diachrony is similar in all these cases.

The phenomenon in question is the strong tendency for morphemes whose primary function is to signal future time reference to also express, directly or as secondary meanings, various modality senses. This tendency has been observed for specific languages, and cross-linguistically by Fries (1927), Ultan (1978), Fleischman (1982), Chung and Timberlake (1985), Dahl (1985) and undoubtedly many others. Most of these authors have assumed some cross-linguistic similarity among what are called 'Future' morphemes in the languages of the world, but this cross-linguistic similarity has been made more precise in the study of Dahl (1985). Dahl reports on the results of a questionnaire survey of sixty-four languages, in which native informants translated more than two hundred sentences designed to cover the major uses of tense and aspect morphemes in the languages of the world. Dahl measured the overlap in the uses of tense and aspect morphemes and postulated a small number of prototypical cross-linguistic categories. A category he labeled FUTURE was one of the most common of these. The uses of this category are defined by the sentences in the questionnaire that most commonly took future marking in the languages of the sample. One very common use of future morphemes in his data is the prediction use: specifically, in sentences in which the speaker is making a prediction about future time, as in Dahl's number (36):

(4) [It's no use trying to swim in the lake tomorrow]
     The water BE COLD (then).[10]

This use probably represents what most linguists would identify as the 'pure' future sense, without modal overtones. This prediction sense is, according to the analysis done by Coates (1983) on both spoken and written corpora of British English, the most common use of the three future markers of English, *will*, *shall* and *be going to*, as illustrated by these examples, some of which come from the corpora studied by Coates and some from that used by Wekker (1976):

(5) I think the bulk of this year's students *will* go into industry. (Coates 1983: 170)

(6) I've given him sedation and he'*ll* be all right for a bit. His beauty *will* be permanently spoiled, but I don't suppose it was ever very much. (Wekker 1976: 61)

(7) We *shall* no doubt live to see stranger things. (Wekker 1976: 44).

(8) (in reference to taking 'just water') Otherwise I *shall* end up like the song The Seven Drunken Knights. (Coates 1983: 186)

(9) Within a few years at the present rate of development, Paris *is going to* look like London, and London like New York. (Wekker 1976: 125)

(10) I think there'*s going to* be a storm. (Coates 1983: 201)

It is important to note that future morphemes in clauses that are not predictions, but do make future time references, are not nearly as common, and in fact, in some cases are not grammatical. Thus in English, *will* does not occur in *when* clauses, even where the clause refers to future time:

(11) When you (*will) see him, give him this message.

(Cf. Dahl's questionnaire, where only seven out of forty-seven languages with future markers use a future in *when* clauses.)

Another extremely common use of morphemes labeled as futures occurs in cases where either prediction (by the speaker) or intention (of the subject of the clause), or both, are signaled, as in the second clause of the following examples from Dahl's questionnaire:

(12) [Said by a young man]
When I GROW old, I BUY a big house.

(13) [The boy is expecting a sum of money.]
When the boy GET the money, he BUY a present for the girl.

These two examples received the highest number of future markings in the languages of Dahl's sample. (Forty-two out of forty-seven languages use the future in these examples.) Note that in (12) with *will* in English ('When I grow old, I'll buy a big house') the most salient interpretation is that this is a statement of the speaker's intentions, and not a simple prediction. The example (13) with *will* ('When the boy gets the money, he'll buy a present for the girl') could be interpreted as a prediction made by the speaker, or as a statement of the subject's intentions. The intention uses of futures, then, represent one case of the oft-cited overlap of future with modal senses.

The data on other modal senses of futures is often more impressionistic. The cross-linguistic survey conducted by Ultan (1978) and the diachronic survey of Fleischman (1982) suggest the following non-temporal uses of future morphemes, some of which are also non-modal: desire, intention, obligation, necessity, habitual, general truth, characteristic behavior, imperative, optative, hortative and supposition.[11] Some of these senses are more closely related to one another than others are. I propose to break them down in the following way, in order to discuss them in groups:

Desire, intention, obligation and necessity are called agent-oriented modalities because they predicate certain conditions on an animate, usually human, agent. (*Desire* in this case does not refer to expressions of the speaker's desire; that is referred to as *optative*.) The corresponding expressions in English would be *want to*, *is going to* and *have got to*, as in the following examples.

(14) She wants to practice her Spanish with you. (*desire*)

(15) She's gonna apply to the graduate school. (*intention*)

(16) She's gotta help her mother on Saturday. (*obligation*)

(17) I gotta get eight hours of sleep or I'm wrecked. (*necessity*)

Obligation and necessity are very closely related: obligation is socially imposed while necessity is physically imposed.

Habitual, general truth and characteristic behavior can be regarded neither as tense nor as modality notions. They are related to each other, however, since they all signal that the same situation holds on different occasions. Examples of future morphemes used in this way are:

(18) Boys will be boys.

(19) Whatever you say to him, he will not answer.

Imperative, polite request, optative and hortative are related in that their function is to get the addressee to do something. They can be regarded as marking a speech act of a certain type, one which either imposes an obligation on the addressee or expresses the speaker's wishes.

Supposition is the term used by Ultan and Fleischman for expressing the epistemic notion of probability. A future marker is sometimes used for stating propositions that are probably true in the present, for example:

(20) *English* (on hearing the phone ring)
That'll be John now.

(21) *Spanish*
Tendrá veinte años.　　She is probably twenty years old.
have – future twenty years

Since future markers fulfilling these same non-tense functions may be found in unrelated languages, some general and non-specific explanation must be sought. Some authors have informally proposed *principles* which attempt to 'explain' the overlap of future and modal semantics by referring to the uncertainty of future events. Consider Ultan's statement:

> The reason for the preponderance of modal applications of future tenses must lie in the fact that most modal categories refer to differing degrees of uncertainty, which correlates with the element of uncertainty inherent in any future event, while past tenses generally refer to completed, hence, certain, events. (pp. 105–6)

Chung and Timberlake hold a very similar view, as seen in the following:

> Situations in the future are inherently uncertain as to actuality. Any future event is potential rather than actual. . . . The future is thus a semantic category where tense and mood merge. (p. 243)

Both of these statements associate future with epistemic modalities of possibility and probability, by noting that the future is uncertain. The problem with this view is that it is too simplistic to say that the past is certain and the future uncertain. Some events in the future are quite certain (for example, 'The sun will rise in the east tomorrow'), while some events in the past may be uncertain in the sense of being unknown and even unknowable (for example 'All human languages developed from a common proto-language'). Moreover, natural languages provide us with various means of expressing uncertainty about the past and present in the form of evidentials or epistemic modals such as *may* and *might* (for example, 'I might have left that book at the office').

Another problem with the view that futures are associated with modalities because the future is inherently uncertain is that many of the non-tense uses of futures do not imply uncertainty at all. The characteristic behavior or general truths use of English *will*, as in 'Water will boil at 100 degrees centigrade', does not give a sense of uncertainty, nor in fact does the prediction sense, illustrated in (5)–(10), where the interpretation is that the speaker actually believes that the event will take place. To see that this is so, consider the same sentences with a better indicator of uncertainty, such as *may* or *might*, in them rather than the future morpheme.

While the statements of Ultan and Chung and Timberlake associate future with epistemic modality, the following statement by Dahl 1985 attempts to associate futurity with the agent-oriented modalities of intention and obligation, as well as with the epistemic modalities:

> Normally, when we talk about the future, we are either talking about someone's plans, intentions or obligations, or we are making a prediction or extrapolation from the present state of the world. As a direct consequence, a sentence which refers to the future will almost

always differ modally from a sentence with non-future time reference. This is the reason why the distinction between tense and mood
becomes blurred when it comes to the future. (p. 103)

While Dahl associates future with a wider range of modalities, his
statement, like the others, does not explain how or why future morphemes
acquire modal uses. Moreover, none of these statements is able to
correctly predict *which* modalities will be associated with future tense.

4.2 *Diachronic lexical sources*

One suggestion (as outlined in Bybee and Pagliuca 1987) is that the
semantics associated with futurity may be accounted for in a general
theory of the development of grammatical morphology.[12] Grammatical
morphemes (henceforth, grams) develop from lexical material, either
single lexical items, such as the Old English verbs *willan* or *sceal*, or
polymorphemic sequences such as *be going to*. We propose that the
original lexical semantics, in conjunction with very general principles of
change, determines the course of development, and that there are certain
universal paths for the development of grams. The evidence for this is the
fact that in many unrelated languages the lexical sources for grams are the
same or very similar. In the case of futures three very common sources are:

  1 *Desire*: an auxiliary verb with an original meaning of 'want' or
'desire', or less commonly a derivational desiderative morpheme, which in
turn has as its source a main verb meaning 'want' or 'desire'.[13]

  2 *Movement towards a goal*: a verb meaning 'movement towards a goal'
or a movement verb in construction with an allative adposition such as *to*,
or less commonly a derivational andative morpheme, which has as its
source a verb meaning 'movement towards a goal'.[14]

  3 *Obligation*: a verb meaning 'to owe' or 'to be obliged', or more
commonly a construction with a copula or possession verb and a non-
finite main verb, such as English *to have to*, or *to be to*.[15]

With their original meanings, these constructions have very specific
semantics, which in each case requires a human, or at least an animate
agent. Their development into future grams requires a loss of some
specific semantic features, which allows an extension to contexts in which
the agent is not human or animate.

Since these three distinct semantic complexes all eventually develop
into expressions of future time reference, their paths must converge at
some point. Our study of the history of *will*, *shall* and *be going to* in
English (which represent the three most common sources of futures)
reveals that the convergence of paths of development begins early as each
of these constructions is used to state the intentions of a first person
subject. *Shall* is frequently used during the Old English period in its
original meaning to express obligation, and also to state an intention by the
speaker. Consider the following example from *Beowulf*.

(22) Ic þæm godan *sceal*, for his mod-thræce, madmas beodan. (Beowulf, line 384)
I shall offer the good (man) treasures for his daring.

Similarly, *will*, which is not frequent in Old English, becomes more
frequent in Middle English and is used both in its original meaning of
'want' and to express the speaker's intention. Consider these examples
from *Sir Gawain and the Green Knight*.

(23) I *wyl* nauther grete ne grone. (line 2157)
I will neither cry nor groan.

(24) Now *wyl* I of hor seruise say yow no more.... (line 130)
Now I will tell you no more of their service.

Be going to is much more recently developed as an expression of intention
or future, dating from the seventeenth century (Scheffer 1975). One of its
current uses is the expression of intention, as in the following examples
from the corpora examined by Coates (1983: 199).

(25) Listen, my dear, I asked you to marry me, didn't I?
And *I'm going to* do my very best to make you happy.

(26) We're not *going to* let you walk home on your own.

These examples show that grams from all three lexical sources develop
a use which expresses the speaker's intention before they progress to the
point of expressing prediction or future time reference. But the convergence at this point is only partial: for while they may all express
intention, they each have other uses that are not shared, uses associated
with their lexical meaning. In addition, there may be different implications
in the expression of intention. An intention may have an external
motivation, in a social obligation or physical necessity, or it may originate
internally in the goals and desires of the agent. Although it is difficult to
know exactly how to interpret *shall* and *will* in the older texts, there may
be, along with the expression of intention, a flavor of obligation for *shall*
and desire for *will* retained from their original lexical senses. Consider the
following example from *Sir Gawain*, where *shall* and *will* are juxtaposed
in the same sentence:

(27) And I *schal* erly ryse, on hunting *wyl* I wende. (lines 1101–2)

If the choice of *shall* and *will* is not random, then it may be that their
positions in this sentence are governed by the expression of obligation and
desire respectively. That is, the speaker *wants to* go hunting, and
consequently he *has to* get up early. (In this context, hunting is a sport, not
a necessity.)

Grams that are used to express intentions are not necessarily future markers. As mentioned above, the defining use of a 'future' is to make a prediction in a future temporal frame. A prediction is a type of assertion made by the speaker, in which the future marking has propositional scope. A prediction will be free of agent-oriented meaning, such as obligation, intention or desire. A marker of prediction can be used in a sentence with a non-animate subject.[16] As illustrated above in sentences (5)–(10), the Modern (British) English *shall*, *will* and *be going to* all qualify as 'futures', since they may all be used in predictions about future situations. Since the Middle English period, then, these future grams have continued to develop by losing more and more of their original lexical meaning, expanding their scope to include the whole proposition and extending to clauses that have inanimate subjects.

Despite the fact that both *shall* and *will* have undergone a long history of development and have reached the stage of expressing prediction, they both retain some remnants of their original lexical meaning in specific contexts. For instance, in the following examples, *will* expresses the willingness of the agent. Willingness is not as strong as desire, but it is related to desire in that it refers to an internally motivated disposition.

(28) Give them the name of someone who *will* sign for it and take it in if you are not home. (Coates 1983: 171)

(29) If he *will* meet us there, it will save a lot of time.

In negative sentences, *won't* often has the sense of 'is unwilling to' or 'refuses to'.

(30) He *won't* eat meat, even if it's offered to him.

Shall can be found in the somewhat archaic expression of obligation in decrees and laws (Coates 1983), but in colloquial British English it is restricted to the first person, where it is used to state intentions, make predictions (see examples above) and in questions to ask the addressee's will.

(31) *Shall* I ring at 11 p.m. one night (English time) in the week after you get back? (Coates 1983: 186)

We argue in Bybee and Pagliuca (1987) that this use is a direct descendant of the obligation sense of *shall*, since it does not speak of internal motivation, but asks for external motivation. Note that *will* is inappropriate in such a sentence, since *will* there could only be interpreted as 'do you predict that I ...' or 'do I want to ...' Note further that in the history of English *shall* does not develop any readings related to desire, and *will* does not develop any readings related to obligation.[17]

4.3 *Universal paths*

Since the same three lexical sources for future grams appear in so many unrelated languages, and since the product of their semantic development is so similar cross-linguistically (see Dahl 1985), it seems safe to assume that the paths of development for future grams are universal. If this is so, then the 'explanation' for the existence of desire, obligation and intention readings for futures is diachronic: desire and obligations are older meanings 'glimmering through' (as Fries 1927 puts it), and intention is a use that predates the development of the pure prediction use, but remains after prediction develops. This theory is also specific about the possible combinations of modal nuances that may co-exist in a particular gram. That is, a future gram may express obligation, intention and prediction, or desire, intention and prediction, but not desire and obligation, since the latter two imply two distinct lexical sources.[18]

Before discussing the other non-temporal uses of future grams, let us consider the nature of the explanation just offered. We have identified what might be called an 'immediate cause' for the existence of readings related to obligation, desire and intention in future grams. Furthermore, by postulating that paths of development for futures are universal, we are able to predict linguistic changes as well as the synchronic range of uses for future grams.

Identifying an immediate cause is necessary to ensure that the search for explanation is on the right track, but it is not the end of the process. Rather, behind the immediate causes are a further set of more general and more interesting questions. In particular it is known that the type of semantic change found in grammaticalization is not restricted to future grams, but can be found in the development of all grammatical morphemes (Givón 1979, Lehmann 1982, Traugott 1982, Heine and Reh 1984, Bybee and Pagliuca 1985). Such change is characterized by three interrelated processes:

1 The gradual loss of specific components of meaning in some contexts, such as the loss of the desire sense of *will*.

2 The generalization of meaning or function with the result that the gram may appear in more contexts. This process is tied closely to the loss of specific meanings, since more specific meanings usually imply more co-occurrence restrictions, for example if *will* means 'desire' it may only occur with an animate agent. If it loses this sense, then it may appear in contexts with inanimate agents as well. Such generalization of function corresponds to an increase in text frequency.

3 Often, grams developing from auxiliary verbs increase their scope from verb phrase scope, which the agent-oriented senses of desire, obligation and intention have, to propositional scope, as found in the prediction sense of futures (for other examples see Bybee and Pagliuca 1985 and Traugott 1982).

These general principles of change can predict a large part of the course of development of futures, as well as that of other grams, such as pasts, perfectives, imperfectives, demonstratives, definite and indefinite articles, and so on. However, these principles are themselves in need of explanation. Why do certain lexical items undergo these related semantic changes and develop grammatical characteristics? To answer this question we are drawn back to the synchronic plane to investigate the way language is used. This part of the investigation has not been undertaken thoroughly as yet, so I will only make a few speculative remarks on some possible directions such an investigation might take.

First it should be observed that there are certain functions that language is called on to perform quite commonly. For instance, linguists who study narrative propose that nearly every sentence of a narrative can be assigned to the foreground of the narrative or to the background (Hopper 1982). For our purposes, spoken face-to-face interaction is more relevant, and here we would hypothesize that the expression of intentions and the making of predictions are very common functions. Some support for this hypothesis comes from Coates (1983), who gives a tally of the frequency of 'modal meanings' (that is, meanings expressed by modal verbs in English) in her corpora of both spoken and written British English. Her figures show indeed that prediction is the most frequently expressed of these 'modal meanings', and that intention is also very frequent, compared to other meanings. That does not imply, of course, that a language must express these functions with grammatical markers. In fact, many languages express these functions with an unmarked verb form. It does mean, however, that linguistic material expressing intention or prediction could have a very generalized range of use.[19]

A second factor is the well-known tendency for people to 'speak as though', that is, to use language metaphorically rather than literally. For instance, Fleischman (1982: 59) comments on the use of *have to* in English to state an intention as though it were born of an obligation, even though it is not:

(32) What are you doing tonight? Oh, I have to go to a party.
      Later today? I have to go jogging at six . . .

Such uses generalize the function of the phrase *have to* and weaken its obligation sense. Another relevant instance of this phenomenon is the use of modal verbs with inanimate objects:

(33) This door doesn't want to open.

A third tendency instrumental in the semantic changes accompanying grammaticization is the tendency to take what one may usually infer from the meaning of an expression to be its actual meaning. Neither *have to* nor *want to* (taken as examples because they are semantically similar to the lexical sources of *shall* and *will*) literally express intention, yet if I say I want to do something, or I have to do something, and it is within my powers to do it, the hearer will infer that I intend to. Since in most cases this inference will be correct, it can become an obligatory inference of the phrase, and as the desire and obligation components weaken, it can become the main function signaled. Similarly, the relation between intention and prediction depends upon inference. Since there is a fairly high level of agreement between our stated intentions and acts carried out, one can usually take a stated intention as predictive.

I would suggest then that function, metaphor and inference are the synchronic phenomena that need to be investigated in order to understand the overlap of modality with future meaning. We reached this conclusion by first identifying the causal mechanisms that bring about the overlap of modal and future meanings. Note that the direction of the investigation is quite different than it would had been if we had tried to investigate the 'uncertainty' of the future more directly. In fact, I would claim, such an enterprise would not have been fruitful at all.

4.4 Probability

Let us turn our attention now to the use of futures to express the epistemic modality of supposition or probability. The particular sense of probability that futures express is a probability about a situation existing at the moment of speech, in other words, in present time. For example:

(34) *English*:
A commotion in the hall ... 'That *will* be Celia', said Janet. (Coates 1983: 177)

(35) *Spanish*:
Ya tú comprenderás cómo nos reímos. 'Now you probably understand (future) how much we laughed.' (Moreno de Alba 1970)

Judging from Dahl's questionnaire data, this is not an extremely common use of futures. It occurs in seven of his forty-seven languages with futures (15 percent). Of these, four are Indo-European languages, and the other three are each from different families.

This use is semantically very close to the prediction use of futures. It does in fact constitute a prediction, but not a prediction about future time, rather a prediction about the present in cases where direct evidence is not available. Besides this semantic relation, there are two indicators that this use develops out of the prediction use of futures. First, it does not seem to be specific to any one lexical source of futures, since it occurs with a desire-derived future in English (as in the example above) and in Greek, with the obligation-derived future in Spanish (again see above) and Italian, and with the future derived from *ir a* 'to go to' in Spanish (Moreno de Alba 1970, no example provided) and a movement-future in Sotho. Second, it appears to be a relatively late development, compared to the development of intention and prediction. This use of *will* in English is documented by the OED from the fifteenth century, while the intention and prediction uses begin in Old English. In the Mexican Spanish corpus studied by Moreno de Alba, the older synthetic future was found in this use in three times as many cases as the newer periphrastic go-future.

4.5 *Imperative*

In some languages the future and the imperative (or optative or hortative) have the same form, or the gram used for future is also used for imperative (for example, in Atchin, Alyawarra, Danish, Maidu, Motu, Nimboran and Yagaria). Thus it could be said that this is another case of mood or modality overlapping with future. These particular mood functions for futures are all directive speech act indicators: an imperative is a speech act by which the speaker assigns an obligation to the addressee. An optative is an expression of the speaker's wish or will, while with a hortative the speaker urges the addressee to action. The use of futures in optatives and hortatives is not so easy to verify, and may involve the use of an additional morpheme along with the future. Let us concentrate on the use of future grams in imperatives.

While philosophers often associate imperative with the deontic modality of obligation, an important distinction must be made for our purposes. The agent-oriented modality of obligation (for example, *must* or *should*) states that an obligation applies to the agent in the clause.

(36) The students must get the permission of the instructor before registering for this course.

An imperative marker, on the other hand, has the whole proposition in its scope, and signals that the speaker is performing a certain type of speech act. The use of the future for direct commands is easy to verify in English (*You will go to bed!*) and in other languages, but this type of imperative is usually secondary, and not the primary means of commanding. Such a use constitutes an indirect speech act, that is, a prediction is made in the second person, which has the force of an imperative, given the social context and intonation. This type of imperative use of the future should be derivable from any of the lexical sources of future, since it is an adaptation of the prediction sense. Another potential source is specific to obligation-derived futures. An imperative gram may derive from the second person of an agent-oriented obligation marker, such as *must* in *You must go to bed*. This path of development is documented in Tamil and Malayalam (Subrahmanyan 1971). If the same obligation marker in other persons developed into a future, then a situation would be created in which a future is used in the imperative. I know of no such documented cases, however.

4.6 *Characteristic behavior*

The aspectual functions attributed to future grams are listed by Ultan as gnomic or general truth, and customary or habitual event. A closer examination of the actual cases, however, reveals that the term 'characteristic behavior' (as used by Fleischman 1982) is a better description and covers both of the categories that Ultan seeks to establish. Gnomic or general truth statements that involve permanent states do not use the future (at least not in English):

(37)   Elephants have long trunks.
(38)   *Elephants will have long trunks.

Rather the type of timeless statements that take the future involve a change of state, or a characteristic behavior.

(39)   The arctic hare will turn white in winter.
(40)   Water will boil at 100 degrees centigrade.

The alleged cases of the future used to mark habitual action also fit better under the rubric of 'characteristic behavior'. For instance in Hausa, the movement-derived future *za* is sometimes used in statements such as the following (Kraft and Kraft 1973):

(41)   Hausa
       (Some men can really tell a tale)
       ai wani sa'ì zā sù fi   mātā   à wurimmù
       well some time fut 3pl surpass women for us
       Even sometimes they'll surpass the women.

Note that the sentence has a non-specific subject. A true habitual could be used with a specific agent.

The relationship between future and characteristic behavior once again has to do with prediction or predictability, and we argued in Bybee and Pagliuca (1987) that this use is an extension of the prediction use. This hypothesis is supported by Dahl's data, which show an exceptionless implicational relation between characteristic behavior and prediction uses. All the languages with characteristic behavior uses in his sample also have prediction uses (16 out of 47), but languages with prediction uses to not necessarily have characteristic behavior uses, in fact 23 out of 47 do not. Moreover, futures from any source may have the characteristic behavior reading: the English and Persian desire-derived future has such a use, as does the Spanish obligation-derived future (Moreno de Alba 1970), and the Hausa and Hindi movement-derived future.

4.7 *Explanation*

In this brief survey I have not discussed all the uses ever attributed to
future grams, but I have covered the ones that are most frequently
mentioned, and the ones that are verifiable across languages. As we
argued in Bybee and Pagliuca 1987, it is possible to show, on the basis of
data from a wide range of languages, that certain uses or semantic nuances
are retentions from the original lexical meaning of a future, while others
develop out of the prediction sense and may appear in futures of any
lexical source. Consider the following diagram that plots the most
commonly occurring paths for the development of the semantics of future:

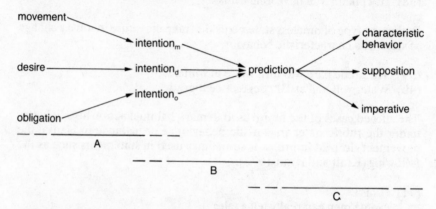

A, B and C are arbitrarily chosen synchronic states. The range of use of a
future gram at any stage, such as A, B or C, is partially determined by the
history of that gram. The history of a gram follows certain general
characterizable processes of change, that is loss of specific lexical meaning
in most contexts with retention in some contexts, loss of co-occurrence
restrictions, increase in frequency and a shift to propositional scope.

This theory is explanatory in a number of respects. It explains why it is
often difficult to find a single abstract meaning to characterize all of the
uses of a grammatical morpheme. It attributes the cross-linguistic similarity of grammatical meaning to similar paths of development, and general
principles of historical development; it explains cross-linguistic differences in the meaning of grams with reference to differences in lexical
source or differences in the extent of development undergone by particular grams. It predicts possible combinations of uses for language-specific
grams. It allows the reconstruction of the lexical source of grams on the
basis of their meaning. Finally, it points to a certain set of dynamic
processes in synchrony that have to be studied further to explain the
nature of grammatical meaning.

The implications of the futures case for explanations of language
universals is that formulating broad principles to cover cross-linguistic

generalizations, such as 'the future is uncertain, thus future tense and modality overlap', does not necessarily lead our investigation in the appropriate direction. However, identifying causal factors helps us to uncover the relevant set of diachronic and synchronic phenomena that will lead to richer and richer explanations. The relation of synchronic generalizations to diachronic processes is the same for the case of the semantics of future morphemes as it is for the more structural phenomena discussed in the first two sections. In each case, if we can identify the factors involved in the establishment of the grammatical conventions, then we can approach a valid explanation. Thus to understand how the ordering of adpositions relates to the ordering of noun and genitive, we must look into how such orders are established when new adpositions arise and when new possessive constructions arise. To find out why suffixes are more common than prefixes, we must refer to the fact that the position of a new affix is determined by the position of that same element before it becomes an affix, and ask what determines its position originally. If we wish to explain why some pairs of elements (such as verb and causative) are more fused than others, we must understand the fusion process itself and what governs it. To understand why frequent words are shorter than infrequent ones, we must investigate how frequent words reduce. To understand case marking patterns, we must investigate how case markers arise, as well as how nouns in different grammatical roles are used in discourse.

I have argued, then, that in order to reach valid explanations for language universals it is necessary to attend to the causal mechanisms operational in the establishment of grammatical conventions, and find the general dynamic principles behind the causal mechanisms. This view requires that explanation – that is, linguistic theory – have both a diachronic dimension and a synchronic dimension. The diachronic dimension plots paths of development of grammatical phenomena across time, and the synchronic dimension fills in the small steps along these paths by referring to the way in which language users manipulate the linguistic conventions they have inherited for their conceptual and communicative purposes.

Notes

I am grateful for comments and suggestions on earlier versions of this paper to the following, none of whom necessarily agrees with all my conclusions: John Corcoran, Julie Gerhardt, Jack Hawkins, Jürgen Klausenburger, William Pagliuca and Revere Perkins. Some of the data used here is from the GRAMCATS sample of eighty languages, constructed by Revere Perkins, with data analyzed by Perkins, William Pagliuca and Roula Svorou. Work on the GRAMCATS project is supported by NSF grant #BNS 8318262. This support is gratefully acknowledged, as is the support of the Netherlands Institute of Advanced Study during the 1983-4 academic year.

1 Since Hawkins (1979, 1983) reformulates the universals to be exceptionless, his statement of this correlation is somewhat different.

2 Adpositional phrases also develop from VO constructions, especially in languages with verb serialization (Givón 1975). In a VO language these constructions will become prepositional, while in an OV language they will be postpositional. Adpositions also develop from adverbs which come to take an object; the factors governing the position of this object have not been investigated, but the placement of the object might be determined on the basis of the VO order, in which case the analogical principle might be involved.

3 There is a use of the notion 'possible state' in historical linguistics that is legitimate, but this is in reconstruction. It is considered justifiable only to reconstruct language states that correspond to documented types.

4 Fleischman does not say exactly what she means by fusion in this case. Apparently she has in mind the fact that the postposed auxiliary is written bound and the preposed one is not.

5 This is a case of diagrammatic iconicity, in which the relation between two elements on the level of meaning is paralleled by the relation of the elements representing them on the level of expression.

6 The mechanism that Zipf proposes for the shortening of frequent words is 'clipping', the process that gives us *fridge*, *lab*, *auto*, etc. Historical documentation shows that clipping is an extremely restricted process which applies only to lexical morphemes (and probably only to nouns), and that the real mechanism behind the shortening of frequent words is phonetic reduction.

7 William Pagliuca (personal communication) points out that this 'typical' information flow is also a matter of cultural convention, pushing back our attempts at explanation one step further.

8 The tendency of the absolutive case to be unmarked, while the ergative is marked, follows from the fact that a marker will arise only in cases where the role of the noun phrase is not the usual one. Thus the following statement by Du Bois is unnecessary: 'a redundancy avoidance principle is best served when the one zero morpheme available in the paradigm is "assigned" to agree with the syntactic category which will in any case be represented by a full noun phrase: the absolutive' (pp. 352-3).

9 Of course many grammatical 'rules' are not categorical, but rather have an extremely high probability of application. Still there is a mechanism that continues to increase the frequency of a structure until it becomes an almost categorical choice.

10 In Dahl's questionnaire the examples were given in English, but the verbs occurred without English inflections in order not to bias the choice of tense and aspect in the translation. I am grateful to Östen Dahl for making available to me his data on the use of future morphemes in each of the forty-seven languages that had them.

11 Omitted from this list are *types* of futures, such as immediate future (or imminence) vs. remote future.

12 Meillet 1948, Givón 1979, Traugott 1982, Lehmann 1982, Heine and Reh 1984.

13 A few languages which have desire-derived futures are English, Central Sierra Miwok, Serbo-Croatian, Mandarin, Chukchi, Modern Greek and Swahili.

14 Movement-derived futures seem to be the most common. A few languages in which they are attested are Southern Sierra Miwok, Haitian Creole, Isthmus Zapotec, Logbara, English, Hausa. See Ultan (1978), Heine and Reh (1984) and Bybee and Pagliuca (1987) for more examples.

15 Obligation-derived futures seem to be the least common cross-linguistically. The only examples we have found of a verb meaning 'to owe' that becomes a future are the Germanic cognates of *shall*. Futures derived with copulas or possession verbs which originally have obligation senses may be found in the Eastern Kru languages, the Western Romance languages and Korean.

16 In Modern British English, *shall* occurs only with first person subjects in spoken discourse.

17 In Bybee and Pagliuca (1987) we also discuss the meaning of *be going to* in terms of its historical source. Remnants of the original lexical semantics of *will* are evident in the way children use *will*, especially as opposed to *be going to*, in negotiatory contexts (Gee and Savasir 1985).

18 Comrie (1985) is too quick to reject the diachronic when he says: 'Finally, one might observe that expressions of future time reference frequently derive diachronically from modal expressions, e.g., of desiderativity, such as English *will*. However, this diachronic relation says nothing of the synchronic status of such forms' (pp. 45–6).

19 A generalized function leads to higher frequency. Frequency plays an important role in grammaticization as it appears to be linked both to the rapid phonological reduction of grams and to their semantic reduction.

References

Berlin, B. and Kay, P. (1969) *Basic Color Terms: Their Universality and Evolution*. Berkeley, Calif.: University of California Press.

Bybee, J. L. (1985a) 'Diagrammatic iconicity in stem-inflection relations'. In J. Haiman (ed.), *Iconicity in Syntax*. Amsterdam: John Benjamins.

(1985b) *Morphology: A Study of the Relation between Meaning and Form*. Amsterdam: John Benjamins.

and Pagliuca, W. (1985) 'Cross-linguistic comparison and the development of grammatical meaning'. In J. Fisiak (ed.), *Historical Semantics and Historical Word Formation*. The Hague: Mouton.

(1987) 'The evolution of future meaning'. In *Papers from the VIIth International Conference on Historical Linguistics*, ed. by A. G. Ramat, O. Carruba and G. Bernini. Amsterdam: John Benjamins.

Chung, S. and Timberlake, A. (1985) 'Tense, aspect and mood'. In T. Shopen (ed.), *Language Typology and Syntactic Description*, vol. 3. Cambridge: Cambridge University Press.

Coates, J. (1983) *The Semantics of Modal Auxiliaries*. London: Croom Helm.

Comrie, B. (1980) 'Morphology and word order reconstruction: problems and prospects'. In J. Fisiak (ed.), *Historical Morphology*. The Hague: Mouton.

(1985) *Tense*. Cambridge: Cambridge University Press.

Cutler, A., J. A. Hawkins and G. Gilligan (1985) 'The suffixing preference: a processing explanation'. *Linguistics*, 23, 723–58.

Dahl, Ö. (1985) *Tense and Aspect Systems*. Oxford: Basil Blackwell.

Dryer, M. S. (1988) 'Universals of negative position'. In M. Hammond, E. Moravcsik and J. Wirth (eds), *Studies in Syntactic Typology*. Amsterdam: John Benjamins.

Du Bois, J. W. (1985) 'Competing motivations'. In J. Haiman (ed.), *Iconicity in Syntax*. Amsterdam: John Benjamins.

Fidelholtz, J. L. (1975) 'Word frequency and vowel reduction in English'. *Proceedings of the Chicago Linguistic Society*, vol. 11.

Fleischman, S. (1982) *The Future in Thought and Language*. Cambridge: Cambridge University Press.

Fries, C. C. (1927) 'The expression of the future'. *Language*, 3, 87–95.

Gee, J. and I. Savasir (1985) 'On the use of WILL and GONNA: towards a description of activity types for child language'. *Discourse Processes*, 8, 143–75.

Givón, T. (1975) 'Serial verbs and syntactic change: Niger-Congo'. In C. Li (ed.), *Word Order and Word Order Change*. Austin, Tex.: University of Texas Press.

(1979) *On Understanding Grammar*. New York: Academic Press.

Greenberg, J. H. (1957) 'Order of affixing: a study in general linguistics'. In J. H. Greenberg (ed.), *Essays in Linguistics*. Chicago: University of Chicago Press.

(1963) 'Some universals of grammar with particular reference to the order of meaningful elements'. In J. H. Greenberg (ed.), *Universals of Language*. Cambridge, Mass.: MIT Press.

Haiman, J. (1983) 'Iconic and economic motivation'. *Language*, 59, 781–819.

Hall, C. J. (this volume) 'Integrating diachronic and processing principles in explaining the suffixing preference'.

Hawkins, J. A. (1979) 'Implicational universals as predictors of word order change'. *Language*, 55, 618–48.

(1983) *Word Order Universals*. New York: Academic Press.

Heine, B. and M. Reh (1984) *Grammaticalization and Reanalysis in African Languages*. Hamburg: Helmut Buske.

Hooper, J. B. (1976) 'Word frequency in lexical diffusion and the source of morphophonological change'. In W. Christie (ed.), *Current Progress in Historical Linguistics*. Amsterdam: North-Holland.

Hopper, P. J. (ed.) (1982) *Tense-Aspect: Between Semantics and Pragmatics*. Amsterdam: John Benjamins.

Itkonen, E. (1983) *Causality in Linguistic Theory*. London: Croom Helm.

Kraft, C. H. and M. G. Kraft (1973) *Introductory Hausa*. Berkeley, Calif.: University of California Press.

Lass, R. (1980) *On Explaining Language Change*. Cambridge: Cambridge University Press.

Lehmann, C. (1982) *Thoughts on Grammaticalization*. Cologne: Arbeiten des Kölner Universalien Projekts, 48.

Mańczak, W. (1978) 'Irregular sound change due to frequency in German'. In J. Fisiak (ed.), *Recent Developments in Historical Phonology*. The Hague: Mouton.

Meillet, A. (1948) 'L'évolution des formes grammaticales'. In A. Meillet (ed.), *Linguistique Historique et Linguistique Générale*. Paris: Champion.

Moreno de Alba, J. G. (1970) 'Vitalidad del futuro del indicativo en la norma culta del español hablado en México'. *Anuario de Letras*, 8, 81–102.

Pagliuca, W. (1976) 'PRE-fixing'. MS, SUNY at Buffalo.

Poppe, N. N. (1960). *Buriat Grammar*. Indiana University Publications in Uralic and Altaic Series, vol. 21. Bloomington, Ind.: Indiana University, and The Hague: Mouton.

Rosch, E. (1978) 'Principles of categorization'. In E. Rosch and B. B. Lloyd (eds), *Cognition and Categorization*. Hillsdale, NJ: Erlbaum.

Sapir, E. (1921) *Language*. New York: Harcourt, Brace & World.

Scheffer, J. (1975) *The Progressive in English*. Amsterdam: North Holland.

Schuchardt, H. (1885) [1972]. 'On sound laws: against the Neogrammarians'. In T. Vennemann and T. H. Wilbur (eds), *Schuchardt, The Neogrammarians and the Transformational Theory of Phonological Change*. Frankfurt-am-Main: Athenäum Verlag.

Subrahmanyan, P. S. (1971) *Dravidian Verb Morphology*. Tamilnadu: Annamalai University.

Traugott, E. C. (1982) 'From propositional to textual and expressive meanings: some semantic-pragmatic aspects of grammaticalization'. In W. Lehmann and Y. Malkiel (eds), *Perspectives on Historical Linguistics*. Amsterdam: John Benjamins.

Ultan, R. (1978) 'The nature of future tenses'. In J. H. Greenberg, C. A. Ferguson and E. A. Moravcsik (eds), *Universals of Human Language*, vol. 3. Stanford, Calif.: Stanford University Press.

Vennemann, T. (1972) 'Analogy in generative grammar: the origin of word order'. Paper presented at the 11th International Congress of Linguists, Bologna.

Vennemann, T. (1973) 'Explanation in syntax'. In J. Kimball (ed.), *Syntax and Semantics 2*. New York: Academic Press.

Wekker, H. C. (1976) *The Expression of Future Time in Contemporary British English*. Amsterdam: North Holland.

Zipf, G. K. (1935) *The Psycho-Biology of Language*. Boston, Mass.: Houghton Mifflin.

SUBJECT INDEX

absolute constructions, 150
absolute universals, 4
absolutive case marking, 115, 195–8,
    199, 361, 376
Accessibility Hierarchy, 10
accusative case marking, 116–17,
    200–1
  Accusative Anaphor Condition, 135
  Accusative Extensions Condition,
    135
acquisition, 6–8, 33–4, 41, 45, 58, 60,
    138–9, 152, 157, 262
  see also computational models of
    language acquisition; Criteria
    Approach; discovery procedures;
    errors; innateness; learnability;
    motherese; negative evidence;
    Piagetian approach; positive
    evidence; Subset Principle;
    weighted hypotheses
adjectives, 8–9, 10, 167–81, 331–2
adpositions, see prepositions/
    postpositions
adverbs (and adverbial clauses), 10,
    150
adversative conjunctions, 145–6,
    148–9, 151
affixes, 116, 146, 164, 202–3, 287,
    301–5, 308–9, 324–5
  derivational, 289–90, 294, 303, 305
  historical origins of, 310–11,
    326–34
  inflectional, 289–90, 294, 301–3,
    305, 355
  ordering of relative to other affixes,
    220, 356

see also Head Ordering Principle;
    infixing; order of computation;
    prefixing; suffixing
agreement, 121–2, 126, 200, 287, 356
  see also Meaning–Form
    Dependency Principle
ambiguity, 10, 110, 116, 119–200
  see also temporary ambiguity
anaphora, 105, 128–39, 174, 176–7,
    179, 186–91, 201, 206, 220, 248
  acquisition of anaphora, 138–9
  essential anaphors, 134–6, 138–9
  long-distance anaphora, 136–7
  syntactically complex anaphors,
    136–7
  see also Binding Theory;
    reciprocals; reflexive pronouns
animacy, 117, 229, 231
  see also Chain of Being
apes, see primates
argument categories, 9–10
articulatory mechanisms, 212–16
aspect, 362
  affixes, 287–8, 292–3
asyndetic clause linking, 150
auditory mechanisms, 212–16
Augmented Transition Network
    (ATN), 42–3

barriers, 38
Binding Theory, 105, 128–40
biological basis of language, see
    innateness
blindness (and language), 228
body part terms, 17, 221–4

INDEX OF LANGUAGES

INDEX OF PROPER NAMES

Contributors' Addresses

Michael A. Arbib, Department of Computer Science, University of Southern California, Los Angeles, CA 90089-0782, USA

Melissa Bowerman, Max-Planck-Institut für Psycholinguistik, NL 6525XD Nijmegen, Wundtlaan 1, The Netherlands

Joan L. Bybee, Department of Linguistics, State University of New York at Buffalo, 685 Baldy Hall, Amherst Campus, Buffalo, NY 14260, USA

Bernard Comrie, Department of Linguistics, University of Southern California, Los Angeles, CA 90089-1693, USA

Anne Cutler, Medical Research Council, Applied Psychology Unit, 15 Chaucer Road, Cambridge CB2 2EF, England

Lyn Frazier, Linguistics Department, University of Massachusetts at Amherst, Amherst, MA 01002, USA

Christopher J. Hall, Department of Linguistics, University of Southern California, Los Angeles, CA 90089-1693, USA

John A. Hawkins, Department of Linguistics, University of Southern California, Los Angeles, CA 90089-1693, USA

Jane C. Hill, Department of Computer Science, Smith College, Northampton, MA 01063, USA

Teun Hoekstra, Department of General Linguistics, University of Leiden, PO Box 9515, 2300 RA Leiden, The Netherlands

Edward L. Keenan, Department of Linguistics, University of California at Los Angeles, Los Angeles, CA 90024, USA

Ekkehard König, Lehrstuhl für Englische Sprachwissenschaft, Technische Universität Hannover, Im Moore 21, 3000 Hannover, West Germany

Jan G. Kooij, Department of General Linguistics, University of Leiden, PO Box 9515, 2300 RA Leiden, The Netherlands

Michael Lee, Department of Linguistics, University of Southern California, Los Angeles, CA 90089-1693, USA

Keith Rayner, Department of Psychology, University of Massachusetts at Amherst, Amherst, MA 01002, USA

Sandra A. Thompson, Department of Linguistics, University of California at Santa Barbara, Santa Barbara, CA 93106, USA